THE HISTORY OF ISLAMIC THEOLOGY

From Muhammad to the Present

The History of Islamic Theology

From Muhammad to the Present

TILMAN NAGEL

Translated from the German by Thomas Thornton

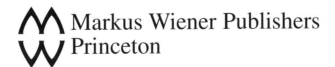 Markus Wiener Publishers
Princeton

The translation of this book into English was supported by
a grant from Inter Nationes.

Cover Illustration: Nineteenth century drawing of Al-Azhar Mosque 973,
Cairo, the world's oldest still functioning university.

For information write to: Markus Wiener Publishers
231 Nassau Street, Princeton, NJ 08542

Library of Congress Cataloging-in-Publication Data

Nagel, Tilman
    [Geschichte der islamischen Theologie. English]
    The history of Islamic theology from Muhammad to the present/
        Tilman Nagel; translated from the German by Thomas Thornton.
    (Princeton series on the Middle East)
    Translation of: Geschichte der islamischen Theologie.
    Includes bibliographical references and index.
    ISBN 1-55876-202-7 hardcover
    ISBN 1-55876-203-5 paper
    1. Islam—Doctrines—History. I. Title. II. Series.
BP166.1.N3413   1999
297.2'09—dc21   99-049828   CIP

Markus Wiener Publishers books are printed in the
United States of America on acid-free paper, and meet
the guidelines for permanence and durability of the
Committee on Production Guidelines for Book
Longevity of the Council on Library Resources.

Table of Contents

Preface   ix

CHAPTER I
The Koran, the Foundation of Islamic Theology   1
  1. The Koran in Islamic Faith   1
  2. Islam   2
  3. Early History of the Koran   11
  4. Central Themes of the Koran's Message   13
    a) Divine "Destination" or "Power   13
    b) The Human Creature   16
    c) Attaining Salvation   21

CHAPTER II
Faith and "Islam"   27
  1. Muslim Views on the Origin of Religious Persuasions   27
  2. On Islamic History between 632 and 750   29
  3. Divine Determination versus Human Determination   35
  4. The Kharijites   41
  5. The Shiites   49
  6. Judgment Postponed   57
  7. The Beginnings of Sunnism   63

CHAPTER III
The Two Types of Islam's Theological Literature   73
  1. The *Hadith*   73
  2. The *Kalam*   82

CHAPTER IV
Early Rationalism   93
  1. Arab-Muslim Society   93
  2. A Glance at the Early Abbasid Period   97

3. The One God and His Revelation   100
4. Human Actions   109
5. Physics and Metaphysics   115
6. Sunnites and Shiites as Opponents of Rationalist Theology   118

CHAPTER V
Rationalism and Tradition   125
1. The Caliphate's Political Decline   125
2. Early Theological Reflection in Sunnism   128
3. Sufism and Rationalism   136
4. Sunnite Rationalism   148
5. The Asharite School   158

CHAPTER VI
Theology and Philosophy   171
1. Exoteric and Esoteric Meaning of the Revelation   171
2. A Glance at the History of the Islamic Mind in the
   High Middle Ages   178
3. Islamic Philosophy   184
4. Re-establishing All Creatures' Power of Being   194
5. Islamic Theology in the High and Late Middle Ages   206

CHAPTER VII
Islam and Gnosis   215
1. Prophetic Message and Gnostic Weltanschauung   215
2. Gnosis and Early Islamic Theology   220
3. Gnosis within Islam   225

CHAPTER VIII
Islamic Orthodoxy   235
1. Sunnism as the Religious Creed of the Majority   235
2. Orthodoxy and the Islamic State   241
3. Shiite Orthodoxy   248

CHAPTER IX
Islam as Ideology   253
  1. Islam Is Knowledge   253
  2. Reform in the Spirit of Orthodoxy   261
  3. Islam as Ideology   271

Epilogue   277
  1. Summary   277
  2. The Tasks   280

Chronology   285

Notes   289

Recommendations for Further Reading   313

Glossary of Arabic Terms   317

Indexes   323
  1. Persons   323
  2. Concepts and Groups   326

Preface

This book is the result of academic teaching. Its entire structure as well as the major part of its content go back to the lecture series "History of Islamic Theology," which I gave in the academic year 1982-83 for the first time and repeated in 1986-87 and 1990-91, both times in revised form. It also includes ideas I first presented in my lectures on the history of Islamic law, the Islamic concept of space, time, and matter (spring semester 1984), on issues raised by cultural anthropology and their applicability to an analysis of Islam (spring semester 1992) as well as on "Islamic History and European Research—Issues and Controversies" (academic year 1989-90). In elaborating on these lectures, I also used seminars on individual aspects of these and similar topics, as well as, of course, my personal research.

Throughout my work on the subject, I have been led by the belief that in the field of Orientalism, just as in any other, academic teaching must not restrict itself to acquainting students with the few clearings in the jungle of extant historical sources that teachers are about to research in the pursuit of their pertinent interests; rather, one should aim for a balanced view of the entire subject, no matter how limited that view still might be. Should teachers avoid that challenge, they would ultimately produce ignorant specialists; what is more, sooner or later such an attitude would turn Orientalism into an insignificant and even useless field of study. The voices of those who know virtually all there is to know about pledges in Islamic law or about late Ash'arite metaphysics but who don't bother to concern themselves with anything else, will not be missed in our country's cultural life, and neither should they complain if charlatans—self-proclaimed experts on the Orient—monopolize public discussion.

We often hear the argument that the educated tend not to be overly keen on learning about non-European cultures: their love affair with their own heritage—which is made up by the traditions of Greek antiquity, early Christianity with its appropriations from the Old Testament, and ideas from medieval Latin and modern Western European sources—has the effect of a shield pierced only rarely and briefly by a hint of the intellectual and cultural importance of anything foreign, at times when political events are being perceived as threatening.

This objection is certainly justified. After a public lecture on a subject related to Islamic theology, for instance, one always has to be prepared to be told by incredulous and skeptical members of the audience that Islam has no theology, all it has is the Koran—that they have read that somewhere in cold print.[1] Where and how could the interested layperson have been better informed? Similar to classical philologists, Orientalists still do not have a general readership, because they hardly ever write for one. They need to develop gradually an audience of general readers—a, as I think, certainly rewarding and thrilling task that does not at all prevent the exploration of new scholarly terrain. Highly specialized individual studies tend to belong in specialized journals; but works that address more universal issues should be written in a language intelligible to the general reader and should develop their topics in a manner that explains the importance of the pertinent subject to a large circle of open-minded readers and extends their knowledge about it.

This brings us to my own approach in writing this book, as well as the book's structure, which is determined by that approach. I define theology as the attempt to explain the message of the founder of a religion—here, Muhammad—in a way so as to produce a coherent body of statements. This attempt, which in different historical contexts can exhibit different tendencies, must be examined without bias and prejudice while at all times considering the insights gained from general and comparative religion. Seen from that angle it will, for instance, turn out that the subject of the theological debate during the Umayyad period (660–750) was not the same as the one in the subsequent period; if seen in its fundamental political and social context, this change in theological themes becomes *comprehensible*—even though it *cannot* be *derived* from it. Rather, the aim of seeing the theological ideas to be portrayed in their concrete historical context is to see them as an essential part of the culture of Islam in general. Not least, this is meant to do justice to Islam's claim to be in a position to blend the religious and the secular into a homogeneous whole.

In short, in this book I will take seriously how Muslims see themselves and their faith; I will not evaluate Islam by outside standards. Nonetheless, the position from which I examine Islamic theology is not an Islamic one. The reason for this is that I will analyze the development of theological theories in connection with *history*. A Muslim's attitude in professing his or her faith and practicing its rites, however, is fundamentally different: he or she views the Prophet's works not as a beginning of something that then evolved over the course of centuries into something else that Muhammad could not have predicted; from an Islamic point of view, Muhammad is already the absolute perfection of the religiosity human beings are able to attain. Therefore a central topic of the first chapters of this book is the question of how the belief in the transhistoricity of the Prophetic message evolved and how it took hold of theology. In order not to blur the borderline between religious doctrines on the one hand—which in many respects are undisputed among Muslims—and what historical-critical scholarship has to say about them on the other hand, I summarize very briefly the Muslim point of view, wherever necessary.

Thus, clearly, this history of Islamic theology is not allied with the zeitgeist, where any "dialogue," any "talk with one another" is considered an act that brings salvation—an act, incidentally, whose background and aims get all the more blurred the more often it is performed in public. My sole purpose is to describe objectively how current historical-philological scholarship interprets and explains what the various Islamic sources from different periods have to say about the Muslims' concept of God and His relationship with human beings. I deliberately refrain from rashly pointing out parallels or similarities between Islam and Christianity, because this tends to be misleading. For what do we learn from an analogy—which is sometimes made—of Christ as the "logos" and the Koran as God's word? Statements of that kind only feign similarities between Islam and Christianity; the naive European reader is led to believe that Islam has a logos theory comparable to that of Christianity. That is utterly wrong! The religious pedagogues' zeal in finding and inventing as many similarities between the world religions in order to reduce tensions by way of a superficial harmony is something I find deplorable—it attests to an (even badly disguised) ignorance of all foreign religions, to an intolerable lack of seriousness. It is more important and helpful to recognize—and accept—the different nature of the other faith. That is the goal to which this book is devoted.

The epilogue summarizes my arguments in the form of theses; it ends with a subchapter entitled "The Tasks," where I outline in retrospect why the Muslim theologians' world of ideas concerns us and that its discoveries, but also its mistakes, are even an integral part of our own history. This realization—in which I am not alone—imposes on scholars, including those researching the Latin Middle Ages, the task to redouble their efforts. In view of the fact that our universities have been increasingly subjected to the political and partisan interests of the day, however, I hardly dare hope that this will happen in the foreseeable future.

Dransfeld,
3 March 1993
Tilman Nagel

CHAPTER I

The Koran, the Foundation of Islamic Theology

1. The Koran in Muslim Faith

The Koran is "protective haven and lasting gift of bliss, excellent argument and conclusive proof, it cures the heart's fear, and makes just determinations whenever there is doubt. It is lucid speech, and final word, not facetiousness; a lamp whose light never extinguishes . . . , an ocean whose depths will never be fathomed. Its oratory stuns reason . . . it combines concise succinctness and inimitable expression."[1] This is a brief quotation from the introduction of a random Islamic introduction to Koran research. For the Muslim believer, the Koran contains the supreme knowledge accessible to humankind, the ultimate, final truth, for it contains God's own words. Quoting its verses equals proclaiming the unshakable truth and being comforted in all adversities. Human reason will never be able to get to the bottom of God's word, whose turns of phrase, forever resisting any attempt at emulation, are distinguished by their amazing accuracy and beauty.

This is exactly the reason why the Koran is the Prophet Muhammad's authenticating miracle. His predecessors—Moses and Jesus—were also divinely endowed with the power to perform miracles, which were universally accepted proofs of their prophetic faculties. However, of all authenticating miracles, the Koran is the most convincing, since it addresses human reason: the laws of rhetoric allow us to prove that the Koran's oratory is unparalleled. Yet it is not only its linguistic magic that humankind cannot surpass, its content, too, opens up ever new insights to those perusing it sincerely and purely in heart and mind. There is no topic which the Koran claims it does not cover.[2] Thus the book is also a road sign which never fails the believer: God's word is an unalterable guide. God established it before the beginning of time, and His messengers delivered it several times to humankind, which was enmeshed in disbelief and obstinacy. Jews and Christians could not preserve it unadulterated; then Muhammad came and delivered it to his people, the Arabs. Muhammad's message was purified of all falsifications and composed in a clear Arabic, which is how Muslims have preserved it to this day.[3]

These facts mark the highpoints of world history, those periods in which a messenger of God delivered the unadulterated original text of God's revelation to the people from whose midst he had been called on to do so, thus founding anew the original religion. The Arab Prophet did this for the last time before the Day of Judgment. Therefore, the delivery of the Koran constitutes the event that ultimately overcame heathenism. Islam, the natural bond between everything that was created and its creator, brings salvation; it has nothing to do with the previous era of aberration and "ignorance."[4] The Koran relates man's entire life to the one God, who takes care that true faith, which He last proclaimed through Muhammad, will spread victoriously over the entire earth.

2. Islam

The emergence of Islam was an extremely complex process, whose major outlines historiography still has not fully grasped. A significant reason for this is that the sources, among which the Koran is the most significant, are not easily accessible. The Koran contains numerous allusions to the course of the Prophet's life, but these can rarely be clearly related to specific, prominent events; while there are numerous additional historical sources on Muhammad, his times and his life, it was not until the eighth century and later that these were put down in the form accessible to us today, and even back then they were overgrown by the fictions of warring religio-political groups.[5] Despite all that, essential facts can be determined, whose knowledge is indispensable for an understanding of the theological essence of early Islamic doctrine.

The sources reveal a society subdivided into tribes and their subgroups. The tribe saw itself as a blood-related community; but it could be enlarged by individuals or groups, or divided by segregation. It did not have a rigid structure. Furthermore, we know of attempts in the sixth century to combine several tribes into confederations, all with the aim of creating expanded political orders.[6] Yet these larger organizational structures proved to be short-lived because factual or alleged descendancy from mutual forebears still provided the, by far, most efficient social glue. Furthermore, the members of a tribe viewed their group as a cult community, which performed its rites in certain places on the Arabian peninsula. Sometimes the deity of a specific sanctuary was worshiped by several tribes, with the result that in that area there was no strict particularity either.[7] In any case, during certain seasons frequent fairs were held at certain places of worship, which made it possible to establish relations that transcended the boundaries of blood relations within a community.[8]

All this prepared the ground for the possibility of one tribe gaining hegemony over the others; it also traced the actual consequences of this hegemony. According to the legend of the City of Mecca, it was a certain Qusayy who, five generations before Muhammad, founded the Quraysh's rule over that place and its sanctuary.

Around the mid-sixth century, the tribal group of the Maadd, which owned the land between Mecca and the southern border to Iran, was loosely dependent on the Lakhmids in Hira, an Arabic dynasty of princes that in turn was in subjection to the rulers of Iran. The Lakhmids tried to extend their influence to Yemen, where they supported the pretender Dh Nuwas, a man of the Jewish faith—and in Medina they also used the Judaicized tribes of the Banu Qurayza and Banu n-Nadir to impose a tribute on the inhabitants of that oasis.[9] Dh Nuwas expelled the Ethiopians from Yemen, and subsequently turned against the Christian Najran, whom he devastated.[10] This made the kings of Hira and Dh Nuwas numerous enemies on the Arabian peninsula, but also caused the Byzantine empire to intervene. As a consequence, the Hirans' supremacy in the Hijaz began to crumble. The Banu Tamim, a powerful tribal community, severed their historic connections with Hira and entered into relations with the Quraysh in Mecca. Around the same time, the latter made agreements with the Bedouins, allowing them to pass through their strip of land. This successfully opened up trade routes to Abessinia, Iraq, and Yemen. According to one source, under Qusayy the Quraysh began to build solid houses in Mecca, which indicates that they had achieved a certain prosperity.[11]

The legend of the City of Mecca also attributes to Qusayy the shape the Kaaba cult eventually took, as well as the revenues the Quraysh received from the pilgrims' festival. Initially the annual rites, which took place at nearby locations and to which people from the entire Arabian peninsula flocked, had nothing to do with "Allah," the deity worshiped at the Kaaba.[12] The blending to a whole of the cult in Mecca and the ceremonies practiced in the urban settlement probably did not take place before Muhammad. A men's association, called *hums*, which included members of several other tribes as well, was considered the core of the pre-Islamic Quraysh community; in literature Mecca was called the "place of the association of the *hums*."[13] What held the association of the *hums* together was the cult at the Kaaba, "the religion of the Quraysh." The members of the Quraysh cult were highly regarded in large parts of the Arabian peninsula; even princes from Yemen and the tribes of the Lakhmides, the Banu Kindas, and the Syrian Ghassanids supposedly went to Mecca and, while performing the rites, obeyed the *hums*' instructions. The members of the association were not equals; rather, each member of a foreign tribe was assigned to a Quraysh *hums* member, called *hirmi*, obliged to obtain food from him and to perform the rites dressed in clothes the *hirmi* gave him. The Quraysh Muhammad was also a member of that association; he was the *hirmi* of a man from the Banu Tamim, who was known by name.

The association of the *hums* provides evidence of the Quraysh's religio-political quest for power, which was symbolically expressed during the pilgrimage season and gradually spread when the Meccans began to have an impact on the organization of the ritual acts in their immediate surroundings. An old custom stipulated that during high holidays all arms be at rest. The Quraysh formed a militia (consisting largely of members of the Banu Tamim) which had to preserve order and mainly fend off attacks by enemy tribes that did not participate in the Kaaba rites. Apart from those two main groups, there were tribes that made pilgrimages to the shrines near the city without being part of the Meccan cult community and were thus independent of the Quraysh. Among these were the Medinese Aws and Khazraj, the Prophet Muhammad's eventual "helpers."[14] For their part, the Quraysh *hums* did not participate in ceremonies outside of Mecca. Muhammad, however, disregarded this restriction after he became God's prophet. He was probably hoping to reach more people that way than would have been possible otherwise.[15]

Let us now take a look at the religious content with which the *hums* members filled the Kaaba cult. The most important source for this is the religious formulas they used to invoke God and announce that they were ready to perform the rites in His honor: the "Lord of the holy Kaaba" was the highest god, the "Lord of Sirius," as a recurring phrase in the Koran states (sura 53, verse 50), and also the lord of the deities Manat, al-Lat, and al-Uzza; the pilgrims, pushing their camels to extreme exhaustion and ignoring all the idols they otherwise still worshiped, had rushed to the place to serve Him.[16] The Koran confirms this tradition. With an undertone of reproach, the Meccans were remonstrated with, on the one hand, believing that "Allah," the "one God," created the world; how could they be, on the other hand, so obtuse as to turn to those three female deities who were no match for the one Lord (sura 39, verses 38-39)?[17]

This belief in one high god, documented in the consecration formula and ascribed to the Meccans in the Koran, is not yet identical with the concept of monotheism, the belief in the *one* God. Perhaps one should best speak of an affective monotheism: during the invocation, the declaration of readiness to perform the rites, the "Lord of Sirius" *was* the only god, lord over the other deities and idols—and they were nothing! This becomes quite clear in some of the formulas mentioned above: at the Kaaba, the wholly divine Lord was worshiped, the prayers were directed only to Him, and so was the vow henceforth to abstain from all sins. The sense of total awe of the noumenon, whose presence overwhelmed the pilgrim, manifested itself in a temporary extinction of all other noumena: the pilgrims standing before the god worshiped at the Kaaba turned to him entirely. It is in that sense that the word "Islam" occurs in the invocation that was customary among the Yemenite Himyarites,[18] and it is precisely in that sense that the term is used in the Koran, along with its verbal and participial derivations. "And who is there that has a fairer religion than he who submits his will to God [who turns his face to God—*aslama*] being a good-doer, and who follows the creed of Abraham, a man of pure faith?" asks sura 4, verse 124.[19]

Untainted relations with someone, relations that were entirely free of all undesired influences—this concept was expressed in the image of the freedom of that person's face. "Kill you Joseph, or cast him forth into some land, that your father's face may be free for you," Joseph's brothers advise each other in sura 12, verse 9. Muhammad was firmly rooted in the religiosity that found its expression in the rites at the Kaaba. What he strove for was not the elimination of the pagan cult, but making the turning to the *one* god permanent, transforming temporary affective monotheism into a permanent worshiping of the highest lord, which would deeply influence people's everyday life and inherited customs. The early Meccan sura 92 castigates the vice of avarice; he who practices generosity, it says, should not do so in expectation of equal remuneration in the hereafter, but only "to seek the Face of his Lord Most High" (verse 20). This concept quickly evolved into the requirement to profess monotheism.[20] "Say: 'O men, if you are in doubt regarding my religion, I serve not those you serve apart from God, but I serve God, who will gather you to Him, and I am commanded to be of the believers, and: "Set thy face to the religion, a man of pure faith, and be thou not of the idolaters . . ." ' " (sura 10, verses 104-105). In the Koran, it is Abraham—whom the Quraysh considered the Kaaba cult's founder—who, owing to his realization of the powerlessness of the astral deities or man-made idols, completely turns to the one God: "I have turned my face to Him who originated the heavens and the earth, a man of pure faith; I am not of the idolaters" (sura 6, verse 79).

As already mentioned, the site of Mecca is said to have been turned into a permanent settlement under Qusayy, the legendary reviver of the Kaaba cult; Kaaba cult and settling share the same historical context. The annual pilgrims' festival, on the other hand, which took place by the nearby shrines, was tailored toward a nomadic way of life; while Mecca was being transformed into a permanent settlement, these shrines remained, and the Banu Tamim and other tribes continued to perform certain rites, which they had done since the days of old. Yet, as the association of the *hums* illustrates, they did enter into firm relations with the Quraysh. If it was Muhammad's intent to make the worship of Allah permanent and he introduced the *daily* ritual prayer in the direction of the Kaaba to this end, he implicitly required the believers to be permanently present at that place—that is to say, to have settled there. This was proved later when the issue was raised of whether a Bedouin could be a "Muslim" in the full meaning of the word.[21] Therefore Islam is also the result of a change in lifestyle that took place among parts of Arabia's population. The integration of nomadic pilgrims' traditions into the Quraysh Kaaba cult, which was not finalized until Muhammad, prevented Mecca from becoming a shrine only for those who had settled there.

The ritual prayers Muhammad had introduced served to make permanent the turning toward the Highest One, the One whose place of worship was the Kaaba. After his expulsion from his father's town, it was difficult to find a replacement for the shrine—always visible in Mecca—to which the believers used to turn their faces. In Medina the believers were not directly face to face with God. To be sure, they could find comfort in this revelation: "To God belong the East and the West; whithersoever you turn, there is the face of God" (sura 2, verse 109). Still, the belief that only when turned in a certain direction could one enter into pure relations with God remained so powerful that prayer took place first in the direction of Jerusalem, but soon Mecca, so the believers could at least symbolically view the place where the presence of the One had always been sensed: "We have seen thee turning thy face about in the heaven; now We will surely turn thee to a direction that shall satisfy thee. Turn thy face towards the Holy Mosque [in Mecca]; and wherever you are, turn your faces towards it" (sura 2, 138, cf. verses 143-44). Only the sense that the direction of the prayer (*qibla*) establishes (symbolic) "eye contact" between the individual believer and God contains the real meaning of the ritual of praying men and women casting themselves down. This is expressed in the belief that if someone interrupts the ritual prayer, it is invalidated. Turned into the direction of his prayer, the praying man stands directly before God: according to the *hadith*, the Prophet, exhibiting all signs of fury, once scrubbed away saliva he had noticed in the *qibla* of Medina's place of worship. "Do any of you want anyone to spit in His direction (or literally: "in His face")? When the worshiper stands up to pray, he is facing his Lord! So he must not spit in front of himself but to the right or left or under his foot, and if it comes over him suddenly, then into his garb!"[22]

Muhammad was not the only one thinking about transforming the ancient Arab faith into a monotheistic belief. Not only he but other men, who appeared as "God-seekers," also proclaimed the belief in the one Creator God and Lord of the forthcoming Day of Judgment, to whom once upon a time Abraham had converted; they, too, were convinced that the cult needed to be rid of the admixtures of polytheism and that people had to be bound to a new, purified morality.[23] However, what is undisputed is that none other than Muhammad, who considered himself the Prophet of the One, was able to express these thoughts in such rousing language.[24] He painted the horrors of the Day of Judgment in gruesome colors and pressed his compatriots hard with the warning that one day God would consider all their deeds with strict justice, no matter how small they were. Thus Allah, the God who had been worshiped at the Kaaba, who had been so profitable and politically significant for the Quraysh, had become menacing: people should consider everything they did with a view toward the end of time that was going to come all of a sudden some day! As he had done when he set out to use the introduction of the ritual prayer to make the turning to the One permanent, beyond the pilgrims' festival, Muhammad also expanded Allah's reign beyond the traditional period of annual rites to include all human activities—a burden hard to bear! The individual was supposed to change his entire life, constantly take his own inventory, and check if what he did and did not do lived up to the strict requirements that had to be met if he wanted to justify himself on the Day of Judgment. There was an unbreakable connection between making affective and temporary monotheism permanent in ritual prayer and categorically abstaining from any act that might be stigmatized as disgraceful. This is clearly expressed in the late Meccan sura 29, verse 44: "Recite what has been revealed to thee of the Book, and perform the prayer; prayer forbids indecency and dishonour."

The faithless and doubting Meccans were told again and again that Allah was the permanent, sole ruler of His creation—and thus about the invalidity of all deities next to Him—with these arguments: He created the world in the beginning, He preserves and directs it, He will, before the dawning of the Day of Judgment, once again transform the dead into human beings in order to consign them to paradise or hell, according to His verdict. Muhammad preached these ideas in numerous variations to his compatriots, and probably also to strangers during the pilgrims' festivals.[25]

Over the years he managed to gather some followers, but who could be surprised if most people found him irritating? His warnings against committing immoral acts, unlawful enrichment, embezzling orphans' inheritances, fornication, and gambling—all that seemed to be aimed at the eco-

nomic and political leaders among the Quraysh. Still, nothing happened
to the Prophet at first. Being a member of the powerful clan of the Banu
Hashim protected him from persecution. The situation did not become
more dangerous until his uncle Abu Talib died; Muhammad owed it largely to him that he was still tolerated in his hometown. Sources indicate that
the Prophet now even brusquely demanded that all deities who were worshiped next to Allah be abandoned. Furthermore, for a considerable period of time, Muhammad had used the pilgrims' festivals to make contact
with people outside the community and promote his faith. This must have
been alarming to the Quraysh, because it could jeopardize their religiously and politically founded predominance in the western part of the
Arabian peninsula. It must have been many small steps that led to the crisis that had been in the offing for some time: Muhammad was expelled
from his hometown, after many of his followers had already fled. Later
on, Islamic historiography turned this into a carefully planned emigration
(*hijra*); the circumstances of this reinterpretation and its far-reaching consequences will be discussed in the following chapter.[26]

In Medina Muhammad found shelter with the Aws clan of the Banu
Adi ibn an-Najjar, followers of his, who, in danger as well, had also
turned to Medina. As already mentioned, the Medinese tribes of the Aws
and Khazraj did not belong to the association of the *hums*, but every year
summoned members for a pilgrimage to Mecca. Therefore they were not
the Quraysh's enemies, although not politically connected to them either.
On his maternal side, Muhammad was related to the above-mentioned
clan; it is said that as a child—he lost his father at an early age—he visited with them for some time.[27] The Banu Adi ibn an-Najjar were already
well informed about Muhammad's teachings, and the Prophet could count
on their being open to his religious calling: Sirma ibn Malik, a member
of the clan, held views similar to that of his distant relative from Mecca,
having long since rejected all idolatry; in a poem ascribed to Sirma, we
read that for years Muhammad had preached monotheism during the pilgrims' festivals, but that nobody had asked the Prophet to visit; only when
he arrived in Medina did God lead true faith to victory.[28] This statement
was of course made in retrospect. Muhammad himself surely did not consider waging a war against his hometown with the support of the Aws and
Khazraj. Rather, he considered Medina to be a temporary haven, which is

proven by the revelation in sura 28, verse 85, said to have been written during the move to Medina: "He who imposed the Recitation upon thee shall surely restore thee to a place of homing."[29]

Soon after his appointment as prophet, Muhammad recognized prominent figures of the Old Testament as his predecessors—Noah, Moses, and Abraham. Some of the revelations he had received were compiled as a "Book"[30] which he took with him to Medina, hoping that he would find an open ear for his teachings, not only among those Aws and Khazraj to whom he could have turned even from Mecca, but also among the Judaicized tribes. Yet to his utter dismay, it was precisely they who radically rejected him. They nagged him with many different questions, for example, about stories from the nonbiblical Jewish tradition, in order to undermine his claim to be a prophet. That is the background of the verse on the people who transgress the Sabbath (sura 7, verses 163ff.) and Dhool Karnayn (the "two-horned," sura 18, verses 83ff.). A number of passages in the Koran reveal Muhammad's despondency and nagging self-doubts at the time: "Perchance thou art leaving part of what has been revealed to thee, and thy breast is straitened by it, because they say: 'Why has a treasure not been sent down upon him, or an angel not come with him?' Thou art only a warner; and God is a Guardian over everything" (sura 11, verse 15).

In Medina, the financial situation of Muhammad and his followers was extremely precarious at first. There were attempts to generate some income by establishing a fair, but this caused disagreements with the natives.[31] The attack in the year 2/624 in Badr on a Meccan caravan was a great success for Muhammad. Aside from rich booty, it secured him enough support in Medina to allow him to risk setting out to destroy the Judaicized tribes. Despite some setbacks, he consolidated his power in Medina in the following years, but always with the aim of conquering Mecca so he could bring his religion back to its place of origin. During the last five years of his activities, the Meccan Quraysh realized that Muhammad, whose reputation quickly spread to all parts of the Arabian peninsula, was ultimately furthering their political goals. For that reason, even obstinate adversaries of his found their way to him, and he proved to be conciliatory. In mid-January 630, after having been absent for approximately eight years, he reentered his hometown. The idols in

Mecca and its surroundings were destroyed. Only a few days later, he led an army against the tribes of the Hawazin and Taqif, who had apparently misinterpreted the latest political development as a sign of weakness on the part of the Quraysh, their enemies. Muhammad returned victorious—the Meccans had been right. The Medinese, who had once received and for a long time supported the refugees, were not at all happy about this turn of events. In its Islamic garb, the Quraysh's old quest for power was more successful than ever! Yet Muhammad did not remain in Mecca, but returned with his "helpers" to Medina, where the anger soon abated. Only after his death in 632 were the ill feelings toward him to erupt with disastrous consequences. For those Meccan leaders who were entirely rooted in the religio-political thinking based on Qusayy, however, the most decisive event of the recent past had not been the transformation of their inherited faith by Muhammad, but the significant expansion of their power. The different interpretations of Muhammad's actions by his younger contemporaries hide a portentous issue, whose theological aspect is discussed in the following chapter.

3. Early History of the Koran

Muslim Koran research divides the 114 suras containing the revelations conveyed by Muhammad into two groups: the Meccan suras comprise those texts originating between the years around 610 to 622, when the Prophet appeared in his hometown; the Medinese suras are those which were written after Muhammad's expulsion from Mecca, during the last ten years of his life. In addition, there is a tradition going back to early Islamic times, according to which a number of Meccan suras reveal insertions from the Medinese period. European research has adopted this rough division into Meccan and Medinese suras and in addition undertaken an analysis of the linguistic style of the texts pertaining to each group. This led to the—essentially still valid—subdivision of the Meccan suras into three subgroups. The oldest subgroup consists of a relatively large number of very short suras containing succinct, lively verses which exhibit elements of the style of ancient Arab prophets.[32] The second subgroup, the output of the so-called middle Meccan period, reveals a decline of poetic power; themes only hinted at in the oldest suras, such as God's incessant work in nature are now defined and substantiated by arguments.[33] In the late Meccan suras, which are stylistically already closely related to the Medinese verses, these themes are treated in longwinded, repetitive explanations, to which edifying sermons are added.[34] The Medinese suras are characterized by a uniform style; yet, since in Medina Muhammad was getting a grip on his tasks as a ruler, these suras often address issues concerning the internal organization of the community, its relations with its enemies, and the determination of ritual-related obligations.[35]

The issue of the composition of the revelations and their compilation to a Holy Book must be carefully separated from the one of their chronology. Scholarly views on the former differ widely. The opinion that it was a very long process lasting perhaps centuries[36] tends to be rightly dismissed; discoveries of Koran fragments dating back to the seventh century refute that opinion.[37] According to Islamic tradition, the version of the Koran generally used today was authorized by Uthman (r. 644–656), Muhammad's third successor. If one accepts that as a historical fact—and an unbiased study of the sources can lead to no other conclusion—then there still remains the controversial issue of what kind of material was used at the time to put together the text that has remained valid until today. It could not have been an amorphous mass of fragments, for even Medinese revelations mention the suras as text units.[38] Reports on non-Uthmanian compilations of the Koran contain different versions that typically do not significantly affect the content and indicate a different order of the suras,[39] but largely confirm the text authorized under Uthman.

In Mecca the Prophet had realized that the words of God which he received and preached were from a holy book whose unalterable text was kept on a tablet in Allah's direct vicinity: just as Moses, who is often mentioned in the Meccan suras, had given his people a copy of that otherworldly book, he, too, apparently intended to offer his compatriots God's word in written form. Altogether twenty-nine suras are from the late Meccan and early Medinese periods. These are introduced by certain groups of letters whose meaning still has not been deciphered; they are almost always succeeded by a formula that identifies what follows as a revelatory text, usually even specifying that it contains verses of the "clear Book."[40] In the Meccan sura 12, which relates the story of Joseph, Islamic tradition regards this formula as an addition from the Medinese period: verse 3 specifically mentions that "before [the revelation,]" the Prophet used to ignore the following story; verse 7, according to Islamic tradition a Medinese insertion, states the reason why the later incorporation of the story of Joseph and his brothers into the book was justified: "In Joseph and his brethren were signs for those who ask questions." It was only in Medina that the Prophet could realize that Joseph's fate resembled his own: he was expelled by relatives and gained influence and renown in a foreign land; finally those same relatives came to him and had to humiliate themselves before him, but he forgave them.[41] This single example must suffice to explain that recording the revelation in written form, selecting the texts to be included in the "Book," as well as supplementing them, was a long process which had already started in Mecca. More research is necessary to clarify the details. The probable reason for the fact that the number of versions of the text with significant differences is small is that the by far largest part of the Koran was indeed authorized by Muhammad.

4. Central Themes of the Koran's Message

A) DIVINE "DESTINATION" OR "POWER"

In a few early parts of the Koran, Allah is praised as the "Lord most High" to whom man must pay reverence. However, as already mentioned, this quickly turned into the realization that Allah is the *only* God. Allah assumes all the tasks which previously were attributed to the other noumena, and, as the only God, He is worthy of *constant* worship. This is true not least because He is no longer the lord over single natural phenomena occurring regularly and determining human life, but because everything that happens, everything that grows and perishes, is a continuous emanation of His workings. This is precisely the Prophet's crucial insight: "Whatsoever is in the heavens and the earth implore Him; every day He is upon some labour" (sura 55, verse 29). "God, there is no god but He, the Living, the Everlasting. Slumber seizeth Him not, neither sleep. . . ." That is how the early Medinese sura 2, verse 256, summarizes this idea. For Muhammad it amounts to sacrilegious self-aggrandizement if the unfaithful do not realize that it is not they who provide what they need to live, but that they owe everything to the One. Again and again, Muhammad endeavors to rid the Meccans, who contentiously speak of their own achievements and riches, of their haughtiness: "He created the heavens and the earth in truth; high be He exalted above that they associate with Him! He created man from a germ-drop; and, behold, he is a manifest adversary. And the cattle—He created them for you; in them is warmth, and uses various; and of them you eat, and there is beauty in them for you, when you bring them home to rest and when you drive them forth abroad to pasture; and they bear your loads unto a land that you never would reach, excepting with great distress. Surely your Lord is All-clement, All-compassionate. And horses, and mules, and asses, for you to ride, and as an adornment; and He creates what you know not. . . . It is He who sends down to you out of heaven water of which you have to drink, and of which trees, for you to pasture your herds, and thereby He brings forth for you crops, and olives, and vines, and all manner of fruit. Surely in that is a sign for a people who reflect. And He subjected to you the night and day, and the sun and moon; and the stars are subjected by His command. Surely in that are signs for a people who understand" (sura 16, verses 3-8 and 10-12).[42]

The Prophet experiences this God, without whose constant care human beings, and even the whole world, cannot exist for one moment, not as an impersonal divine being, but as a personal God with human features: He sits on a throne, creates with His hands, and His countenance appears to express His nontemporal quintessence: "All that dwells upon the earth is perishing, yet still abides the face of thy Lord, majestic, splendid" (sura 55, verses 26-27). It is this God who talks to Muhammad, recognizes his innermost thoughts, comforts and, if necessary, reprimands him: "Did He not find thee an orphan, and shelter thee? . . . Did He not find thee needy, and suffice thee? As for the orphan, do not oppress him, and as for the beggar, scold him not" (sura 93, verses 6 and 8-10).

The realm of the "unseen," that which is inaccessible to the human senses, is attributed to God, who conveys to the Prophet what happens there (for instance, sura 3, verse 39); it is the other human beings' duty to believe that that realm exists in which God's works, of which the events happening in the world are only signs, take place directly. What is at work in the hidden domain is the "destination" or "power" which God permanently emanates or yields,[43] the medium through which He rules His creation. In Koranic thinking, this "destination" or "power" is ceaselessly carried into creation either by the angels or the Holy Spirit. Thus sura 17, verse 87, says: "They will question thee concerning the Spirit. Say: 'The Spirit is of the bidding of my Lord. You have been given of knowledge nothing except a little." In sura 97 the concept of "destination" or "power" is associated with the Koran: "Behold, We have sent it [the Koran] down on the night of Power; And what shall teach thee what is the night of Power? The Night of Power is better than a thousand months; in it the angels and the Spirit descend, by the leave of their Lord, upon every command. Peace it is, till the rising of dawn."

Even in the early Meccan period the concept of "power," whose concrete meaning originated from this God-seeking,[44] assumed a narrower meaning: "Even so We have sent to thee a Spirit [Gabriel] of Our bidding. Thou knewest not what the Book was, nor belief" (sura, 42, verse 52). In this context "bidding" (power) is God's message of salvation and law; but more on this later.

It should be noted that around the same time as the concept of God's constant care evolved, the idea gained significance that "in the beginning" God created the world in six days and put Himself on His throne.[45] Even though the Koran does not contain any stories comparable to the Old Testament's account of distributing the days of creation over the individual days of the week, we must assume that, with the introduction of this concept, Muhammad took up a highly religious tradition that had originated in Judaism. By no means was it necessarily in direct contradiction to God's ceaseless exercise of "power," but it brought a new aspect into focus: the single straight line of the course of world history from the act of Creation to the Day of Judgment. Indirectly this also emphasizes the linear course of human life; missed opportunities to collect good deeds for the Day of Judgment will never recur! This promoted the necessity to find rules for human life in view of the ultimate judgment, rules that, if obeyed, would guarantee salvation.[46] The ground for developments in Medina was now prepared.

B) THE HUMAN CREATURE

In light of Allah's all-encompassing authority, man is put into a place of overall dependency—he becomes a creature of the one God, and he neither can nor must be anything beyond that. Human beings are called upon to recognize and accept themselves as creatures. Time and again Muhammad called on them to do so, which is why he repeatedly preached to them verses describing God's workings in nature as the ever-present sign of His incessant creative power. Seen from this angle, the unbridgeable ontological gap between the one God and man appears as the distinction between "creating" (*khaliq*) and "created" (*makhluq*)—a central theme of Islamic theology. To be sure, the Koran does not engage in ontology proper. Rather, it wrestles with the issue of how human beings can be made to realize that being created is the one determinative factor of their existence and that the realization of this necessarily leads to the belief in the one Allah. Recognizing this brings salvation, and Abraham, the God-seeker, is the one illustrating how that knowledge can be attained: he recognized the vanity of all idolatry; God wanted him to "be of those having sure faith." Abraham raised his gaze to the nocturnal sky; his thoughts were being spellbound by a bright star, the moon, and finally the rising disk of the sun, but he hoped in vain to find in them the supreme deity, the one superior to all idols. While he recognized the star, the moon, and the sun one after the other as his lords who were far above anything on earth, their rule was never permanent, they all set again. He said, "O my people, surely I am quit of that you associate. I have turned my face to Him who originated the heavens and the earth, a man of pure faith [i.e., a *hanif*, or God-seeker]; I am not of the idolaters" (sura 6, verses 74-79). He who follows Abraham's example and entirely turns toward the one creator, turning his face toward Him just as the pilgrims turned toward the deity of the shrine, takes the decisive step toward attaining salvation.

With this step, he submits his entire life to the meaning engendered by his acceptance of his identity as a creature, as which he owes his Creator total gratitude. In the Koran, denying one's debt of gratitude is the quintessence of unbelief.[47] Yet how can man clear his permanent debt? Precisely by constantly being aware of being a creature, by worshiping God day after day in ritual prayer, by never forgetting that, at the end of time, God will sit in judgment over His creatures! Thus confessing one's identity as a creature necessitates a profound change in thinking, which also transforms the way the believer acts: arrogance, pride of property, bragging about one's numerous and powerful kin—all that resulted from the lack of acknowledging one's identity as a creature, which was now considered reprehensible; greed, cheating in measuring and weighing, embezzling someone else's property, severe verbal abuse of someone weaker than oneself, using force—all that had to be renounced so that Allah, who painstakingly kept a record of everything, did not end up with a balance sheet where one's evil acts outweighed the good ones. Therefore, one could not preserve an unmarred relationship with God through rites, even though they were performed several times a day; but one must change one's entire lifestyle. Thus, we read in the Medinese sura 4 (verses 121-24): "But those that believe, and do things of right-eousness, them we shall bring to gardens underneath which rivers flow, therein dwelling for ever and ever; God's promise in truth; and who is truer in speech than God? . . . Whosoever does evil shall be recompensed for it, and will not find for him, apart from God, a friend or helper. And whosoever does deeds of righteousness, be it male or female, believing—they shall enter Paradise, and not be wronged a single date-spot. And who is there that has a fairer religion than he who submits his will to God being a good-doer, and who follows the creed of Abraham, a man of pure faith? And God took Abraham for a friend." Here the believer's direct, pure relationship with God is associated with right acting, which is deter-mined by his acknowledging his essence as a creature. What right acting consists of was mentioned only indirectly in Mecca; all that was neces-sary were the words of exhortation, the descriptions of judgment and the horrors of hell, and the depiction of bliss in paradise. In Medina, howev-er, the quest for clear-cut rules of conduct—laws—became palpable.[48]

Before we return to this issue, we first have to examine another aspect of man's substance as a creature, which is crucial to Islamic theology as well as for an understanding of this religion's claim to absolute truth. Turning one's face to God, turning one's being over to Him, as the pil-grims did in their invocations, is the prototypical religious gesture, which is a ritual representation of the state of grace—"Islam"—proper. Performed with the knowledge of one's essence as a creature, it will lead to the transformation of the believer's entire life. Yet in Islamic thought this does not require forming one's life anew; rather, it is an actualization of man's original destination to be saved, which is implied in the concept of being a creature to begin with. Man in his essence is not thrown into disgrace as a creature; it is only wrong developments that have more or less led to the obfuscation of his destination to be saved, which he shares with all creatures. For this reason, it is not the Prophet's task to elevate man into a state of grace that never existed before, but to lay bare his original destination. "So set thy face to religion, a man of pure faith [*hanif*]— God's original upon which He originated mankind. There is no changing God's creation. That is the right religion; but most men know it not." This is the confident message of sura 30, verse 29. In other words, man is created in God's direction. By turning toward God and accepting his essence as a creature, his original destination to be saved is fulfilled. Sin—moving away from God—is not part of man's nature; rather, it is something with which he was endowed by Satan. The Koran contains numerous passages documenting this, of which only one—sura 8, verse 50—shall be quoted. The Meccans are about to go to war against Muhammad: "And when Satan decked out their deeds fair to them, and said, 'Today no man shall overcome you, for I shall be your neighbor.' But when the two hosts sighted each other, he withdrew upon his heels, saying, 'I am quit of you; for I see what you do not see. I fear God; and God is terrible in retribution.'"

As a creature, man is created in the direction of God; if his nature can develop without being influenced from outside, he is good. Yet man can be tempted. God gave him reason, thus making him master over His creation—He appointed him His deputy on earth.[49] Reason, however, is an ambiguous gift of grace: it can use arguments to lead man astray, just like Satan made waging the war against the Prophet palatable to the Meccans; furthermore, one can get caught up in wrong conclusions. Satan was the first to whom this happened: God ordered him to pay tribute to man, whom He had just created, but Satan, employing his faculty of reason, refused to comply, for paying reverence to a created being did not make sense to him, as reverence was due only to God.[50] Reason is supposed to contribute to the restraining of instincts and desires and not to be misused to speculative attempts to comprehend the essence of God and His cre-

ation. For it is not the faculty of reason that is the opposite of dissolute-
ness and passion, but the irrefutable knowledge of what is right, which
one obtains from God.[51]

To define and ground this knowledge in every believer with absolute
certainty is the highest goal of all Islamic theology. This goal is already
outlined in the revelation that all theology's efforts will fail unless the gift
of human reason is employed, but that reason invariably has to be sacri-
ficed before that goal is reached. The question of how far away from that
goal this sacrifice has to be made is a distinctive feature of the various
schools of thought examined in the following chapters.

We have seen that at the decisive moment Satan did not relinquish reason, which is why his thinking led him astray and he became haughty
toward God, who punished him by expelling him from paradise. Just
when he was about to leave paradise, he asked God, "My Lord, respite me
till the day they shall be raised." God replied: "Thou art among the respited until the day of a known time." Satan, who felt God had expelled him
unjustly, threatened he would take revenge on people for the disgrace he
had suffered: "My Lord, for Thy perverting me I shall deck all fair to
them in the earth, and I shall pervert them, all together, Excepting those
Thy servants among them that are devoted." Allah had made monotheism
the angel Satan's obligation, yet also given him the faculty of reason and
on that fateful day ordered him to prostrate himself before Adam, who
had been created out of clay. Satan refused to obey; his reason, the gift
from God, led him astray. Now he wanted to prove that Adam, too, was
prone to independent thinking and acting and, therefore, would extricate
himself from his relationship of salvation with God. However, even at that
point it seemed clear that there would be some human beings who would
not be tempted: those who on this earth already possessed "firm knowledge." God replied to Satan's threat: "[O]ver My servants thou shalt have
no authority, except those that follow thee, being perverse; Gehenna shall
be their promised land all together. Seven gates it has, and unto each gate
a set portion of them belongs. But the godfearing shall be amidst gardens
and fountains" (sura 15, verses 26-45).

Sura 7, verses 18 to 23, describes even more strikingly how, after the
Creator has cursed man and expelled him from paradise, He gives Satan
permission to lay traps for him. Satan entices Adam and Eve to eat the

forbidden fruits, and they are banished along with him. The same story is told in sura 2, verse 35, where it is continued as follows: "Thereafter Adam received certain words from his Lord, and He turned towards him; truly He turns, and is All-compassionate. We said, 'Get you down from out of it, all together; yet there shall come to you guidance from Me, and whosoever follows My guidance, no fear shall be on them, neither shall they sorrow. As for the unbelievers who cry lies to Our signs, those shall be the inhabitants of the Fire, therein dwelling forever." Since the time of Adam, man has carried within him the promise that he is destined to be saved; despite his expulsion from paradise, he does not carry the burden of an original sin, for he has the option to accept and follow God's directions, which have been conveyed to him through the prophets. Only, he once again must profess to God his essence as a creature, just as all individuals have done even before their earthly existence began. "And when thy Lord took from the Children of Adam, from their loins, their seed, and made them testify touching themselves, 'Am I not your Lord?' They said, 'Yes, we testify'—lest you should say on the Day of Resurrection, 'As for us, we were heedless of this" (sura 7, verse 171).

Islam's claim to the absolute truth is rooted in the recognition of man's essence as a creature and, as a result, his destination to be saved. It is a claim that in Medina was formulated as a radical contrast to Christians and Jews, "those to whom the Scriptures have been given"[52]: "Fight those who believe not in God and the Last Day and do not forbid what God and His Messenger have forbidden—such men as practice not the religion of truth, being of those who have been given the Book—until they pay the tribute out of hand and have been humbled." These unambiguous words in sura 9, verse 29, are followed by the charge that in their long history, in which priests and monks appropriated the tradition, Jews and Christians deviated from true monotheism; that the Jews claimed Ezra,[53] and the Christians Jesus to be the son of God, thus lapsing into polytheism. It was argued that the Prophet, who did not base himself on any old and therefore distorted scripture, went back behind those two religions of revelation; that he gained his knowledge directly at the source, from God, which was why his faith was the original faith, the belief of Abraham: "Abraham in truth was not a Jew, neither a Christian; but he was a Muslim and one pure of faith; certainly he was never of the idolaters. Surely the people standing closest to Abraham are those who followed him, and this Prophet, and those who believe; and God is the protector of the believers" (sura 3, verses 60-61).[54]

C) ATTAINING SALVATION

God created human beings toward Himself. If they realize this basic fact—that they are creatures—and internally turn toward the One, they have the chance of entering paradise. This all-decisive step is their sole responsibility; there are no priests or monks who can give them their necessary share from a treasure of grace administrated by some human institution. The Koran mentions quite brusquely that each individual is responsible for his or her own salvation; during the strict final judgment all individuals alone are accountable for their acts of commission and omission on earth: "When the earth is shaken with a mighty shaking and earth brings forth her burdens, and Man says, 'What ails her?' upon that day she shall tell her tidings for that her Lord has inspired her. Upon that day men shall issue in scatterings to see their works, and whoso has done an atom's worth of good shall see it, and whoso has done an atom's worth of evil shall see it" (sura 99).

The God-seekers also believed in resurrection, in that people would be sentenced according to their earthly deeds, and in paradise and hell. They, too, held that the one God, "to whose Face we pay reverence and respect," determined duration and circumstances of each individual's life. This all-encompassing care led them to conclude that the dead did not have to wither in their graves for all eternity.[55] The resurrection at the end of days, at once promise and threat, gives a definite goal to everything human beings do and say on earth—and what distinguishes Muhammad from the God-seekers is that he clearly recognized, and actually even saw, how truly frightening the conclusions from this realization must be. In view of the looming final judgment, it was no longer enough to settle privately one's record with the God of Abraham. All human beings must be warned of that danger—all of them who, superficial, frivolous, oblivious as they were, do not even realize what is in store for them! They must not simply live for the day but should know that it is their salvation that is at stake, and that they have to struggle day after day to attain it: "By the afternoon![56] Surely Man is in the way of loss, save those who believe, and do righteous deeds, and counsel each other unto the truth, and counsel each other to be steadfast" (sura 103).

Under the impact of premonitions and visions of the end of times, Muhammad called on people to take stock of themselves and act rightly so they would not forfeit their salvation. To begin with, right action—a consequence of one's turning toward God, of one's natural destination to salvation being actualized[57]—was up to each individual. Yet as soon as a community had been formed, a purely individual about-face was no longer sufficient, for it could have too many different effects in daily life. What was most important was that all those who had heeded the Prophet's call asked the alarming question: "Am I really doing everything right?" They must not be at a loss for an answer to this question, which is why it was necessary to establish general guidelines, rules, and laws. In the first place, these referred specifically to the worship of God, but soon also affected all other areas of life. Human beings, destined to be saved and personally responsible for their "original" closeness to God, could not turn to mediators, and so all they could do was to adapt to the daily rites of turning to God as well as to the other Islamic ceremonies, which essentially tried to express precisely this: Friday worship and pilgrimage to Mecca. To this day, the believers' active participation in the religious rites has preserved infinitely more meaning than in European Christendom, which in its rational condescension toward any formally established procedure has lost a great deal of its numinous attraction.

What remains for the Muslim is the fulfillment of God's will, which initially could be determined more or less indirectly in stories about good and bad behavior, but in Medina increasingly assumed the character of commandments; disregarding them resulted in punishment on earth and in the hereafter. Verses 53 to 56 of the Meccan sura 39, which according to Islamic tradition must be regarded as a Medinese insertion, illustrate very succinctly how intertwined the concepts of recognizing one's essence as a creature, turning toward God as a consequence of this, and observing His laws are: "Do they know that God outspreads and straitens His provision to whomsoever He will? Surely in that are signs for a people who believe. Say: 'O my people who have been prodigal against yourselves, do not despair of God's mercy; surely God forgives sins altogether; surely He is the All-forgiving, the All-compassionate. Turn [your faces] unto your Lord and surrender to Him, ere the chastisement comes upon you suddenly while you are unaware.'" Here the believers are reminded that they can find a way that pleases God precisely by following what God has sent down to them as a guideline. By obeying God's commandments, one secures salvation and protection from the punishment of hell. Here the turning toward God, which applies to the believer's total existence, is being transformed into pious obedience. And, indeed, in Medina the law was the actual means by which the continuously growing community of believers was held together in its turning toward God, in Islam.

Obeying God and His messengers now became the crucial criterion for turning toward God and belonging to His community. Thus we read in sura 4, verses 82-85: "Whosoever obeys the Messenger, thereby obeys God; and whosoever turns his back—We have not sent thee to be a watcher over them. They say, 'Obedience!'; but when they sally forth from thee, a party of them meditate all night on other than what thou sayest. God writes down their meditations; so turn away from them, and put thy trust in God; God suffices for a guardian. Why do they not ponder the Koran? If it had been from other than God, surely they would have found in it much inconsistency. When there comes to them a matter, be it of security or fear, they broadcast it; if they had referred it to the Messenger and to those in authority among them, those of them whose task it is to investigate would have known the matter. And but for the bounty of God to you, and His mercy, you would surely have followed Satan, except a few." This transformed Islam, man's existential turning toward his Creator and the reformation of his way of life from inside, into externally obeying the law. This law and the measures Muhammad took in certain emergencies transformed the Muslims' lives from outside, which paved the way for the concept of righteousness of one's deeds. It was important that human beings do what was right and adhere to the right way of doing it, not only while performing the rites. Thus, it became possible to observe from outside if someone had turned toward the right faith. Attaining salvation, which originally was a purely individual affair, now also took place under the eyes of the community of fellow believers and the Prophet. The community's self-concept changed unnoticeably, but irrevocably. It was no longer so much a group of individuals who had been transformed internally and who joined together for ritual prayer, thus proving every day anew their inner transformation; rather, it became a community of believers that was ready to execute God's will on earth. Muhammad and his followers now formed the one community that complied as strictly as possible with God's law. That was the reason the community had attained the highest possible degree of certainty that it would be saved. This is expressed in sura 3, verse 106: "You are the best nation ever brought forth to men, bidding to honour, and forbidding dishonour, and believing in God."

If Muhammad and his followers now saw themselves as a community that had already attained salvation, their view was diametrically opposed to the oldest revelations, which spoke about the threat to the individual's salvation in rousing terms. Now, in the late Medinese period, the believers' membership in the community alone seemed to guarantee their salvation; it was virtually ensured in the collective. Still, even in its late suras the Koran stresses again and again that merely joining Muhammad's community did not suffice; there must be corresponding deeds if turning toward God was to lead to one's salvation. The converts needed to transform themselves into real believers, who in sura 8, verses 2-4 are described as follows: "Believers are they only whose hearts fill with fear when God is named, and whose faith increaseth at each recital of his signs, and who put their trust in their Lord; Who observe the prayers, and give alms out of that with which we have supplied them; These are the believers: their due grade awaiteth them in the presence of their Lord, and forgiveness, and a generous provision." Thus, even in the late Medinese concept of faith there is consideration of the individual's deeds, which must follow entirely new standards. For the first decades after Muhammad's death, the community he had founded referred to itself as "the believers" (*al-mu'minun*). His second successor, Umar (r. 634–644), adopted the title of "commander of the believers" (*amir al-mu'minin*), referring to the connection between the individual's membership in the community founded by the Prophet on the one hand and the life which it was his responsibility to lead according to God's law on the other, a connection Muhammad had emphasized time and again, but which was now in jeopardy.

That professing one's faith and inner change were not necessarily identical, because there were people who only formally joined the community and through that step alone tried to secure their salvation, was something Muhammad had learned largely from the Bedouins. Sura 49, verses 14 and 15, contains the following lament: "The Bedouins say, 'We believe.' Say: 'You do not believe; rather say, "We surrender"'; for belief has not yet entered your hearts. If ye obey God and His Messenger, He will not diminish you anything of your works. God is All-forgiving, All-compassionate.' The believers are those who believe in God and His Messenger, then have not doubted, and have struggled with their possessions and their selves in the way of God; those—they are the truthful ones." In this passage "Islam," the act of turning one's face toward the one God, which is done every single day during ritual prayer, appears as an external mark that has not yet led to inner change, not yet to true faith. We do not know precisely under what circumstances the terms "Islam" and "Muslim" became generally accepted terms for the new faith and its followers.[58] However, that it did is indicative of another development: the assumption that mere membership in the community of the Prophet and one's participation in its rites guaranteed salvation became more and more attractive compared with the idea of the individual being obligated to secure his or her own salvation. Again and again, the unbridgeable gap between these two concepts gave Islamic theology an impulse to reflect on the relationship between God and man.

CHAPTER II

Faith and "Islam"

1. Muslim Views on the Origin of Religious Persuasions

Muslim interpretations of the events during the first decades following Muhammad's death have been quite varied, depending on the observer's religious persuasion. Wherever appropriate, this chapter will have to examine the various interpretations in more detail. They agree only on some very general issues: for example, the Prophet was God's personal messenger who conveyed His word and laws, and ruled the community of the faithful in His name; his death marked the end of direct guidance and thus, irrevocably, the end of the complete satisfaction of the Creator's will—a satisfaction that had ensured salvation. From that point of view, history, as it evolved from that point on, has moved away from salvation and appears as a painfully long process of irreversible decay; it is not until immediately before the end of the world that a millenarian "divinely guided leader" (*al-mahdi*) will force a change toward the superior way, destroy the legions of the evil liar (*ad-daggal*), and reestablish the wholesome conditions of the Prophet's original community.

The Muslims found in the Koran itself information on events detrimental to salvation—events that have subverted and almost destroyed their Prophet's work. As is documented for Jews and Christians (see sura 9, verses 30ff.), wrong interpretations of God's word lead the believers away from their predestined salvation, which Muhammad had made them recognize for the last time in world history. This also means the end of harmony within the community (sura 3, verse 101) which after all can last only as long as each individual turns his or her face toward God alone, fending off any personal sentiment and anything foreign that may try to interfere. And indeed, we are told, even before Muhammad was buried, harmony among the believers had been destroyed; they had begun to argue about who should become the Prophet's religious and political heir. In the Muslim view, even the appointment of Muhammad's first successor, his old companion Abu Bakr, therefore implied a certain devaluation of the state of salvation that had been achieved. In 634 Abu Bakr was succeeded by 'Umar, who after his death in 644 was succeeded by 'Uthman. 'Uthman reigned for twelve years—the first six entirely dedicated to the original community's ideals, and thereafter, deviating from them more and more. After a twelve-year rule he was murdered, which paved the way for 'Ali ibn Abi Talib, Muhammad's cousin and son-in-law, who became caliph but also threw the community of believers into the disastrous First Civil War (656-660): the split of which the Koran had warned so emphatically had become a reality.

That, in any case, is how the Sunnites view the early history of Islam. The Shiites have a different take. As far as they are concerned, even the caliphates of Abu Bakr, 'Umar, and 'Uthman were periods in which the majority of early Muslims committed the most serious offenses. For it was not those three, but 'Ali alone who should have been leader—immediately after Muhammad's death. He alone had had the right to become the Prophet's heir, since he was his daughter Fatima's husband. In the Shiites' opinion, only very few believers had opposed the wrong that began with Abu Bakr's appointment: the predecessors of "Ali's party (*shi'a*), which had actively supported the first caliph during the First Civil War. 'Ali, they say, had almost succeeded, and with him, truth and justice, yet he had been cunningly denied the success that was already within reach.

In 660, finally, the Umayyad Mu'awiya became caliph, a man from the Quraysh clan of the Abd Shams, whose prominent members Muhammad had once fought with particular tenacity and who had not converted to Islam until the very last minute. In short, someone unworthy took over the rule of the community Muhammad had founded at God's command; the caliphate degenerated into a mere kingdom[1], into an exercise of power unrestrained by divine law. This is the charge both factions, the Sunnites and the Shiites, leveled against the Umayyads, who until 750 built and ruled the Arab-Islamic empire from Damascus. The imams from 'Ali's family felt they had been cheated of their right; the Shiites view their early history as a battle against the Umayyads'—in their opinion illegitimate—caliphate, as a fight for the preservation of true Islam, a task which they alone were able to live up to and called upon to perform. The

Sunnites lay the same claim for themselves, even though they never went as far in their (belated) condemnation of the Umayyads as their Shiite rivals.

2. On Islamic History between 632 and 750

The picture the Shiites and Sunnites paint of the first century of Islamic history is not all that distorted. The very fact that we have to use the term "Islamic history" rather than the history of the community of "believers" hints at the schism that—from the Shiites' and early Sunnites' perspective—existed between the Prophet's original community and its political successor structures. In the original Medinese community, "Islam" implied the external profession of the Prophet's message—simply the performance of the rites it prescribed. Sura 49, verse 14, for instance, insinuates that "faith" had not yet entered some Bedouins' hearts, which was why they were wrong to call themselves believers; they should simply have said truthfully, "We profess Islam [turn our face to God—*aslam-nah*]"—that is to say, perform ritual prayer. There is a break between "Islamic" history and the history of the "believers": the former comprises, certainly since Caliph Mu'awiya, the fate of a powerful and successful dynasty, while the latter contains the efforts of a quite motley pious movement which tried to bind an empire and its rulers to its own ideals.[2]

After Muhammad had entered Mecca in 630 without having to resort to force, he reconciled with his former Quraysh enemies and, as already hinted at, appropriated their political aims—which could not have been entirely alien to him, since he was himself a Quraysh. His Medinese "helpers," above all those tribes with an ancient Quraysh frame of mind who had just been formally accepted into the community of believers, were uneasy about that turn of events. As soon as Muhammad died, the tensions erupted. The helpers demanded their own leader in the planned armed conflict; he was to secure the believers' supremacy on the Arabian peninsula. The tribes that had always opposed the Quraysh's quest for power now considered themselves released from their pledge of allegiance to the Prophet, refused to pay their obligatory tribute, and at best were ready to declare that they would continue to abide by the new religion, without however accepting any political duties. In the meantime, those of Muhammad's old companions in faith who had gone from Mecca to Medina had taken charge there. Whenever the Prophet had set out from Medina for a campaign, he had appointed a deputy (*khalifa*) who on his behalf had to direct the ritual prayers of those who had stayed behind. Immediately after the death of God's messenger, Abu Bakr took over that task, and the old companions made sure that functioning as Muhammad's deputy *during the rites* was soon interpreted as being his political successor as well.

It was Abu Bakr's most important task to again subjugate the tribes that had broken away from Medina. For that purpose, he took advantage of the many connections and expertise in military leadership of the Quraysh, who until recently had been the believers' enemies. In short, he continued the policy Muhammad had initiated after 630. The Medinese "helpers" allowed this to happen, because for the moment it was advantageous to them. The campaigns ended in—albeit hard-won—victories; Medina's rule was expanded over the peninsula, as well as in areas in the east that had probably not been subject to the Prophet's community of believers during Muhammad's lifetime.

Now the Quraysh leaders were very close to reaching their goals. Therefore, it is not surprising that their representatives, who had been so successful of late, considered that "deputy of God" in Medina a lightweight. To be sure, Abu Bakr, too, was a Quraysh, but only from a clan that had not had much say in Meccan politics. When he died in 634, it was high time for the Medinese community of believers to assert itself if the Prophet's work was to remain more than an episode along Quraysh Mecca's route to supremacy on the Arabian peninsula. 'Umar ibn al-Khattab—also one of Muhammad's old brothers in arms who had fled to Medina—turned out to be the right man for the task. That he was able to tackle it successfully proves that the idea of using a religious message for establishing a community that transcended tribal boundaries had kept its attraction even after Muhammad's death. 'Umar took a number of different measures to curtail the Quraysh elite's power. He assigned important tasks not to late converts among the Quraysh, but to old companions of the Prophet, and he tried to keep the old Meccan leaders from participating in the early expeditions against the badly ailing Sasanid empire and

Egypt. He assumed the title of "commander of the *believers*" and introduced the *hijra* calendar, a visible sign of his new policy, which the
Quraysh elite found outrageous. The developing empire's tradition was to
be derived from the Prophet's leaving his original homeplace, the *hijra*,
and all religio-political thinking dating further back—and thus affirming
the Quraysh nobility's claim to power—was banished behind that historical turning point, into the dark era of idolatry that had been overcome.

For more than a decade, it looked as if the Prophet's old companions,
proclaiming they were continuing Muhammad's work, were firmly in
charge; 'Umar was succeeded in 644 by 'Uthman, another man from their
midst, who, however, had the advantage of being a descendant of the
noble Quraysh clan of the Abd Shams and therefore was probably acceptable even to those circles that could not have been pleased with 'Umar.
'Uthman has been charged with deliberately promoting, at least during
the second half of his caliphate, the revival of the Quraysh elite, which his
predecessor had pushed out of many positions of power; this is contradicted by a careful analysis of the sources. Under 'Uthman the young
community entered into the phase of its fastest expansion; ample war
booty was a powerful bait. How then could he have been able to keep the
Quraysh back in Mecca? How could he have stayed in control over what
was happening in the garrison towns and at the fronts? Under him, members of formerly leading clans rose to the positions of governor, and some
of them failed or caused scandals. In the Hijaz itself, where 'Uthman had
had the least difficulty in asserting himself, he took steps to curtail the
impious luxury of Quraysh *nouveaux riches* dandies, making himself
unpopular precisely in those circles that others suspected him of favoring.
And so, toward the end of his reign he became controversial all around;
he had not been able to live up to the task of fairly distributing the profit
from his conquests. The Prophet's old companions and their descendants
felt they had been betrayed to the Quraysh nobility and gathered around
'A'isha, Abu Bakr's daughter and the Prophet's widow, as well as az-
Zubayr and Talha, the former a relative of Muhammad's first wife
Khadija, and the latter a member of the same clan as Abu Bakr.

The forces that declared 'Ali ibn abi Talib caliph after 'Uthman's assassination in 656 were much stronger, but at the same time much less homogeneous. 'Ali had once been among those Quraysh who disapproved of

Abu Bakr's rise to the rank of Muhammad's successor. After all, 'Ali, like the Prophet himself, was a descendant of the prominent clan of the Banu Hashim; that was one of the main reasons why the Prophet had made him contract political marriages with daughters of certain leaders whose tribes had been incorporated into the Quraysh league only after they had accepted Islam, at a time when the Quraysh were basically governed from Medina. After the Prophet's death, these tribes tried to take advantage of the uncertain situation by deciding no longer to obey the Islamized Quraysh, whose subjects they had just become, but armed force convinced them of who was now in power. They had to submit to the Prophet's successors in Medina. 'Ali objected to Muhammad's old companions' rule; after the most recent events, those tribes who, until a few years ago, had been the Quraysh's enemies, surely must have been irked by the Medinese regime. They supported 'Ali's ambitions, which he justified by pointing out—and it certainly was a convincing argument—that he was related to the Prophet. People also flocked to him from the circles of warriors who had risked their lives during the first wars of conquest, but were now dissatisfied with their share of the booty, which was allocated to them in proportion to the low esteem in which their tribe was held. Finally, both the Medinese "helpers" and their descendants were furious about the new political development. Their fear—which they had voiced even under Muhammad—of being but useful tools in a political game about the power in Arabia that was cleverly arranged by the Quraysh, increasingly seemed to be borne out. And so many of them began to discover they liked 'Ali.

In 656 'Ali's party was no doubt the largest; Talhah, Zubayr, and 'A'isha could not stand up to him in Medina, and avoided a confrontation by going to southern Iraq. 'Ali's followers were agreed on not reviving the rule of the Prophet's old companions with Talhah or Zubayr as leaders. They managed as early as 657 to defeat both of them in the famous Battle of the Camel near Basra, and to take 'A'isha prisoner; for the time being, these factions were put out of commission. Yet 'Ali's followers still had to pass the real acid test: Mu'awiya ibn abi Sufyan, a close relative of the murdered 'Uthman, accused 'Ali of making common cause with the assassins and demanded their extradition so they could be subjected to vendetta. Mu'awiya had been governor of Damascus for over ten years.

Even in pre-Islamic times, the clan of the 'Abd Shams had kept close relations with the Arabian tribes in Syria and Palestine. Furthermore, the situation there was basically under control, since the country, which had long been Arabized, did not suffer from random attacks by greedy warriors from Arabia. That was what was happening in Iraq, where the early collapse of the Sasanid rule had quickly made the situation hopelessly unmanageable; first efforts at gaining some control had been made by founding the garrison towns of Basra and Kufa, but the situation was still anything but under control. In the course of the war against Tulhah and Zubayr, 'Ali had got himself right in the middle of that witches' cauldron in Iraq. Mu'awiya, however, advanced his units up to the middle Euphrates, where at Siffin battles between him and 'Ali were fought for several months in 658. In the end, they agreed to submit to arbitration on whether Mu'awiya had the right to demand vendetta for 'Uthman's murder. The decision was in favor of Mu'awiya and had disastrous consequences for 'Ali.

Those little-respected groups that, even years before, had gone to Iraq to wage armed battles for the new faith and a little booty, felt betrayed by 'Ali; they felt they had devoted their lives to the fight against the unbelievers, just like all those who three decades before had moved to Medina to join the Prophet. They had entirely surrendered to God and now had to witness 'Ali subjecting himself to human judgment. So they had been wrong about him, that prominent Quraysh who let formerly anti-Quraysh tribes glorify him as an "imam," a leader with religio-political authority totally unattainable to ordinary men, no matter how astute and brave they were. That hurt their plebeian self-image, which was saturated with pious ardor, and, burning with hatred, they turned against 'Ali. He spent the rest of his life in Iraq battling those renegades who later were called Kharijites; in 660 he was killed by one of their men.

And so, thanks to favorable circumstances, Mu'awiya was victorious in the Arab-Islamic power struggle, the so-called First Civil War. It was probably shortly before 'Ali's death that the governor of Syria declared himself caliph; yet, from the mouth of the son of a prominent Quraysh enemy of Muhammad, this title sounded quite different than it used to. "The messenger's deputy," that interpretation of the title, whose historical background was outlined above, was hardly possible for Mu'awiya. The

old Quraysh elite could not regard Muhammad as the one who had established their power, only as the one who had expanded it. The measures
'Umar had taken had turned against the Quraysh and their pre-Islamic
claim to power, but they could not erase at one bold stroke the reality that
was decisive for Mu'awiya in Damascus: at the least, he had not gained
his dynastic power only through Islam; as already mentioned, it was,
rather, also based on already established connections, and the position he
as a Quraysh claimed within the community of Arabian tribes was due to
the alleged reform of the Kaaba cult ascribed to Qusayy. It was at that
point, and not simply because of Muhammad, that in this historical interpretation the Quraysh became the ritual servants of Allah who were distinguished among all Arabs. Therefore, the sovereign title of "caliph,"
which the Prophet's old companions had established, no longer denoted
Mu'awiya as the "deputy of God's messenger," but as "God's deputy"
(*khalifat Allah*), just as Umayyad court poetry has documented it. God
Himself—without the Prophet as intermediary—put sovereign power into
the hands of the Umayyads.[3]

With the rise of the Umayyads, those forces gained political power
who knew how to use Islam for their purposes, but did not justify their
actions by their religion alone. This put them in direct opposition—initially with no possibility of compromise—to the representatives of the
movement, which, strong but at variance with itself, saw in Muhammad
the climax of the history of salvation and believed that the individual's
life as well as the standards of political rule were derived from him. The
more the followers of that movement felt their hope for the quick realization of these ideals waning, the more obstinately did they cling to the
memory of that blessed period, painting in their memory a picture of it
that was more beautiful than it had actually been, and wanting to hold on
always to whatever was left of it, or even to reestablish forcefully those
conditions of which they dreamed. The Umayyad caliphate and its servants did not remain entirely untouched by this turbulence, but in the long
run they could not manage to exploit it for their purposes and make up for
the lack of legitimacy from which they suffered in the eyes of their enemies, who insisted that Muhammad's works were at the center of their
religion. For these reasons they lost, in the mid-eighth century, their
power to a movement whose leaders had been deft at integrating the pious

opposition's most important issues, at least for the purposes of political propaganda. That movement, which fought for the establishment of a Hashim[4] caliphate, brought the Abbasids to power, a Hashim clan whose members claimed to be descendants of 'Abbas, one of the Prophet's uncles.[5]

3. Divine Determination versus Human Determination

We have seen that the fact that man was created makes him grateful to his Creator and subjects everything he does and does not do to His fair judgment.[6] Even during Muhammad's lifetime, there were objections to this sort of individual responsibility for one's salvation. Various kinds of argument were raised: on the one hand, what people did was determined by the particular circumstances of their individual lives, which were the result of God's inscrutable ways—the world was not entirely at man's disposal. On the other hand, if the individual believers became part of the community that performed the rites God had instated, and if they obeyed His law, then reflecting on a personal path to salvation was not necessary. Thus, obedience toward "God and His messenger" was the benchmark of the "best community," which was destined to attain salvation: membership in the Prophetic community relieved the individual of the burden to have to take care of his or her own salvation. It was precisely this element of greater-than-individual responsibility that made Muhammad's political work possible and kept his religion from running dry in some God-seeking individualism; outlasting him, this element carried the development that led to the establishment of an Arabian empire that at least partly overcame the tribes' inherited particularism. Ultimately it created a community comprising many different peoples—if only by destroying the Damascene caliphate, whose rulers were accused of halting the process of social change once Arabian supremacy was established, and of refusing to take the necessary step toward the "Islamic empire."

In the course of the development of a community that transcended the borders between tribes and eventually even ethnic differences, the religious justification of obedience to the rules, which even Muhammad had demanded back in Medina, was bound to become crucial. Thanks to their well-known close relationship with Muhammad, the Prophet's first three successors, and probably 'Ali ibn Abi Talib as well, were probably able to derive some authority from the Prophet's works. Mu'awiya and the caliphs after him could no longer do that. The close connection between the first Muslim dynasty's ancestors and the rise of Islam no longer existed. That is the reason why the Umayyads' interpretation of the events in the first half of the seventh century deviated fundamentally from that of the Prophet's old companions, such as 'Umar ibn al-Khattab: the Umayyads regarded Muhammad's work as only *one* benchmark along the Quraysh's way to power over the Arabs. The idea that the obedience demanded of Muslims was based on God's express wish, which is often emphasized in the Medinese suras, was certainly fascinating to the Umayyads and their eulogists, for it gave more clout to the Quraysh's claim to power, which they had expressed even in pre-Islamic times.[7] The "successor to God's messenger" became "God's deputy," the executor of the supreme will, to which the "herd"[8] had to succumb without protest.

The Umayyad caliphs, however, were not prophets, nor did they ever claim to be. It was this lack of authority that led up to the question of the *content* of their sovereign commands, which was difficult to answer: Why was it that God wanted exactly this and nothing else? There was still no Islamic law, not even in rough outlines. Under such circumstances, could obedience to the rulers really guarantee their subjects' salvation? Did the caliphs convey the "guidelines to righteousness" that were so fervently sought? The charge leveled at the Umayyads time and again by a broad movement of discontent, that they were nothing but "kings," proves that that question had to be answered in the negative if one compared the situation with the ideal image that was painted of the Prophet's original community. Indeed, being a prophet and being an Umayyad caliph were two entirely different matters. Muhammad had always held that ruling the believers was by no means his ultimate goal; he was the conveyor of a message, a warner who did not even have the power to enforce the commands God had revealed to him: "Say: 'He is able to send forth upon you chastisement, from above you or from under your feet, or to confuse you in sects and to make you taste the violence of one another.' Behold how We turn about the signs; happily they will understand. Thy people have cried it lies; yet it is the truth. Say: 'I am not a guardian over you. Every tiding has its time appointed; you will surely know.'" That is how the late Meccan sura 6 puts it (verses 65-67).

In Mecca the political and social situation had forced Muhammad to show such restraint; yet the same concept determined his self-image in Medina as well. If he demanded obedience from the believers, he always did so in the name of God, and even as a prophet he was subject to the law the Supreme One had him proclaim, just like all other members of the community were. In that sense, Muhammad was always on the same level with all the other believers. Quite differently, however, the Umayyad ruler as "God's deputy"! He acted on God's behalf and—to use the phrase in sura 6, verse 67—was certainly the guardian of all his subjects, the "herd."

In the young community of followers of the new belief, a community that was barely held together by clearly defined tenets or a binding tradition, this momentous shifting of weights was felt very keenly. For lack of clear concepts, the community members argued heatedly about the caliphs' tyranny and injustice (zulm), all the more so since, under 'Abd al-Malik (r. 685–705), profitable expeditions were hardly possible any longer, and he established a strict order at home, where there was so much destruction after extended civil wars. That is the historical background for the earliest specifically theological documents Islam has produced. These sources center around the Arabic term qadar, which in the Koran refers to the measurement of something, a measurement determined by God[9]; as a verb, the root qadar expresses God's determining measures that irrevocably influence human fate: as far back as when He created the world, He determined once and for all the food supply for each individual (sura 41, verse 9); he also determined the stations of the moon (sura 36, verse 39). Thus the verb qadara refers to God's independently disposing of what He has created, about which man can do nothing[10]; in relation to God the idols worshiped by the Meccans—which were created, just like those worshiping them were—were pathetic slaves who could not determine anything of their own volition.[11] In other words, the concept of divine qadar occupies that area of meaning where God's ever-active care merges with the predetermination of the individual's fate.[12]

Where do we find that gray area in real life? This was the question which stirred up fierce arguments at the time; there were some scattered audacious men who did not want that area to begin until far beyond all human activities and endeavors, men who tried to maintain that the individual was endowed with a large degree of self-determination. They granted human beings virtually their own, independent *qadar*, and we find them in the history of Islamic dogma under the name of "Qadarites."

Obviously, "God's deputy" could not be pleased with views of this sort. To be sure, the Qadarites did not assail the Umayyad ideology of power directly, but people who are convinced they have their own *qadar* are bad sheep in a herd that is supposed to wait passively for the orders of "God's deputy." 'Abd al-Malik was concerned and asked one of the most prominent advocates of these new ideas, al-Hasan al-Basri (d. 728)[13], what the *qadar* was all about. After all, it was not long since 'Abd al-Malik's governor al-Hajjaj ibn Yusuf had given by now famous speeches in which he demanded unqualified obedience from the Iraqis, who had been forced back under Umayyad rule, and threatened draconian measures in response to all kinds of transgressions. Each shepherd, the speaker was suddenly yelled at from the crowd, was responsible for his own herd—the caliph, he was told, was not God's governor who was above everything, which meant that he was—as was even the Prophet himself—accountable to the Creator. Al-Hasan al-Basri shared that view.[14]

In his response to the caliph, al-Hasan confirmed that he believed human beings possessed a certain degree of self-determination, quite in accordance with the view their ancestors—the Prophet's original community—had held. It was an opinion based on the revelation which said: "I have not created jinn and mankind except to serve Me" (sura 51, verse 56). It was absurd, al-Hasan argued, to believe that God had created human beings for a certain purpose whose fulfillment was their salvation, if He deliberately kept some of them from achieving that goal—that is to say, if He personally caused their insubordination; only a tyrant could deal with his subjects in such a malicious manner. It was, al-Hasan continued, precisely in absurd thought processes of that kind, which took evil to be the result of an unfathomable, divine exercise of power, that he recognized a disturbing renunciation of their forefathers' faith, which he, constantly pointing out pertinent passages in the Koran, said he believed needed to be reversed. After thus having the highest authority—the ancestors' faith with its basis in the revelation—corroborate his view, he discussed numerous verses in the Koran, which at first glance seemed to confirm the predestinarians' opinion, but, as al-Hasan explained, only at first glance. He managed—not always without splitting hairs—to interpret all of them in a way that supported his view. Not even sura 7, verse 178 he said, contradicted his interpretation: "We have created for Gehenna many jinn and men; they have hearts, but understand not with them; they have eyes, but perceive not with them; they have ears, but they hear not with them. They are like cattle; nay, rather they are further astray. Those—they are the heedless." This passage, he claimed, only seemingly talked about predestination for hell. He argued that in actuality obduracy, blindness, and deafness were not invariable characteristics such as complexion. "For Gehenna" (hell), he says, did not refer to those jinns' and to people's existential destination; frequently, for instance, people said that they were building houses only for time to destroy them again; but this was not at all the purpose of building them. Now al-Hasan permitted himself a pointed polemical remark directed at the predestinarians: Most of those who claimed their faith or unbelief was predestined by God were careful not to let their worldly businesses run themselves, without personally interfering!

All human beings had the faculty (*istita'a*) to fend off evil. Sura 18, verses 59ff., tells the story of how Moses once met a friend whom he wanted to accompany. That stranger committed three acts which Moses found entirely incomprehensible: he knocked a leak into a ship; he killed a boy; he shored up a wall that was about to collapse. Moses demanded an explanation and learned the following: "As for the ship, it belonged to certain poor men, who toiled upon the sea; and I desired to damage it, for behind them there was a king who was seizing every ship by brutal force. As for the lad, his parents were believers; and we were afraid he would impose on them insolence and unbelief; so we desired that their Lord should give to them in exchange one better than he in purity, and nearer in tenderness. As for the wall, it belonged to two orphan lads in the city, and under it was a treasure belonging to them. Their father was a righteous man; and thy Lord desired that they should come of age and then bring forth their treasure as a mercy from thy Lord. I did it not of my own bidding. This is the interpretation of that thou couldst not bear patiently'" (verses 79-82). The stranger knew about the bad things that could happen if he did not interfere. Therefore, he acted in order to prevent disaster. Every human being, al-Hasan al-Basri argued, could do likewise to avert evil, of which he would be guilty otherwise. The conclusion of the letter to the caliph was a stern warning: "Comprehend and always realize that God will not prevent the enforcement of His commands by destining part of mankind to evil. God did not send out the messengers to make people do the opposite of what He has decreed for them and then to punish these people for all eternity for not obeying Him when He never even gave them the option to do so."[15]

Early on, during the confusion in the first years of 'Abd al-Malik's caliphate, a pretender to the throne was said to have promoted himself in Damascus with the following words: "Before me, no Quraysh preaching from this pulpit failed to claim that paradise and hell were at his disposal, and that he was sending all those to paradise who obeyed him, and all those to hell who opposed him. I, however, am telling you, paradise and hell are in God's hand!"[16] Ascribing the *qadar*—which the predestinarians ascribed to God, and His deputies, therefore, claimed for themselves—to every human being was a politically explosive theological statement. This becomes once again clear in this context. Caliph 'Abd al-Malik was not able to contain the Qadarites' polemics, which, under his successor al-Walid (r. 705–15), took a distinct anti-Umayyad turn; the Qadarites had already been involved in a rebellion in Iraq around 700.[17] During the last two decades of the Umayyads' Damascene reign, the subversive character of a Qadariyya, that by now had turned politically radical, became fatefully obvious. Ghailan, one of its leaders, seems to have promoted the idea that, since all believers were responsible for their own salvation, there was no compelling reason why the ruler should be from the tribe of the Quraysh. Anyone who applied the Koran and the *sunna* correctly could be caliph; yet if a ruler violated the divine law, he should be dethroned—if everyone had to obey God, ultimately no "deputy of God" was necessary. Now the Umayyads struck out against the Qadarites; Ghailan paid with his life.[18] These disturbances weakened the Damascene caliphate, which was already seriously shaken by other quarrels, even further. During 744, a caliph was, for a brief time, even devoted to the Qadarites; expressing their opinion, he proclaimed in his inauguration speech: "No obedience to any creature that is disobedient to his

Creator!"[19]

The example of the Qadarites illustrates the Islamic idiosyncrasy of dogmatic and political views being inextricably intertwined. The individual's personal responsibility for his or her salvation restricts institutional authority on earth, which in turn affirms its claim to power by declaring that it rules as an agency of God, and, when enforcing its measures, by stressing the supra-individual traits of the Prophet's original community—which ultimately means that the individual Muslim's deeds are more or less externally determined. The individual's external determination, it is suggested, originated in God, which in view of God's care for His creation, as stressed everywhere in the Koran, does make sense.

At this point we are already getting a glimpse of yet another characteristic of Islamic thinking: any interpretation of current events has to refer to the period of the original community; al-Hasan al-Basri called the predestinarians' thoughts novel, which stripped them of all authority; conversely, he presented himself as the preserver of the forefathers' teachings. His adversaries would, of course, make similar claims about their own convictions. This means that all dogmatic or religio-political movements developed their own interpretations of earliest Islamic history; this analytic construct allowed them to discover, in a circular conclusion, their predecessors in the original community, whose true heirs they felt they were and whose work they were continuing. We will presently deal with this phenomenon.

4. The Kharijites

Although the Qadarites' teachings contained a good deal of politically explosive material that, if interpreted radically, might even question the lawfulness of a Quraysh caliphate, they still were mainly directed at the individual believers, reminding them that they were responsible for their own salvation. A wholesale condemnation of the Umayyad caliphate and the thesis that only a revolution could pave the way for the creation of a true community of believers were not part of their platform; even those Qadarites who in 744 temporarily seized power enthroned an Umayyad of their choice (who however did have to accede to their religio-political demands). Other groups were much more radical. They rejected the direction history had taken after the Prophet's death as absolutely detrimental to salvation and claimed to be the only true believers continuing Muhammad's Medinese works. Preserving that tradition was the only way of obtaining legitimacy, and only the cooperation within a community that was firmly committed to the ideal of the Prophet's original community could ensure entry into paradise. These factions did not believe salvation could be obtained in a "kingdom" where the attempt to realize the Quraysh's claim to power sometimes came even above Islam. The Kharijites fought adamantly and with the greatest tenacity for perpetuating Islam's Medinese past in this spirit.

Let us recall that 'Ali ibn Abi Talib was murdered by a member of that sect. When he had agreed on submitting to arbitration, a large part of his followers broke away from him. Even before the pronouncement of the fateful verdict, they had moved on to Haraura, a location near Kufa; this is the reason al-Harauriya is one of the oldest terms for the early Kharijite movement. In addition, they were called al-Muhakkima, after their slogan "*lah hukma illah lillah!*," translated: "God alone has the right to judge!" Initially this was a reference to the decision in the dispute between 'Ali and Mu'awiya, yet the slogan was perfectly suitable for generalization and for taking on an anarchist twist. After arbitration had been unfavorable for 'Ali, the movement gained even more followers. It now called itself ash-Shurat, those who "have sold" their lives for God's cause. This term is in reference to sura 4, verses 76-77, and similar passages in the Koran. There it says: "So let them fight in the way of God who sell the present life for the world to come; and whosoever fights in the way of God and is slain, or conquers, We shall bring him a mighty wage. How is it with you, that you do not fight in the way of God, and for the men, women, and children who, being abased, say, 'Our Lord, bring us forth from this city whose people are evildoers, and appoint to us from Thee a helper'? The believers fight in the way of God, and the unbelievers fight in the idols' way. Fight you, therefore, against the friends of Satan; surely the guile of Satan is ever feeble."

The term *ash-Shurat* indicates the radical personal commitment all Kharijites and likeminded people were expected to make. Securing one's individual salvation took on more and more extreme forms: only a martyr's death would guarantee one a place in paradise. The first Kharijites praised themselves in numerous poems for holding these beliefs. "You, who wish to contend with me in a duel, approach that I may hand you the poisoned beverage of death; There is no shame in passing one another the cup which slays those who put their lips to it; pour it out for me then, and drink it yourself." The following three verses are ascribed to an Amazone: "I bear the weight of a head I am tired of carrying, I have had enough of oiling and washing it. Is there not a brave man who will relieve me of such a burden?"[20]

'Ali could not rein in the hatred and bellicosity expressed in such words, and Ziyad, Mu'awiya's governor in Iraq, soon had his own problems with the Kharijites. At that time, their centers were at the lower left bank of the Tigris, from where they could quickly escape into the Iranian highlands in the event of peril, and to the marshlands around the young garrison town of Basra. At the time he took office in Basra, Ziyad gave a famous speech in which he voiced his reliance on God's authority, which, he said, had been transferred to the Umayyads; public safety should be strictly restored. For that purpose the city was divided into districts, in each of which were appointed spokesmen who were accountable to the governor; in the event of violations of the new statutes they were to be held responsible if the real perpetrators could not be found. It was a Kharijite who allegedly objected to this decree: quoting sura 53, verse 39—"That no soul laden bears the load of another"—he insisted that such measures were in contradiction to the revelation.[21] We once again recognize the basic pattern of the conflict which pushed the Qadarites into opposition against the Umayyads.

Except the Kharijites were not in the least willing to recognize the Umayyads as rulers of an Islamic community. They formed their own communities with their own leaders, which, in the first decades of the eighth century, removed large areas in southern Iran as well as northern Africa from the caliph's influence, and in Iraq and the Hijaz, too, they often pressed the Umayyad governors hard. That the Kharijites never won a decisive victory with far-reaching consequences was because, even during 'Abd al-Malik's reign, their movement was hopelessly splintered into many factions. Their rigorous attitudes and ceaseless striving for individual salvation concealed a large measure of anarchy. Even before some

Qadarites issued the slogan that a caliph disobedient to God should be deposed, the pious fanatics fought for precisely that idea, and apparently practiced it, too, in their communities. They thought nothing of the concept of legitimacy by virtue of birth, holding instead that all that counted was fear of God. Many of them even doubted if there had to be a ruler at all, arguing that only during military campaigns should someone be in command.

The Prophet was dead, but as far as the Kharijites were concerned, the conditions of the original community in Medina had to remain intact—the conditions, that is, before Muhammad had reconciled with Mecca. Typically, that event was considered the end of the period in which one could gain religious merit by subjecting oneself to the Prophet, by abandoning one's pre-Islamic way of life, and by moving to Medina: for, after the quarrel with Mecca had been settled, Islam became "Quraysh," and the new message prevailed. Around the turn of the eighth century, the Kharijite movement took a different view. It held that those, and only those, who put themselves entirely at the Kharijite leader's disposal and were willing to live as part of his band of warriors—that is to say, those who made the *hijra*[22]—had really found true belief. That belief had to be realized every day by strictly observing God's commandments. Those who violated these commandments were considered apostates by some Kharijites and had to leave the community of believers, to which they could not return even if they admitted their guilt and repented. Some factions are said not even to have stopped short of murder in such cases. For in Islam, those who have broken away from the true faith, have forfeited their lives, even though later legal handbooks granted them the chance of penitently disavowing their fateful conduct.[23]

It is rather difficult to decide whether these Kharijite beliefs were actually practiced very often, and if they were, in how many factions and splinter groups. It is conceivable that individual responsibility for one's salvation, carried to an extreme, might have taken on those forms. However, certainly not all Kharijites were willing to accept such extremes. Some recognized that the more they exhausted themselves in senseless battles, the more they were removed from their religious and political goals. These more prudent members were called—mockingly?—the "ones who are sitting," as opposed to their bellicose brothers in faith, the "ones going to battle." That moderate faction's leader and first theologian during the reign of Caliph 'Abd al-Malik was 'Abdallah ibn Ibad from al-Basra. In contrast to their more radical fellow Kharijites, the members of this faction did not insist on forcefully reestablishing the Prophet's community, but were content to be in possession of the true gospel in an environment which they still could not (yet) structure according to their tenets. Perhaps they were even somewhat skeptical of their own ability to emulate those early believers under Muhammad's stewardship; for we are told that 'Abdallah ibn Ibad's successor, Jabir ibn Zaid al-Azdi, had members of the community address him as "imam of the Muslims" rather than "of the believers"[24]: he who professed his faith not arms in hand but exercising restraint, merely performed the daily rites (comparable to the Bedouins Muhammad had once rebuked[25]); without letting go of his convictions, he accepted for the time being the fact that the present political situation did not allow him to meet fully the requirements of his belief. In Shia Islam we will again encounter the willingness temporarily to abstain from making a revolution; even though "faith" and "state" were to be one according to the model of the original community, their dualism was grudgingly accepted. Still, situations could occur at any time in which it was possible to unleash a civil war against the rulers and the Muslims of different persuasion, with the goal of reestablishing that unity of "faith" and "state." We should note that it is here, among the early Ibadi Kharijites, that the word "Muslims," as an Islamic community's term for itself, occurred for the first time with its clearly defined, specific meaning.

We are also familiar with 'Abdallah ibn Ibad's beliefs from a missive he sent to 'Abd al-Malik. Like al-Hasan al-Basri's letter, it seems to have been a response to an inquiry by the caliph, who had announced that he would not tolerate the Kharijites' harsh criticism of 'Uthman. In any case, Ibn Ibad began his discourse by stating that, after the Prophet's death, the Koran was the only source of divine guidance. Muhammad himself had abided by the revelation and so had his closest companions, among them, 'Uthman. Even under Abu Bakr and 'Umar, the Koran's rules had been undisputed. Only after 'Uthman became caliph were there deviations. For this reason his caliphate was already overshadowed by tyranny (*jabrut*). In the term "tyranny" we recognize a close connection with the contemporary Qadarites. They, too, denigrated the caliph, who, in their opinion, arbitrarily imposed laws on his subjects like a "tyrant" (*jabbar*), with the root *j-b-r* also denoting the arbitrariness which a deterministically minded creator—if, indeed, there were one—would be inflicting on his creatures. In short, we are dealing with a key word here that plays an important part in various anti-Umayyad currents and movements. The Shiites, too, consider the Umayyad caliph a despot (*jabbar*), comparable to Pharaoh, from whose tyranny Moses had to suffer. However, they state a different reason for their opinion, citing the—in their opinion illegal— seizure of power by Mu'awiya and his successors.

But back to 'Abdallah ibn Ibad. He concluded a listing of some of the offenses against the Koran of which 'Uthman had been guilty in his position as caliph with the following quote from sura 47, verse 27: "Those who have turned back in their traces after the guidance has become clear to them, Satan it was that tempted them, and God respited them." That is the verse on which the Kharijites based their tenet concerning the sinner's apostasy. According to Kharijite doctrine, all believers have to defect from 'Uthman, the apostate! From this, in turn, followed the obligation to the holy war (*jihad*), which 'Ali had accepted at the beginning of his reign. In his charges against the Kharijites, 'Abd al-Malik had apparently pointed out 'Ali's special status as a relative of the Prophet. The caliph probably meant this as a criticism of the hatred with which the Kharijites had persecuted 'Ali and which ultimately led them to reject any kind of reign based on genealogical legitimization. 'Abdallah ibn Ibad was trying to preempt that criticism, stating that he was still convinced of 'Ali's dignity. Yet, he continued, salvation did not lie in being a blood relative of Muhammad, but only in the law as revealed to him, which 'Ali had clearly abandoned near Siffin, thus becoming entangled in unbelief. "Know that it is the sign of that community's unbelief that it reaches decisions according to something other than the revelation!" Someone, he argued, who pursued his own goals was simply not fit to preserve the faith; salvation could be gained only by complying with the Koran. He also categorically rejected 'Abd al-Malik's contention that God had guided Mu'awiya's hand during the vendetta. That statement of the caliph once more documents the Umayyad concept of "governorship" in God's name, which the Qadarites rejected as a limitation of the human *qadar* they postulated, but which 'Abdallah ibn Ibad rejected because it justified a ruler's actions that the Koran neither prescribed nor approved. The fact, he argued, that a ruler was victorious did not indicate that he was executing God's will; initially Pharaoh, too, had triumphed, and yet he had been God's declared enemy from the start. If, therefore, Mu'awiya had demanded vendetta for 'Uthman in a manner the Koran clearly did not approve, one had to break away from Mu'awiya, even if success seemed to validate him.

Ibn Ibad proceeded to shift his focus on another term, that of "exaggeration" (*guluw*). Apparently 'Abd al-Malik had accused the Kharijites of being "exaggerators" because of their stubbornness and unconciliatory stance in regard to Mu'awiya. 'Abdallah ibn Ibad contended that "exaggeration" was nothing but a deviation from the norm God had established; in short, he returned the charge to his critic. After all, 'Abd al-Malik had accused the Kharijites of having left the community of the Muslims. Naturally, 'Abdallah ibn Ibad had a different take. He claimed that the ancestors—whom he, of course, viewed as the Kharijites' predecessors—had always been genuinely devoted (*tawalla*) to Abu Bakr and 'Umar, for Muhammad's first two successors had truly inherited the power over the Prophet's community. Both had been guided by the Koran and, thus, continued Muhammad's rule. Yet it had been impossible to support 'Uthman, 'Ali, and Mu'awiya because they had brushed aside the divine decrees as revealed by the Prophet. "O believers, fight the unbelievers who are near to you, and let them find in you a harshness; and know that God is with the godfearing." That verse from the Koran (sura 9, verse 125) served Ibn Ibad to justify Kharijite rebellions, even though, in his opinion, this divine word no longer explained the extremists' obsession with war; they had become apostates themselves, infidels from whom he and the moderates were disassociating themselves. Ibn Ibad urged the caliph to base his rule solely on the provisions established in God's Book; he once more emphasized that that was what the Prophet and his first two successors had done, and their example (*sunna*) must be emulated so as to put an end to discord and bloodshed.[26]

The extremist movements within Kharijite Islam were short-lived. Yet the Ibadiyya established their own imamate in Oman, whose history has lasted until the present time. They were successful in northern Africa, too, in the eighth century, particularly among the Berbers; they founded their own imamates in the areas of what today constitutes Algeria and Djebel Nefusa near Tripoli in Libya. The Kharijites were not able to influence crucially Islam's main course in history. Yet, within the development of Islamic theology as a whole, they assume a prominent place, for it was in their thoughts that certain fundamental views evolved for the very first time. Like the Qadarites, they stressed the believer's individual responsibility for his or her own salvation; however, they went far beyond the Qadarites in that they tried to force upon the Muslims a firm yardstick for correct conduct: the Koran. In their crusade for that tenet, they offered a deliberate contrast to the political and religious conditions of the early Umayyad period. Their main concern was not merely to establish a theological foundation for the individual's personal responsibility for his or her salvation. Rather, they committed themselves to a way of life based entirely on the Koran; by adopting and following the Koranic way of life, every believer would gain entry into paradise. As in the original community and, they believed, under Abu Bakr and 'Umar, everything one said and did should be directly inspired by the revelation, which became the institution ensuring prophetic "guidance" even after the Prophet's death.[27]

The Kharijites outlined their views of early Islamic history according to these beliefs: Muhammad himself, as well as Abu Bakr and 'Umar after him, were positive figures; one had to turn away from 'Ali and the Umayyads, because they had ignored the "guidance" and were "imams of error."[28] Aside from the conviction to have found in the institution of the Koran a substitute[29] for the Prophet's guidance, which made it possible to continue the conditions of the original community that guaranteed salvation, it was that view of history that was the Kharijites' most efficient unifying force. Adopting it meant to have broken away from the Umayyads as well as the Shiites, who considered 'Ali and his successors to be the leaders toward salvation. Caliph 'Umar ibn Abd al-Aziz (r. 717–720), who wanted to ease the religio-political tensions in his empire, tried to dissuade the Kharijites from their exaggerated veneration of Abu Bakr and 'Umar, arguing that those two had been guilty of committing offenses as well, without the Kharijites' ancestors raising their swords against them.[30] It goes without saying that 'Umar ibn 'Abd al-'Aziz did not succeed in wresting the Kharijites' integrating figures away from them.

5. The Shiites

Originally the Shiites were 'Ali's party (*shi'at 'Ali*) during the First Civil War. After the secession of those who were later called Kharijites and his political defeat in the struggle against Mu'awiya, 'Ali's situation had become hopeless. He could regard only Mesopotamia as his empire, and even that not without qualification, for there the Kharijites fought him extremely tenaciously. After his father was murdered, his oldest son, al-Hasan, whose mother was Muhammad's daughter Fatima, thought it advisable to decline the inheritance his father's followers had offered him, to seek an agreement with Mu'awiya, and otherwise lead the certainly not uncomfortable life of a grandson of the Prophet in the Hijaz. His younger brother al-Husayn was enticed by 'Ali's Kufan party to lead a rebellion against the Umayyads, which disintegrated pitifully as soon as it became serious. Until this day the Shiites remember al-Husayn's bloody end near Karbala in 681 as the shocking triumph of the evil forces rebelling against God, against whom the Prophet's younger grandson had waged a heroic but hopeless battle; yet his martyr's death, the Shiites hold, should be seen as a beacon of their just cause, and the grief over his death be turned into aggressiveness against the Islamic state as long as it is not Shiite.

The Second Civil War, the Umayyad caliphate's profound crisis, in the course of which power was transferred to the dynasty's Marwanid branch, gave the Shiites a new boost, especially in Iraq. Under the leadership of al-Mukhtar ibn Abi 'Ubayd, an Arab from the tribe of the Banu Taqif, they defied until 687 'Abd al-Malik's efforts to bring Mesopotamia back under firm Umayyad control. Al-Mukhtar had claimed to be leading the Shia at the behest of a third son of 'Ali, the Muhammad "ibn al-Hanafiyya," who was born to a woman from the tribe of the Banu Hanifa; whether there is truth to that claim, has to be left open.[31]

The historical chronicles note numerous smaller Shii rebellions before the end of the Umayyad period, particularly in or originating in Iraq. Yet the Damascene caliphs were in no serious danger until Shiite ideas and the forces they had gathered merged into one broad-based movement directed against the Umayyads. This movement incited the masses with the demand that the rule of the Banu Abd Shams, who allegedly were sinners, be replaced by a truly Islamic caliphate held by a man from the Banu

Hashim, "one from Muhammad's lineage who has unanimous approval."[32] The promised caliph from the Prophet's lineage who was raised to the throne in Kufa in 750 was as-Saffah—a descendant of 'Abbas and uncle of Muhammad. 'Ali's party had been outmaneuvered by the "Hashimiyya movement." The Abbasids persecuted the Shiites no less harshly than the Umayyads had, and did everything they could to blur the memory of the fact that they originally owed their rise to the Shia.

In order to outline the contribution of 'Ali's early party to the development of Islamic theology, we have to revisit the period of the original Medinese community. In 630 Muhammad reconciled with the Meccans, which hurt the Medinese "helpers," at least in their view. Their ill feeling must have lingered on; during the First Civil War, many of them supported 'Ali, who—as his expedition against Talha and az-Zubayr illustrates— seemed to put an end to the rule of the old Meccan clique, who had come to Medina in the wake of Muhammad's flight and seized power there. Furthermore, in the genealogical system of the time, the Aws and Khazraj were considered southern Arabs and not northern Arabs like the Quraysh. 'Ali, however, was related through marriage to southern Arabian tribes.[33] The mother of his above-mentioned son Muhammad was a member of the tribe among which the prophet Musaylima, a serious competitor of the Quraysh Muhammad, had lived and worked. Furthermore, as a vassal of the Sasanid shah, the Banu Hanifa's leader had worn a crown himself[34]— in view of which the Quraysh's claim to power must have been perceived as the insolence of a parvenu. And so, in response to the Quraysh challenge, the southern Arabs pointed out the much older—and, in part, fictitious—historic tradition, which during the Umayyad period had been handed down in a slew of poetic legends.[35]

We have just struck one of the roots of Shiite thought: charismatic rule can be bequeathed within a dynasty by way of a testamentary disposition. Muhammad the Prophet should have been succeeded by 'Ali, the heir (*wasi*) said to have been explicitly named. According to a document summarizing the views of 'Abdallah ibn Saba', a Yemenite Jew who had converted to Islam and been the early Shia's main theoretical influence, every prophet had an heir to his mission. As Muhammad was the prophets' seal, so 'Ali was the heirs' seal; preventing 'Ali from performing the tasks assigned to him by way of the Prophet's testamentary disposition was the worst injustice imaginable. 'Uthman was guilty of that crime; therefore, it was high time to strike back! That legitimist concepts of this kind were bandied about among southern Arabian tribes is documented in the legends mentioned above, in which the term "testament" (*wasiya*) is used for the transition of rule from one "crowned king" to another. As the events after his death illustrate, Mu'awiya, the founder of the Umayyad dynasty, had not managed to ensure his son Yazid's smooth succession to the throne; a Quraysh northern Arabian "kingdom" was considered an extraordinary novelty, and the Prophet's former companions vehemently disapproved of any effort in this direction.

Yet that was precisely what the Shia were fighting for, albeit with a radically different take than the Umayyads: the Shiites wanted to pass on the Prophet's charisma, which had a religious basis, among the descendants of his son-in-law 'Ali; the believers' Shiite leader was supposed to be the "imam." On the Day of Judgment all human beings would stand before God in groups, each one led by its "imam," as is revealed in sura 17, verse 73. That seems to be the origin of the Shiite and Kharijite concept and usage of the term "imamate." It was the institutionalized rule of the community of *believers*, who had dedicated their entire lives to following God's rules; therefore, the imamate is fundamentally different from that "kingdom" which the Umayyads embodied and which, in the Quraysh's view, dated back to the time before Muhammad, the period of wretched paganism. Early Shiites and Kharijites used the term "imamate"[36] in the sense of leadership over a community of warriors, the, in their opinion, only true heir to the Prophet's original community. This lays bare the archaic roots common to both movements; still, after their split their interpretations of the imamate were incompatible with each other. To the Kharijites, it meant leadership, to be bestowed on someone with proven abilities, for the purpose of fighting for the preservation and expansion of the community of believers; to the Shiites it was the office of the ruler that was endowed with religious charisma and could be passed on only via decree by the preceding imam, and only among 'Ali's descendants. Since in the Kharijites' view charisma was not genealogically based, they held that the imamate could evolve into the leadership over a community of *Muslims* which united in the performance of rites; to the Shiites, however, the imam was always more than that: since he had within him a prophetic core, he assumed the traits of a conveyor of salvation.

When Muhammad fled to Medina, sura 28, verse 85, was revealed to him: "He who imposed the Recitation upon thee shall surely restore thee to a place of homing." 'Abdallah ibn Saba' is said to have offered the following idiosyncratic interpretation of these words: Muhammad's return to earth was more certain than Jesus' return.[37] Here we have touched upon Shiite Islam's second root: its general millenarian tone. The promised day of absolute fulfillment, of the divine law's unqualified rule, still has not broken, but it is imminent; soon God will put the rule into the hand of the rightful heir among Muhammad's descendants, of the true imam! With announcements such as this, Shiite movements have swept people away time and again during the course of history; more than once they have toppled the existing order, for example, the Umayyads' Damascene caliphate. Such millenarianism was alien to the Kharijites, whose understanding of the imamate was so different. They took things entirely into their own hands. In Shia Islam, however, the promises, together with the charisma ascribed to the leader from the Prophet's lineage, led more or less to a watering down of the individual's responsibility for his or her own salvation: owing to his close kinship with the Prophet, 'Ali, like Muhammad, had divine guidance; everyone who rejected 'Ali's leadership, was caught in religious error. The imam gradually became a guarantor of guidance, of the right path to salvation; swearing loyalty to the imam took its place next to, and in extreme cases replaced, right action, for the imam possessed the unshakable, divinely inspired knowledge of the interpretation and correct application of the commandments that were revealed to the Prophet. This concept can be documented in Shiite circles as far back as the end of the Umayyad period. "Neither in the East nor in the West will you find true knowledge, except what had its origin in the Prophet's family." The following phrase has been put into the mouth of Muhammad himself: "I am a city of knowledge, and 'Ali is its gate. He who wants to gain knowledge, walk through the gate!"[38]

Turning to the imam in matters of faith became for Shiites the only safe way to salvation on the Day of Judgment. The imams from the line of 'Ali's descendants increasingly assumed the parts of saviors. Ja'far as-Sadiq (d. 765), the man in the center of the early development of Shiite dogma, impressed upon his followers: "If you, my people, experience riots, as if you had to traverse the dark night, riots where the fast rider, the eloquent preacher, the leader and his followers perish, turn to Muhammad's family! Its members will lead you to paradise and will call you there on the Day of Resurrection. And rely on 'Ali! By God, we have assured him of our loyalty to him as well as to the Prophet. Whatever has entered people's minds? Envy perchance? Cain envied Abel and had no faith!" Ja'far as-Sadiq further explained that under the prophet Moses, the people had turned away from his deputies, Aaron and Joshua, and became entrapped in the sin of apostasy. God punished them for this, "and this community is just like the Israelites. Why are you letting yourself be seduced? What do I have in common with Abu Bakr and that 'Umar? Woe unto you! I really do not know whether you are dumb or only acting dumb. I do not know whether you have forgotten or only pretend to be forgetful. Muhammad's family shall have the same rank among you as the head does within the body, and even as the eye among the head's sensory organs!"

The redeeming function of 'Ali's descendants is illustrated in numerous additional Shiite traditions. "We are the cave for him who takes refuge with us; a light for him who lets himself be illuminated by us; a shield to him who seeks our protection. He who loves us is on the highest peak, he who abandons us, plunges into the fire!" "Among this community, my family is like Noah's Ark on the high sea: he who enters it, will be saved; he who does not, will drown."[39]

The role of redeemer could hardly be expressed more clearly. Yet since there are no messiahs and even the Prophet has to content himself with passing on the divine message—to which the Koran frequently calls attention[40]—Shiite imams must not be called "redeemers." The term chosen for them was that of "argument" (hujja): probably following sura 4, verse 163, the imam living among the believers becomes God's argument for humankind, which on Judgment Day in view of its guilt wants to plead ignorance or insufficient knowledge of God's laws. "Since Adam's (the first prophet's) death, God never left the earth without an imam as a path to God. That is the argument God offers His servants. Those who abandon the imam, will perish; those who hold on to him, will truly be saved toward God."[41]

As already demonstrated with the example of the Kharijites, each religious persuasion's dogma and concept of history were tightly interwoven. The same holds true for 'Ali's party. At the outset, it probably needed to justify 'Ali's making common cause with 'Uthman's murderers. The Shiites could point out that the Quraysh themselves did not help 'Uthman during the siege of Medina. What became more important for the Shia's concept of history, however, was the poetic glorification of the events of Siffin with its ancient Arabian motifs. Even during Muhammad's lifetime 'Ali was said to have performed mighty deeds in battle; now there was new material for exalting him to the status of hero. The verses by an-Najashi ibn al-Harith ibn Ka'b are considerably younger.[42] He praised 'Ali's steadfastness and maintained that it was God's will that he be obeyed: "What 'Ali believes to be beneficial to us, we agree with, even if it should happen in the future that our noses will be cut off. Above all other members of the family of God's messenger, he was given his authority, he is his heir, even above his older paternal uncles."[43] The last line could be a later addition, since it rejects the "Hashimiya movement's" liberal interpretation of the term "Muhammad's family." Yet the idea that 'Ali was the executor of the Prophet's legacy and, therefore, had special privileges, was known since 'Abdallah ibn Saba'.

If this idea is projected back into the past, the conclusion is that not only 'Uthman, but also his two predecessors were usurpers, no different from any of the "tyrannical" Umayyads under whose rule there had been so much suffering. This raises the original feud between 'Ali and Mu'awiya to a new level. Now the question is no longer whether Mu'awiya could demand vendetta for his relative 'Uthman and whether 'Ali was allowed to make common cause with the murderers—now the problem is why 'Ali could not enter upon the Prophet's inheritance from the start. This necessitates a reinterpretation of Islam's entire early history: as *wasi*, 'Ali was Muhammad's true successor! This can be deduced from history as well as indications given by the tradition concerning Muhammad. Historiographers did not shy away from elevating 'Ali to the oldest believer after the Prophet himself, even though he must have been only a small child at the time Muhammad was appointed. Early on, numerous documents reflect that new image of 'Ali. It is more appropriate for a legend of saints than a realistic account, but found acceptance not only among Shiite circles. Even al-Hasan al-Basri, who was not an avowed Shiite, is said to have subscribed to the view that 'Ali had been the first to follow Muhammad's call and perform the ritual prayers.[44] This kind of worship bestowed on the figure of 'Ali was increased by the gushy story about his taking care of the Prophet's ritually correct funeral, while Muhammad's other companions started haggling, right after his death, over who should be his successor, and about 'Ali being so angry and sad about this that, for a while, he refused Abu Bakr the oath of allegiance. As explained above, 'Ali's reticence had probably quite different reasons.

Around the year 700, these and other stories led up to the Shiite doctrine of the rejection (rafd) of the caliphates of 'Ali's three predecessors. In particular those Shiites who looked for their imams among al-Husayn's descendants were zealous proponents of the "rejection" theory. A Book of the Visitation of the Believers' Prince, a prime example of the misuse of history for religious purposes, circulated among these circles: it claimed that while the Prophet's evil companions were haggling over the succession to Muhammad, 'Ali had exercised restraint, because he wanted to preserve harmony and peace among the believers; he had preserved peace twice more by putting his own right last—when 'Umar was given power, and when 'Uthman was made caliph. "Had I raised myself to the position and then called on the community to support me, it could have taken one of two stands toward me and my cause: one part would have followed me, fighting or getting killed in battle if everyone had not followed me. Others would have abandoned me, becoming infidels by failing to help me or by refusing to obey me." 'Ali claimed he had waged the war against Mu'awiya only under duress. Soon he had been abandoned by many of his followers and had had reason to fear his sons al-Hasan and al-Husayn might be harmed; therefore, he had agreed to arbitration.[45] Whereas Abu Bakr, 'Umar, and 'Uthman appear as the principal villains in this short text, while the Prophet's other companions remain in the background without being explicitly condemned, subsequent interpretations soon became increasingly extremist. As early as 750, the Husayni Shia was convinced that all the Prophet's companions had become unbelievers and fallen prey to erroneous religious belief, because they had not joined 'Ali. In this more radical concept of history we can recognize the reflection of the Husaynite doctrine of Islam: 'Ali was the only true leader of the believers, the imam ensuring salvation; those who did not recognize him as such could, therefore, only be unbelievers and would be condemned to hell.[46]

To be sure, other Shiite movements abstained from such extremism. Above all the Zaydites deserve mention. Zayd, also a descendant of the Husayn line, had gone from Medina to Kufa around 740. There various Shiites urged him to rise up against the Umayyad rule. Zayd, politically perhaps the most astute among 'Ali's descendants, had managed to gather followers around him who were not exclusively "Husaynites"; even some Kharijites had joined his camp. Therefore, Zayd's rebellion can be viewed as a prelude to the "Hashimite movement," which, ten years later, would abolish the Umayyad caliphate. Since Zayd wanted political and military success, he had to foreswear sectarian extremism; he sought compromise instead. This also becomes evident when we look at the Zaydi Shiites' concept of history. For them, Abu Bakr and 'Umar were by no means apostates and infidels; their caliphate certainly had validity. Yet they assumed that both of them were far inferior to 'Ali in virtue. However, as far as the Zaydites were concerned, all this was neither a disaster nor an indication of erroneous religious belief. According to their doctrine, a historical situation can develop where the "imamate of the inferior in virtue" (*imamat al-mafdul*) becomes meaningful. Therefore the imam could never assume the role of guarantor of salvation in the Zaydi Shia. Rather, he had always been someone who called on the people to go to battle, and surely also to pleasing God and securing the afterlife, for which, however, the individual believer continued to bear sole responsibility.[47]

Both Kharijites and Shiites wanted to build a community of believers based strictly on the conditions that had existed under Muhammad in Medina. Obeisance to the law as it had been revealed was supposed to determine everyday life. The two groups differed, however, in how this concept should be realized. While the Kharijites wanted to rely on the Koran as a surrogate institution for the Prophet's guidance, the Shiites insisted on a charismatic imamate, with the imam personifying the continuity of Prophetic guidance—but only on the level of the *interpretation* of the law, which had already been revealed and could not possibly be expanded, so as not to violate the doctrine of Muhammad as the seal of the prophets. By espousing a self-concept based solely on the original community, they could capitalize on the universalist features of Muhammad's message in a way the Umayyads with their Quraysh tradition of aiming toward dominating the Arabs never could. Since, furthermore, both early Kharijites and Shiites considered themselves to be the original community's only legitimate heirs, they inhibited the transition from an activist religiosity to a rite-oriented piousness, to "Islam," at least within their own ranks. As we shall see, that development happened very quickly and powerfully outside of these two movements from the late seventh century on. One consequence of this was that, from the viewpoint of later observers, Kharijite Islam and the Shia came to be perceived as diversions of mainstream Islam, even though they, more than any of the other groups, exhibited archaic traits. Both Kharijites and Shiites drew a large following from non-Arab converts; therefore, it is in those two movements that the intellectual climate was prepared that, influenced mainly by the Arabic language but also by ideas of various origins, could lead to theological speculation during the early Abbasid period. This speculation started with attempts to prove that the Koran's core statements were universally valid and mutually inclusive. Here we have an early indication that mainstream Islam suspected all rational theology of being sectarian and, not getting involved in these disputes until late, picked up and processed theological ideas only with some reluctance and reservations.

6. Judgment Postponed

Shiites and Kharijites could not wait to continue fully the work Prophet Muhammad had left behind, and they were convinced they were equipped with the only proper means to do so: solely the Koran or its authoritative interpretation by the imams from among 'Ali's descendants. Such a firm conviction is expressed not only in a desire to correct everything that is flawed; it also invariably implies an unwavering certainty about what each individual believer should and should not do, what the community should be like, and how the leader should rule. In short, everything in the world, down to the last detail, must fit into the divine plan of salvation as revealed to the believers. This assumption leads to two dilemmas. One, might that absolute certainty not be treacherous? The doctrine of the imam's inspiration helped the Shiites to cross those shallows. Yet it was impossible for them to circumnavigate the second difficulty: man's actions sometimes fail or lead to surprising, entirely unexpected results!

After all, the Kharijite and Shiite groups' plan to perpetuate the circumstances of the original community of believers had by no means led to peace and harmony, but to division, hatred, and bloodshed. In upholding the human freedom of action, the Qadarites too, whose more theologically inclined speculations had led them to believe that a just God could never condemn anyone to hell from the outset, became vulnerable to the question of whether they were not by far overestimating human possibilities and abilities; for the basis of human efforts was not determined by human beings but externally—by God. Who could always make out the borderline between the result of the actions for which they were responsible and the circumstances that were determined by God's inscrutable ways? Yet, if that could ultimately not be decided, then believing that human reason could ascertain what was and what was not a right action was an illusion. Merely considering the result of an action and assuming God, too, would judge only by that result on the Day of Judgment, implied that one had to ignore those very circumstances that every so often cause lawful actions to fail—that is to say, that God was not just. Therefore, preserving one's belief in God's justice required nonacceptance of the Qadarites' superficial view of the righteousness of one's deeds, which, incidentally, some of them cautiously expressed toward the end of the Umayyad period.[48] Rather, one had to admit that human beings, who could not determine that borderline with precision, must not anticipate God's judgment, because He alone knew all the facts about every action.

It is easy to see why, during the turbulent times of the Second Civil War, in which Shiites, Kharijites, Umayyads, and others contended for the supremacy of their concepts of the caliphate and the religious community, ideas of this kind began to develop and soon thereafter stirred up a theological debate. The probably oldest pertinent document is connected with the name of al-Hasan, a son of Muhammad ibn al-Hanafiyya. Around 687 al-Hasan was in al-Mukhtar's camp, but—possibly shocked by the sectarianism he witnessed there—he soon left him in order to reconcile with the Umayyads.[49]

Al-Hasan ibn Muhammad was the author of a short treatise that critically deals with the Qadarites' teachings; it contains almost forty questions put to the proponents of an unlimited human *qadar*. The questions are designed in a way so as to drive al-Hasan's opponents into a corner and ultimately make them realize that their ideas are untenable.[50] Initially al-Hasan used arguments from the doctrine of salvation: the prophets were appointed by God, and whatever they said, from that moment on, was necessarily in agreement with Him; even if they had wanted to, they could have neither concealed nor adulterated the message entrusted to them! That was a point the Qadarites must concede; otherwise, they would have had to doubt the authority of Islam's essential revelation. Another example reveals how al-Hasan ibn Muhammad drew his arguments from the history of salvation: the Qadarites would have to assume that God had created Adam and Eve for paradise, and that they were personally accountable for the sin for which they were expelled; yet al-Hasan pointed out that it had been decided from the outset that human beings were to live and die on earth, and on the Day of Judgment would again be brought forth from the earth[51]—therefore, the decision to lapse was not their own. If God had planned human beings to be nothing but good, which would be the logical conclusion of the thesis that Adam and Eve had been destined to remain in paradise forever, why then did He create hell?

According to al-Hasan, human beings cannot forget what God once taught them: that He, the Creator, exists and that He created day and night, this world and the next; only impudent liars, he argued, could deny that. If, however, God created everything, then surely He also created human speech. Again the Qadarites would have to agree. Yet human speech, the author continued, contained truths and falsehoods, the profession of God's oneness as well as that of polytheism, which was the worst possible insult to God. This turn of argument prepared the ground for an understanding of all human sensations and deeds, man's life span, beliefs, or disbeliefs as a result of God's inscrutable ways, or at least for the assumption that they were influenced by them. This standpoint could directly lead to the belief that every single event was predetermined by

God: according to sura 8, verse 7, God promised the Prophet's followers before the Battle of Badr that, before long, they would seize the trade caravan returning from Syria to Mecca, or they would defeat the army sent for its protection. If someone were to assume that Muhammad's companions could still have decided not to fight the battle, this would imply that it was conceivable God would not keep His promise! Al-Hasan presented to the reader numerous additional examples of this kind. They were all meant to prove that God deliberately made creatures that were destined to hell and to paradise, and that it was impossible for them to oppose God's will—just as impossible as to alter one's natural physique.[52]

This brings into focus the wide gap between al-Hasan ibn Muhammad and the Qadarites; it also shows us the many different views that were at that time mentioned to connect plausibly God's omnipotence and human responsibility for attaining salvation, and we realize how difficult it was to find arguments simultaneously to corroborate both lines of reasoning. In one of his writings, al-Hasan al-Basri, who defended the Qadarites before Caliph 'Abd al-Malik, later allowed that no one could determine his or her physique or life span,[53] but he not once generalized this opinion the way al-Hasran ibn Muhammad did. The latter thought logically and was suddenly in danger of glossing over the individual's responsibility for his or her own salvation. The radical Qadarites had been similarly emphatic in insisting on the human capacity for self-determination. Pointing out that God determined the conditions of one's actions, al-Hasan had exhorted people to be prudent lest they forget the Creator's superior power. Therefore, al-Hasan al-Basri was not merely a rational interpreter of Islamic faith; he earned posthumous fame largely as the leading representative of early Islamic piousness. Sufism regards him, whose thoughts mainly centered around the spiritual aspect of Muhammad's message and from there ventured into theology,[54] as one of its most eminent forerunners. This leads us to a basic fact in the history of Islamic theology: strict logic will never be able to solve the contradiction between, on the one hand, God's determining and guiding everyone and everything in the world, and on the other, man's subjection to a law he has to follow because he is a creature. Nonetheless, immersing oneself into the essence of the One makes it possible to see the two as an identical, indissoluble whole. We will see that in the course of Islamic history, Sufi ideas repeatedly revived theology when it was hopelessly lost in impasses and paved its way for another round of trying to reconcile what can ultimately not be reconciled rationally.

But back to al-Hasan ibn Muhammad. If we knew only his writings against the Qadarites, we could be led to believe that by and large he came to agree with the doctrine of the predestination of human actions. Yet what made him pick up the quill was by no means his stand a staunch predestinarian. In turning away from al-Mukhtar, who wanted to establish the community of true believers by supporting the imam, al-Hasan ibn Muhammad had quite a different objective.

In a short treatise known as the *Book of Postponement*, he revealed his religio-political goals, in whose light his rejection of the Qadariyya is to be understood as well. God, he began his reflections, sent Muhammad to transmit a certain message—His order to invalidate heathen customs. What kinds of customs did he mean? When we read on, we realize that he was thinking of the discord and constant tribal feuds that had never ceased to endanger peoples' lives.[55] God selected for Muhammad the "emigrants" and "helpers" so he could satisfy that message's religio-political demand, and He made them all victorious. At the same time God established ritual rules and laws; obeying them must be understood as a path leading to repentance and thus to gaining or regaining one's allegiance to Islam. This Islam had become a reality in the Medinese community. That is why al-Hasan could state, "The efforts in behalf of God's cause and keeping the middle course grounded in the divine norms (*sunna*)—neither the earthly luxury it brought could distract that community from all that, nor did it abandon it in the face of the worst disaster it met." The oldest Muslims, he argued, proceeded according to God's commands, spontaneously and sure of their faith. "Then this community encountered the discord (*fitna*) God had foretold, in view of which some people broke with the others, and other people declared their solidarity with still others." Here al-Hasan used the terms employed by the Kharijites and Shiites to distinguish their followers from their enemies, mutually disputing their opponents' faith. "If anyone wants to know our opinion on this: we are God's our Lord's people; Islam is our religion, the Koran our imam, Muhammad our Prophet. We rely on him. We entrust our cause to God and His messenger. We agree with Abu Bakr and 'Umar, who are among our imams; we approve of showing them obedience, are indignant when they are disobeyed; it is for them that we fight their enemies. And we postpone (*nurji'u*) judgment on the first among the Prophet's companions who were guilty of the split (i.e., 'Uthman, 'Ali, and their followers). We support Abu Bakr and 'Umar so that people may be in solidarity with them. For there has been no fight between them in the community, there has been no discord, no doubt in the believers' cause. Postponement is called for especially in the case of someone whom people reproach even though we did not meet him."[56]

We can see that the point was by no means to promote predestinarian doctrines—it was to not anticipate God's judgment on man, especially if one had not witnessed their actions. Al-Hasan ibn Muhammad knew that the ancestors' accomplishments in spreading the faith and forming the community did not fall into their laps; yet neither were they a result of "God's help." If, in the dispute with the Qadarites, he stressed the aspect of actions not determined by man, he merely did so to protest against judging the ancestors' actions simply by their results, which only led to constant quarrel. Postponing judgment, which also meant renouncing all-too-carelessly relying on human *qadar*, seemed to be the cure for a community torn by religio-political discord when the fact remained that the community as a whole was founded upon one incident, Muhammad's appointment as Prophet. "Islam" was supposed to be the community's unifying center of life. The "postponers," in historiography known as "al-Murji'a," were afraid of feuds in a new era of paganism; yet al-Hasan and the few likeminded friends he may have had certainly were not able to serve as the focus of a powerful movement for the unification of all Muslims. What they lacked most was the clout of a convincing interpretation of early Islamic history that could have attracted and united a large number of people, and neither did they have their own theory on how to continue the Prophet's work. However, what they did realize was that one must not insist on an activist interpretation of the concept of faith, but that only a much wider concept of "Islam" could be the basis of the community created by Muhammad. That was a realization the Murjiites shared with their Ibadi contemporaries. Yet the future was to show that there was a historically much more powerful movement which had subscribed to that principle, without however formulating it as clearly as the Murjiites.

7. The Beginnings of Sunnism

In the early Umayyad period, two models of continuing the Prophet's original community, the Kharijite and the Shiite model, had taken shape. Both started out from the concept of faith that was established in the Koran—in sura 49, verse 14, for instance—one of active transcendence of mere Islam, the ritual turning toward God's face. The Bedouins, in whose hearts belief "has not yet entered," are denied the rank of true believers. Yet they are not simply rejected. "If you obey God and His Messenger," they are promised, "He will not diminish you anything of your works." This is immediately followed by a description of the true believers: "those who believe in God and His Messenger, then have not doubted, and have struggled with their possessions and their selves in the way of God . . ." Those, into whose hearts God has written faith, follow the divine messenger's words, even if they have to turn against their own kin. That is the reason God is pleased with them, and they with God (sura 58, verse 22). It pleased God, for example, when in 628 the believers followed Muhammad on his way to Mecca and pledged their allegiance in Hudaybiyya (sura 48, verse 18), even though the outcome of that bold enterprise was extremely uncertain.

It was that spirit of sacrifice "along God's path" that the Kharijites had in mind when thinking of the "community of believers." This attitude was to prove itself during the fight against the Umayyads' "kingdom." Yet that it could not be sustained forever becomes clear when we look at the Ibadi. One could not always be on the battlefield, one also had to be able to lead a life without constantly fighting—"sitting" at home, as they worded it—and be allowed to make the performance of the rites the distinguishing sign of the new community formed by the Prophet's message. The constant battles were vividly reminiscent of the raids and tribal feuds of the pagan period they thought they had left behind. Al-Hasan ibn Muhammad, the "postponer," reminded his readers that the Prophet's community was expressly meant to distinguish itself from all former communities by the harmony among its members. In stressing that aspect of the Prophet's work, he came to realize that he should make his peace with the Umayyads: despite their ancestors', the Banu Abd Shams', hostile attitude toward the Prophet, a member of the Banu Hashim clan, they were now the only political force that could hope to reestablish harmony. Under Caliph 'Abd al-Malik they apparently quite pointedly brought to bear the Koranic command to create a united community of believers. Yet they did not entirely manage without an interpretation of early Islamic history that contained a symbolic enemy; every Friday they had 'Ali ibn Abi Talib condemned from their pulpits as the original unity's destroyer. What was more important, however, was that they praised the year 73 h (which began on 4 June 691), the end of the Second Civil War, as the "year of the harmonious community" ('am al-jama'a).[57]

Yet criticism of the "pagan" discord was voiced not only among the caliph's surroundings and the "postponers." Over time, in the memory of several of the Prophet's former companions or their sons the image of the community was glorified into an era which had been immune to religious quarreling. And that was how it was supposed to be again; therefore it was urgently advised to keep out of the controversy and put all ambition aside. 'Abdallah, 'Umar ibn al-Khattab's son, was considered the man who most impressively lived according to that ideal. Three times, it is said, he was offered the post of caliph: after 'Uthman's assassination, during the battles near Siffin, and after Mu'awiya's son Yazid's death. Each time he refused,[58] stating that not even a cupful of blood should be shed for him; ascetic caution would gradually put an end to all feuds in the community. This, in any case, is how later sources described 'Abdallah's principles; he did not, they said, wish to compete with the Quraysh for power, because he feared God. "Fight [the unbelievers], till there is no persecution and the religion is God's." This command in sura 2, verse 189, we are told, was being obeyed in Medina, and now only the one God was being worshiped; those who still fought wars did so for some other belief[59] and were, therefore, moving away from the state of salvation that had already been achieved. The following, frequently quoted, words were put into the mouths of each of the two arbitrators in the case of 'Ali versus Mu'awiya, as well as other known figures of early Islam: "You will experience persecutions[60] . . . in which the one who is sitting acts better than the one who is standing; the one who is walking, better than the one climbing a horse. . . . Therefore lie in your houses just like your mats!"[61]

In this way of thinking, the Umayyads came to view the "harmonious community," referred to by the term jama'a and used in the sense explained above, as an important part of the inheritance the Prophet bequeathed to his followers. However, the word was now loaded with religious meaning to a degree we cannot easily understand; it became the quintessence of a way of living whose only goal was to gain entry into paradise. The Prophet, we are told, explicitly exhorted us not to leave the *jama'a*,[62] for the fact that it existed was a sign of God's grace; schism, on the other hand, signified punishment.[63] Those who relinquished the "harmonious community," associated with Satan,[64] and when they died it was as if they had died during the era of paganism[65]; they had no chance of being saved! Therefore the *jama'a* was not realized by fighting against other movements that also claimed to be preserving and expanding the Prophet's legacy; "faith" in the sense described above could *not* be its unifying center. That is why it gave the concept of faith a different meaning. One day, it is said, a commission from the 'Abd Qais appeared before Muhammad, complained that their tribe, separated from Medina by a strip of land occupied by pagan Bedouins, was forced to wander about at a very long distance from the source of religious calling, and finally asked for succinct but clear instructions that would pave the way to paradise. Muhammad, the tradition continues, told them they should always believe in the one God, and when they confessed they did not know what that belief consisted of, the Prophet personally explained to them, "Professing that there is no God besides Allah, and that Muhammad is Allah's messenger; performing ritual prayer; paying the alms tax; the fast of Ramadan; handing over one fifth of your war booty!"[66] We also find these demands in the Koran in connection with "faith,"[67] but there they are always associated with the invisible element of the fear of God.[68] Verse 14 of sura 49, quoted above, clearly points out that one should speak of "faith" only if the rites, performed while turning toward the face of God, entirely fill the new convert's being and separate him from his natural attachments; formally obeying ritual and fiscal rules alone is not sufficient, it is only "Islam."

In the Prophet's *hadith*, the expression of the Islamic movement discussed here,[69] the above set of demands is often no longer associated with the word "faith," but identified as the "content" of Islam. That "Islam" and "faith" mean two different things is not forgotten. However, this difference loses its edge when God's messenger establishes that "faith" means "that you believe in God, His angels and His Book, in facing Him (in the hereafter), in His messengers, in resurrection, and in the full degree of God's power of determination (qadar)."[70] Again a series of clearly defined statements has assumed the place of personal devotion and of actively living one's faith, which is difficult to ascertain.[71]

A pious movement of a quietist mold developed which recognized 'Abdallah ibn 'Umar and soon all the Prophet's prominent companions, including 'Ali, as its predecessors. This movement is difficult to make out in the narrative historical documents on the Umayad period. That is not surprising since the members of this movement were repulsed by inner-Islamic wars, which they considered relapses into paganism. Because they stayed away from these feuds the chroniclers paid almost no attention to them. We can only indirectly detect their growing influence, and as early as around the turn of the eighth century, during the decades when the seeds of Islamic theology began to sprout, their presence was felt in many different ways; their—at a superficial glance—simple way of looking at things began to have an impact on the discussion of central religio-political issues.

Aided by the Koran—or more precisely, the Koran and its interpretation by the inspired imams—the Shiites and Kharijites tried to save the community founded by Muhammad. Yet those looking at the "harmonious" community knew a different path toward salvation, one that must have been much closer to a culture like ancient Arabia with its belief that its forefathers' merits determined the present: it was the path (sunna) the ancestors had cleared. At that time no one could tell what exactly that sunna consisted of; it was still impossible to determine whether the Prophet's first successors or all his companions or only Muhammad himself had represented it in what they did and said. Only one thing seemed to be certain: that following the sunna meant avoiding disastrous splits. Apparently sunna was used in that sense even back during the arbitration after Siffin.[72] In his defense of the qadariyya against Caliph 'Abd al-Malik, al-Hasan al-Basri explicitly referred to the ancestors' sunna. In his Book of Postponement, al-Hasan ibn Muhammad mentioned the sunna, evidently applying it to the totality of specific Islamic manners of conduct; "an effort on behalf of God's cause and keeping the middle ground based in the sunna," he wrote, had been the principles from which neither prosperity nor poverty had been able to dissuade the early Muslims.[73] 'Abdallah ibn Ibad used the term *sunna* similarly. He wrote that Abu Bakr and 'Umar had followed God's Book and acted according to the *sunna*; that was how they preserved harmony within the community. 'Uthman, on the other hand, had deviated from his two predecessors' path. Therefore he had been warned about and reminded of God's Book and the "*sunna* of believers before him." 'Abdallah ibn Ibad then discussed the concept of exaggeration (*guluw*), a kind of conduct for which the Ibadiyya criticized their Azraqi rivals. His understanding of exaggeration was that of failing the *sunna*, as having the audacity to state anything but the truth about God and to act according to something other than the Book of God and the *sunna*. 'Ali, he argued, had been guilty of that transgression when he accepted arbitration. Those who left 'Ali "followed God's messengers, Abu Bakr and 'Umar, in their faith and their modus operandi (*sunna*)." That, he argued, was how a good imam would always act; only an imam of error will follow his own course.[74]

Eventually the term *bid'a* was used as an antonym to *sunna*, stigmatizing as "innovations" practices that did not conform to the ancestors' way. *Bid'a* quickly evolved into a religio-political slogan intended to silence opponents. For example, the Umayyad 'Umar II (r. 717–20), who—albeit unsuccessfully in the long run—tried to combine blossoming Sunnism and the caliphate, accused the Qadarites of *bid'a*, coupled with "exaggeration" (*guluw*) in the sense in which 'Abdallah ibn Ibad had used it before.[75]

'Umar's pamphlet against the Qadarites brings us to the issue of what to make of the human responsibility and freedom of choice. As noted above, that was the specific theological issue tenaciously argued about during the Umayyad period. Similarly to al-Hasan ibn Muhammad, 'Umar II supported the view that God significantly limited the human ability to choose. Guidance and error, good and evil, he argued, were determined for every creature by God according to His free will.[76] 'Umar II continued by stating that God created Adam, immediately afterward examined his offspring, and determined which of them would enter paradise or be condemned to hell; all their future acts had been recorded ahead of time.[77] In conclusion, 'Umar II pointed out to the Qadarites, "God's messenger said: 'Islam rests on three acts: fight (against the unbe-

lievers) from the time of the messenger's appointment by God until the
day when a troop of believers attacks the Antichrist. . . . second, that you
may not condemn as infidels for committing a sin those who profess
God's oneness, that you may not charge them with (the crime of) polytheism, and not exclude them from Islam for something they did! Third,
that everything that has been imposed on man, good and evil, comes from
God's *qadar*!' You, on the other hand, took the religious war out of Islam,
abandoned it through your innovation (*bid'a*), and have denied that everything is determined by God—one's life span, acts, and subsistence. No
longer do you hold in your hands that on which Islam is based, you have
rejected and abandoned everything!"[78]

This once again vividly illustrates the contrast between "Islam" and
"faith": the Qadarites, who around that time became politically very
active,[79] laid sole claim to the right faith, which they—similarly to the
Kharijites before them—combined with the fight against all other Muslim
movements, whose members they denounced as infidels; that, in any case,
was the charge 'Umar II leveled against them. In the caliph's opinion,
"Islam" was to be the tie uniting the community, and while that community was no stranger to religious wars, these were only wars against members of a different faith and never against opponents within Islam's own
ranks. "Islam" demanded surrendering to the events God had determined,
and not believing that one's own insight created the opportunity to correct
the course of events, not even if it was one's goal to enforce obedience to
God's law. For "Islam" truly to become the common inheritance of all
members of the community, the Qadarites, therefore, had to desist from
imposing their faith on other Muslims; they should—and this was similar
to what al-Hasan ibn Muhammad had suggested—refrain from judging
other Muslims. Furthermore, they had to understand that one's acts were
predetermined. That was the first step Sunnism dared go beyond al-
Hasan. Postponing judgment still left open the possibility of considering
the conditions and circumstances of human action, even though it was
clear that this consideration would not lead to conclusive results. The
Sunnites, on the other hand, demanded that one's own judgment be abandoned and that everything be left up to God from the outset. No split must
occur within the community!

"O men, if you are in doubt as to the Uprising, surely We created you of dust then of a sperm-drop, ten of a blood clot, then of a lump of flesh, formed and unformed that We may make clear to you. And We establish in the wombs what We will, till a stated term, then We deliver you as infants, then that you may come of age; and some of you die, and some of you are kept back unto the vilest state of life, that after knowing somewhat, they may know nothing. . . ." That the fetus grows in the mother's womb is, in this Koranic passage (sura 22, verse 5), proof of God's ability to bring the dead back to life, which the Meccans doubted. The second part of this verse, however, sounds the theme of the predestination of life, even though that line of argument is not what Muhammad had had in mind. As the following sentences mentioning that vegetation is made to sprout by rain, make clear, his intention had solely been to "prove" resurrection—and the subsequent Day of Judgment.[80] In the sayings ascribed to Muhammad, the *hadith*, that verse is often referred to, but now clearly with the true focus on predestination: "God's messenger . . . told us: 'When one of you is created, he is put together in his mother's womb for forty days. Then he is a blood clot there. Then he is a clump of flesh there. Then an angel is sent who has four words of instruction: (the unborn man's) subsistence, his date of death, and whether he will die condemned or in bliss.' By God! One of you acts as the paradise dwellers act, until there is but an ell between him and paradise; but then the record (of predestined deeds) gets the better of him, and he acts as the hell dwellers act, and he goes to hell. Another one of you acts as the hell dwellers act and there is but an ell between him and hell; but then the record gets the better of him, and he acts as the paradise dwellers act, and he enters paradise."[81]

He who chooses the *sunna* for a yardstick makes the survival of the uniform Islamic community possible, for he accepts everything that has happened as divinely determined. That is one side of *sunna* piousness. The other side is manifested in the Sunnite certainty that something comparable is also true with regard to the difficult issue of how to shape that community. Neither the ruler nor the Muslims are obliged to struggle with the issue of how to build and rule an Islamic empire, and they do not need to quarrel over it. "In His Book, which God taught you, and in the *sunna* rules which God's messenger introduced and which ignore none of your religious and worldly matters, there is great proof of mercy and a firm obligation to give thanks to God, as God gave you guidance and taught you what you did not know. Therefore, no one needs to do anything with God's Book and the *sunna* of God's messenger but to implement their content and fight for it."[82] These words were proclaimed on the occasion of 'Umar II's ascendancy to the throne. They cast doubt on whether the Sunnites really believed in predestination. Our doubts grow when we read these sentences in the same speech: "My actions and the tribulations God had planned for me were (such that) the effect of what I did was (really) due to Him, or they prevented by His might what I prevented. All the good things I did were the result of being instructed and guided by God, and I ask God to bless me. Everything else, for which I have to take responsibility (myself), the sickness of sin, I ask the mighty God to forgive me in His mercy."[83]

What should we do about this lack of clarity? In Sunnism—this much is clear—the *sunna* becomes the surrogate institution that makes it possible to preserve or regain the wholesome conditions of the Prophet's original community. The Prophet is said to have comforted his community shortly before his death by vowing to leave them God's Book as an invaluable inheritance.[84] According to the Sunnite tradition, that vow is much better known in a different version: Muhammad promised his community to bequeath to them two important things, God's Book and the *sunna*. In the Shia, incidentally, a third version circulated, in accordance with the movement's own concept of guidance: Muhammad bequeathed to the Muslims God's Book and his family.[85] Elevating the *sunna* to the most valuable source of guidance next to the Koran does not necessarily imply the adoption of a predestinarian point of view. Only if we remind ourselves to what degree religio-political forces pervade all theological thinking do we understand the elective affinity in subsequent Islamic history between Sunnism and the doctrine of the predestination of one's deeds, no matter what 'Umar II pronounced. One of Sunnism's intentions is always to apply immediately theological insights or constructs to reality; like the Murjia's theses, the concept of the *sunna* is meant to end and prevent future factional quarrels. Seen from that angle, it should be interpreted to the effect that Islam's controversial figures were not responsible for what they did. The ruler could promise to put his efforts behind the fulfillment of the *sunna*'s norms; but that did not mean he could claim to have his own *qadar*—and perhaps that would not even make sense. Even if 'Umar II mentioned that he was responsible for his subjects as a shepherd was for his herd,[86] in the final analysis everything was left undecided. We begin to have an idea of what the fact that in Islam religion and politics are—or are meant to be—one, means for theology.

CHAPTER III

The Two Types of Islam's Theological Literature

1. The Hadith

In his attack on the Qadarites, 'Umar II quoted not only verses from the Koran but also repeatedly referred to other sources, which he introduced by using the term "news" (*khabar*) or "speech of God's messenger" (*hadith rasul Allah*). The Qadarites denied that it was God who assigned belief or unbelief to man; 'Umar argued that in order to support their, in his opinion, erroneous view, they "interpreted the speech of God's messenger, which the proponents of the *sunna* quote—and this speech does support the revealed Book—in a way as if the point had been some disgraceful offense (plus restitution for it), about which 'Umar (ibn al-Khattab) asked the Prophet (in these words): 'What do you think, is what we have been doing settled for good or can we tackle it anew?' Then the Prophet replied, 'Of course it is settled for good!'" In other words, 'Umar II argued, in order to save their theory of free will, the Qadarites had got set on claiming that that question had addressed an utterly banal fact, whereas what 'Umar ibn al-Khattab really wanted to know was whether all human actions were already executed—determined once and for all—according to God's ways, even before they were actually committed. As far as 'Umar II was concerned, the predestinarian meaning of the question and answer was a firmly established fact, and he sharply criticized the Qadarites for arguing that, if that were true, God would be a despot committing an injustice to His creation.

In order to support his dismissal of the Qadarites' view, 'Umar II then mentioned the "news" we already know: that God had examined Adam's offspring and consigned them to hell or paradise. "And in the battle of Siffin Sahl ibn Hunayf said, 'You people, be mistrustful of your own views of your religion! For by Him in Whose hands is my soul! I still see us on the day of Abu Jandal! If we had been able to reject the order of God's deputy then, we would have! We always hanged the sword around our shoulders so that it might facilitate our admission to a goal we knew—except in the matter before us!'"[1] During the battles of Siffin Sahl ibn Hunayf, a companion of the Prophet, who fought on 'Ali's side, was afraid that the enemy parties' own plans might spell disaster for the community. He pointed out that under Muhammad people had put their own opinions aside and according to the agreements made in the recent treaty of Hudaybiyya extradited Abu Jandal, who had defected from the Meccans to the Prophet—a measure which upset some Muslims.[2] 'Umar II recalled this incident in order to make the Qadarites realize that in the Prophet's original community people's "own opinions" were suppressed and—according to God's will?— could not even be brought to bear; whereas later, after Siffin, they did immeasurable damage.

As the reader will recall, al-Hasan al-Basri, al-Hasan ibn Muhammad, and 'Abdallah ibn Ibad often referred to the ancestors' example, which they implied should be understood as an obligation. 'Umar II's statements, written between 717 and 720, contain a rather large number of examples documenting the development of a new literary genre which formulated models of acting and speaking that expressed current views. 'Umar II paid close attention to the evolving genre and tried to support it as much as he could. For instance, he asked Salim, 'Abdallah ibn 'Umar's son, to write down for him how "'Umar ibn al-Khattab had ruled the people of the direction of prayer and the people of the contract,[3] for I wish to rule like he did, as long as God aids me."[4] Several sources document 'Umar II's other attempts to procure material suited to fill with content the idea of attaining salvation by emulating the original community.[5]

None of these oldest collections are extant. Still, we can make out their literary form with some accuracy. No doubt each treatise was not composed as a whole, but as a compilation of statements on many different issues, in almost no particular order; for instance, in his treatise on the Qadarites, 'Umar II could talk very generally about the "news" that God "sowed" human beings in their preexistence "over His hand" and then determined who would eventually go to paradise and who to hell. Later this kind of carelessly dealing with the traditions was increasingly looked down upon—precisely to the degree in which they were revalued as a source of guidance originating from God, like the Koran. At the time of 'Umar II, this concept was still far in the future, but it was already outlined. After all, as long as one followed it, the ancestors' example (*sunna*) was supposed to implement the "harmonious community" that had existed under the Prophet's leadership in Medina. In short, the traditions were soon believed to convey a vivid and realistic picture of those early times and basically even to express authentically what the ancestors said and did. This was the concept that fomented this literary genre during the eighth century.[6]

In the *hadith* collections that are approximately one century younger— the earliest extant ones of their kind—the "news" 'Umar II mentioned occurs in its peculiar disguise that directly reveals something about character and function of that "tradition." Let us first examine the story about the examination of Adam's offspring. Here it appears as a commentary on sura 7, verse 172: "And when thy Lord took from the Children of Adam, from their loins, their seed, and made them testify touching themselves, 'Am I not thy Lord?' They said, 'Yes, we testify'—lest you should say on the Day of Resurrection, 'As for us, we were heedless of this.'" Then someone approaches 'Umar ibn al-Khattab to ask him to explain this passage, which, as the reader will have noticed, has nothing to do with the issue of predestination, but is really meant to corroborate Muhammad's belief that in their essence human beings are created toward God.[7] 'Umar ibn Khattab, however, claims that this proves the Sunnites' view of all creatures' limited responsibility for their salvation, and he calls the Prophet as his witness: "God's messenger was (once also) asked about this, and he replied: 'God created Adam and ran his right hand over his groin, retrieved from it (part of his) offspring and said, 'These here I have created for paradise, and they will act like (future) paradise dwellers.' Then he ran his hand once more over Adam's groin and said, 'These here I have created for hell, and they will act like (future) hell dwellers!' Someone then interjected: 'Messenger of God, what are one's works good for then?' Whereupon he explained: 'When God has created someone for paradise, He makes him act like (future) paradise dwellers in such a way that he will die during such an act, and He takes him to paradise because of that act. And when God creates someone for hell, he makes him act like (future) paradise dwellers in such a way that he will die during such an act, and He takes him to hell because of that act.'"[8]

The "news" 'Umar II once mentioned has now been manipulated to fit the narrative motifs of the Koran passage as whose interpretation it is presented: God does not examine in His palm humankind in its preexistence, but He brings it forth from Adam's groin (Adam's sons, according to the Koran). Yet the story fits the Koran only formally; as for its theological content, a reinterpretation has taken place, as was already mentioned: a meaning that conforms with Sunnism has been superimposed on the verse in the revelation.[9] In order to preclude any uncertainty, the logical construct of the "final act,"[10] which we have previously encountered in a different context,[11] is now being added. The expanded "news," which in this form appears in Ahmad ibn Hanbal (d. 845)[12] and, with minor text variations, in later, similar handbooks, consists of set pieces which were put together to corroborate a certain doctrine—not so much with polished arguments, but by endowing it with the authority of the original community and giving the listener the impression that these words represent a part of the present, not past, history of salvation.

This example of a *hadith* compels us to look more closely at that narrative genre.

In Ahmad ibn Hanbal's version, the events sketched in a rough outline by 'Umar II have been turned into a lively scene. If one compares this version with numerous formally similar traditions, this literary genre's most standard features become recognizable: an unnamed (or often fictitiously named) member of the generation following the generation of the Prophet's companions inquires with an—if possible, prominent—companion of Muhammad about some religious or ritual matter; this very often takes place after the Prophet's death. The respondent's typical reply consists of a quote from God's messenger; frequently, however, he outlines a brief scene which has something to do with the issue on which Muhammad will make a statement, and this statement is, of course, also an answer to the question by that possibly fictitious member of the generation following that of the Prophet's companions. Some Muslim experts still remembered that around the time when 'Umar II used to refer to the *hadith*, such standard scenes were employed in—as al-Hakim an-Naisaburi (d. 1014) worded it—an attempt to strengthen religion.[13]

Obviously, this was done by recalling a past that had been adjusted to the needs of the present, by bringing to life a view of history that brought the idealized "Back Then" to the "Now" and gradually obliterated the general understanding of specific historical circumstances and conditions—that is to say, it left it up to God to judge, precisely in line with what the Murjiites and Sunnites considered imperative. Stripped of their original context, only those fragments that seemed suitable were thrown into the maelstrom of the *hadith*'s genesis. This, too, is illustrated by the paragraph from 'Umar II's pamphlet against the Qadarites quoted above—by those sentences of Sahl ibn Hunayf that exhort the readers to form their own opinion and to act accordingly. Later collections sometimes still contain the passages quoted by 'Umar II.[14] In addition, there is a version in which Sahl ibn Hunayf appears as a preacher near Siffin; what is mentioned is not the affair concerning Abu Jandal—instead, 'Umar ibn al-Khattab approaches the Prophet to be reassured that the believers, the proponents of truth, will never be abandoned by God.[15] A third version ends with the same sermon by Sahl ibn Hunayf, but places it within the prehistory of the battle of Nahrawan, in which 'Ali had won a great victory over the Kharijites.[16] In all these cases the point is not the historical figure of Sahl ibn Hunayf, but the advice "Distrust yourselves, your own opinions!" 'Umar II used this as proof of the correctness of his own theological standpoint; in the *hadith*, which was written later, it was used in various different scenarios, with 'Umar ibn al-Khattab again appearing as the character requesting from the Prophet confirmation that that advice was correct and on that occasion receiving further instruction.

It is direct speech that carries the *hadith*'s actual content; the stock scenes merely serve to place the speakers credibly, especially the Prophet's companion and the Prophet himself. As soon as that model was generally accepted—around the mid-eighth century—the use of written notes that did not yet contain the by now modern *hadith*'s characteristics were considered inadequate. Oral rendition, which in many cases included clarification of the scenes' purpose by way of gestures, now became standard; it is documented that, in the second half of the eighth-century text, material was revised with that principle in mind, and that often it was falsely claimed that the texts were rendered orally. In connection with this stage of the *hadith*'s development it seemed to make sense—and was even imperative—to document the various stages of how the tradition, which was now considered an authentic representation of the wholesome beginnings, was passed on orally: using a chain of authorities (*isnad*) before the *hadith* proper, and sometimes even smoothly becoming part of it, became standard. The extant *hadith* collections, which go back only to the turn of the ninth century, all offer the material in its fully developed form but allow us to draw conclusions about the way it had been arranged previously.[17] Yet the reader, especially if he is a Sunnite, has the impression that he is directly involved in what Muhammad says and does: only the perfectly structured *hadith* literature turns the *sunna* into a surrogate institution for the Prophet's guidance.

Al-Humaydi passed on to us—Sufyan (ibn Uyayna) passed on to us—'Ata' ibn as Sa'ib passed on to us; he said: My father told me: I heard 'Abdallah ibn Mar ibn al-'As say: God's messenger—may God pray for him and greet him with "*Salam!*"—spoke: "There are two things, insignificant to be sure and a small burden to him who follows them, but every Muslim who adheres to them will enter paradise!" "What are they, o messenger of God?" was the question. He replied: "After each prayer you shall say ten times 'Praise be to God!,' ten times '*Allahu akbar!*,' ten times 'Glory be to God!'; when you lay down to sleep, you shall say thirty-three times 'Praise be to God!,' and thirty-four times '*Allahu akbar*', " Sufyan (ibn Uyayna) explained: "One of the three phrases thirty-four times, that makes two-hundred and fifty times[18] with your tongue, that makes two-thousand-five-hundred on the scale (of good deeds)." 'Abdallah ibn 'Amr said: "I observed God's messenger counting this with his fingers. Then he asked: 'Is there someone among you who can commit two-thousand-five-hundred sins in one day and one night?' Thereupon (those who were listening to the Prophet) exclaimed: 'Messenger of God! How could it happen that one forgets those words!?' Muhammad replied: 'Well, Satan approaches one of you and whispers to him: Don't forget to think of this, don't forget to think of that! And already that man gets up without having said them.'" Sufyan ibn Uyayna commented: "This was the very first (tradition) about which we asked 'Ata'. When 'Ata' arrived in Basra, Aiyyub (as-Sakhtiyyani) had told people to call on him and ask him to recite this *hadith* to them."[19]

This was a *hadith* in its developed form. It was taken from the collection of al-Humaydi (d. 833) and written down approximately one century after 'Umar II's polemic against the Qadarites. The Meccan al-Humaydi owes almost all of his material to the well-known and highly esteemed chronicler Sufyan ibn Uyayna (d. 813), whose lectures he is said to have attended for twenty years. 'Ata' ibn as-Sa'ib (d. 754) was from Kufa and traveled twice to Basra to recite traditions to an audience. Among those the one quoted above was considered particularly valuable and important.[20] 'Ata' mentions 'Abdallah ibn 'Amr ibn al-'As as a companion of the Prophet, who claimed to have closely observed Muhammad when that recommendation was announced to him—"I observed God's messenger counting it with his hands." 'Abdallah ibn 'Amr ibn al-'As was said to have "southern Arabian" inclinations, which is why he may have acquired in Kufa, which was on 'Ali's side, the reputation of being a suitable source.[21]

So 'Ata' arrived in Basra, and the city's native Aiyyub, his contemporary,[22] advised the believers to have someone recite to them the *hadith* on gaining religious merit by frequently repeating the praise of God, a *hadith* whose contents were apparently known: by referring to the authority of the sources, who were all said to have heard the tradition's oral rendition and performance, the speaker was able to render faithfully and intelligibly the Prophet's alleged speech as well as the elucidating gestures that went with it, and only by listening to him directly did the important message of salvation become real and effective; thus the era of the Prophet had survived into the present era, no matter how many years it may have been past. The desire for orally represented Prophetic guidance was so strong that Sufyan ibn Uyayna apparently pretended to have been a witness to that memorable passing-on of the *hadith* in Basra. 'Ata' died sixty years before him; since Sufyan was born in 725, it is not impossible that he had heard 'Ata'. Yet nowhere are Sufyan's connections in Basra mentioned; he was from Kufa and lived in Mecca from 780 until he died.[23] Nonetheless, he stressed that he was present when 'Ata' *came*—Sufyan preferred not to add "to Basra"—and was asked about that tradition. It was said, incidentally, that the Basrans had not been pleased with 'Ata'; he had been with them twice, the second time already somewhat mentally confused, which was why only his early Basran acts of passing on traditions, among them our *hadith*, could be taken seriously. Al-Humaydi documented that Sufyan adopted the Basran criticism of 'Ata', but again without mentioning Basra: "I had heard 'Ata' ibn as-Sa'ib earlier, when he came to visit us. Then I heard him pass on some of what I had heard from him (previously)—and he mixed it up! Thereupon I avoided him. . . ."[24] If we remember that Sufyan falsely claimed to have received the *hadiths* in an oral rendition by az-Zuhri, the famous collector who had died seventy-five years before him,[25] we can be almost certain that in the case of the tradition being passed on by 'Ata', we are looking again at a pious fraud. We have already learned that a *sunna* made concrete in the form of a *hadith* was ultimately considered one of the "two important things" Muhammad left his community[26]: tradition and Koran factually become sources of equal value.

What the *hadith*—which given these circumstances can only be the proof of a *sunna* of the *Prophet*[27]—conveys, is sometimes presented as the direct result of a revelation. Abu Sa'id al-Khudari, a companion of the Prophet who is often called on as a witness, supposedly told the following story: "What I fear for you most is the earth's plants, this world's splendor of the blossoms God makes sprout from the earth!" Someone asked the Prophet three times why something good could turn out to be bad. "God's messenger was silent; then we noticed that something was sent down on him. For when he received a revelation, he had to contort his face as if he were blinded, and he broke out in a sweat."[28] As soon as Muhammad came to, he called the man who had asked him and told him that good begot only good; however, one could eat too much of the fruits of this earth; therefore, one should beware of insatiable voracity. "Sufyan ibn Uyayna said: 'Al-A'mash (d. 762)[29] asked me only too often, whenever I visited him, to repeat this *hadith*.'"[30] Sufyan ibn Uyayna's connection with al-A'mash, who was also from Kufa, is reliably documented.[31] Al-A'mash, who was the by far older of the two, asked him again and again to recite this *hadith*, which elevates the general tone of asceticism of early Sunni piousness[32] to the realization of a revelation. This is how much al-Amash, who is explicitly said not to have dealt with written documents,[33] desired to hear this scene which the younger man had been reliably told by someone else!

The more firmly the conviction was established that what Muhammad did and said, and that the divine guidance as it was so strongly felt in the original community became palpable in the *hadith*, the more the *hadith*'s content was apt to reveal its practical usefulness for providing binding rules for Islamic everyday life. Now, toward the end of the eighth century, there was finally something at hand to which one could refer on issues regarding rites and secular life. Only fifty years earlier, right after the Abbasids had come to power, people had been searching desperately for a firm guideline for establishing an Islamic empire; it is documented that at that time people referred to the ancestors' customs all too easily, without being able to determine their content, let alone connect that content with Muhammad.[34] Now people no longer had to be that uncertain. The *hadith* became by far the most important source of early Islamic jurisprudence[35] ; the last part of al-Humaydi's work already reveals the desire to organize traditions under the aspects of rite and important legal institutes.[36] In the canonic collections, which had been put together since the end of the ninth century, this system completely replaced the older one, where traditions were always kept together under the name of the oldest "witness," typically a companion of the Prophet.

One example may serve to illustrate the way the *hadith* was used as a legal source; it can also further document the characteristics of that literary genre that were outlined above. Sufyan ibn Uyayna reports that, after the victory against an anti-Quraysh tribal coalition near Hunayn in the spring of 630, a companion of the Prophet by the name of Ya'la ibn Umayya accompanied Muhammad on his way to al-Ji'rana, from where the Prophet wanted to go on the so-called lesser pilgrimage (*'umra*) to Mecca.[37] A stranger, wearing perfume and a linen garment, approached the Prophet to ask if it was permissible for him to have entered the sacred state of the lesser pilgrimage in his extravagant outfit. Muhammad asked him what he had done during the major pilgrimage, and the stranger assured him that he had always washed the perfume off his body and taken off his fine clothes. That, the Prophet replied, was precisely what he should also do before the lesser pilgrimage. It became a rule in ritual law that one should accept the sacred state during the major as well as the lesser pilgrimage only after taking off all fine clothes.[38] Sufyan was also familiar with a second version. As in the first one, a chain of witnesses includes 'Ata ibn Abi Rabah, a Meccan who died around 733 and was considered an expert on pilgrimage law[39]; however, the witness between him and Sufyan is someone else. In this version, the Prophet's companion Ya'la ibn Umayya asked a rather long time ago 'Umar ibn al-Khattab's permission to be present when Muhammad received a revelation. His time had finally come near al-Ji'rana. 'Umar called for him. The Prophet was lying on the ground as if he were dead, wrapped in a robe.[40] " 'Umar uncovered Muhammad's face for me, and lo, it had turned red." When the Prophet came to, he immediately asked for the stranger who had inquired with him about wearing elegant clothes and perfume at the beginning of the lesser pilgrimage.[41]

2. The Kalam

The *hadith* was the literary genre that offered the chance of leading the quasi-sacred life of the ancestors to those Muslims who rejected in retrospect the splinter movements of the Kharijites and Shiites. The "unifying sunna," which around the turn of the ninth century had been narrowed down to the "Prophet's sunna,"[42] now appeared as the obliging, richly detailed, and nearly all-comprehensive standard of life which Muhammad had personally established. The time was ripe for the work of the great legal theoretician ash-Shafi'i (d. 820), who assumed the task of proving that all laws can, in part directly and in part indirectly, be traced back to the Koran, and especially to the *sunna*.[43] When we look back at 'Umar II's polemic against the Qadarites, we can already sense that the tradition about the Prophet was also be apt to affect profoundly the entire field of theology; 'Umar II quoted Sahl ibn Hunayf in order to invalidate the conclusions reached by reason: they did not ensure salvation! We have also seen that the *hadith* elevated the acceptance without complaint of the divine *qadar* to the status of a religious doctrine, and once the *hadiths* were recognized as parallel revelations, it was bound to be difficult to argue rationally against their theological implications; but that is not yet our concern here. A speculative theology developed quite unimpeded by the *hadith* until far into the ninth century, and one can say with some authority that the Islamization of society that took place along with the development of the Prophet's tradition cleared the view for the fact that the issue of "predestination or personal responsibility for one's salvation" needed to be examined not only with regard to the opposition between "faith" and "Islam," but also required that profound issues be dealt with that reached into the realm of metaphysics. As will be shown at the beginning of the next chapter, Islamization delivered the Muslims' rational theology.

While the *hadith* is dogmatic in character—the Prophet answers one of his companions' questions or evaluates roughly outlined facts—the special quality of the *kalam*, the literary genre that rationally penetrates and develops theological and metaphysical statements, is that antagonistic views are settled. *Hadith* literally refers to an oral report or a story told; *kalam* refers to the act of speaking and does not imply a final, given set of facts or a decision that has already been reached. In the *kalam* speakers and counter-speakers appear to advance a train of thought; therefore, the *kalam* always has a polemical trait. It is not characterized by the dispassionate and objective development and consideration of pertinent arguments, but by the opponents' attempt to secure advantages for themselves, even if this is done disingenuously. Refined tactics, a subtle sense of the opponent's weaknesses, and sometimes even coming on strong and rude, are the *mutakallim*'s indispensable equipment. To be sure, there were certain rules of proper conduct, which were to ensure that the opponent would be done justice. His thesis had to be presented undistorted, and he must not be personally intimidated.

And so, since the end of the eighth century, a culture of arguing evolved that soon afterwards was adopted by Islamic jurisprudence.[44] Being able not only to prove one's opponent wrong but to put oneself in his place, was considered praiseworthy. The literary thinker al-Jahiz (d. 869), the eminent representative of the early Abbasid period's intellectualism, particularly distinguished himself in this respect.[45] It was not always immediately clear whether or not he stood behind a particular view that he substantiated with all kinds of arguments. That gives his discourses a chameleonlike character. Still, this way of discussing an issue is eminently valuable, as it provides insights into very different trains of thought. However, when dealing with the *kalam*, one always has to remember one thing: the arguments that were written down—and they are all we know—are always suspect of being modified to the author's advantage, for after all, it was he who had the final word. All that may have been quite different during the dispute itself, which took place in front of a possibly biased audience.

Before it began, the participants' parts were determined precisely. Only the one asking the questions was in a favorable position, for he could determine the course of the argument. His counterpart was forced to substantiate the antitheses his responses contained. The questioner set traps for his opponent, who had to anticipate them as well as, probably, the trick questions he would have to fend off if he parried this way or that.[46] At the beginning of the ninth century people still hoped that this way they would, step by step, reach a religious form of Islam that was founded in reason and, therefore, true and generally accepted—for hadn't God endowed man with reason?—and thus end all quarrels once and for all: all reasonable human beings would bow to the more convincing argument. Toward the end of that same century, it became clear that this hope had been treacherous. Disputes without roots in a firm and unquestionable basis of belief did not decrease hatred and quarrel, but vastly increased it.[47]

But back to the *kalam* as a literary genre. It consists of disputes that were recorded the way they should, in the opinion of the authors, go or have gone in order for the doctrines they supported to win out. The *kalam*'s basic polemical trait is accompanied by an effort to give helpful instructions. The opponent's potential replies or subterfuges are rehearsed so that the reader, who has to adopt tacitly the author's opinions, is prepared for everything.

The characteristics just outlined can be found in an early source such as al-Hasan ibn Muhammad's polemic against the Qadarites, which the Zaydi imam Yahya ibn al-Husayn (859-910)[48] copied and "disproved" question by question. A paragraph from that work shall serve as an illustration of some of the characteristics particular to the *kalam* literature.

Let us recall that al-Hasan ibn Muhammad, the Murjiite, was firmly convinced that human beings did not create the circumstances of their actions, which is why it was not possible to judge justly their success or lack of success in retrospect; only God, who created those circumstances, was in a position to do so. Al-Hasan ibn Muhammad had written his treatise under the impression of the Second Civil War, and had been interested in moderating the destructive quarrel between the parties. He had searched for convincing examples to buttress his arguments, but as we have seen, this had brought him in dangerously close proximity to the doctrine of predestination, which had not at all suited his purposes. Yahya ibn al-Husayn did not give the least consideration to al-Hasan's historical circumstances, but saw his work as a testimony of pure belief in predestination (*jabriyya*). For al-Hasan it had been perfectly clear that Muhammad had been appointed Prophet by God and, therefore, had been able to act only as Prophet and not against his calling; this had constituted the divinely created circumstances of everything he said and did. Therefore, al-Hasan had asked the Qadarites whether God's messengers were able to desist from preaching the revelation.

Yahya faithfully repeats the arguments directed against the Qadarites: "If (the Qadarites) say, 'Yes, God accorded them opportunity and ability to refrain from preaching. If (the prophets) had wanted to, they could have altered His . . . revelation!' then they become caught up in an even worse contention than the one they rejected, namely, that if God's messengers wanted to, they could fail to worship God by proclaiming His oneness and by disobeying Him. In this regard, the Qadarites even maintain that the messengers could conceal from them their divine inspiration! Therefore, one asks them (if indeed they should have gone so far as to believe that): 'So you do not know whether or not the messengers have preached the entire revelation and all the rules that were conveyed to them?' If (the Qadarites) reply, 'Yes, God's messengers can . . . fail to tell you all that if they want to!' then (this) will be used against them.[49] But if they say: 'God's messengers were unable to conceal the revelation, to change the duties of faith, to refrain from preaching, then God compelled them to do all that . . . ,' then they give the (correct) answer and thus disprove their own opinion."[50]

This quote from al-Hasan ibn Muhammad's treatise shall suffice. Yahya ibn al-Husayn begins his discussion of this apparently conclusive argument by reformulating the original question. This illustrates how quickly the level of disputation has been raised since the times of 'Abd al-Malik. "The first thing about which he (al-Hasan ibn Muhammad) inquired was whether prophets are able to commit two opposite acts in two different states." Can prophets be obedient at one time and then again, under different circumstances, disobedient? What this version of the question secretly contains is the dispute about the relationship between the manifold world as it was created and the one Creator, a dispute that had emerged toward the end of the eighth century. God must be one, and also uniform, otherwise one could differentiate Him into multiple entities. The world's multiplicity, however, is not only caused by the multitude of the particles of matter of which a body consists, as well as the different *accidentes* these contain, but also by time, which is subdivided into countless moments and in which changing circumstances and activities accompany the changes in the construct made of particles and *accidentes*. Whether we may presume that the created entity's own laws and, as far as human beings are concerned, the movements of will ruled by reason can direct this change, or whether it is always directly and completely implemented by God—this is now more or less how the question of individual responsibility versus predestination is put.

"We teach concerning (the thus reformulated question): 'God's messengers executed His order, in the manner He had determined and without reservations. In all of this they attached the greatest importance to God's order and remained obedient to Him. Furthermore, God did not require them to convey the message until He gave them the necessary ability to do so. . . . So they passed on from Him what He had told them to, by choosing freely (to do so), preferring to be obedient, and endeavoring to please God. Hence, He did not force them to pass on the message! . . . Rather, He ordered them to do so, and they transmitted the message, and He encouraged them to hold out patiently, and they were patient: O Messenger, deliver that which has been sent down to thee from thy Lord; for if thou dost not, thou wilt not have delivered His Message (and are disobedient), God says (sura 5, verse 71).' " If Muhammad did not inherently have the capacity to execute or refuse the order, Yahya continues, the order would not make sense, and "doing" also implies an action, not something being done passively. "Never does God issue an order to someone without knowing that the person could also do the opposite." Hence the encouragement, hence the prohibitions, and finally also the exhortation to be patient in failure! Were it any different, the Koran would not say, "So be thou patient, as the Messengers possessed of constancy were also patient" (sura 64, verse 34), but "We made thou patient as we made them patient." One would have to consider God to be foolish if He gave orders that could not be carried out.

Yahya ibn al-Husayn points out that in the Koran God distinguishes very clearly between what He does and what His creatures do. "It is We who give life, and make to die," He says in sura 50, verse 42. He gave human beings eyes and ears—why else but for them to use them themselves? Yahya ibn al-Husayn concludes this train of thought with one of the *kalam*'s favorite lines of logical argument, whose purpose it was to expose the opponent to ridicule. Quite often the Meccans disdainfully dismissed Muhammad's message concerning the resurrection of the dead on the Day of Judgment as "fairy-tales of the ancients"; that derisive phrase is mentioned in sura 16, verse 25. "If human beings could not choose freely and were incapable of achieving what they want, and if it were the Lord of the Worlds who leads their hand in everything they do, it also would be He Himself, and not they, who would denounce the truth of what He has revealed as 'fairy-tales of the ancients'!" No, God only wants what is good, as the believers recognize correctly! And He sends only good down to His creation! This thought, which is derived from sura 16, verse 32, is the basis of the next step.

Al-Hasan ibn Muhammad had made the assumption that, if God's messengers could act of their own volition, one could not be sure if they really preached the entire message or if they falsified it. The thesis that God's sole intention was to send down good to His creation opens up the opportunity for Yahya to argue cogently, "Do you not know, questioner, that God considers honest only someone who is truly honest and noble?" Never would He elect a scoundrel prophet!

We have just touched upon a basic trait of the *kalam*, one that often makes its arguments difficult to understand for an outsider. Even though they were really bound to intellectual honesty and quite willing to present their opponents' trains of thought accurately —as we have noted, Yahya adhered to that principle—the contenders still consider their own views to be absolute. They argue from that perspective, not from that of the issue itself.

Since he was convinced that one's divinely created circumstances significantly restricted man's freedom of choice and action, al-Hasan ibn Muhammad had to consider what the Prophet did and said as something determined by God; otherwise there was no assurance that the message conveyed by Muhammad would be complete and pure. Yahya does not address this motive of al-Hasan but in his arguments presupposes what he considers to be true: that God always has His creation's well-being in mind. If both authors had been able to enter into an actual dispute, they would have talked at cross-purposes. Still, Yahya concludes his argument with al-Hasan being absolutely convinced that he has been thoroughly victorious: "Therefore the argument of the man who wanted to criticize the divinely guided prophets"—a nasty imputation in itself!—"is moot! Praise be to God, and His 'Salam' to all messengers!"[51]

This was an example of how the opinion of an author who had died a long time ago was disproved; its stylistic pattern was direct speech versus counter-speech: Yahya addressed al-Hasan ibn Muhammad, indignant about the latter's alleged ignorance that made him ask absurd questions. The *kalam*'s textbooks are more succinct and designed in such a way as to prepare students for intellectual battles. They endeavor to present the entire subject matter of theology systematically. A very early work of this genre is Ibn al-Baqillani's (d. 1013) *Book of Introduction*. A glance at the chapter on the human ability to act (*istita'a*) may serve to illustrate this characteristic feature: "When someone asks, 'Are you teaching that human beings have the ability to acquire their acts?'[52] the answer is, 'Yes.' If the next question is, 'Why do you teach that?' we reply, 'Because man recognizes the difference between whether he is standing, sitting, or talking—movements that occur according to his volition and intention—or between acts to which he is forced, but which he cannot commit because he lacks the strength on account of an illness, as someone who is paralyzed cannot move. Both (the movement executed intentionally and the one prevented on account of illness) cannot be distinguished from one another either in regard to their category or to one's knowledge of them, or in regard to their different substratum or intent to execute them. Consequently, the act occurs at the moment in which it is acquired in its pertinent quality, precisely because the one executing it has the power to commit it.' If (the opponent) now asks, 'Are you claiming that the actor acquired the act owing to a power of his own or to a power he is given from somewhere outside of him?' we respond, "Not (owing to his own power) but to a power which is generated in him (at that moment). This is proven by the fact that at one time the actor had the power to execute the movement, but not at another time—or at yet another time to commit an act comparable (to the movement).' "[53]

Let us for the time being ignore the presupposed concepts in this passage. What we can clearly recognize is the attempt to anticipate the course of a dispute and—in this case—to prepare the proponent of man's severely limited freedom to act for possible tricky objections; I have quoted only a very small part from the chapter Ibn al-Baqillani devoted to this issue. At the conclusion of this quick glance at the *kalam*, we still need to pursue the question regarding its significance within the eighth- and ninth-century intellectual and social process we have characterized by the terms "from faith to 'Islam.'" The answer to that question will in part overlap with what we have said about the *hadith*.

Initially the *kalam* was supposed to mediate between the inimical Islamic movements, similarly to the *hadith*, but on another level. Al-Hasan's treatise on postponing judgment had already stated this intention. During the early eighth century, the proponents of the evolving *kalam* would employ a line of argument that can be compared to the Murjiites' way of thinking. It had the advantage of staying clear of predestinarian teachings and thus of preserving one of the *kalam*'s main concerns, the rational evaluation of human actions.[54] The two parties in the First Civil War were compared to a husband and wife arguing about the paternity of a child suspected to be illegitimate. In such cases Islamic law applied the procedure of *li'an*: husband and wife had to corroborate their mutually contradictory statements by cursing each other; if both were ready to do so, paternity was of course not established, but the marriage was considered dissolved. The rationale behind this was that one could not tell which of the two was lying, but one had lied in any case and was therefore in the wrong. In the eighth and ninth centuries a literature evolved which tried to determine even the subtlest possible motives of the opponents 'Ali and Mu'awiya. This body of work was written in the spirit of the *kalam* and reached its peak in numerous writings by the above-mentioned al-Jahiz. Rational arguments were supposed to depict the events of early Islamic history in a way to which all Muslims could agree.[55] Rationality was supposed to create forcibly what the Sunnites were hoping to gain by remembering the beginnings, by eradicating what was, in their view, a disastrous history.

Yet while the *hadith* could influence the Islamic community only internally—because it presupposed the belief in Muhammad as God's Prophet—the *kalam* was apt to wage an intellectual battle with other religions. This was infinitely more important to Muslims than for, say, the Christians in medieval Europe. Apart from Judaism, which basically refrained from proselytizing, there was no highly religious competition in Europe, whereas Islam had to assert itself in the Near East, a region that had been molded by other universal religions before Islam arrived.

Still, the Muslims did not so much consider the representatives of the oriental Christian churches and the followers of Zoroastrianism as a threat to their faith as they did the intellectuals of an urban mold. They were hard to understand, steeped in syncretistic and skeptical ideas, and are sometimes considered to have been Manicheans; with the bureaucratization of the empire, which had begun during the late Umayyad period, they had become indispensable. They served their new—the Islamic—masters, learned Arabic extremely well, shone with their wit and education, and made fun of the Muslim faith's lack of sophistication and intellectual inadequacy. "Their god sits on a throne; then he draws near until he is suspended two bows'-length away" (sura 53, verse 8), mocks 'Abdallah ibn al-Muqaffa' (d. 756), an administrative official of Iranian descent who rose from the ranks during the early Abbasid period. He wrote a treatise—it has survived in quotes—on the absurdities and silliness of the Koran.[56] Attacks of this kind had to be fought off; yet it was also necessary to answer questions arising from camps close to Jewish and Christian doctrines; both were rooted in a theology that was centuries old. It was impossible to avoid confronting these issues on the same level. It is not surprising that early representatives of the *kalam* boastfully claimed they had proved all foreign religions wrong.[57] Ibn al-Baqillani's handbook devotes long passages to discussions of Jews, Christians, Zoroastrians, as well as followers of star faith and movements of natural philosophy.

However, accomplishing tasks of this kind internally, within the Islamic community, and externally was not the *mutakallimun*'s primary goal; assuming this would fail to recognize its religious fervor. Their— ultimately unreachable—goal, which spurred them on to ever greater efforts and occasionally propelled them to get carried away in extravagant sophistries, was to systematize convincingly the Prophet's message in a manner entirely accessible to human reason. In short, the *mutakallimun* struggled for a solution to the central issue the Koran had imposed on the Muslims: to bring into agreement worldly causality (and thus responsibility for one's actions) and the one Creator's incessantly manifesting omnipotence.[58]

CHAPTER IV

Early Rationalism

1. Arab-Muslim Society

The Abbasid caliph al-Mu'tasim (r. 833–42) had built a new capital: Samarra. Baghdad, which was not founded until around 760, had been razed during the civil war following the dispute between his two predecessors al-Amin (r. 809–13) and al-Ma'mun (r. 813–33) about the rightful succession to the throne. Yet this alone was not the reason for making a new beginning. Al-Mu'tasim realized that if he wanted to rule without interference from the parties that had supported the inimical brothers al-Amin and al-Ma'mun, he had to build an army that was loyal only to him and that he would best keep from having too close contact with the political establishment. Enlisting mercenaries was not difficult—new territories for Islam had been gained in battles in Central Asia. Turkish war slaves formed the basis of his new army, to which he assigned closed quarters in Samarra.[1]

Sons of Turkish princes had also arrived in Mesopotamia; as officers of the guards, they soon gained considerable influence on the caliphs. Among them was al-Fath ibn Khaqan, the undisputed favorite of al-Mutawakkil (r. 847–61), the second successor of al-Mu'tasim. Al-Fath and his sponsor gathered a circle of illustrious literati, among them al-Jahiz, who dedicated to his Turkish patron a short treatise on the advantages of the new troop of mercenaries. In this treatise he praised the Turks' courage in battle and their manly virtue to the skies, but also attributed to them a talent for profound religious and philosophical insights; in addition, he praised their nomadic way of life, which, he said, was a better preparation for battle.[2] Yet, al-Jahiz writes, in a discussion during al-Mu'tasim's reign, al-Fath ibn Khaqan had been compelled to defend himself against an ardent follower of the old party in Khurasan, to which the Abbasids owed the caliphate. The Khurasanians' loss of power, at least in Iraq, and the rise of the mercenaries were the top domestic policy issues under al-Mu'tasim. Back then al-Fath had informed al-Jahiz of the altercation; the latter had then summarized the arguments in a brief report, which, however, because of certain "reasons which it would take too long to mention," he had not passed on to al-Fath. But, be that as it may, the conflict al-Jahiz recorded in such detail does deserve a closer look.

The Khurasanian had triggered the dispute by thanking God for the fact that even though the Abbasid army consisted of five different peoples who were strangers to one another—Khurasanians, Turks, Mawali[3], Arabs, and descendants of Arabs who had immigrated to Iran—it was united in its obedience to the caliph. All five of them, he maintained, had their own claim to fame. This had been elaborated on in some depth during the—alleged—conversation, except that the Turks had been mentioned only rather briefly. Yet, al-Jahiz assures his readers, al-Fath ibn Khaqan did not even demand the same eulogies for them but was in favor of leveling those distinctions that his anonymous opponent had so eloquently emphasized. Khurasanians and Turks, he said, were by no means as clearly distinct from one another as Arabs and non-Arabs or as Byzantines and Slavs; rather, they formed two parts of one and the same people, and were distinguishable only by their different ways of life—just as some members of the Arabian tribe of the Taiy lived in the mountains and some in the plains. In order to determine to which larger group someone belonged, it was, he argued, not one's genealogy that was important but the individual's living conditions, as well as the nonmaterial circumstances that determined them. These circumstances, he said, carried more weight than consanguinity. Neither, al-Jahiz informed his readers, was one's language community a determining factor: initially Isma'il, the Arabs' ancestor, had not spoken any Arabic at all; God had taught him that language, the same way that everybody who entered paradise began to talk in the language customarily spoken there. Why, the author asked, was the clan of the Banu 'Abd al-Muttalib, from which the Prophet came, considered the noblest among the Quraysh? Not on account of some superior genealogical quality, but because 'Ukasha ibn Muhsin,[4] the ancient Arabs' most courageous knight, was one of them—but only as an ally! Owing to their battle skills, "the Turks became Arabs despite all other qualities that separate them from them."[5] God chose His servants, whether they were Arabs or members of some other people, whether Quraysh or Negroes, so those five peoples who made up the caliph's army were actually one people and what connected them was stronger than what separated them.[6]

Al-Jahiz explained that under al-Mu'tasim, al-Fath ibn Khaqan presented himself as someone who supported among the most important strata of the army and the empire a sense of unity that was based on Islam; however, the Arabs should clearly have superiority, because the Prophet had been one of them. Now, under al-Mutawakkil, the author felt compelled to add to his report on the dispute a eulogy about the Turks—noble lords such as al-Fath ibn Khaqan did appreciate flattery. However, al-Jahiz assured the reader, he was going to be strictly honest and keep a fair middle ground between exaggeration and paucity of praise. Otherwise, he said, his treatise would consist of lies, of artificial verbal noise, and would beg for criticism. "For one achieves the form of praise that is most useful to the one doing the praising, most fruitful to the one being praised, and most lasting and beautiful, if it is truthful and really appropriate to how we perceive the person being praised . . . ; this is achieved only if the words characterizing him describe how he (actually) is.[7] Furthermore, I believe that if one could express the Turks' glorious names only by criticizing the other contingents of the army, it would be better to leave the whole thing be. . . . Even if much praise is bestowed on many of these groups, this does not compensate for the criticism of only a few of them (plus the caliph's army would appear in a bad light). For praising almost all of them is like a ritual act that goes beyond one's duties; it expresses overzealousness, and criticizing almost no one means being guilty of neglecting one's duty. The little of our duty serves us more than the plenty of overzealousness. All human beings have faults and assume a certain degree of guilt. Therefore, they are distinguished by the number of their good and bad sides. Never has anyone heard of someone having all conceivable good and no bad qualities. . . . Bashshar ibn Burd[8] wrote: 'If you only ever criticize your companion, well, you will never find one who has no faults! Stay by yourself or stick with your brother, who now commits a sin, and now avoids committing one! If you cannot drink anything murky now and then, then die of thirst! For whose drink is always pure?'
" The majority of people, he argues, act according to this insight, and

even the caliph, whom God elevated above all other Muslims in many respects, had to be forbearing and, when appropriate, forgiving.⁹ These considerations were followed by the above-mentioned honorable description of the Turks, in whom, however, al-Jahiz also detected traits of barbaric savageness, so that in his own estimation he was preserving the objectivity he had promised.

What is telling in these reflections is that al-Jahiz tacitly distanced himself from two forms of poetry that were characteristic of ancient Arab paganism: the panegyric (*madih*) and the invective (*hija'*). He alluded to both of them: "This treatise is not intended to be boundless in its praise (*madih*) of people or to carry its disparagement (*hija'*) of others too far."¹⁰ He rejected both as untruthful. In Arabia's pre-Islamic times, it was permitted to indulge in the exuberance of one's words, of the verses that— according to al-Jahiz—had nothing to do with reality. The noblemen of one's own tribe were praised downright excessively, and one's enemies were inveighed against as if one wanted to destroy them. Islam, on the other hand, provided a standard for judging people—all people: this standard was the divine law. If it was applied—which made it imperative to control one's potential feelings of love or hatred—then everyone had a mixture of virtues and vices. The caliph's army was not made up of groups with their pertinent distinct collective characteristics, but of individual warriors who all had to be judged by universally valid guidelines and who formed a unit, inasmuch as they fought for the Islamic empire.

To al-Jahiz Islam signified the breakthrough to worldly wisdom gained pursuant to sensible, God-given rules. This conviction pervades his entire oeuvre, which to the careless observer seems incoherent. Al-Jahiz was by no means alone in his view of Islam. It is a perspective that became more open to the degree in which ancient Arabian values and rules of conduct have changed under the influence of Islam. The period of paganism, the era of impetuous action determined by uncontrollable bursts of emotion, was gradually looked at as a strange, inferior phenomenon of the past; Muhammad's appointment as Prophet marked the beginning of civilization, of considering word and deed dispassionately. The wailing lamentation of the dead, enraptured, even frenzied screaming, scratching one's face, and tearing one's garment to shreds—these customs from pre-Islamic times were now considered improper; exercising self-control, having patience in view of the certainty that it was God who determined the term of everyone's life—this was now considered commendable conduct; the *hadith* portrays the mourning Prophet as weeping quietly, the expression of genuine, heartfelt grief.[11] What was now considered desirable was no longer the generosity, exaggerated to the point of self-destruction, with which pre-Islamic heroes obtained utmost glory, but clemency, exercised with constant regard of the one Creator and judge whose simple gifts relieved the stranger's predicament. The Allah Muhammad had proclaimed, who was in charge of everything, was also the Lord over the believer's most intimate emotions: what the Koran demanded of a select group of new converts and what branded them as outsiders who had to leave their native environment, was now taken for the Muslims' unifying, natural view of the world and way of life. Again, as with al-Jahiz, the issue of truthfulness arose; now, however, it was augmented by a new aspect: were grief and noblemindedness indeed in absolute agreement with the impulses of the heart, or were they merely pretentious and hypocritical? We can recognize in early rationalism's speculations that the issue of truthfulness, which testifies to the profound change in the guidelines for living which Islam has brought about,[12] was approached from two different angles: the linguistic and the ethic-moral perspective. It would turn out that they could not be answered without taking a stand on the issue of how God and His creation related to one another, in short: not without metaphysics.

2. A Glance at the Early Abbasid Period

The question, raised back in Medina, of what was Islam and what was faith, how they related to each other and which of the two should govern the community specified in Muhammad's revelation, had toward the end of the Umayyad period been decided in favor of Islam. As we have seen, the Damascene caliphs had no longer profited from that decision. To be sure, amidst the crisis of the waning dynasty the Hashimiyya movement, propelled by a radical religiosity, was able to release an unscrupulous energy[13]—an energy that overthrew the powers that be, replacing them by the unifying ideal of the community of believers in the newly founded caliph's empire. This was possible not least because of the legitimacy derived from the caliph's descendance from the Prophet's lineage; some members of the Hashimiyya movement did not want to stop the revolution once it had brought to power a caliph from among the Prophet's descendants.

Yet it was not merely their excessive behavior—invariably a quality of radicals—that led al-Mansur (r. 754–75), the consolidator of Abbasid power, to destroy them relentlessly.[14] People who surrounded him realized that the new caliphate would have to be supported by the majority of the population. What was needed was not hot-blooded bellicosity but an ordered everyday life that would accommodate a large number of people. Accordingly, in a memorandum Ibn al-Muqaffa' described the new ruler as a legislator who collected the legal customs of the various areas of his empire. By virtue of his insight, which on account of his descendancy from Muhammad's family was deeper than that of ordinary humans, he selected and codified the most suitable rules.[15] This put al-Muqaffa' far ahead of his time, for the *sunna* was still in the process of turning into the literary genre of the *hadith* as we know it today. However, the subjects' Islamization had progressed so far that, if a ruler acted in a way that could not be brought into agreement with Islam, it was considered illegal and reprehensible. The Umayyads had been almost relentlessly accused of violating Islamic principles, and during the turbulent days of the upheaval it was announced that, from now on, power was finally going to be exercised in the name of the Prophet and the religion established by God.[16] Therefore, what would have been in accord with how people felt—and what Ibn al-Muqaffa was absolutely right to propose—could still not be granted.

For this reason, al-Mansur and his successor al-Mahdi (r. 775–85) took a different approach. Making the particular faculty of insight of which the members of the Prophet's clan were capable—and at which Ibn al-Muqaffa' had hinted as well—the new caliphate's highest authority on earth, they spread a version of Islam's early history that supported their view of the principles and legitimization of power. According to this ideology, 'Ali, whom all Shiite movements, including the Hashimiyya, claimed as their spiritual ancestor, had been forced to recognize that it was not he and his descendants who had been chosen to be rulers, but

'Abbas, in whose family the legacy of being destined to be caliph had been passed on as if subterraneously until it could be brought to the light of day in 750.[17] The Abbasids thus placed themselves above all Islamic persuasions. With this, the feuds and the discord that darkened the Muslims' lives before the overthrow were declared a consequence of the illegitimate exercise of power, which had now been overcome. Finally the moment had arrived to bring about the harmony that Muhammad's community had been promised.

It is not surprising that the Shiites did not accept this tenet quietly. They rebelled on various occasions and had to be rigorously persecuted. The Abbasids' relationship with the *sunna* experts was always reserved as well; being employed by the new caliphs was considered frivolous, for it exposed one to the danger of forfeiting paradise by becoming entangled in reprehensible deeds: there were too many cases where the Abbasids and their cronies did not act according to the Prophet's *sunna*.[18] Yet the Abbasids found support among the circles of the literati and scholars, who, enticed by the magnificent court of the "prince of believers" and the equally luxurious life-style of his noblest servants, rushed to Baghdad to display their intellectual abilities as their sponsors' acolytes.

All this prepared a fertile ground in which the seeds of a rational concept of religion could grow. It was Caliph al-Ma'mun, a son of Harun ar-Rashid (r. 786–809), who personally supported the blossoming of rationalism with particular zeal. Educated at the court of the vizier's family of the Barmakids, he had become familiar with that intellectualist movement from an early age. In his fight for power with his brother, he stuck with the followers of rationalism, whose political support consisted of the old pro-Abbasid forces within the Hashimiyya movement. These circles, predominantly seated in Kharasan, had to face al-Amin, whose followers were among the large strata of Baghdad's population that supported the Sunnites. After all al-Ma'mun had achieved, he did everything he could to curtail the influence of the intellectual leaders of the Sunni in Baghdad. In the end he even established an inquisition that was to examine their religious beliefs and make them subscribe to the doctrine of the Koran as a creation, the shibboleth of rationalism. Only al-Mutawakkil dissolved that institution; it had not fulfilled its purpose and instead only widened the gap between the population and the caliphs, and brought ill repute to rational theology.

How different this was from al-Ma'mun's dreams! He had himself celebrated as the "imam of right guidance," as a caliph equipped with superior insight who had wanted to watch like an arbitrator over the rational arguments among all religions and Islamic persuasions, to bring them to a successful conclusion in peace and harmony. Did not all human beings have the same faculty of reason? Would they, therefore, not all submit to the rational insights which would lead to a unified Islam that would be recognized as true by everyone?[19]

3. The One God and His Revelation

Rationalist theology made the believers aware of the theological issues evolving from the content of the revelation and forced them to extract a meaning from the Koran's words when general categories of thought were applied in their analysis. The discussion of foreign religions could not go beyond a trite profession of one's own views until that analysis had taken place. In the mid-eighth century the caliphs ruled over a vast territory in which the older religions were far from extinguished. There was significant tension between Islam's radical monotheism and Christendom, which was accused of deifying Jesus. Dualistic ideas, which view the entire history of the world as a conflict between a good and an evil principle, thrived on Iranian soil as before. Islam had to explain why, when all was said and done, good and evil were derived from one single force, the one God. The Gnostic world religion of Manichaeism, which was generally very flexible, challenged Islamic monotheism. While it had an entirely transcendent god, he was ultimately idle—he did not interfere in the battle between good and evil on earth, for the world was not his creation but the product of a malicious demiurg. Finally, there were also "natural philosophers"[20]—a tradition passed on from antiquity—who explained everything that happened in the world as an interplay between eternal forces and eternal matter. They, too, had to reject Islam's concept of God, for they considered it unlikely for a *creator*, especially a personal one, to produce the vast number of phenomena in the world.

When monotheism was viewed from an Islamic angle, there did not seem to be a problem at first. The argument over the separation into areas of divine action and human action, however, which was fought behind the banners of "faith" and "Islam," contained difficulties enough. As soon as questions were asked about the exact meaning of the words by which the Koran describes God, these difficulties were bound to come to the surface. On the one hand, the one God is supposed to always be present in His creation, giving it direction. The Koran wants us to perceive with our senses, apply our names to, and consider the way He guides His creation; God has many different ways of recognizing the world and acting in it. Furthermore, these ways are comparable to humankind's, except that they are far superior to them inasmuch as they comprise everything there is and, owing to God's universal responsibility, cannot be thwarted: He sees and hears everything, no one can defy Him, especially not the idols the Meccans worshiped![21] He pervades everything, in which regard He is comparable to the "natures" of the ancient traditions, and at the same time He is supposed to be entirely different from His creation.[22] He is a person with human features, and yet this is exactly what He must not be—a disconcerting dilemma!

This dilemma could be avoided most easily by de-emphasizing one aspect in favor of the other, which was attempted as early as the end of the Umayyad era. A certain Ja'd ibn Dirham, whom tradition connects to the last Umayyad, Marwan II (r. 744–750), is supposed to have said that Abraham could not have been God's friend, and God could not have talked to Moses either. Statements like this must have been perceived as shocking denials of what the Koran stated. Whether they are the reason Ja'd was executed in Kufa or Wasit around 743 is uncertain.[23] What is clear, however, is the thrust of his arguments: God's transcendent character did not allow direct contact with Him; consequently, the truth of statements in the revelation claiming the opposite was eminently doubtful. The awareness of contradictions of this kind inevitably led to the nature of the revelation itself becoming a subject of debate.

Jahm ibn Safwan (d. 746) was given to similar reflections. He was from Tirmidh or Samarkand and was active in the eastern part of the Islamic empire. Tradition has it that he conducted disputes with the so-called Sumaniyya, a movement that apparently did not believe in a personal god. The Sumaniyya[24] may have been Buddhists; at that time Tirmidh was the center of Central Asian Buddhism, which was still in full bloom. It is certainly conceivable that in his discussions with the Buddhists Jahm ibn Safwan felt compelled to struggle for a rational and transcendent concept of God.

In his theology Jahm made a clear distinction between God and everything he termed a "thing" (*shai'*). One must not call God a "thing." This was entirely in agreement with the Koran, for in sura 39, verse 63, we read that God is the Creator "of every thing," and sura 42, verse 9, states that "like Him there is naught." Therefore, the Koran, too, was created.

One could say of all "things" that they were created in time (*mudhath*), and that it was God alone who made everything a "thing." Jahm ibn Safwan used "thing" as a technical term. By definition, God's being absolutely transcended the being of every "thing." One must by no means ascribe the quality of a "thing"—which was created in time—to God; this would imply a similarity between God and the created things. This also meant that all definitions applicable to a "thing" could not apply to God. One must not state that God had dimensions, boundaries, a direction, a color, etc. God had none of the qualities whatsoever that we perceived here on earth and according to which we could group the "things" and arrange them within a comprehensive system.[25]

The theological movement of the Jahmiyya blossomed particularly in the Islamic world's eastern part in the second half of the eighth century. We are familiar with it especially through the polemical statements leveled against it that disparaged them as "deflating" (*al-mu'attila*), precisely because it divested the concept of God of all conceivability.

Ad-Darimi (d. 869), a Sunnite from Samarkand, wrote a treatise against the Jahmiyya in which he accused it of robbing God of all attributes: "They spoke great words about God and disparaged Him most disgracefully, attributed ignorance to Him, and gradually robbed Him of His attributes. Finally they also took His pre-knowledge (of events) (*al-'ilm as-sabiq*), His speech, His hearing, His sight, everything."[26] In this treatise al-Darimi explained how the Jahmiyya defended its arguments. When, for instance, the Koran talks about God's hand, the Jahmiyya claimed that this did not really refer to His hand, but that the word was a metaphor for the benevolent deeds God had done for His creation. The interpretation of Koran passages mentioning that after creating the world God had sat down on His throne (sura 32, verse 3, or sura 10, verse 3) was an issue that was heatedly debated. Most Muslims certainly understood these passages quite anthropomorphically, as analogies to what happened here on earth. According to ad-Darimi, a Jahmite was once asked, "Do you admit that above the seventh heaven God has a real and definable throne which is carried by the angels, and that God is above that place, as He has said of Himself, separate from His creation?" The Jahmite is said to have been unable to come up with a clear answer—for the Jahmiyya believed that the word "throne" referred to God's magnificence and majesty. Ad-Darimi complained: "This group of people professes these verses with their tongues, and claims to believe in them. Thereupon they disprove their argument by another argument, saying: 'God is in every place, and no place is without Him.' We argue: 'You disprove that you believe God is sitting on the throne if you simultaneously claim that He is in every place.' They reply: 'In our view, this has to be interpreted to the effect that He took possession and control of it.'" In the Jahmites' view, the expression that after creating the world God straightened Himself in His throne meant no more than that God held the universe in His power and inspires it with His power.[27]

Another way in which the Jahmiyya expressed its tenet that God was different was by stating that He was limitless. This was meant in a spatial as well as temporal sense[28]: no place was free of God; God Himself was not *more* present in one place than in another. Human reason, the Jahmiyya argued, could not comprehend this. God, it said, was neither above nor below, neither to the right nor to the left, neither light nor heavy. Positing that He was first above and then below contained two different statements about Him, which was a violation of the law of God's absolute oneness. The word "face"[29] was used as a synecdoche; at the same time it indicated that bliss was guaranteed the believer for as long as he turned his face toward God and God for His part turned His face toward him. Yet, in the Jahmites' understanding, "face" referred to the totality of the ever-present divine being. It is in this connection that we have to see their frequently used phrase that the faculty to hear or see is an absolute and unlimited expression of His divine being. In contrast, the human senses of sight and hearing are inferior, for they were created by

Him; they have essential limits.[30]

The Jahmites came to understand God's oneness as an omnipresence of His being, which was incomprehensible to human reason. God had personally revealed Himself in His Book, which was created and subjected to the boundaries of time, like everything that surrounds us and that we apprehend. But, if He were so inconceivable and transcendent, could one really say that God revealed Himself? And, if one took the Jahmiyya's tenets seriously, was He not also immanent in His creation in a quite unexpected way? Ibn Taymiyya (d. 1328), the Sunnis' great thinker of the late Middle Ages, compared pantheistic theology, which was so prevalent during his time, to the Jahmiyya for a reason![31] What is more, the Jahmiyya, which had hoped that its tenets would serve to delineate sufficiently God's ontological otherness and infinite superiority, put itself in danger of concealing the Creator's subject-object relation to His work, which is one of the essential traits of the Koran's concept of God. The Prophet had a direct experience of God as an actor—not only in nature's growth and decay, but also in the fate of peoples and God's messengers. How could that be reasonably explained within the context of the Jahmite God's utterly undefinable being?

The Jahmiyya's tenets even influenced Muslims who did not explicitly endorse it. Abu Hanifa (d. 767), the famous legal scholar, is said to have shocked his contemporaries by saying that one could not doubt that the Kaaba existed, but that it was that house in Mecca—worshiping God was not restricted to certain localities, because God Himself was not three-dimensional; Abu Hanifa is said to have drawn the seemingly frivolous conclusion that one was also allowed to choose a sandal for the direction of one's prayer, as long as the worshiper had God in his heart.[32] If left unopposed, Jahmite ideas would not shy away from trying to change the rites, the essential glue of Islamic society.

It was difficult to go back behind the abstraction of the concept of God the Jahmites had formed, except by simply confining oneself to the holy texts—including, by now, the *hadith*. This abstraction as well as the level of rationality it had reached had to be preserved, and yet God must be thought of as the personal Creator and ruler of the world. The theories of God's attributes by Abu l-Hudhayl al-'Allaf (b. circa 750, since 818 in Baghdad, d. 840) represent the first well-documented attempt to overcome this difficulty. At first glance, his solution appears to be a merely formulaic compromise. Still, it showed the way into the future. According to Abu l-Hudhayl, God knew by virtue of a knowledge which was entirely Him; He had the power to act because it was a power which was entirely Him and in a manner of speaking identical with His being. By positing that God knew, Abu l-Hudhayl argued, one claimed that He had a knowledge that was identical with His being and one denied that He was not knowing, ignorant; at the same time, however, one was referring to an object which existed or would exist.[33] Abu l-Hudhayl tried to show that God was *one*, that His attributes did not indicate that His being had many different layers, but that we only perceived it as having many different layers. It was *we* who classified God's acting upon His creation by using the categories "seeing," "hearing," "being powerful," "knowing," and so forth; that, Abu l-Hudhayl said, was nothing but a very imperfect device we used to illustrate the overwhelming reality of God's actions.

We also have to see Abu l-Hudhayl's theory of the attributes against the backdrop of the references in the Koran—of which there is an increasing number from the middle Meccan period on—to human beings who pondered growth and decay in nature, reaching the conclusion that they owed all this to a never-resting Creator-God. In light of the well-ordered course of the world there must be a ruler with knowledge, for it was also true that, within the space given us human beings on earth, only someone with knowledge could produce a well-ordered work. Yet since God's being was identical with His attributes—in this case, His knowledge—it manifested not only on certain occasions, but constantly. The divine omnipresence of Jahmite thought developed a Koranic figure of thought into a comprehensive subject-object relation between Creator and creation. Thus an idea was born that initially was fascinating to theologians, but over the next centuries was to turn more and more into a Greek gift.

Approximately since the time of Abu l-Hudhayl, rationalist Islamic theology has been referred to by the collective term Mu'tazila, whose original meaning is being debated. In the Mu'tazilites' own interpretation, it refers to the withdrawal (*i'tizal*) from the arguments between the factions that were formed during the First Civil War[34]; rational reasons were put forth for striving toward a position beyond these factions, toward a stand with which everyone could agree. In this respect the Mu'tazila carries the spiritual legacy of the "postponer" al-Hasan ibn Muhammad, and it is in accord with al-Ma'mun's ideology of the imamate of right guidance. It was during his caliphate that the Mu'tazila reached the height of its influence. Among its circles, Abu l-Hudhayl's theories were heatedly debated and advanced in various ways.[35] One conclusion one could draw from Abu l-Hudhayl's reflections was frightening and dangerous to the Islamic dogma of God's oneness: the knowledge, hearing, and so forth that were identical with God's being were such diverse manifestations that it was no longer possible to recognize what it was that held together those hypostasized qualities that made up "God's nature." Was it perhaps only a concept devoid of meaning?

In order to understand the Mu'tazila's efforts to escape that danger, we have to examine a contemporary of Abu l-Hudhayl, Dirar ibn 'Amr. He was active in Basra during Harun ar-Rashid's reign and cultivated relations with the viziers' family of the Barmakids. Dirar ibn 'Amr had come to the realization that (1) God's existence could be assumed, and (2) he had certain qualities, a certain essence. We human beings, however, basically know only of God's existence (*anniyya*), but nothing about his essence (*mahiyya*). According to Dirar ibn 'Amr, we may conclude from God's works only that He exists; it is impossible to draw conclusions about His qualities. As we know from experience, our secret sensations cannot be entirely deduced from our actions; yet one can deduce *something* from them. This was similar with regard to God. Dirar, however, was convinced that we would not be able to gain more detailed knowledge about Him until we were in paradise. This, he said, was precisely what was meant by the Koran's promise that we would see God. However, this seeing must not be equated with our seeing something here on earth. God could not be perceived by our visual sense. Instead, Dirar suggested, in paradise we would be equipped with a sixth sense, with whose aid we would be able to comprehend part of God's fullness of being.[36]

Let us now consider theology as it evolved from the Jahmiyya via Dirar ibn 'Amr to Abu l-Hudhayl al-'Allaf! The Jahmiyya considered God to be everywhere and always, in other words, to be without limitations of time and space. In that regard, His being was necessarily different from the domain of His creation; therefore, it was also impossible to think of Him as relating to an object. Dirar ibn 'Amr discovered the difference between

God's existence and His essence. Yet the problem of how God extended His knowledge or sight to objects was still unresolved in his theology. That was achieved only by Abu l-Hudhayl, who postulated that God knew by virtue of a knowledge which He was entirely. This was the foundation of a rational theory of attributes. If God's essence was not to collapse into hypostasized attributes, it had to bring them back into itself, as it were. One must no longer speak of God's knowledge, sight, and hearing. God always had to be thought of as someone who possessed these attributes: He knew, saw, and heard. The uninterrupted acts of His knowing, seeing, and hearing originated in Him, the subject that could not be grasped in the fullness of His being, and extended to His creation, the object He had called into existence.

This has brought us right back to the Koran's statements about God. The Koran, too, presents God as an actor who never rests. In Dirar ibn 'Amr's theory, the attributes of God's acting were notably devoid of content; to him, describing God as knowing, powerful, and so forth, meant to negate the negation: God was not ignorant, not weak, not deaf, etc. Accusing God of weakness or inability would have been blasphemous.[37]

An-Nazzam, an early ninth-century Mu'tazilite who was called from Basra to Baghdad in 818, seems to have been familiar with Dirar ibn 'Amr's ideas. He formulated the solution to the theory of attributes as follows: knowing was a (object-related) confirmation of God's general existence and the negation of His ignorance; "powerful" was another confirmation of His existence, and a negation of His inability. An-Nazzam believed he could interpret an attribute such as "knowing" to mean that God *was* (*anniyya*), and that He could not have any attributes denoting inability.[38] The doctrine of the attributes of God's actions, which was modified in many different ways from the ninth century on, explained Him in His oneness and simultaneously as Him being the one who incessantly acted. Thus, the anthropomorphic interpretation of the attributes ascribed to Him in the revelation was also avoided. This was clearly possible only if many statements about Him in the Koran were read as metaphors, and especially when attacked in a polemic, the Mu'tazilites were often lumped together with the "deflated," the Jahmites.[39] This motivated the Mu'tazilites to keep refining their doctrine of God's oneness (*tauhid*). Since Sunni Islam had become so strong—which will be dealt with in the next chapter—the Mu'tazilites felt increasingly under pressure. After all, the point was not only to grasp God's oneness rationally and to understand in what way God acted upon the world. The pious believers did not want to recognize God only with their reason, but to have the One's being also light up their hearts; they yearned to experience Him as a personal God. Thus, in the tenth century the Mu'tazila was made to modify its doctrine about the divine attributes, which initiated the end of its leading role within Islamic theology. We will have to deal with this in more detail when examining Sunni rationalism.

The Jahmiyya's God, who inspired the world, could hardly be understood to be a personal Creator and preserver of the world; it was also impossible to ascertain how He could convey His word to this world. Furthermore, the domain of that which was uncreated—God Himself—could not be labeled with the words of a human language; as for us, we creatures were unable to make an image of the transcendent and translate it into words. What was called the revealed word was necessarily part of the domain of the created and could not exhibit any otherworldly characteristics. When dealing with the issue of whether or not the Prophet could have withheld part of the word of God he had received, we already realized that the Koran's truth is connected to the thesis about the Koran's divine origin.[40] This is doubtless Islam's most significant tenet of faith, and Jahmite teachings raised doubts about it!

Dirar ibn 'Amr saved the revelation's supreme dignity by differentiating between an original Koran which, as sura 85, verse 22, says, was written down on a guarded tablet, and the words of its recitation, which lie within the human realm of experience. The original Koran was obviously created by God and for this reason had no transtemporal qualities, but it was the only created thing to be in God's direct vicinity: "The Koran is an *accidens* on the well-preserved tablet; it has an independent existence in the tablet and cannot possibly disappear from it. Yet every time someone recites, writes, or knows (it) by heart, God creates (the Koran) anew. It was first created on the tablet, and this Koran on the well-preserved tablet cannot possibly be something someone acquires. When someone recites it, God creates this recitation (in the person reciting it) in that moment as his or her acquisition, and the Koran is being created a second time. It is at once God's creation and the reciter's acquisition. Likewise, in the lines of the writer and the memory of the person who has memorized it, it is God's creation and at the same time the acquisition of the writer or the person who has memorized it. What is God's creation is simultaneously their acquisition. Yet what is both God's creation and its acquisition is at the same time the Koran that was created on the well-preserved tablet before (the recitation, the writing, that which has been memorized) were created."[41]

The Mu'tazilites tried to prove beyond any doubt that the Koran, just like God's hearing or His power, could not possibly be a hypostasis of the divine being. Mu'tazilite teachings are exemplified in Caliph al-Ma'mun's proclamation of 218 h (which began on 27 January 833). The tenet that the Holy Book was created was first corroborated by quotes from the Koran itself. Sura 43, verse 2, says: "We have *made* it an Arabic Koran." In Mu'tazilite interpretation, this clearly says that the Koran was created. According to this interpretation, the passage regarding the well-preserved tablet has the same meaning. God gives the following assurance in sura 41, verse 42: "[F]alsehood comes not to it from before it nor from behind it." The expressions "before it" and "behind it," the argument went, indubitably referred to the Koran's limitations. Having limitations, however, was an unmistakable sign of something that was created. Therefore the Koran itself was created. In Arabic terminology, it was *makhluq*, and for the Mu'tazilites, just as for the Jahmites, the only alternative to this was *khaliq*, an attribute applicable only to God. Those who assumed that the Koran was not created were therefore claiming that it was *khaliq*, that is to say, identical with God.[42]

4. Human Actions

This differentiation between *khaliq* and *makhluq* was derived from the Koran. If one thinks this concept out and turns it into a general ontological statement, its logical conclusion is that creatures cannot perform creative acts. As described above, the Qadarites defended human responsibility for oneself and human freedom to act; Kharijites and Shiites, who acknowledged the "faith" only of those who proved it by their actions, thought along similar lines, if only with qualifications. The Murjiites did not declare human beings to be unfree, but argued that it was God who had created the necessary requirements for the individual's attempt to shape his or her life according to the divine law. It was He alone who could pass fair judgment on the result of an action.

Murjiite thought did not disappear along with the end of the Umayyad empire. It found a crucial follower in Abu Hanifa. This, in any case, is what his *Religious Doctrines* indicate, which are associated with his name but certainly went through several revisions. The probably oldest extant version mentions the postponement of judgment, but already with a distinct predestinarian trait[43]: "We do not consider anyone to be an infidel on account of sin; nor do we deny his faith. We enjoin what is just and prohibit what is evil. What reaches you could not possibly have missed you, and that what misses you could not possibly have reached you. We disavow none of the Companions of the Apostle of Allah; nor do we adhere to any of them exclusively. We leave the question of 'Uthman and 'Ali to Allah, who knoweth the secret and hidden things."[44]

There exists another, more comprehensive text version of this creed. It begins with the definition of faith. Faith is to confess with one's tongue, to consider to be true with one's reason, and to know in one's heart. The emphasis on knowledge indicates this source's Murjiite origin, for according to the "postponers" faith was realized in the knowledge of what the Koran and the Prophet taught. Jahm ibn Safwan had argued similarly; he considered faith to be the knowledge of everything God had revealed. According to him, even someone who had denied God remained a believer, as long as he had had knowledge of God just once.[45] In other words, faith could neither grow nor diminish in people. All this meant that it was entirely independent of actions. The Jahmites' motivation for shying away from relating one's faith and works to one another could no longer simply be attributable to the lack of knowledge of the circumstances of human action, but also to the strong emphasis on God's transcendence. As we have seen in the example of the revelation, this transcendence made it impossible to apply a uniform terminology to the omnipresent God and the world; all that remained for acting human beings was the option to take in the knowledge of Him and to believe in Him.

Jahm ibn Safwan considered the omnipresent God the only real actor (*fa'il*). Since Jahm radically distinguished between the transcendent God and this world, a being that in its essence belonged to this world could never be a *fa'il* in the full meaning of the word. He argued that one could only metaphorically say that creatures act, as in, "The river flows," or "The mill is turning." The nature of physical bodies do not contain a cause of movement or activity. Therefore, human beings have no strength or activity whatsoever within themselves. Neither, Jahm continued, can they be described as beings who have the faculty (*istita'a*) of acting. In fact, they have no power (*qudra*), no will (*irada*), no freedom of choice (*ikhti-yar*) at all. It is God who creates actions in people, the same way He can create in all other bodies actions that are metaphorically ascribed to them. Just as skin color, height, and similar qualities that were once recognized by al-Hasan al-Basri as circumstances that accompanied actions and were independent of human will, so were now, in Jahm ibn Safwan's view, actions and impulses of will themselves.[46]

Jahm gave al-Hasan al-Basri's argument against man's total freedom of choice a predestinarian spin. Still, it would be inappropriate to suggest that Jahm believed in unqualified determinism. His point had been God's transcendence, not relieving human beings of their responsibility for their own salvation. His concept of the metaphoric character of actions in this world was entirely in agreement with the doctrine of the Koran as something created: his tenet was that everything human beings knew about God was inevitably created in them and could be attributed to them only figuratively; this meant they could not destroy it themselves either—faith could not increase or decrease. Consequently, the message the Prophet conveyed to human beings could fall only under the category of things that were created.

Abu l-Hudhayl al-'Allaf and Dirar ibn 'Amr served the Mu'tazilites as a foundation on which they reconstructed a concept that comprised this world and the next world, which had been broken apart by the Jahmiyya. This was accomplished while God's transcendence was strictly preserved. Previously, the theory of the *li'an*, which is attributed to the Mu'tazila's precursors, had postulated human responsibility for one's actions, which however could be assessed only vaguely in this world. Yet there was a log-ical connection, an increase in precision and justice between the judgment human beings could pronounce and God's judgment: we knew that *one* of the opposition factions acted reprehensibly during the First Civil War, but

God also knew *which one*.[47]

The seed the Qadarites had sown germinated during the transition of power from the Umayyads to the Abbasids. This was the time in which 'Amr ibn 'Ubaid lived, an ascetic man critical of all institutionalized power. He was so steeped in the concept of the profound interconnectedness of action in this world and judgment in the next that he rejected as forged *hadiths* and Koran passages contradicting this notion. "Perish the hands of Abu Lahab, and perish he!" (sura 111, verse 1); "Leave me with him whom I created alone" (sura 74, verse 11); "I shall roast him in Sakar" (sura 74, verse 26)—surely none of this could have been in God's original revelation! He pointed out the following word of God: "By the Clear Book, behold, We have made it an Arabic Koran; haply you will understand; and behold it is in the Essence of the Book, with Us; sublime indeed, wise" (sura 43, verses 1-3). The original copy of the Koran, 'Amr ibn 'Ubaid said, was a clear, logical Book which any sensible human being could comprehend.[48] The principle of work and compensation was so powerful that statements contradicting it could not be part of the revelation.

Before we look at the way the early Mu'tazila developed the Qadarites' teachings on where human beings stand with regard to God, we need to examine Dirar ibn 'Amr's theories, the same way we analyzed his concept of God. We have seen that he distinguished between God's mere existence, of which we do possess firm knowledge, and His essence, which we do not know; Dirar ibn 'Amr did *not* think of God as entirely unfathomable. Neither did he view human actions from only one perspective. The Jahmiyya had postulated that creatures entirely lacked the ability to act of themselves. Everything, it had taught, they did was ultimately God's work. The Qadarites, by contrast, were convinced that human beings decided on their own what they committed or omitted, for which they had to assume full responsibility. Dirar, however, recognized two actors in every action: God and the human being committing it. We are familiar with this way of thinking from his theory about the nature of the Koran.[49]

"What distinguishes Dirar ibn 'Amr from the Mu'tazila," al-Ash'ari (d. 935), the irreplaceable chronicler of the history of early Islamic dogma, wrote, "is his theory that human actions are created, and that one single act has two actors, one of whom—God—creates it, while the other acquires it for himself (*iktasaba-hu*)—man. (Dirar further teaches) that in reality God creates human deeds and that human beings create them in reality as well." In this Dirar ibn 'Amr clearly distinguished himself from the Jahmiyya, which held that human beings acted only metaphorically, whereas God was the actual actor. "Dirar maintained that the ability to act (*istita'a*) exists both before and during the act, and that it is a part of the person who possesses it."[50] Dirar ibn 'Amr attributed to human beings an ability to act which was located within them and belonged only to them; it "exists before the act." Yet this ability could probably be actualized only once God stepped in. However, neither were these acts of God, in which human beings participated and which appeared to be acts of human beings, conceivable without these human beings' active participation.

Abu l-Hudhayl al-'Allaf had recognized that God's knowledge and power, which were supposedly identical with His being, acted upon the world; there was an intimate connection between God as the actor of creation and the creation upon which this action was performed.[51] As soon as God discontinued His creative acts, everything would die, paradise and hell would at some point at the end of history freeze, for everything that was created and existed only by virtue of these acts, was temporal. From this belief one might draw the conclusion that man's acts were determined by God. Yet Abu l-Hudhayl, rehearsing al-Hasan al-Basri's standpoint, admitted divine determination only for human beings' lifespan and subsistence. Abu l-Hudhayl certainly picked up the ethical element on which 'Amr ibn 'Ubaid had placed so much emphasis. At a lower level, this world, which depended on God's creative acts, was subject to rules which human beings could recognize and use, if not to the degree they would like: at least we were accountable for the predictable consequences of our actions! God's creative acts and human action interlocked, but from where we stood, we had only an extremely limited view of the network of consequential effects, consisting of countless loops. That, however, did not suffice to postulate that human beings were fully accountable for their actions.[52]

We have seen that the Qadarites argued that God would be a tyrant if He decreed laws and arbitrarily allowed to comply or kept believers from complying with them.[53] This argument constituted a strong motive for thinking further about these issues. If God imposed a law on human beings (*taklif*), then it logically only followed that He also gave them the power (*qaudra*) to carry it out. In short, the Mu'tazilites agreed with Dirar's teachings, which said that human beings possessed a capacity (*istita'a*) to act even before they acted. Human beings used this capacity, but without God guiding their hands: this is exactly the point where the Mu'tazila went beyond Dirar ibn 'Amr. Human beings' power (*qaudra*) became visible during the act. They had the *qaudra* to commit an act or omit it, or to do the opposite of what they had been told. Neither *istita'a* nor *qaudra forced* human beings to commit an act. They were only potentials. In contrast, Jahm ibn Safwan considered human *istita'a* to be entirely dependent on God; if God planted it in human beings, the action, which was metaphorically attributed to human beings but in reality originated from God, followed.

Like Abu l-Hudhayl, the Mu'tazila tended to regard the consequences of human actions in terms of cause and effect: the consequences were generated (*tawallud*) by the actions. If someone threw a stone and this stone hit someone else and caused him pain, then that pain was caused by the thrower and nothing else. We can see how this way of thinking was bound to turn the Jahmite concept of metaphoric human action into its opposite. To be sure, not all Mu'tazilites were willing to go this far. Some limited human impact on the throwing of the stone alone. They claimed that the act of flying originated in the stone itself. Furthermore, the hit body's pain should be attributed to that body. Here we are touching on a web of issues that is difficult to disentangle into individual threads. Once again the early dispute about *qadar*—determining the borderline between human responsibility for actions and God's determination—comes into view, augmented by the issue of causality in nature. It was a point that occupied the Mu'tazilites a great deal; the most varied, and at times bizarre, theories were developed. The Mu'tazilites never lost sight of the basic concept of responsibility. They were far from letting action disappear in a determinism of natural causes. They performed with keen psychological perception sophisticated analyses of the actor's impulses of will and his motivations, similar to their attempt to comprehend the parties' motives during the First Civil War.

As a result, they got lost in endless constructions of cause and effect, in establishing complex facts that served them to rehearse their mental faculties. Let us assume a murderer dies when still young precluding any chance to do good deeds that might counterbalance his grave sin: he is condemned to go to hell. Had he lived longer, would he then not have been able to reach paradise? Is his condemnation attributable only to the fact that God granted him but a brief life, and did not God Himself condemn him? The Mu'tazila hoped to avoid such questions by establishing the theory that God was benevolent and merciful (*latif*) in every respect. This line of thought was briefly summarized in the concept of the good or suitable (*al-aslah*) caused by God in any given case.

This theory was spread mainly by the great Mu'tazilite an-Nazzam (d. 845); Abu l-Hudhayl had employed it as well. It was intrinsic to God that He could not generate anything but the best. Everything He did was perfect and complete. An-Nazzam's perspective on this "best" was the human standpoint, holding that human beings were superior to all other creatures. In turn for this distinction, they must accept God's law, or else distinguishing them would make no sense. Since human beings could either observe or violate the law, they were either rewarded or punished accordingly. Consequently, the distinguished position of human beings was justified by the fact that they had an individual responsibility for their salvation.

Yet the triumphant mood at having reached this conclusion did not last long. The more people reflected about all this and finally also threw the animals' suffering into the debate, the uneasier became the feeling that it would be impossible to establish the hoped-for clear and simple connection between action and judgment. What for brief moments had seemed to be the resolution of the contradiction between divine omnipotence and human responsibility seemed to seep through the fingers like trickling sand.

5. *Physics and Metaphysics*

The Koran distinguishes two areas of reality, the "unseen" (*ghayb*) and the "visible" (*shahada*). "Visible" are the phenomena of this world that we can perceive with our senses; "unseen" is the area of divine being located in the heavens, but also everything that lies in the past or has not yet happened. Part of what is "unseen" will one day enter the state of the "visible"; the Koran does not make a clear ontological distinction between the two domains. However, in its totality the "unseen" is reserved for God: he knows *both* domains well (sura 6, verse 73, and *passim*). The Jahmiyya had dissolved God into a formless, omnipresent being who was not even supposed to be understood as a being opposite the world, but the message about the judging Creator-God could not do without such an opposition. Hence, the comparability of "visible" and "unseen" reality, which in early Islamic theological thought had been an unspoken presupposition, now had to be substantiated with arguments and even generated in the first place. We have already seen that Abu l-Hudhayl made an essential contribution to this in his theory of attributes. Furthermore, the discussion of the *qadar* was extended by the issue of observable causality in nature; it went beyond a purely ethical consideration of the issue of human responsibility.

The Jahmites had taught that divine, creative being was ontologically distinct from created earthly being by postulating that the term "thing" (*shai'*) was applicable only to creatures; there was no third being next to or between "thing" and "God." In an utterly simplified way, "thing" was considered an aggregate of atoms of matter and *accidentes* existing within these. The Mu'tazila essentially adopted this ontological theory: every body consisted of matter (substance, *jauhar*) which consisted of tiny particles. Whether these were atoms or could be split into an indefinite number of parts was a matter of debate. Taken individually, they could not be defined by their location—neither by "above" nor "under." There had to be at least two atoms in each dimension before one could speak of a body. The matter of these bodies carried the *accidentes* (*a'rad*). That term comprised everything that could not be conceived of without the matter as carrier—mainly odor, color, taste, flexibility, or firmness; frequently, however, it was also argued that the functions of the sensory organs, such as hearing or seeing, were *accidentes* inherent to the substratum. Life, or being alive, fit even worse into that theoretical pattern. One could of course argue that life, too was an *accidens*. Yet if this theory were expanded to include nonmaterial facts, such as will, there arose the difficulty of having to regard will as created. That was in contradiction to the theory of free will so will could certainly not have been created by God. In this predicament, some Mu'tazilites seemed to have a vague notion of the concept of the organism: sight, they said, was not inherent to certain particles of matter, but was the result of the synergy of many particles with different *accidentes*. Once this idea was accepted, it was possible to speak of a creature's own power to act, even if the laws of physics could be applied to subdivide that power into a finite sum of particles with their various *accidentes*.

No matter how sophisticated this ontology, which vacillated between physics and metaphysics, became, it was entirely useless for an ethical evaluation of human actions. The Mu'tazilites traced the motivations for an action, took impulses of will into account, considered desires and passions and the ability to moderate them—and all that with the modest ontological concept of particle and *accidens*.[54] One can easily imagine the dilemma in which the Mu'tazilites quickly found themselves. All mental-psychological processes had to be attributed to changing constellations of *accidentes*. Argument and counterargument—both equally unsubstantiatable—begot each other ad infinitum.[55]

Working out the details of the theory of matter and *accidens* had established the basis for examining the "thing" in this world and its function in different causal relations within the "visible." How this was connected to the "unseen" was still an open question. The Mu'tazilites realized that all they could do was to infer, by way of bold analogies, from facts of this world to phenomena of the transcendent realm, which, after all, the Koran had encouraged the Meccans to do. Following this line of thought, the perfect order of the course of the world then became a sign of the Creator's wisdom, and, since only someone with knowledge acted prudently and wisely, God, too, must have knowledge. He revealed this knowledge to us in the "visible" realm, but He also applied it in the "unseen," outside of human experience. The inference from the "visible" to the "unseen" preserved the plausibility of reward or punishment in the next world for deeds committed in this world. It thus formed the basis of the Mu'tazilite theory of the freedom of will and responsibility for one's salvation. Yet the Mu'tazilites connected the two realms of being with each other not only through that theoretical formula. Daring to go a significant step further, they set out to extend the concept of metaphysics accordingly. Breaking with the Jahmites' restriction of the "thing" to this world, they assumed instead that everything that was known was a "thing"; from this it followed that God, too, could be called a "thing,"[56] which signified the discovery of an—albeit largely empty—similarity between the two realms of being.

6. Sunnites and Shiites as Opponents of Rationalist Theology

The Mu'tazilite school of thought was too diverse to produce a uniform theology. The caliphs employed it to fight Sunnism, and the Mu'tazila's doctrine of the Koran as something created—a consequence of its reflections on God's oneness—temporarily gained the quality of a political dogma. This doctrine is not, however, among the five basic principles of the Mu'tazila's theology formulating the thrust of the Mu'tazilites' line of thought rather than the final truth of a clearly defined philosophical construct. Generally these principles are subdivided into two large ones, God's "justice" (al-'adl) and God's "oneness" (at-tauhid), and three minor ones, which can be derived from the large ones: first, the "threat of punishment in hell and the promise of the reward in paradise" are true— one's deeds in this world will be weighed strictly, and neither is there a secret way out of facing judgment on the Last Day nor the possibility of having considered anything (such as Muhammad's interceding for his community or one's declaration of loyalty to the imam from the Prophet's lineage) but one's actions; second, that the grave sinners are in a "borderland" is true—it is not known who of them is guilty and, therefore, condemned to hell, but in no event must Mu'awiya be considered a model companion of the Prophet (as many Sunnites did), or 'Ali as the imam who always had right guidance (as the Shiites did); third, the Mu'tazilites stressed the "bidding to honour and forbidding dishonour,"[57] the active struggle for the observance of God's law that the Koran (sura 3, verse 110) demands.

The Sunnites and Shiites did not deny God's oneness and justice, even if their concept of it was different from that of the Mu'tazilites. That "bidding and forbidding" were necessary in order to protect the community's Islamic character was considered to be beyond doubt as well. However, it is the first two minor principles that exactly describe the areas where a dispute was bound to flare up. Neither the Sunnites nor the Shiites could accept a "borderland" for the opponents in the civil war; the Shiites did not accept 'Ali, the imam, as being even in the slightest suspected of having violated the divine law, and the Sunnites could not bear the thought of the Prophet's companions, among them 'Uthman and Mu'awiya, being guilty of offenses—they, who had now become guarantors of the Prophetic *sunna*! To the Sunnites, Muhammad's companions, who by now simply included all those who were born during the Prophet's lifetime, had gradually become purified, unassailable saints. Ahmad ibn Hanbal (d. 855), at the time the eminent representative of Sunnism in Baghdad, wrote a catechism in which he made it the duty of his brothers in faith to abstain from any criticism of the ancestors and to speak only well of them.[58] Consequently, Ahmad rejected 'Ali's condemnation—a position that the Sunnites generally still shared at that time—insisting that the Prophet's son-in-law be acknowledged as the fourth "rightly guided caliph" after Abu Bakr, 'Umar, and 'Uthman, and to honor him accordingly.[59] The Sunnites also seemed to have settled the argument about who was responsible for the First Civil War, but in a curious way: everything that was questionable and could have aroused suspicion, was supposed to be hushed up. That certain questions became taboo is understandable if one is familiar with the Mu'tazilites' opinion of the *hadith*. They certainly could not fail to recognize how contradictory and sometimes strange the content of the traditions was. The Sunnites firmly relied on the most popular companions of the Prophet as witnesses who served to corroborate a great many tenets. Yet, if the *hadiths* were taken literally, their reliability was seriously called into question. The Mu'tazilites sarcastically picked on odd and ridiculous details,[60] which made it quite difficult for the Sunnites to explain away and smooth over certain inconsistencies.[61]

The gap that opened up on the issue of "promise and threat" between the Mu'tazilites on the one hand and the Shiites and Sunnites on the other, was virtually unbridgeable; this gap did not only have a theological basis but also one of profound differences in a general attitude toward life. We have seen that there were certain *hadiths* that traced back to Muhammad the belief in the predestination of each individual creature's fate after death.[62] Ahmad ibn Hanbal's *hadith* collection contains the following tradition, which presupposes this idea, but trivializes it by applying it to the banality of this world: 'Abdallah ibn 'Abbas relates that one day the Prophet told him: "My son, I will teach you a few words! Preserve Allah, then He will preserve you! Preserve Allah, then you will find Him within you; when you ask for something, ask Allah, and when you call for help, call Allah for help! Know that even if an entire people joined together to obtain some benefit for you, it could get you only the benefit Allah has intended for you. And even if an entire people joined together to do you harm, it could do you only the harm Allah intended for you. The quills have been taken off (the parchment), the hieroglyphs are dry!"[63]

Another *hadith*, from the collection of at-Tirmidhi (d. 892), answers the question of how Sunnis should conduct themselves in view of the disconcerting fact that the decision about their salvation has long been made—the desire to influence favorably the judgment on the Last Day simply never completely disappears. Mu'adh ibn Jabal[64] asked the Prophet: "O messenger of God, name an action that will get me into paradise and move me away from hell!" Muhammad replied: "You are asking about a serious matter. But it is simple for him whom Allah assists. Serve Allah, do not put anything next to Him, perform the ritual prayer, pay the ablution tax, fast during Ramadan, and make the pilgrimage to the Kaaba!" Then he continued: "Shall I point you toward the gates of good? Fasting is a protection, alms extinguish sins as water extinguishes fire; (and what helps is) a man's prayer in the middle of the night." The Prophet then recited: "Their sides shun their couches as they call on their Lord in fear and hope; and they expend of that which We have provided. No soul knows what comfort is laid up for them secretly, as a recompense for what they were doing" (sura 32, verses 16–17). Then he said: "Shall I tell you what the beginning of our religion is, its support and apex?" I answered: "Please do, o messenger of God!" He explained: "The beginning of religion is Islam, its support is ritual prayer, but its apex is religious struggle. . . . Shall I also tell you what the basis of everything is?" "Please, o messenger of God!" Thereupon he touched his tongue and said: "Beware of this!" I asked: "O messenger of God, we have to account for what we say?" He replied: "May your mother lose you! Does anything throw people on their faces, even in hell, but the evil their tongues speak?"[65]

In this *hadith* the connection between right, lawful action and entry into paradise has been significantly watered down. Having been replaced by the obligation to observe the rites, they assume an almost magical quality. While "religious struggle" is mentioned, this no longer refers to the war against those who confess to other religions, but to controlling one's tongue, to pert speech, frivolous intellectual arrogance, in short, the struggle against a kind of rationalism that is considered unfounded and condescending!

This exhortation was aimed at the fundamental attitude of those writers and theologians who reveled in their own insights and knew how to relish debates with witty quips and turns of phrase. "His friends carouse until the wee hours of the morning, eagerly investigating whether the Koran was created," people scoffed at the grand inquisitor's gregarious circle.[66] What a difference to the way the chief Sunnites viewed the world! Not haughtiness, but scrupulous fear of the Last Day was supposed to characterize their attitude. Many sources attest to this. 'Abdallah ibn Mubarak (d. 797) was one of those *sunna* scholars who preached pious asceticism. Someone is said to have once asked him who he thought were the most important people. "The scholars!" he allegedly replied, that is to say those who aspired to gain knowledge of the Koran and the *sunna*. "And who then are the kings?" was the next question. "The ascetics!" "And who are the inferior people?" "Those who live at the expense of their belief!"[67] The faithful Sunnites of the late eighth and ninth centuries struggled to lead a life that pleased God, painstakingly performed the rites, and observed the commandments. Yet they did not inquire after their content. What is important is that they committed no act automatically and possibly carelessly. They always had to examine their thoughts while performing their deeds. Being superficially in agreement with God's law did not suffice; it was crucial that they be executed with a corresponding inner attitude.

The basis of the Shiites' discussion of rationalist theology was different from that of the Sunnites. Their rejection of rationalism was not completely homogeneous. The strongest influence on the Zaydi movement was the Mu'tazila. The Zaydites did not regard the imam as a conveyor of salvation; as we have seen, they even accepted the view of the "imamate of the man surpassed in virtue," which implies that they really adopted an intermediary stand toward the factions in the First Civil War, which was the view the Mu'tazilites supported as well. Less clear-cut is the attitude toward rationalist theology of the Husaynite Shia, which in the waning ninth-century split into the two branches of the Twelvers and the Seveners. Their doctrine of the imam's significance for salvation stood in almost direct contrast to the Mu'tazilites' emphasis on the believers' responsibility for their salvation. Still, sources say that Ja'far as-Sadiq, the sixth imam of both movements of the Husaynite Shia, was well-versed in the methods of rationalist speculation.

As demonstrated above, the Mu'tazilite theory of attributes culminated in the doctrine of the Koran as something that was created. Shiite thought contained parallels to this: the imams possessed knowledge that was significant for salvation; they put into perspective the revelation Muhammad had received so that it took on the qualities of a temporal event and, in the Shiite view, was not complete since it did not contain allusions to the imamate. Some Shiite circles defended the idea of *bada'*, the possibility of God's revisiting certain pronouncements and decisions if they should not turn out to be useful. Yet, as soon as such a maneuver is performed and God's word carried into the realm of the created world, a God who can be defined only negatively is easier to tolerate.

In the area of human conduct and God's assessment of it, the Husaynite Shia had principles that suggest an elective affinity for the Mu'tazilite view of the consequences of righteous deeds; this was the legacy of the early belief that faith could be proved by one's actions. This legacy surfaced whenever the Shia's latent millenarianism entered a phase where it expected the end, that is to say, when the Shiites believed they would have to fight weapon in hand for the imminent appearance of the ruler at the end of time. The basis of this was the differentiation between "Islam" and "faith." "Islam" was interpreted as the external system which ruled the everyday; "Islam" meant the rules of the marriage contract, the law of inheritance, and rituals. By contrast, "faith" was the area where human beings actually proved themselves before God. Internalizing the law and love of God were the characteristics of "faith," and it was they that would be taken into account on the Day of Judgment.[68] Yet, contrary to the Mu'tazila, this "faith" with its focus on the action that brought salvation was not founded in rationalist speculation. Rather, its point of departure was veneration of the imam. The Shiites' actions, for which they were responsible, their battle for the beginning of the era of salvation on earth, were rooted in their hope for the end of time. What was promised was the establishment of justice on earth. The Mu'tazila lacked precisely this millenarian element, and it was largely foreign to the Zaydi Shia as well. During the long periods when the Shiite empire of justice seems to be lying far in the future, veneration of the imam outweighs all considerations of righteous acts; the necessary requirement for obtaining salvation cannot be met. The troubled believers must be guaranteed salvation by reverentially professing their belief in what they expect will come to pass. It may even be advisable to conceal one's true faith from anyone uninitiated, in other words, to deny that one is a follower of the imams. This is the very opposite of the belief in righteousness based on one's actions.

Like the Sunnite *hadith*, therefore, the Husaynite *hadith*, which was attributed to the imams, developed with a pronounced emphasis on cultic-ritual piousness. Furthermore, according to Shiite tradition, the love of the Prophet's family was proved by empathizing with the manifold sufferings of its members. Repeating *"Allahu akbar"* one hundred times is— again a parallel to the Sunnites—also recommended.[69] Finally, there was the suggestion to submit to Muhammad's example in everything one did and said.[70]

CHAPTER V

Rationalism and Tradition

1. The Caliphate's Political Decline

The predominance of Mu'tazilite rationalism, decreed by the caliphs, began to wane as early as the mid-ninth century. Al-Mutawakkil put an end to the inquisition. It had exerted great pressure on several heads of Sunnite schools, but some of them had resisted, among them men who had let themselves be coerced into making feigned verbal confessions, and others who had steadfastly stood by their conviction, knowing that all the pain they were suffering only helped to further fuel the masses' anger toward the caliphate. Ahmad ibn Hanbal had been among those few Sunnites who had withstood the inquisitors' interrogation technique of trying to corner him; he had simply refused to comment on the rationalists' views, his contention being that he was not one of them.[1] Only a few Sunnis followed his example; others recognized that it would be prudent to adopt the Mu'tazilites' methods. Thus, the inquisition had sowed the seeds of discord among the Sunnis; it was to flare up two hundred years later.

Still, it had failed to achieve its goal of superimposing a rationalist dogma on the empire. Since al-Mutawakkil, formal cooperation with the Mu'tazila was no longer feasible for the caliphs. When al-Mu'tadid (r. 892–902) set out to instate the policies of al-Ma'mun, whom he admired, the courtiers tried their best to dissuade him from his plan.[2] The caliph, they reasoned, should not waste the few options that were left to him to exercise power in the battle against the majority of the capital's population; the state of the empire was much more critical than it had been under al-Ma'mun. Andalusia had long since been lost to the Umayyads' descendants; for all intents and purposes, northern Africa was independent under the Aglabis residing in Cairuan; in Egypt the governors of Turkish descent had wrested ever more liberties from the Abbasids; in Yemen a Zaydi imamate was being established; and in the east, around Bukhara, the Samanids, who officially were also the Abbasids' governors, strove for more and more independence. In short, the empire was crumbling, and in the waning tenth century this development had progressed to such an extent that a contemporary observed that every village now had its own lord.[3]

While this did not topple the caliphate, for several decades the Abbasids were profoundly humiliated. They had to transfer all official duties to usurpers, and their power went no further than the thresholds of their dilapidated palaces at best. War lords and adventurers adorned themselves with the title of "grand emir," did as they pleased, and, if necessary, even collected some moneys due the caliphs. However, they were not able to establish a stable situation even in Iraq. Only when members of the large family of the Buyids, who ruled in western Iran, took over the "emirate," did the situation improve temporarily.

The Buyids were Shiites; they leaned toward the movement of the Twelvers, who were supported by the population of several rather important districts in Baghdad.—In the waning tenth and early eleventh centuries a number of bitter fights flared up between the capital's Shiite and Sunnite quarters. Why did the Buyids in this situation continue to back the caliphs, who clearly leaned toward the Sunnites and eventually acted as their advocates? The Twelvers taught that the twelfth and last imam from 'Ali's clan, Muhammad, had been carried off and was not supposed to return to earth until the end of all days, in order to "fill it with justice, just as it is filled with injustice now." Since then, the Twelvers lived in the era of "absence," and they could recognize only Muhammad, "the expected one," as their legitimate imam and ruler. However, the main reason for continuing a caliphate that increasingly followed Sunnite lines was the power-political balance in whose grip the Islamic world was held from approximately 980 on.

In Egypt the Fatimids, the Shiite caliphate of the Seveners, had usurped power[4] and attempted to remove their rivals in Baghdad, whom they considered illegitimate. This also would have meant the end of the Buyid "great emirate." The Twelvers and Seveners hated each other; the Seveners derided the Twelvers' attentism, and in return, the Twelvers charged that the Seveners' imam and caliph in Cairo was not a descendant of 'Ali. Secret supporters of the Seveners dared infiltrate the highest circles of the Baghdad Twelvers and the Buyids' provincial courts: Buyids and Twelver Shiites were afraid of the Fatimids. In the meantime, directly after the turn of the millennium, a new empire was established in what is today Afghanistan. It was governed by a bold military commander, Mahmud of Ghaznah. Of Turkish descent and a Shiite, he had conquered new territories for Islam in India, amassing legendary riches through raids. He gradually extended his territory to Iran as well, entered into diplomatic relations with the caliph in Baghdad, and had him officially appoint him governor of all territories already conquered and yet to be conquered. In return, he hinted that he would soon move westward in order to put an end to all Shiite wantonness. While this plan was not realized, the Buyids, who on several occasions felt the thrust of the Ghaznahvid armies, now were even more reticent than ever to touch the Abbasid.

The balance that had been achieved by all higher-level Islamic rulers holding each other in check collapsed around the middle of the eleventh century. Nomadic Turkish tribes from Central Asia intermittently advanced westward under a leader from Saljuq's clan. Around the same time, the "great emirate's" power was weakened by an endless family feud among the Buyids. In early 1058 the Saljuq Togrilbeg arrived with his army in Baghdad. The caliph had to crown him, who for some time had called himself Mahmud of Ghaznah's political executor and professed to be a zealous Sunnite "king of the East and West"[5]—in other words, he was compelled to transfer all actual power to him. That is how the sultanate was established, an institution of power that ultimately possessed all of the caliphate's authority, except that the sultan needed the caliph's official legitimization.[6] Disputes within the Saljuq dynasty, which like that of the Buyids was split into numerous local branches, enabled the Abbasids from the mid-twelfth century on until the destruction of Baghdad by the Mongols in 1258, once again to rule their own empire, whose borders were approximately those of modern-day Iraq.

In the Iranian Nizam al-Mulk the early Saljuq sultanate had a talented and circumspect administrator of the dynasty's power. Like al-Ma'mun he tried to achieve internal harmony and peace by creating an Islamic state religion, but this time with a Sunni slant. He prepared the country to fight armed battles against the opposing movements, in particular the

Isma'ilites, or Sevener Shiites; as before, they were the Saljuqs' bitter enemies, working underground and leaning on the Fatimids from Cairuan. Shahfur Tahir al-Isfara'ini's (d. 1071) *Book of Sects* dates from that time. It states that, according to the Prophet, Islam would split up into seventy-three different movements, of which only one, the Sunni movement, would attain salvation. There were indications that this prophecy was about to come true: numerous different sects battled each other, innovators enticed people to commit evil deeds, from among the Mu'tazilites to Isma'ilites, those Sevener Shiites who were also called "people of the esoteric meaning" of the revelation. All of them, Shahfur warned, were persecuting the Sunnites, sometimes in clever disguise! Therefore, it was the duty of all good Muslims who believed in the Prophet's tradition and supported the "harmonious community" to become familiar with the one true theology, and specifically, with all rational proofs pertinent to its doctrines. Only then, Shahfur continued, would they be immune to all deceptions and not be taken in by those who wanted to lure them away from the safe haven of Sunnism.[7]

2. Early Theological Reflection in Sunnism

Sunnism did not remain untouched by the speculative theology initially of the Jahmiyya, and later of the Mu'tazila. Questions raised by theology had to be answered, even by those who wanted to constrict the life of Muslims to emulating the Prophet. Al-Humaydi (d. 834), a pupil of Sufyan ibn 'Uyayna's (d. 811), wrote a short catechism. He introduced it with the doctrine of the divine *qadar* in which everybody must believe; we are familiar with this doctrine as part of a phrase regarding "Islam's" integral parts that was ascribed to Muhammad.[8] Faith, al-Humaydi continued, consisted of words and deeds, and could either increase or decrease; yet professing one's faith and deeds was worthless unless these were the consequences of deliberate intent[9]; intention grounded both of them firmly in the *sunna*. Then al-Humaydi took up themes from the early ninth century, the era of the inquisition: he repudiated criticism of the Prophet's companions—criticism as it was voiced, for instance, by the Mu'tazilite an-Nazzam when he set out to prove how contradictory some *hadiths* were.[10] He also rejected the dogma of the Koran's createdness, to which he juxtaposed Sufyan ibn 'Uyayna's statement that it was "God's speech."[11]

Al-Humaydi also called on Sufyan as a witness to support the statement that faith could either increase or decrease. In contrast, he said, Sufyan's brother Ibrahim had ascribed to faith an indestructible quality, but that view had been categorically rejected. Sunnism at the end of the eighth century, full of an ascetic piousness and with a nostalgic, idealized image of the original community,[12] sought to preserve the obligation to act in a way that pleased God, as long as one's acts were an emulation of the example the Prophet had set. In this context Ibrahim appears as a follower of the "postponers'" successors, whose belief was based on Abu Hanifa's teachings.[13] Then al-Humaydi addressed the Jahmites; he affirmed the *visio beatifica*, which they had declared impossible, and demanded that the Sunnites accept without qualification the anthropomorphisms in the Koran and the *hadith*. Finally he once again illuminated the issue of one's actions, but from a different perspective: unbelief, he said, was not the result of a grave sin, as the Kharijites thought, but solely of neglecting the five ritual obligations on which "Islam" was based.[14]

Ahmad ibn Hanbal explained the Sunnites' theories much more comprehensively. He described the Murjiites' concept of the essence of faith before proceeding to the issue of predestination: each human being's fate in the hereafter, each evil and each good deed were predetermined by God, about which human beings must not argue with Him. "If someone says that lechering does not originate in (divine) *qadar*, the counterargument is: 'And this woman here, who became pregnant after lechering and bore a child, did God want to create this child? Was this predestined in His prior knowledge?' If the opponent denies that, then he assumes that there is another creator besides God, and that is blatant polytheism! And those who maintain that theft, imbibing wine, and consumption of stolen goods do not occur according to God's ways and *qadar*, are also maintaining that one can consume the subsistence (God gave someone else). That is sheer sorcery![15] Conversely, everyone consumes only his own subsistence, of which God decided that he should consume it in this and no other way."[16] Ahmad had learned his lesson from the battles with the inquisitors; we can recognize the basic polemical trait we have described

as characteristic of rationalist theology. One can also recognize the quality that is characteristic of later Sunni rationalism, that of each process
being judged only by its result rather than by examining the preconditions
for an event's result, as the Murjiites and Mu'tazilites had done. On the
other hand, Ahmad at one point pointed out that everyone was obliged to
provide for his relatives as well as for himself, and that everyone had the
basic right to use his inheritance or the profit from his business for himself. The "opposing rationalists" (*mutakallimun*) denied that by apparently considering, not only the results, but also the different *ways* of acquisition.[17] However, the contradiction between good business sense and the
predestination of human actions dissolves if one follows Ahmad ibn
Hanbal in considering each person's profit as precisely the subsistence
God has allotted him.

Even though Ahmad exhibited much more distinctly than al-Humaydi
Sunnism's predestinarian traits, the events of the Last Day, the inventory
of actions, expressed an indispensable truth of faith his work contains;
these events lost their frightening aspect because of Muhammad's intercession on behalf of the Muslims. Paradise and hell had already been created, and they would never disappear. Abu l-Hudhayl al-'Allaf had maintained that at the end of God's acts of creation, they would be beset by
rigor mortis[18]; an eternal hereafter was hard to reconcile with the sharp
division into divine and created—and hence temporal—being. The same
was true for the image of God on His throne, but Ahmad declared it to be
part of Sunni faith in all its details, just like all the anthropomorphisms in
the Koran and the *hadith*. "The Koran is God's speech, which He
expressed; it is uncreated. He who claims the opposite is a Jahmite, an
infidel. And he who says, 'The Koran is God's speech,' and stops there
without adding 'uncreated,' speaks even more abominably than the former. He who maintains that our sounds (which render the Koran) and our
recitation of the Koran are created, is (also) a Jahmite, and he who does
not declare all those people infidels is like them! God spoke to Moses
with His mouth and put the Torah into his hand with His own hand. God
has not ceased to speak. He is full of bliss, the best of all creators!"[19]
God's uncreated word was present even in everyday recitations; merely
professing that the Koran was God's speech did not suffice for Ahmad ibn
Hanbal. He rejected this equivocal phrase, which some Sunnites had used

to escape the inquisition's torture.

Ahmad ibn Hanbal explained that the Prophet's companions should be revered and were exempt from all criticism: religion rested on the Koran and the traditions, which were passed on reliably by trustworthy sources, and in that manner one could trace one's way back to God's messenger. The Sunnis "use neither analogies nor their own judgment. Analogies in matters of faith are invalid; so is one's own judgment, and it is even worse. Those who employ them in religion are of the innovators who have fallen prey to error. Exempt are (only those cases) where we have a tradition (justifying the use of one's own reason) from one of the trustworthy ancestors."[20] After outlining the Sunnis' doctrines, Ahmad put together a list of those movements that failed to obtain salvation because they had left the firm ground of the Prophet's norms, or apparently transformed their faith by way of analogies or their "own judgment." He briefly sketched typical doctrines of the Murjiites, Qadarites, Jahmites, and so forth, without the reader having any idea of the context in which these very significantly abbreviated statements appeared. In conclusion, Ahmad ibn Hanbal listed the derisive nicknames their opponents used for the Sunnis. "Oh God, refute the Murjiites' lies, weaken the Qadarites' perfidy, . . . take your revenge on the Jahmites soon!"[21]

Ibn Khuzayma (d. 923), a *sunna* scholar from Nishapur, discussed the Jahmites in a very different way. He barely rehearsed theological arguments but justified the anthropomorphisms of which the Sunnites were accused as expressions of a profound religiosity that had its source in the Sunnites' reverence for the Creator, who was not intentionally compared to His creatures. The Koran said that everything would one day perish, but not the magnificent face of God (sura 55, verse 27). Ibn Khuzayma assured his readers that, in this passage, it was impossible to confuse God's face with that of a mortal human being. "We and all scholars of our movement, whether in the Hijaz, the Tihama, in Yemen, Iraq, Syria, or Egypt—we all say about God what He said about Himself, and we profess this with our tongues and believe in it in our hearts, without equating God's face with that of one of His creatures. . . . We and all our scholars in all our lands say that the one we worship has a face, as God told us in His clear revelation, which ascribed to it magnificence and venerability, declaring it to be eternal and denying that it will ever perish. We furthermore say that our Lord's face radiates so much bright light, so much splendor that if one lifted the veil covering it, its glory would scorch everything in its scope. The gaze of the denizens of this world is protected from the beam of its eyes; no man will ever see Him during his earthly life. And we say that our Lord's face has no beginning and no end, it was always part of the One who remains and never perishes. Therefore, He denied (the possibility) that it could perish."

How different human beings' faces were in contrast! They lacked all glory, all radiance; the gaze their eyes emitted could be withstood without difficulty, it did not scorch so much as anyone's hair. "Human beings' faces are rooted in time and were created, . . . they will all perish. They will be dead and molder," and God would resurrect them for Judgment Day. "Oh you sensible ones, could it ever really occur to anybody who is wise, has his full intellectual faculty and knows Arabic . . . and knows what it means to compare, that this (transient) face could be compared to that one? Does this, oh you discerning ones, mean that we claim God's face . . . has a resemblance with the faces of human beings beyond the corresponding term 'face' . . . ?" If the Sunni scholars' view ultimately implied that God resembled His creation, then it would also be true that the faces of human beings resembled those of pigs, monkeys, dogs, serpents, and scorpions. Even the most astute Jahmite would burst with anger, Ibn Khuzayma insinuated maliciously, if his dearest friend compared his face to that of a pig or monkey.[22]

To support his arguments, Ibn Khuzayma leaned largely on the Koran and the traditions passed on as the Prophet's words; he would not let himself be forced into a debate in the manner of the rationalists, and perhaps he did not know how to debate that way. Yet defected Mu'tazilites did a tremendous service for the development of a Sunni theology, which was capable of using the tools of rationalism well. Disappointed about those debaters' inability to reach an agreement on the doctrines, and repelled by extreme arrogance and haughtiness, they sought firm ground on which to base their belief, thus discovering Sunnism's advantages. Among these defected Mu'tazilites was Ibn Qutayba (d. 889), who defended the *hadith* against the Mu'tazilites' contempt in an extensive treatise.[23] In another short essay he addressed three significant problems of theology, which he discussed from a Sunni point of view. He had the least difficulties with the issue concerning which of the enemies was to blame for the First Civil War. Following the Zaydi doctrine concerning the imam, the Mu'tazila under al-Ma'mun had maintained that 'Ali had been Muhammad's most suitable successor, but that historical circumstances had made it impossible to appoint him immediately after the Prophet's death. Therefore, Abu Bakr's, 'Umar's, and 'Uthman's rules had been legitimate. Ahmad ibn Hanbal had suggested that the Sunnites remembered all of the Prophet's companions, in particular 'Ali, with reverence. In this sense Ibn Qutayba wrote that 'Ali's good qualities were documented in reliable sources and that all Sunnites should recognize them; neither love nor resentment of him should be excessive. Ibn Qutayba then explained why 'Ali was held in such high regard during Islam's early history: the Prophet had become his brother-in-law; 'Ali had consistently displayed great bravery during the battles in Medina; being always close to the Prophet, he had had extraordinarily reliable knowledge in all religious matters, which the other companions had certainly acknowledged. 'Ali should be praised, but this praise implied anything but a disparagement of Mu'awiya. Ibn Qutayba was hoping for a reconciliation of all parties, with the tradition serving as the basis for mutual understanding. If that happened, he argued, one could do without the sophistry in historical matters in which the rationalist theologians indulged with a similar purpose.

Ibn Qutayba commented extensively on the Koran's createdness and on the issue of anthropomorphism. He rejected the Jahmites' "deflating" the concept of God of any specific content. It was a certain kind of *hadith*, he said, that made Sunnism an easy target for the Jahmites' criticism. In these traditions, the divine was equated with the human in an offensive way. Yet by no means was it necessary to interpret these traditions metaphorically; one should simply have applied a certain critical method, then it would have been noticed how badly documented those statements were. One should have never taken seriously and interpreted as a metaphorical speech on God's grace such a *hadith* as completely absurd as "The believer's heart is between two fingers of God."

Here Ibn Qutayba abandoned Ahmad ibn Hanbal's principle of regarding everything as true "without asking how," for if one gave the Prophet's alleged saying serious consideration, one would arrive at the conclusion that God's dignity was being questioned. Like Ibn Khuzayma, Ibn Qutayba rejected all the facile anthropomorphisms that must have been prevalent in the Sunnism of Ahmad ibn Hanbal's time. He did not shy away from writing in his outline of Sunni faith that God "gradually descends to the lowest heaven, just as He pleases. The hearts of men are between two fingers of the Merciful, which he uses to turn them this way and that, as He pleases, inspiring them with what He wishes."[24] More *hadiths* of this kind were being bandied about: "I saw my Lord in Mina dressed in a jacket, on an ash-colored male camel." "God created the angels from a hair of His lower arms and His chest." "I saw my Lord as a frizzy-haired, beardless youth in a green robe." "When God gets angry, He swells up on His throne so that it becomes hard for its carriers to hold Him."[25] Ibn Qutayba dealt with some of these odd traditions in his work in defense of the *hadith*.[26]

Those who entirely drained the concept of God of all content and made it abstract had gone astray, just like the anthropomorphists, Ibn Qutayba argued in his theological treatise. "God has made the middle between the two extremes the path to justice; in matters of our faith He even prohibited exaggerations that are much less significant than the issue of God's qualities, and how much more so, then, when it comes to this issue! He did not leave us to ponder about how He was, how He decided something, how He created; He did not assign to us tasks that we are not made and able to perform. A fair assessment of these traditions (describing God's qualities and His knowledge) is that we should believe all those that must be true because reliable men have passed them on to us. Consequently, we must believe that we can see (God in paradise) and that He will manifest Himself; we must believe that He is astonished, that He descends to heaven, that He sits down on His throne. We believe that He has a soul and two hands, without, however, assuming any details in that regard or that there are any limitations, and without making an analogy between what was passed on to us and that which we were not told. We hope that with this firm doctrine, tomorrow—if God wills it—we will be on our path to salvation."

Ibn Qutayba also sought a middle course in trying to decide whether human beings had free will or whether their actions were predetermined. He believed both parties were wrong, arguing that if human beings could

shape their own future, brave people would always prevail and the courageous would never founder. In addition, he considered the fact that some
people lived in more favorable climate zones than others, who were
always fighting an uphill battle, as an argument in support of the predestinarian view. History, he maintained, taught us the same lesson; for why
had the Arabs been distinguished by Muhammad's appointment as
Prophet, and why did the Negroes have to vegetate in ignorance and
poverty? God's inscrutable ways would always remain a secret; He had to
be accepted in pious fear. "God does not owe anybody anything, no one
has any rights before Him. When He grants something, He does so
through His grace; when He denies something, He does so in His justice.
Yet human beings have the capacity for action, and they act and are
judged according to what they acquire of good and evil deeds. For God
disposes of a subtle substance which He gives to whomever He pleases
before all beginnings; He blesses those He loves by putting this substance
into their hearts, so that the thusly chosen prove themselves to be obedient. Those, however, who deserve His word of condemnation, are refused
this subtle substance. This is the entire knowledge the son of Adam can
obtain about God's Providence; anything beyond that is kept from him."[27]

This last sentence, with its phrase "son of Adam," is acutely reminiscent of al-Hasan al-Basri's choice of words and might go back to him.
Like him, so Ibn Qutayba had realized that God's being and His acts upon
creation could not be comprehended through reason alone. The unqualified inference from the "visible" to the "unseen" could be maintained
only if sophistries of any sort were accepted. Sophistry, however, undermined the numinous quality of the Koran and the traditions, and even of
respect for religion in general. The "visible" and the "unseen" were not
related to each other in a strictly "logical" sense, but ontologically still
clearly distinct from one another. It was a third ontological element,
somewhere between *khaliq* and *makhluq*, that established a connection
between them. For Ibn Qutayba it was a fine substance that God created
and that guided the believers. This had a parallel in Sufyan ibn 'Uyayna's
doctrine of the revelation as "God's speech." Sufyan equated it with an
incessant act of Providence (*amr*) that originated in God and would return
to Him at the end of time. It is likely that the Sunnites, who during the
time of the inquisition subscribed to the phrase of the Koran as "God's

speech," were thinking of this view of Sufyan ibn 'Uyayna, which was very close to Koranic concepts.[28] This concept softened the flagrant contradiction between "creating" and "created," and human actions were no longer strictly determined by certain predictable judgments of God, as the defenders of the freedom of will claimed; yet neither were human action and divine judgment entirely separate from each other, as the Jahmites had taught. Still, this concept, which was so convenient for a theology that mediated between the two movements, disappeared from the general debate for several centuries. It did not reappear until much later, and under radically different circumstances: the ontology that acknowledged only the categories of "creating" and "created" being was too fascinating; it needed to be pushed into its absurd extreme until these issues could be revisited.

What showed the way into the future in Qutayba's treatise was the realization that naive anthropomorphisms, which ultimately Ahmad ibn Hanbal, too, had endorsed, would not be tenable in the long run. Particularly a profound piousness had to reject its consequences. It was best simply to base one's doctrines on the Koran—which did not mention a beardless youth! The Mu'tazila was also on its way to restricting its assessment of God's potential attributes to statements concerning creation and the perception of the events taking place in it. The further one walked on this path of abstraction, however, the closer one got to the predicament of being in a position where one merely said that God *was*, and that He related to His creation in a way that might be expressed in human terms, but that still remained incomprehensible.

3. Sufism and Rationalism

'Abdallah ibn Mubarak is an example of a philosophy of life which a great many Sunnis shared. We have described this philosophy as one of scrupulous self-exploration on the part of the believers who strove painstakingly to imitate the Prophet, their model. Considering the dangers of an error that would jeopardize their salvation, they had to moderate their enthusiasm for unbridled speculation on religious issues; trying to know more than the Koran and the *hadith*—sources that originated in

God—was a sign of blasphemous haughtiness.[29] This kind of attitude could easily deplete religious belief of its depth by turning into an automatic—even though certainly pious—observance of rituals. Some *hadiths* we have discussed illustrate Sunnism's tendency to take the rites to be everything. The more this movement within Islam became that of the great majority of believers, the more this latent tendency came to the fore. The exhortation in ritual law to perform everything absolutely consciously proves that there was concern about this development. Yet a Sunni could also go in a different direction—that of the strict performance of rites and of bridling one's haughtiness. This route led to the extinction of the ego, whose impulses—and even whose mere existence—interfered with the direct connection to God which the believer desired. Repressing the ego in order to open oneself entirely and submit to the One was the ambitious aim of a pious movement within Sunnism during the ninth to eleventh centuries. It was called "Sufism."

Its roots reach quite clearly back to the period of the Umayyads. At that time people had begun to form an image of Muhammad, of what he used to do or say, so they could hold it up to the impious present with its endless bickering between different parties.[30] Living up to the standard the Prophet had set did not necessarily mean only meeting his norms, but could also mean adopting the philosophy of life that was the source of his God-pleasing actions. To the Sunnites, "knowledge" (*'ilm*) meant secure and detailed knowledge of the model the Prophet had personified.[31] In Sufism it took on a deeper meaning, coming to signify the adoption of the philosophy of life that was behind Muhammad's individual actions, and emulation of unqualified surrendering of the self to God. "Beware of miserliness!" was one of the recommendations a Sufi received in the eighth century. "For human beings who are bound to the earthly realm, miserliness means giving nothing away of what one owns. For those who look toward the hereafter, miserliness means keeping the self from God. Yet is it not true: when someone gives God his self, his heart receives right guidance and fear of God as an inheritance, and it acquires the calmness of the certainty of salvation, the knowledge that offsets everything else, and perfect reason."[32] A Sufi who lived at the turn of the ninth to the tenth centuries worded the ideal of the profound adoption of the *sunna* as follows: "Knowledge does not consist of passing on a great many traditions; rather, he knows who *follows* his knowledge, applies it, and emulates the Prophet's norms, even if he does not have much knowledge."[33] This phrase dates from the same period: "Only people of (the) love (of God) have reached perfection in striving (toward Him), and they have reached it solely by following the *sunna* and avoiding innovations. Of all human beings, God's messenger possessed the most perfect striving (toward God) and came closer to God than anyone else!"[34] "Which way leads to God?" a ninth-century Sufi was asked. "The ways to Him are numerous! The best, and best developed, way that is least likely to entangle you in doubts is in following the *sunna* in word and deed, in inner firmness and resolution, in deliberate intent!" "And how does one get to follow the *sunna*?" "By avoiding innovations, holding firm to what the early scholars of Islam agreed upon, and staying away from the circles of the *kalam*. . . ."[35]

An important representative of that pious movement in the ninth century was al-Harith al-Muhasibi. He was born around 780 in Basra and worked in Baghdad, where he died in 857. This makes him a contemporary of Ahmad ibn Hanbal. He studied the Prophet's *hadith*, but was no traditionalist. Sources relate that, when he was young, he went through a bitter fight with his father, who was an alleged member of some unspecified Shiite movement. Like Ibn Qutayba, al-Muhasibi began to seek firm ground for his faith in the period of confusion during the civil war between al-Amin and al-Ma'mun, and afterwards, when religious passions were fueled by the inquisition. In an autobiographical passage he described how much the events he was witnessing disconcerted him: "All my life I incessantly thought of the discord in the community and searched for the true, straight path. . . . And I viewed its discord as a deep sea in which many drowned and from which only a small number of people emerged safely. I witnessed how each group among them claimed that salvation lay in its own doctrines and that their opponents were doomed to perish. I saw that there were (other) kinds of people: the one with knowledge, who prefers the next world, hard to find, a precious discovery! He who does not know: a blessing not to be near him! The pseudo-scholar, who is keen on his world and gives it preference! The one who does have religious knowledge but is not trustworthy in religious matters and tries to acquire esteem and happiness through his knowledge! The one who has knowledge but does not know the meaning of what there is inside of him! Fake ascetics, devils personified!—And so I sought guidance through knowledge, became engrossed in thought, and reflected for a long time; then I saw the light in God's Book and the community's consensus, that the pursuit of one's own (unfounded) views makes one blind to right guidance and leads away from wisdom. And so I began to banish desire from my heart, and out of fear of heretic views sought the group of salvation. Then I discovered in the Book of God that had been given to the Prophet, in agreement with the community's consensus, that the path of salvation lies in preserving one's fear of God, fulfilling one's obligation toward God, being scrupulous in matters He has forbidden, striving for that which He has permitted, and observing all His rules. . . ." Like his younger contemporary Ibn Qutayba, Muhasibi turned away from intellectualism, which could lead to despair; and like Ibn Qutayba, he looked for a firm and reliable foundation for faith. This he found in the strict observance of the law.

"You will meet no one among us who does not criticize others and is not criticized by others, who is not disliked by others or who trusts others, or is trusted by others—except in connection with the desire for deceit and pretense! We cannot find a friend who could comfort us or whom we could follow. . . . And so we remain helpless; we seek sincerity, and yet there is no path toward it. Do you know, oh sensible one, who I am describing? I am describing the people of our time, among them the teachers of the Koran, the scholars, those who pray to God, people who claim to be equipped with reason. . . . So when you live during a time in which it is dangerous to speak the truth before those who claim to be scholars, what will the state of the discovery and knowledge of the truth be? You are drifting in an ocean whose waves are breaking over you! He who swims in it, how long can he survive before he drowns? He who cannot swim drowns. That today anyone should survive is inconceivable. How could he, if he builds castles in the air and delays everything until tomorrow?"[36]

At such a time of intellectual and spiritual uncertainty and confusion, it was advisable to choose a path between all extremes. That was what al-Muhasibi recommended his readers as well. As for the concept of God, he said, one should neither approve of the method of "deflating," which the

Jahmites practiced, nor must one lean toward anthropomorphist views. The pure freedom of will the Qadarites and, in their wake, the Mu'tazilites taught should be rejected. Instead, al-Muhasibi developed the concept of a certain alignment of God's actions and those of His creatures,[37] a concept we became acquainted with in our discussion of Dirar ibn Amr. However, the large majority of the traditionalists, as which al-Muhasibi basically considered himself, were not yet ready to walk the path of the theology al-Muhasibi and Ibn Qutayba showed them. To Ahmad ibn Hanal, who by his own assessment could not answer the inquisitors' questions appropriately, any such middle course was utterly foreign. Only a predicament could force one to study the *kalam*,[38] he said, and the only predicament Ahmad would accept seemed to have been mortal danger. Suffering on account of the currently pressing issues seems to have been incomprehensible to him, and he refused to accept the argument that rationalism should not be condemned wholesale but taken seriously for taking up actually existing issues, as opposed to issues that originated in the frivolous fantasies of some heretics. Yet trying to bring the desperately contradictory answers of speculative theology into agreement with one another meant admitting that the issues behind them were real.

Most of the information we have on the Abbasid empire concerns its center. Yet that was not the only place where issues were dealt with that rationalism had formulated and answered in its own way; and not only in Iraq were these answers considered insufficient because they lacked uniformity and, above all, seemed to sacrifice the affective aspect of faith all too casually to bottomless academic reasoning. The example of al-Maturidi (d. 944) of Samarkand illustrates that in the Islamic world, the objections against unbridled rationalism were not exclusively based on a deep rootedness in the Prophet's *sunna*. However, al-Maturidi's criticism also came from a discomfort about the kind of speculation that came close to touching on God's dignity and, even more importantly, was suspected of losing sight of the core of Islam's message of salvation. Al-Maturidi lived in eastern Iran, where at the time a factually independent local Islamic empire was developing under the Samanids, whose rulers generously supported literature and scholarship. The first height of Persian poetry goes to their credit. In the translation of the great Koran commentary by at-Tabari (d. 922), which was produced at the instigation of

Mansur ibn Nuh (r. 961–76), the author at one point briefly digressed to describe the tasks Sufism had set itself. It had begun to be organized in orderly communities. Regular meeting locations had been established, that commentary explained, where people devoted themselves to the acquisition of knowledge so that "the teachers will be educated and can be useful to people, and so that they can . . . preserve Islam, the *sunna*, and God's law; for if these teachers did not exist, if they did not advise and exhort people, and if they did not preserve the law, people would have to live like cattle, and religion and law would disappear."[39]

Aside from his annotation to the Koran, al-Maturidi left us an extensive theological treatise, the *Book of Oneness*. It took up the Murjiite tradition, which had been conveyed by Abu Hanifa and become prevalent in the eastern part of the Islamic world.[40] Al-Maturidi devoted a major part of this work to the discussion of various dualistic religions that in his homeland might have been so strong that they represented a challenge to Islam. Several of them, however, can no longer be documented in Samarkand for the first half of the tenth century.[41] Yet if al-Maturidi had mentioned dualistic movements that were already extinct, the reason for this would not have been his desire to be comprehensive, but part of his main reason for studying the doctrine of God's oneness to begin with: the Mu'tazilites had failed in one crucial regard! They wanted to defend Islam, particularly against the dualists, but along the way they themselves came shockingly close to their opinions. Al-Maturidi wanted to turn his readers' attention to this dangerous fact, which in his view was a negative consequence of the Mu'tazilites' exaggerated trust in speculative reason at the expense of striving toward intuitive knowledge (*ma'rifa*). That was what motivated him. In his didactic dialogues he enjoined this on his— Sufi?—students, the "community of my brothers,"[42] whom he sometimes challenged to reflect on certain facts that seemed significant to him.[43] The style of the *Book of Oneness*, often lacking in elegance and even confusing, is probably attributable to the fact that it is the written record of his lectures.

Al-Maturidi started out his discussion by inquiring after the origin of how human beings found out about religion. He explained that this had happened in two ways: by hearing authoritative statements and by way of reason. Prophecy and political rule were based on listening—on statements conveyed through preaching and through traditions. It was the function of reason to derive insights from analyzing the world. The world consisted of two different "natures" that even worked against one another; for forcing this conflict to result in productive synergy, a guiding medium was required that was at work in all living organisms, telling them to do what was necessary for their continued existence. For it would not be a sign of wisdom if this world had been created only in order to decay. It must have certain means and forces at its disposal so that it could make sure it stayed alive. As far as human beings were concerned, this force was reason. It prepared decisions by weighing advantages and disadvantages against each other. Yet what was advantageous and what was disadvantageous? Some scholars claimed that the heart recognized both intuitively; others believed divine inspiration was necessary to do this. Al-Maturidi regarded both explanations as insufficient; he saw the bitter fight between the proponents of the various religions as proof of this. For if one or the other were true, harmony would be bound to reign.[44]

The cognitive theory al-Maturidi developed on the basis of this fundamental principle granted the created world a certain degree of ontological independence. The Mu'tazilites had done so as well, otherwise their theory of the freedom to act and of the human responsibility for one's salvation would have had no basis. Al-Maturidi, however, was convinced that what happened in this world did not say much about the "unseen." In this respect he differed from the Mu'tazilites: God's acts were performed spontaneously, at any given time; in His omnipotence He created what He wanted, unbound by any requirements such as matter, instruments, and so forth.[45] Al-Maturidi battled the Mu'tazilites' inability to disprove dualistic religions and to corroborate sufficiently Islamic belief in God's oneness. The Qadarites had been derided as "sorcerers of this community," precisely because they postulated a second, independent actor besides God—man.[46] If al-Maturidi wanted to attack this theory, he had to explain in what way divine and human actions were different from each other. What was true for the realm of the "visible" could not be transferable to the "unseen." Requirements of innerworldly actions could not guarantee the *perfect* results one must assume for God's actions, which ran their course according to the rules of the "unseen." When people assumed only some kind of advantage or disadvantage—however these may have been defined—as a motive for action, they arrived at contradictory interpretations and actions, which explained the discord in human society. Only if we desisted from explaining actions within the sole context of this world would we attain salvation.

Yet if we advocated the refusal to explain—and in light of our disastrous reality we must!—then we also had to abandon the concept of human beings as independent actors. Toward the dualists, al-Matiridi advanced the argument that the evil in this world could not be changed at all if this evil were one of two independent ontological principles.[47] Yet Islam was a message of hope that overcame the Gnostics' despair of worldly existence and hatred of the world in which we human beings live. This was possible by having trust in the kindness of the one Creator-God. Al-Maturidi exhorted his readers: "We have mentioned the views (of the dualists) so that you know God hates all those who oppose Him, who disobey Him and do not humbly reflect on His creation and do not beg Him for help in leading them toward the happiness of His true religion and opening for them the gates of truth, but who cling to this world and their own desires. . . ."[48]

Sufi belief in scrupulousness and an ascetic life in this world turned into an impulse to overcome Gnostic pessimism, whose contempt for the world sometimes took on even orgiastic forms.[49] The Sufi world must be quite different from the dualistic world, which could be most easily demonstrated by looking at the cognitive value al-Maturidi ascribed to the inference form the "visible" as opposed to the "unseen." Perceiving a phenomenon in this world did not at all mean having an analogy in the other world! It was similarly erroneous to assume that what the senses perceived in this world was logically primary, and that it had a corresponding derivative in the "unseen." Most likely, al-Maturidi assumed, the opposite was true. From the fact that the world existed did not logically follow that there was an *eternal* Creator. "Considered solely from the standpoint of reason, everything that comes into being because of something else in the realm of the 'visible' is outside of the substance of that (to which it owes its existence), such as an architectural structure or handwriting. Any kind of actions and words which are ontologically separate from that which brought them about must not be linked to the latter either substantially or in terms of their inner structure. . . ."[50] Handwriting indicated someone who had written something; but it did not reveal if that someone was a human being, a jinn, or an angel. In short, it did not reveal anything about that being's nature—all it proved was that that unknown being had written something. The same was true for the world: all it revealed was *that* there was someone who had created it.[51]

Another passage in the *Book of Oneness* deals with the question of whether God could be seen in paradise. Al-Maturidi recommended that we refrain from answering this question; the difficulties, he said, of conceiving of an encounter between human perception and divine being were insurmountable. Furthermore, sura 6, verse 103, stated that while man's "eyes attain [literally: perceive] Him not," he was perceived by Him. How human beings would be able to behold him, must remain an open question. In contrast, to make the inference from the "visible" to the "unseen" permissible, the eastern Iranian Mu'tazilite al-Ka'bi (d. 931), whom al-Maturidi would not cease to attack,[52] explained that what was taking place in the original Koranic passage was an act of "perceiving," a very general term rather than one making a clear determination of how "seeing" and "being seen" occurred. Still, the elements of seeing were there: possibility of eye contact, the increasing shrinking in size of what was seen the further one got away from it, and so forth, "and if another kind of seeing were conceivable, then having knowledge of it would be conceivable, too." The only way seeing was possible was the one we were practicing, which in the "unseen" was no different than it was here.

After having thus sketched al-Ka'bi's view, al-Maturidi argued that "perceiving" always implied the perception of limits; but God did not have any limits—which not only meant that the Koran's statement in sura 6, verse 103, frustrated al-Ka'bi's attempt to evade the issue by focusing on the word "perception," but also that in view of God's limitlessness this attempt was unmasked as misleading. Furthermore, al-Maturidi argued, we were certainly familiar with the kind of seeing that took place under different conditions than the ones al-Ka'bi had listed, which were seeing light, shadows, and darkness. To be sure, al-Maturidi did not know a solution to these difficulties,[53] but the inference from the "visible" to the "unseen" was certainly much more complicated than the Mu'tazilites were ready to acknowledge. Their naiveté made them "comparers," whose concepts of the other world coincided with what they perceived in this world.[54]

In order to relate back to creation the Jahmites' God, who was omnipresent but in His being strictly separated from the world, the Muʻtazilites had extended the term "thing" to include Him as well, defining "thing" as anything that was known.[55] Al-Maturidi considered this line of argument to be invalid as well, for its logical conclusion was that even something that did not exist was a "thing." It was not God's act of creation that had produced it; God only transferred it from nonbeing into being. Therefore, there were countless "things"; there was an eternal world! In the final analysis, al-Maturidi argued, the proponents of the world's eternity were more logical than the Muʻtazilites, for reason was simply unable to explain why God had existed for all eternity and then created the world at a certain point in time.[56] The path of reason ultimately led to the loss of the faith Muhammad had preached.

Preserving this faith while relating God and the world to each other as something "unseen" and something "visible" was possible only if this world was regarded as no more than an indication of the Creator's wise actions without relating them to His being—in short, if, as al-Maturidi noted, it was conceded that there was a relationship between master and work, between writer and handwriting, and if one ascribed an entirely different mode of being to the work rather than to the master. This, according to al-Maturidi, was the real meaning of the theory of substance versus accidens, which explained matters in this world—and only in this world!—but was invalid for the domain of the "unseen." In addition, this theory had the advantage of describing God as the permanent director of His work. As al-Maturidi explained, the natural philosophers had in this manner deduced the changing fate of the eternal world from the constantly changing admixture of its constituent elements; mixing colors, they argued, made new colors: the latter were not generated out of nothing. Al-Maturidi's response to this argument was that colors never mixed by themselves; there must be someone who made them do that. If one mixed colors, they made an ugly tone, and the result was different only when the wise ruler of the world interfered. The "elements" were nothing but substances with their different accidentes; it was the latter that determined the quality of the substance carrying them, and not a mixture of elementary matters.[57] Al-Maturidi regarded the Muʻtazilites' extremely complicated atom theory with suspicion. He probably considered it to be a science that was always in great danger of explaining what was happening in the world by pushing the *one* cause, "God," far into the background. This would again advance the dualism between God and eternal matter. It was better, he argued, to content oneself with assuming that substances existed solely because of their *accidentes* and that they, therefore, could not be eternal.[58]

Al-Maturidi was not quite sure to what extent the creation's power of being had to be restricted in order for God's power to remain untouched and His profoundly felt venerability to stay undiminished, despite all enticing dualistic theories. Al-Maturidi was grounded in the Murjiite tradition passed on by Abu Hanifa, which already tells us that we may expect significant restrictions on the human freedom to act. Yet, before we can measure that freedom, al-Maturidi had to say a few things about God's actions. Again we detect the rejection of dualistic concepts. Al-Maturidi suggested that the theory propagated by the Mu'tazilites, that God always created the best (*aslah*) for His creatures, was supposed to refute the dualists; for the good and the evil principle could function only in accordance with what they were, and therefore only effected what they were meant to. The wise God of Islam, however, was not restricted to His own being and, therefore, was able to work toward the advantage of others. Al-Maturidi agreed with this view, but only under the condition that God's wisdom was not limited to helping human beings. God was unpredictable, He could not be subjugated to human rationality in the sense that He—as many Mu'tazilites thought—would have to make up for a loss He had unjustly caused someone. Again we recognize the basic motif of al-Maturidi's theology, the preservation of Allah's numinous fullness of being. God's independence expressed itself in His ability to create out of nothing, that is to say, without being restricted by material preconditions or concerns.[59]

Once again we have touched, on a higher level of intellectual comprehension, the Murjiite motif of determining the limits of human actions.[60] If one accepted this motif, then, al-Maturidi's arguments made clear, a just evaluation of actions was impossible for us, because in contrast to God, we could never act in a "pure" way, independently of external circumstances—out of nothing. These circumstances always existed before human beings got involved; they never occurred while we were already acting. The "natures" al-Maturidi had mentioned at the beginning of his *Book of Oneness*[61] made up the matter human beings had to deal with, as it were, and whose harmful or useful application they had to consider. Human beings acted really, not only metaphorically, as the Jahmites taught. Yet utilitarian rationality was not man's only guiding principle. God also created faith in Him, which in the Murjiites' view was indestructible. Faith was indispensable as a guiding principle, for what was advantageous or harmful from a utilitarian point of view was not necessarily identical to what fell under the categories of good and evil. Al-Maturidi accused the Mu'tazilites of having blended the two levels of evaluation.[62]

Matter, which was a given, weighing the advantages and the harm an action would cause, and the law handed down by God via the Prophet's mouth—or the faith created in man—all became part of human actions; they were never acts of "creation," which, as we have seen, produced something out of nothing. Rather, they were acts of "acquisition" because they were based on the appropriation and potentially fruitful usage of conditions "created" by God. Man's every deed, al-Maturidi explained, had two sides. He comprehended one of these because he understood matter, usefulness, and lawfulness; in this respect it was his deed. The other side was incomprehensible to him; it was beyond his capacities. The same was true for the constellation at the beginning of an action; it could never be reproduced. Neither could the result of an action always be correctly determined; clear predictions were impossible.[63]

Al-Maturidi was one of the tenth century's most fascinating theologians. Grounded in Murjiite tradition, he put great effort into working his way through the ideas he had inherited. On the one hand, this enabled him to prepare them for a confrontation with the issues the rationalism of the previous generation had raised, and, on the other, finally to reach what he considered to be rationalism's main goal: the refutation of dualistic theories. Al-Maturidi firmly believed that this must be done while strictly preserving the rank Islam had given Allah: being the apex of everything human beings could possibly experience. While al-Maturidi's theology was influenced by rationalism's way of reasoning, in the firm knowledge of its definite limits its logic was consistently put into its proper perspective. We could, he believed, only guess with awe at the ineffable fullness of God's being, and he hoped that this vague notion may penetrate us and lead us out of our helplessness in which all theology ended that relied on reason alone.

4. Sunnite Rationalism

Sufi piousness was nothing foreign to Abu l-Hasan al-Ash'ari (d. 935), the thinker whom historiography credits with making the *kalam* serve Sunnism's purposes. The Sunni component of Sufism[64] is much more discernible in him than in al-Maturidi. It consists of viewing the world as the place where the Prophet's example is constantly being repeated. No matter how minor the details of this example appear to be, Sunnis wholly immerse themselves in all these minutiae. In al-Ash'ari we will encounter similar theological issues as in al-Maturidi. His responses will lead in a similar direction; yet, if we look closely, they are fundamentally different from al-Maturidi's. After the victory of al-Ash'ari's school, al-Maturidi's heirs would feel compelled to examine what their master taught and to interpret his theories—a regrettable fact. Until most recently it has veiled the Transoxianan's achievements and banished the richness of his reflection from theological debate in favor of Ash'arite simplicity.

Since soon after his death al-Ash'ari was monopolized as the founder of a specifically Sunnite theological school, his heirs sometimes ascribed views to him that had not even been developed yet. Even a brief overview of the history of Islamic theology must try to distinguish between the historic Al-Ash'ari, his students, and their students. Owing to sufficient source material and a rather large number of scholarly studies, this is now possible.

Muslim biographical literature can tell us only few details about al-Ash'ari. He was born in Basra in 873. There he became one of the ablest students of the theologian Abu 'Ali al-Jubba'i (d. 915) and perhaps the rival of the latter's son, Abu Hashim (d. 933). In any case, there seems to have been a quarrel between the two. Al-Ash'ari moved to Baghdad, the city with the great Sunni past in which the memory of Ahmad ibn Hanbal was still very much alive. Al-Ash'ari died there in 935.

Ash'arite sources describe his break with the circle around Abu 'Ali al-Jubba'i as the consequence of a conversion which supposedly took place around 912. That al-Ash'ari was approximately forty years old at that time reminds us of Muhammad's appointment as Prophet; we cannot exclude the possibility that his biography was somewhat glamorized and his conversion even made up. In any event, legend has it that al-Ash'ari remained in his house for fifteen days, then entered a mosque, and proclaimed: "I remained hidden from you for such a long time, devoting myself to speculation! I found that all proofs were equally convincing, nothing had more weight than anything else." Ibn Qutayba and al-Muhasibi had also complained that rationalist speculation ultimately led to all arguments being equally valid.[65] "I asked God for guidance, and He led me to the faith I proclaim in my writings, and now I am abandoning my former faith just as I am taking off my garment here." Al-Ash'ari, the story continues, took off his garment and threw it away. He supposedly distributed among his audience the writings he had produced in his house during that time. They were all in defense of the *sunna*.[66]

There are also other versions of al-Ash'ari's conversion to Sunnism. One of them relates that Muhammad appeared to him three times in a dream. He had, it is said, instructed him to defend the traditional teachings by virtue of the Prophet's authority. Thereupon al-Ash'ari abandoned the *kalam*. During the night before 27 Ramadan, in which according to Muslim belief the Koran was revealed, he had one last dream about the Prophet. Muhammad exhorted him, "By no means should you abandon the *kalam*; but you shall support that which was revealed. God will assist you." Now al-Ash'ari was convinced that he had understood God's message correctly: he should not reject rationalism but put it in the service of the *sunna*. And so he began to defend by means of rationalism the *hadiths* about man seeing God in paradise and about the Prophet's intercession. These sources were the very traditions the Mu'tazilites had dismissed as absurd: since God was in His essence so fundamentally different from human beings, human eyes could not behold Him; and since man's actions were the only basis for judging him on the Last Day, the theory of Muhammad's intercession on behalf of his community must be rejected. As explained above, al-Maturidi used the issue of human beings beholding God to disprove the Mu'tazilites' theory of the connection between the "visible" and the "unseen" and to restrict the human freedom of action in favor of God's power, which created out of nothing. We then learn that al-Ash'ari found, in part in the *kalam*, new proof of the *visio beatifica* and Muhammad's intercession.

There are also reports that supposedly reveal what triggered the change in al-Ash'ari's intellectual development. One day he discussed with his teacher Abu 'Ali al-Jubba'i the issue of how an infidel, a believer, and a minor child would be judged on the Last Day. Abu 'Ali's response, we are told, was entirely in agreement with Mu'tazilite views: the believer was in paradise, the infidel in hell, and the minor child at a "place of deliverance." Al-Ash'ari then asked what would have to happen for the child to enter paradise. Abu 'Ali strictly denied that possibility, since gaining paradise required that one had committed acts of obedience. Thereupon al-Ash'ari replied that the child could argue he was not to blame for having died before reaching maturity. For had he grown up, he might have committed acts of obedience. If God told the wailing child He knew that he would commit crimes if he grew up, and He had only had the child's best interest in mind when He made him die so young, the infidel could interject that he did not have the chance to die as a child; that he remained an unbeliever and was, therefore, condemned to hell. Why had God not had his best interest in mind? Abu 'Ali al-Jubba'i did not know what to say. This story brought the Mu'tazilite theory of the calculability of fate in the hereafter to its absurd conclusion. Al-Maturidi also discussed this issue extensively, with the same intention.

That the Mu'tazilites believed that there was such a direct connection between actions in the next world and God's judgment undermined His omnipotence. He was no longer free in His decision, but must decide according to what human beings did. The idea that the sovereign of a country—and God, after all, was the sovereign of the Islamic state, whose heads ruled only in His name!—was bound by the very laws he had decreed, was not brought up. Back then, the Umayyad caliphs had been accused of believing that they were chosen rulers who could dispose of the believers as they wished. All believers, including their highest ruler on earth, should have the same distance from God. Yet this God could be thought of only as a despot. By accepting and acknowledging that one was subjugated to him, it might have been possible to invoke His mercy and to make Him allow His favorite messenger, the Prophet Muhammad, to intercede on the subjects' behalf, with whom He otherwise did as He pleased, as was His right. The Sunnis' God had no limitations, and His despotism was mitigated only by His mercy, which one could not, however, demand of Him.

How did al-Ash'ari defend these views against the Mu'tazilites? A Hanbalite credo from the late tenth century tersely said that one must believe in intercession, for the Prophet had said, "My intercession is for those who have burdened themselves with grave sins."[67] Al-Ash'ari did not believe it was as simple as that. In his portrait of Sunnism, which he wrote after his conversion and in which he repeatedly praised Ahmad ibn Hanbal as the great teacher of Islam, he wrote that the Muslims agreed that the Prophet was entitled to intercede. But on whose behalf was Muhammad allowed to intercede? The criminals' or only the believers'? According to Sunnite belief, Muhammad may intercede for the criminals within his community. The other standpoint, that Muhammad's word should benefit only the believers, who are promised paradise anyway, had to be objected to, as it made no sense because God certainly never broke His promise. Yet that was the only kind of intercession the Mu'tazilites could accept—after all, they firmly believed that threat and promise should be taken absolutely literally. If one could consider the possibility of intercession at all, then it could only be as a confirmation of what was to be expected in any event.

Al-Ash'ari sternly protested this way of thinking, which imposed restrictions on God. He argued that one must not maintain that the believers deserved paradise on account of their deeds, or that it was God's duty to admit them. Certainly, nothing escaped God's attention, not even a tiny piece of dust or the smallest deed. Yet one should not argue that God would be unjust if He refused the believers entry into paradise. God, he said, was always just, and those who requested intercession on the *believers'* behalf insinuated that now and then He did something unjust. Yet, should the Mu'tazilites argue that intercession took place so that God would be even more merciful to the believers but not admit them to paradise, this would contradict sura 4, verse 172: "As for the believers, who do deeds of righteousness, He will pay them in full their wages, and He will give them more, of His bounty." Even without Muhammad interceding on the believers' behalf, they received more than they deserved. All this, al-Ash'ari argued, indicated that intercession was possible only on behalf of those who deserved to be punished for how they had lived. After having based his arguments on the Koran up until this point, al-Ash'ari then proceeded to quote the tradition. The Prophet clearly said, "My intercession is for those who have burdened themselves with grave sins." The minor sinners were going to escape the fire of hell anyway, as long as they were believers. This, too, was a *hadith*, which al-Ash'ari used to buttress his contention.[68]

Thanks to his Mu'tazilite training, al-Ash'ari mastered the rationalists' art of the dispute. Both al-Humaydi and Ahmad ibn Hanbal had very cautiously used this approach, even if the latter had brusquely declared that analogies in matters of faith were invalid.[69] Al-Ash'ari attempted to legitimize rationalism within Sunnism by pointing out that certain methods of proof developed by the Mu'tazilites originated in the Koran. "Why, were there gods in earth and heaven other than God, they would surely go to ruin," sura 21, verse 22, says. Was this not the starting point of the "proof with mutual obstruction"? This alludes to a way of thinking that was often reflected upon and was supposed to prove beyond doubt God's oneness: two omnipotent beings would mutually interfere with each other's acts of creation. Furthermore, al-Ash'ari argued, the *hadith* documented abundantly that Muhammad had mastered the art of the *kalam*; yet he had to refer to it only rarely, since at that time the questions that so puzzled those that came later had not even been discovered yet.[70] This justification of a theology that reasoned rationally makes clear how necessarily jeopardized it always was from a Sunni point of view. The *kalam* was not un-Islamic, but it was a byproduct (an inevitable one, according to Al-Ash'ari) of the collapse of the unquestioned piousness of the early days. If that piousness were to be regained—and this, after all, was the goal of all *sunna* piousness—then the *kalam* would be unnecessary! Theological rationalism's function was limited by the definitive standards not only of the revelation but also of the *hadith* with its much fuller content; to Sunnism it could only be an aid to be used when necessary.

Simply by justifying the use of the rational method of arguing within the set framework of the *sunna*, al-Ash'ari had, of course, not yet formed a specifically Sunnite theology of reason. Only his pupils were to realize and deal with the difficulties that were created by the step he had taken. Al-Ash'ari himself practiced theology entirely within the set of issues that were prevalent at his time: that of the inference from the "visible" to the "unseen," and of what we could know about God's being without defining it so narrowly with the terms of the world which our senses perceived, that it was deprived of its numinous force. The Mu'tazilites had come to the realization that God's one and uniform being was manifested for us, the creatures, in His being creating, speaking, knowing, and so forth. Thus the Mu'tazilites had escaped the Jahmite danger of "deflating" the concept of God. Yet this did not prevent them from piously reflecting on God's actions in and upon creation. In view of the many, very worldly qualities that characterized the experience of God, which was guided by religious feeling, that theological compromise remained pale and inadequate. So what about those of "God's names" that were put together in lists of ninety-nine and repeated again and again during religious edification in order to open up the believer's heart for the overwhelming fullness of Allah's being? There were names such as "the one who remains," "the helping one," or "the noble-minded one," but Allah's essence was fully contained only in His secret one hundredth name.[71] Did all this not stand for a reality of which the believers had no concept but which they could experience after all? The Basran Mu'tazilites had realized that in the long run rationalist theology could not ignore the experience of the One—an experience the Sufis described so powerfully— unless they were willing to accept the "deflation" of the concept of God: without that experience, the barely one-hundred-year-old formula about God's essence as something that in various ways related to the world as if to an object was going to be discredited. In order to fend off that danger, Abu 'Ali al-Jubba'i's circles had developed the theory of the states: God was in the states of knowing, of being powerful, being alive, and existent; these four states led to a fifth state, that of divinity (*ilahiyya*), which contained the four states in which were manifested God's works in His creation. The Mu'tazilites believed that states were neither existent nor nonexistent; they did not have their own being or nonbeing. That is why it was possible to talk about them as states of the eternal God without simultaneously affirming other eternal beings next to Him. Abu l-Husayn al-Basri, a contemporary of Abu 'Ali al-Jubba'i, had proposed a similar theory: he had come to believe that God's state of knowing, for example, was contained in His all-comprehensive being.[72]

The Mu'tazilite formula of God's relating to the world as if to an object, which Abu l-Hudhayl had prepared, was now generally considered as signifying the total "deflation" of the concept of God; al-Ash'ari's opposition to this "deflation" followed a trend of his time. Yet he also always spoke out against viewing God as entirely similar to His creation, the way some Sunni circles did. Al-Ash'ari tried to walk a middle course between the two. As far as he was concerned, from the analogy between God and the world there perforce followed the reality of the divine attributes. They were not merely some phantom of the necessarily human language of the revelation. To be sure, when the Koran spoke of God's hands, it meant something that exclusively referred to God's reality, but it also had a comparable reference point in the realm of human experience. Al-Ash'ari attempted to summarize God's attributes in his explanation of Sunni belief as follows: God, he stated, said in the Koran, "Say: 'He is God, One, God, the Everlasting Refuge, who has not begotten, and has not been begotten, and equal to Him is not any one' " (sura 112). How could the Koran be the word created by God and thus different from Him if God's name itself was contained in the Koran? This would imply that all of God's names were created; yet if God's names were created, then His oneness would also have to have been created, just like His knowledge and His power. Al-Ash'ari insisted that the Jahmites' belief in the Koran as the *created* word was entirely wrong. For in this case the name "God" could not be part of the Koran. Yet God said in the Koran: "Praise the name of thy Lord, the Sublime, Who has created . . ." It was possible that the "name of thy Lord Who has created" was also created. If God's word was created, then the condemnation of Satan was also created. If God's created word disappeared, then the condemnation of Satan also disappeared, al-Ash'ari argued at another point in the same treatise. Yet, just as God's word had a reality, so did all the other qualities mentioned in the revelation. Expressions in the revelations such as hand, face, etc., which God Himself chose, were by no means metaphors! But neither must they be understood in purely human-physical terms. Rather, they were real attributes whose true nature man was not able to recognize.[73]

In a collection of al-Ash'ari's teachings recorded and compiled by his students, we can detect his efforts to condense the terms for God's nature and works into a few basic concepts. The category "talking" also contained the attributes "saying" and "speaking"; likewise, God's "insight," "recognition," as well as His "reason," His "sensation," and His "realization" were declared synonyms.[74] This created a distance between God's nature and the complex events in this world. The reason Al-Ash'ari gave for thus restricting our ways of defining God's nature was that the attributes we deduced from certain divine actions perceived by us were flawed in that they focused on only a tiny part of what God did, a part that was thus disconnected from the fullness of His being. Such arrogance was surely not appropriate. If we wanted to regard God with the awe He deserved, we should employ only the terms used in the revelation and approved by Him, and we should recognize that each of them touched no more than a small part of God's all-comprehensive actions upon and within His creation. The more inclusive our understanding of the meaning of these sanctioned attributes, the better, for the closer we would come to the never reachable goal of completely describing God.[75]

Yet not only in his adherence to the exact words of the revelation did Al-Ash'ari go beyond the five "states"[76] conceived in Abu 'Ali al-Jubba'i's circles; he invalidated that construct by declaring God's attributes terms for kinds of expression of His nature that were actually part of Him—*kinds* of expression" again only from the perspective of created human beings, whose concepts were imperfect and who perceived differences where in reality there was uniformity. These kinds of expression were God's nature, from eternity to eternity, independent of whether or not they were manifested.[77] God Himself was ahistorical, but creatures' perceptions and the words given them were historical. The text of the Koran was eternal and uncreated, the recitation of its words was created and temporal.[78]

Thus the inference from the "visible" to the "unseen," which even al-Maturidi no longer quite trusted, had become less and less plausible, for whatever human beings conceived of God's works was only an insufficient fragment of a whole that transcended their capacity to understand. The conclusion that was so popular during early rationalism was turning into an empty formula: the attribute "knowing" could be ascribed to a human being as well as to God, but what this term meant in the domain of the "unseen" remained incomprehensible.[79] Thus in connection with the question about the *visio beatifica* al-Ash'ari explained that the possibility of seeing something implied only that it existed, nothing more; and the fact that it existed at a certain moment only meant that its being seen existed. Closeness or distance, mass of the object seen, reflection of one's gaze off the object, and additional details of the process of seeing, he argued, should not be interpreted as qualities of the perceived object, and neither were they the cause of their visibility. "Mere seeing [or being seen, respectively] must be discounted in the analogy, as well as the inference from the 'visible' to the 'unseen,' unless the content of what the proof determines has been established as well. Thus [al-Ash'ari] made a distinction between qualities, causes, conditions, and essence; he did not relate to essence what should have been viewed as a quality. Hence he would say that the visible, created things with their qualities, which transcend existence, are seen, no matter whether or not these qualities are given, for these [additional qualities, such as the seen object's placement opposite the observer] do not impact its visibility or the lack thereof. And he would teach that something lying opposite one is not being seen for its quality of being opposite because even before being seen it had the quality of being opposite. Rather, it was encountered by seeing as something that had the quality of being opposite."[80] "And, regarding the inference from the 'visible' to the 'unseen,' he used to teach: If someone asks, 'What about someone who lives in an area where he sees only black people, or surrounded by a lake in which he gets to know only freshwater, must he conclude from this that there are only freshwater and black people?' we have to explain as follows: 'He must not make these inferences, for the human beings he sees are not human beings because they are black. Do you not notice that their hands are [also] black, but these hands are surely no human beings?' And the questioner was informed: 'We call everyone with this kind of anatomy a human being, and everything of that color black, because that is what the language experts have taught us, not because we saw it this and not any other way.'" We use the term "freshwater" in the second example only because that is what we were taught, "and with regard to the power of the One who created this quality, we have to admit that He can also create another quality."[81]

We can discern that al-Ash'ari's doubts in the validity of the inference from the "visible" to the "unseen" are no longer restricted to a theological level but begin to include the possibility of causal connections in this world. He explicitly rejected the theory of the "nature" of created things, which al-Maturidi had recognized and which enabled him to leave creatures in Murjiite fashion a certain degree of their own power of being and responsibility: "Everything that happens is a deed (af'al) of God, is a result of His choice, His will, His direction and terms. . . ."[82] When something happened, when it entered into existence, then only because God assigned to it a certain faculty or weakness, or existence: "Al-Ash'ari denied that the heaviness of the burden keeps the carrier from carrying and the fettered from walking; rather, the substratum is different [from one moment to the next] Obstruction occurs only because [that particular moment]the pertinent substratum contains the opposite of walking or carrying. . . ."[83]

And so in al-Ash'ari is outlined what would become characteristic of his school: the victory of metaphysics over physics. The Mu'tazilites had focused their attention strictly on causality in nature in order to understand better the nature of the Creator-God and to explain why human beings, who were obliged to act in this world, were rewarded and punished in the next world. Perhaps as a consequence of the highly unsatisfying and contradictory results of these efforts, al-Ash'ari's reflections were turned in the opposite direction. God was now the one overwhelming reality which all theology had to take as its point of departure. Compared with the fullness of His being, that which was created was almost nothing and, in any case, dependent on Him. Apparently al-Ash'ari was not clearly aware of the inevitable consequences of this for human actions, which they were after all supposed to account for before God. He picked up the already existing theory of the acquisition of actions, which were really committed by God,[84] and in the end tended to believe that even the capacity for this acquisition would have to be created simultaneously with the execution of this action. Yet he had also expressed his belief that the acquirer needed to possess knowledge and will—in short, to add something of his own. According to Ibn Furak (d. 1015), to whom we owe a large collection of al-Ash'ari's teachings, he ultimately did end up believing that the process of acquisition was caused by God in *all* of its aspects, because he was convinced that "what does not (yet) exist is neither 'thing' nor 'essence,' 'substance,' '*accidens*,' 'white,' 'black,' 'ugly,' or 'beautiful,' and all these qualities can be ascribed only to the One who creates the pertinent essence with its (individual) characteristics, just as he also assigns to it the characteristics of 'existence' and 'being created in time.' "[85] Not, as the Mu'tazilites thought, what was "known," but what was "in existence," was considered "a thing" in the opinion of al-Ash'ari and his school. This implied that every "thing" was directly related to God and that He caused every action. This removal of the creature's power was inevitable, and the expulsion of causality from this world was absolutely necessary in order to cut the ground from under the feet of natural-philosophical speculation; the proponents of natural philosophy declared everything they could not themselves perceive—the Prophet's alleged miracles[86]—to be impossible, which meant that they cast doubt on the very core of Islam.

5. The Ash'arite School

One accusation al-Maturidi brought against the Mu'tazilites was that their way of practicing theology unintentionally worked into the hands of the dualists; al-Ash'ari was afraid that what the natural philosophers taught might in the end appeal to people. In both cases, the ostensibly logical consequence was going to be that what was created would lose its power. Al-Ash'ari himself stressed this power all the more when he preserved atomism, with which he had become familiar during his education in the Mu'tazilite school. Yet atomism without an even vague idea of the synergy of particles inevitably led to explaining even the most banal processes, and even the mere existence of the simplest bodies, by way of God's interference. Even though this contradicted direct human experience in many respects, he and his school were ready to accept that disadvantage, as long as Islam could be successfully defended. The *kalam* was not in itself a desirable path of theology but an area of intellectual activity that should be entered only when absolutely necessary. This was how al-Ash'ari justified what he taught—after all, people were no longer as firm in their belief as they had been in the beginning—and this is how the historical philosopher and universal scholar Ibn Khaldun (1406) viewed the issue five hundred years later: *kalam*, he said, had become superfluous since Islam's enemies had been vanquished.[87]

Yet, in the Islamic world, rationalist theology was not practiced without any enjoyment whatsoever of using the intellectual tools that had been created, nor was it done without any curiosity about whether all conceivable problems would be solved with its aid and about whether God and the world could fit smugly into an intellectual construct. Al-Ash'ari's treatise, in which he justified his, a Sunnite's, occupation with the *kalam*, was based on the assumption that the Koran and the *sunna* made statements about God and creation which were accessible to, and even required, sensible exegesis. For the signs by which the Creator manifested Himself were not easily comprehensible to everyone. Classifying the phenomena of the created world that could be perceived by the senses and by reason was apt to lead to a meaningful image which would remain hidden without the *kalam*. This image could be used apologetically, with the aim of defending the faith in the one Creator and preserver of the world. It was in this sense that Shahfur Tahir al-Isfara'ini and other theologians spoke about the Muslims' duty to familiarize themselves with the rational explanation of faith. Yet, even without this goal, it was possible to struggle toward an understanding of the ontology of creation and the Creator.[88]

That this happened is documented by the complete reproductions of the *kalam* since the tenth century. These portray their topics according to a certain pattern, which Al-Ash'ari briefly outlined: the first part must explain that the world was not eternal but was created; then it had to be shown that it was the work of only one Creator; next must come the proof that Muhammad was God's messenger; finally, it must be shown that the commandments God proclaimed through Muhammad must be obeyed so that paradise would be gained.[89] This way of thinking both served its apologetic purpose and conveyed to the pious Muslims deeper insight into the nature of the Creator and of that of His creation in general, as well as of the human beings acting in it. It was a pattern that must have developed in the ninth century within the Mu'tazilite school; yet the oldest sources document it only indirectly. One of these is the first book of the hexaemeron commentary by Moses bar Kepha (d. 903), the Jacobite bishop of Mossul from 863 until his death.[90] The first part of al-Maturidi's *Book of Oneness* followed the same model; as in Moses bar Kepha's work, its introduction was an epistemology (which, however, is missing in al-Ash'ari's study).[91]

This structure—epistemology, createdness of the world, humankind's duties, and how these can be carried out—was the norm for the theology of al-Ash'ari's school, which flowered in the tenth and eleventh centuries. Mu'tazilite handbooks continued to follow this model as well. A theologically key work of the Ash'arite school is the *Book of Introduction*, by Ibn al-Baqillani (d. 1013) from Baghdad. In this work ontology is the firm ground on whose basis the author tried to prove the essential truths of Islamic faith. Al-Ash'ari's methodology had been very strict—before making inferences from the "visible" to the "unseen" it was always necessary to decide for which partial aspect the inference was valid. Ibn al-Baqillani was even much stricter: he postulated that for any proof to be absolutely unshakable, it must be possible to generalize and reverse it; the two parts on each side of the equation a definition constituted must be exchangeable.[92]

Let us now look at the main characteristics of the ontology Ibn al-Baqillani developed in his *Book of Introduction*. He wrote that everything that was known was either existent or nonexistent. Everything that existed could be termed a "thing." This gave Ibn al-Baqillani his first definition: everything that existed was a "thing"; every "thing" existed. This illustrates the exchangeability of definition and what was defined, which Ibn al-Baqillani had stipulated. A trivial-sounding definition such as this was already the decisive step away from the Mu'tazilites' ontology. The Mu'tazilites had postulated that everything that was known, whether or not it existed, could be subsumed under the term "thing." This is extremely significant inasmuch as both that which once existed and that which would one day exist could be included in philosophical speculation. Therefore the past and the future had a certain reality—they related to one another via that which existed in the present. The cosmos had a history that could be rationally interpreted and was open to analysis. How different was the Ash'arite Ibn al-Baqillani! As far as he was concerned, only that which was immediately present could be analyzed and comprehended. Only what existed could be termed a "thing" and be the object of analysis. Ash'arite thinking was decidedly ahistorical. This was in agreement with Sunnism's attempt to destroy history and instead to hold on to its salutary beginnings. As shown above, the literary genre of the *hadith* served precisely that purpose.

Ibn al-Baqillani recognized a number of distinctions in the realm of the existent. As content of knowledge, the nonexistent was the impossible; for instance, it was impossible for two contradictory statements to come true at the same time and at the same place, or that two bodies were in one and the same location. While an additional category of the nonexistent had to be regarded as possible, it never became real. In this connection Ibn al-Baqillani mentioned the return of the dead to this world. Then there was that which was nonexistent in our time—such as the resurrection of the dead—as well as that which was no longer existent in our time, in other words, everything that had become part of history. In all of this the nonexistent was the object of our knowledge, but, of course, without the ontological status of the "thing" the Mu'tazilites would have ascribed to it. There was also that which was nonexistent yet possible, even though it was impossible for us to know anything about it. We could never know whether or not God would move something. These distinctions of certain categories of the nonexistent echoed Mu'tazilite views. They also represented a connection to later developments that were triggered by the impact of philosophy.[93] Yet Ash'arism also knew the radical view of the absolute negation of the nonexistent, about which no statements could be made.

Opposite the nonexistent was the existent. It was either eternal or contingent. The contingent consisted of composite bodies which in turn consisted of particles of matter, of everything that could carry one of the various *accidentes*. The *accidentes* appeared in the particles but were without any continuity, as the entire course of time was thought of as a finite sequence of tiny atoms of time. In each atom of time various *accidentes* again attached themselves to such a particle. Since "existent" was a quality as well, which had to be renewed in each atom of time, both the particles as well as the bodies lacked any kind of permanence. Ibn al-Baqillani saw proof of the existence of *accidentes*, which in this concept of the world were the crucial element, in the following consideration: if a body moved of its own accord, it would be inconceivable for it to be still; it had to be moving on account of an external reason (*'illa*). This movement was assigned to the body, hence it was an *accidens*; the same was true of colors and other physical qualities.[94]

Equipped with these relatively modest metaphysical means, Ibn al-Baqillani hoped to be able to resolve all theological issues definitively, conclusively, and logically. He believed he would gain unshakable, secure knowledge. In his definition, knowledge meant recognizing what was known for what it was; this definition, he said, contained what was known in its entirety, it did not add anything to it or leave anything out. "If the definition contains that which must be defined in this manner, it must be a correct, unshakable definition. And everything that defines knowledge or other concepts by delineating and differentiating it from other concepts, and comprehending them the way we do in our definition of knowledge, must be recognized as true."[95]

Ibn al-Baqillani's discussion of the scholarly view of God as a body (*al-mujassima*) may illustrate the way that he believed this postulate could be verified. "What argument do you use to deny that God is a body?" Ibn al-Baqillani let his opponents' party open the dispute. "Because of our definition of the term 'body': the body is a composite. Since the eternal One cannot be a composite, He is not a body." His opponents insisted: "What is your argument for proving that He cannot be a composite?" This gave Ibn al-Baqillani the opportunity to go further back. The concept of the body implied space, he said, and it was perforce inconceivable that any of God's limbs touched another limb in more than just one place. For two bodies had contact with another at a certain place, and at that very spot they could not simultaneously touch a third body. That was the inevitable consequence of spatiality. Ibn al-Baqillani also saw this as a consequence of the rule that the same two *accidentes* could never be inherent to one and the same particle of matter. Particle N could never contain the *accidens* "contact with A" *and* the *accidens* "contact with B." If God were a body, all of His limbs would have to follow the law of spatiality and thus also the laws of substance and *accidens*. These, however, were valid only for the created things. Yet the eternal One could not be created, therefore He could not be a composite body possessing spatiality.

The issue of God's spatiality was of great significance to Islamic theology. According to sura 2, verse 257, God's throne comprises all of creation. Other verses frequently mention that God sat down on His throne after finishing His work. Gnostic movements could interpret this Koranic statement to the effect that God was entirely outside of His creation and, therefore, not constantly working in it.

Ibn al-Baqillani had not yet concluded his proof of God's noncorporeality. If one thought of the eternal One in terms of a body made of different parts, all of these individual parts would have had to be carriers of qualities. As we have seen, the Ash'arites had rejected the Mu'tazilites' early attempts to see living bodies as organisms.[96] Al-Ash'ari had understood the term "knowing" to be an *accidens* subsisting in only one or a few very specific particles, and being independent of all the other particles of the body. If God were a body consisting of particles, each of these would, in Ash'arite view, possess divinity. Furthermore, one could then assume that these individual particles could never find their way to a uniform will.[97] After Ibn al-Baqillani had presented this Ash'arite view, it was the opposition's turn to ask, "Why then is man able to coordinate his limbs?" It seemed obvious that not all particles obstructed one another, which at best would have had to lead to a complete standstill. Ibn al-Baqillani's answer again started from a viewpoint of Ash'arite metaphysics. The substratum of the acts of two created actors could never be one, since it was impossible that the act of each of them transcended the substratum of his ability to act at that pertinent moment. The Ash'arites did not believe human beings had the capacity to act of themselves upon something else. A created actor simply received from God the power to work upon an individual substratum during the duration of an atom of the time in which he acted. There would be mutual obstruction of the individual particles of which the human body consisted only if they tried to act of themselves on a substratum. Within the framework of Ash'arite metaphysics the question about the human ability to coordinate the movements of the limbs of the body became meaningless.[98]

Ibn al-Baqillani continued, "Someone asks: 'What is the argument with which you deny that He whom we praise as the Creator is a body, yet not a created body, which is in agreement with your opinion that He is a thing, even though not like the created things?' The response is: 'Only because our term "thing" is neither restricted to a certain species nor implies being a composite. . . .' Now one could argue, 'What is the argument you use to deny that it is conceivable to call Him a body, even though not in the sense this noun was given in language?' The response is: 'We deny this because in that case this term . . . would then be proven by the revealed law or the authority of doctrine at best; for reason does not require this term (for God), and even rejects it, because the eternal One, who is without beginning—praise be to Him!—is not a composite. Nowhere in the sources that can serve as proof and are perceived via hearing—the Koran, the *sunna*, the Islamic community's consensus and what can be deduced from it—is there anything that would indicate the necessity of this term, or even the conceivability of this term. Therefore, what you are saying is invalid.' "[99]

For Ibn al-Baqillani, the Ash'arite, and for many like him, the point of departure for theological reflection was ontology. The Koran and the *sunna* were of course consulted, but as the last sentences of the above quote indicate, they did not really determine the course of the argument. On the contrary, Ibn al-Baqillani expressed his relief because in the case of the term "body" they did not interfere with his own thoughts. Trying to derive Ash'arism's entire theology from the revelation and the *hadith* would probably have been doomed to fail,[100] but that was not Ibn al-Baqillani's point. His Ash'arite theology was Sunnite in that it combined some important basic principles of Sunnism and rational arguments: God's determination of human action, which was illustrated in the discontinuity of everything that was created; and also, touching on this, the ahistoricity of all events in this world, which were viewed as directly related to God and, from the point of view of creation, did not exhibit an independent development.

The victory of metaphysics over physics, the perfection of Ash'arite theology, is most distinct in the work of Abu l-Maali al-Juwayni (d. 1085). It was his ultimate intention to fix in his life's work those flaws that he had discovered in Ibn al-Baqillani's reflections. However, al-Juwayni's creative zeal was already tainted by the premonition that despite all his efforts, this would ultimately not provide him with the certainty of faith he sought—and that al-Baqillani had in fact been overly sanguine in many respects. For instance, the Ash'arite claimed that the definition contained in its entirety that which was being defined, even its essence, so that both were exchangeable with each other. Al-Juwayni, who had studied the issue extensively, did not share this optimistic view.

He realized that all a definition could achieve was to approach gradually that which was being defined by using synonymous expressions. It was impossible to explain or define anything to those who did not know these expressions. All definitions were merely attempts to make someone understand the essence of what was being defined; the very struggle for a definition distinguished it from other, similar things. It was quite clear that any attempt to follow this theory and find a definition could not possibly ever reach its ultimate goal. One could get closer, but never really reach it, which was what Ibn al-Baqillani had tacitly presupposed. It follows from al-Juwayni's insight that definitions could never lead to ultimate certainties, to whole, fundamental truths of faith.[101] Even though al-Juwayni did not state this explicitly, those doubts are clearly implied in his work. If all that intellectual work could achieve was to bring us closer to its essence, the revealed sources were the final, decisive authority. In this sense al-Juwayni's theology seemed to be more in line with al-Ash'ari's goals than Ibn al-Baqillani's theories were.

But why had the identity of definition and what was being defined, of proof and what was being proven, been so important to Ibn al-Baqillani? Al-Juwayni stated that his precursor had reflected on the contingency of the world and on the world as a sign; the contingent world referred to its ontologically infinitely superior Creator even when no one pointed out this reference. If what could be reached via a definition or proof was only the *knowledge* of what was being defined or proven, then the latter would not exist as long as no one defined or proved it, and the world was not a sign unless someone defined it, nor, consequently, did the One exist of whom the world was a sign.[102]

Al-Juwayni could not dismiss Ibn al-Baqillani's misgivings; in vain had been Ibn al-Baqillani's monumental effort to keep from crumbling altogether the rock on which Islamic theology had rested until then: the stringency of the inference from the "visible" to the "unseen" that had been doubted since al-Ash'ari. According to al-Juwayni, Ibn al-Baqillani had taught that if two objects were considered equal, *all* their characteristics, the most specific as well as the most general ones, needed to have something in common. In this Ibn al-Baqillani took up al-Ash'ari's criticism of the carelessness with which the Mu'tazilites had established analogies between both the two ontological domains and the facts in this world. Ibn al-Baqillani, al-Juwayni continued, had warned that one must not simply ascertain an agreement of the pertinent "most specific" characteristics and from this draw the conclusion that all other characteristics were in agreement as well. If two characteristics of an object related to one another in an identical manner, this never meant that there was necessarily an analogous relationship between the two in another object. There was no hierarchy of qualities; everything must be individually examined case by case. Al-Juwayni tried to make absolutely clear the unrelatedness of qualities which Ibn al-Baqillani had expressed before him: "In our opinion, the fact that someone has knowledge is caused by his knowledge, which holds true for the created world as well as the domain of the uncreated. The point of view from which knowledge is the cause of someone having knowledge is also true in both domains. To clarify this: knowledge in one of us does not cause that person to gain knowledge because it has been engendered in time or is an *accidens* or because it exists. No, these latter qualities can also be confirmed for everything that runs counter to knowledge. Therefore we hold that it lets someone have knowledge only inasmuch as it is knowledge, and in this there is no difference between the knowledge of the eternal God and that of a creature. This proves that both kinds of knowledge are united in the quality that gives someone knowledge. What compels us to assess that someone is 'knowing'—in this the two kinds of knowledge are not different; rather, they have it in common. Yet as far as the other qualities are concerned in which the two kinds of knowledge are different from one another, it is not they that produce the assessment 'knowing.' "

"While the two kinds of knowledge are different from one another, they are united by the fact that they are two kinds of knowledge, and even though they must certainly be assessed differently, they are united in that they relate in the same way to one and the same object. If knowledge is affirmed in the domain of the created, and this knowledge, in order to be knowing, requires the substratum in which it subsists, then nothing can be affirmed that would not share with the substratum this quality but would invest it with a different assessment, because there is no knowledge that does not imply this assessment of the substratum as 'having knowledge.' It is this fact that we mean when we say 'being united.' That this is correct is shown by the created knowledge differing from the 'being united' that holds true for the eternal God only inasmuch as the former was created accidentally, with a possible existence and without the possibility of permanence, whereas the eternal knowledge of such inferior being is superior to it."[103]

The assessment "having knowledge" must be ascribed to the created substratum as well as the Creator because both had "knowledge" concerning one and the same object or fact. It was no longer possible to determine what it meant that they had something in common. The bringing together of the "visible" and the "unseen" which Abu l-Hudhayl and the Mu'tazilites had attempted had become a mere word. Human knowledge was an *accidens* that subsisted in it as the substratum, investing it with the assessment "having knowledge." As a quality of God this knowledge could obviously not be an *accidens*, because God was not a substratum. That is why the Ash'arites did not speak of *accidens* qualities in regard to God either, but of "qualities of meaning." God's knowledge revealed those character traits of the divine being that subsisted in itself—character traits through which this being acquired sense or meaning for creation. Without these "qualities of meaning," God would have been an entirely self-sufficient being that neither could have produced a creation nor would preserve it. "If it is certain that the world was made by the Creator, and if reasonable people recognize its subtlety and they realize how harmonically and artfully, how skillfully and masterfully the heavens and the earth and everything in between is arranged, they perforce reach the conclusion that all this came about only through the work of someone who has the knowledge and power to do this."[104]

It was with the courage of despair—or the obstinacy of someone who refuses to acknowledge his failure—that al-Juwayni drew this conclusion: there was only "necessary" knowledge, whose content had been established in the revelation and which could be clarified through reflection.[105] This knowledge was "necessary" because it was not gained through human effort but caused by God, like all phenomena in the domain of the created, occurring without the creature's doing. This certainly left a bitter aftertaste, for it turned out that the triumph of metaphysics did not entail the *rational* certainty of faith that had been hoped for. As he became older, al-Juwayni increasingly turned toward jurisprudence—for where, if not in this field, was there the kind of knowledge that was established by

God and that could be penetrated by reason, but whose body could not be augmented![106] The provisions of the law, which were passed by God and, therefore, could not be questioned, had the advantage of being looked at as independent entities, without the need to relate them to creation. God's speech was His law, which was beyond all history! Far back, under pressure from the inquisition, the Sunnites had begun to develop the idea that God's speech was an integral part of His being, just like omniscience and omnipotence; the way this supratemporal speech was expressed on earth, however, was in a form that was created.[107] Al-Juwayni relentlessly drew conclusions from this about the content of God's speech: there could not be any relation between this content and concrete facts that could be deduced from causes and illuminated by the knowledge of accompanying circumstances.[108] One reason for the fact that al-Juwayni, who after all was a legal scholar, was not shocked at this turn of his thoughts, was the peculiarity of Islamic law, which does not grow out of concrete experience, but tries to subsume the vast variety of everyday life under the finite number of divine provisions.[109] The other reason was his being firmly grounded in ascetic Sufism, whose center of life was the strict compliance with all rules in the Koran and the *sunna*. The greater the compliance, the greater the certainty to have been selected by God for paradise before the beginning of time.[110]

Let us, at the conclusion of this chapter, attempt to gain clarity on the place of Ash'arite theology within the whole of Islam's religious history. Early rationalism marked an important step on the path away from the feeling-centered nature of paganism (*jahiliyya*). The *hadith*, which could reshape everyday life much more effectively than rationalist theology, worked in exactly this direction: what was being created was the Arab-Islamic society, united by a certain way of thinking, of relating to one's fellow human being, and of perceiving the world—a way that was founded in religion and constantly necessitated by it.[111] The rejection of pagan traditions,[112] which indirectly became an obligation with the introduction of the Muslim calendar, turned into a reality by the turn of the third Islamic century. Still, the traditional views on Arabia's pre-Islamic identity retained their significance as a source of the blossoming of philology. Philology was the most important field of "Arab" scholarship, since it was absolutely essential for interpreting the Koran. As raw material for philological research, and sometimes also as a romanticized alternative to the Islamic urban life, that tradition caught the attention of scholars, who considered it a matter of course that Arabic, the language of the revelation, was Islam's only suitable means of expression, the means chosen by God. Arabic philology and Mu'tazilite theology—the discussion of the subtleties of the inference from the "visible" to the "unseen"—depended on one another and were intertwined. This way of exploring the relationship between this world and the next lived on the rich nuances of the Arabic vocabulary.

However, was Arabic really that "meta-language" that contained the unabridged and unadulterated, transtemporal[113] word of God? Ibn Khuzayma noted that the Arabic word for "face" could not be applied to God without qualification,[114] and the Mu'tazilites of the early tenth century and especially Al-Ash'ari,[115] their renegade, voiced skepticism about the wealth of attributes the Arabic language provided for those who wanted to explain the "unseen" by way of the "visible." Al-Ash'ari's search for a few superordinate terms that could summarize and make abstract the vast number of nuances of Arabic words released theology to some degree from its deep embeddedness in the Arabic vocabulary. Ibn al-Baqillani[116] joined al-Ash'ari in his criticism and turned it into the doctrine that it must be possible to generalize and reverse any logical proof; as we shall see in the next chapter, al-Juwayni would finally abandon the conventional method of deriving the existence of the one Creator, who was infinitely superior to His work, from postulating the world's createdness.[117] In the encounter between and mutual penetration of the Mu'tazilite *kalam*, which endorsed history, and the *hadith*, which wanted history to end with the idealized original community, it became at least possible to overcome the purely Arabic foundation of Islam.

A glance at philology reveals precisely this developmental leap. The grammarian az-Zajjaji (d. 949), for instance, described Arabic as a web of causal relations: the particle *inna*, which introduces a sentence, puts the subject following it into the accusative case *because* this particle itself "resembles a transitive verb."[118] Statements of this kind are not applicable to any other language. The dependency of the early theory of grammar on the essence of Arabic becomes even clearer when we look at the opinion of some scholars who claim that the active participle of the first verb stem can implicitly contain the meaning of the personal pronoun *because* this participle has the same sequence of vowels as the finite form of the verb: the words "*khadim*" (serving) and "*yakhdim*" (he serves) distribute the vowels "a" and "i" in exactly the same sequence over the root *kh-d-m*.[119] "Explanations" of this kind make sense only for Arabic; they are entirely inapplicable to other languages.

The Andalusian Ibn Hazm (d. 1064), on the other hand, the proponent of a kind of jurisprudence and theology that was firmly based on the tradition, was seeking a philology that would distill from the revelation's Arabic words the meaning God had had in mind; in other words, he believed that the Arabic phrases were not a direct expression of the content of God's message. He taught that language went back to divine teachings, but in the course of human history it had changed. It was impossible to know today what language God had taught Adam; its words had probably fit very clearly the things and facts they named,[120] an ideal state of affairs that Ibn Hazm believed was no longer true even for Arabic. Arabic sank down to the level of humankind's other languages, and now it was the scholars' task to find out the real meaning of Arabic texts and to protect them from distortion.

The partial profaning of Arabic became the necessary requirement for equating the entire treasure of the meaningful and useful knowledge humankind can gain with the revelation that was conveyed first to Adam and in the end to Muhammad, which is why it could be appropriated as part of "Islam," regardless of the cultures in which fragments of this knowledge were first recorded. This process of equating the two occurred in the late nineteenth century and will be discussed in the last chapter of this book.

CHAPTER VI

Theology and Philosophy

1. Exoteric and Esoteric Meaning of the Revelation

The Ash'arite school put the method of practicing theology as developed by the Mu'tazila into the service of a faith in whose center was the
emulation of the Prophet's *sunna*. The Ash'arites had significantly modified the content of Mu'tazilite theology according to their Sunni convictions; the direction of speculation had changed. The Mu'tazilites had tried
to deduce God's way of acting from creation's character as a sign, and,
therefore, subtly reflected on human nature and behavior. In contrast, for
Ash'arites it was the sense of the creature's complete dependency on the
One's inscrutable ways that was *the* basic fact to which all theology had
to bow. Yet what Mu'tazilites and Ash'arites still had in common was the
concept of the ultimate goal of Islamic theology: defending faith against
outside influence and building a construct of arguments that were related
to, but not contradicting, one another—arguments that were supposed to
make the principles of Islam unassailable and give Muslims the certainty
of possessing the definitive truth.

Ibn Khaldun's (d. 1406) introduction to historiography includes a look
at the development of Islamic theology. As already noted, he supported
the general view that the *kalam* had been developed for the purpose of
fending off anti-Islamic theories.[1] Now, he argued, in the fourteenth century, there was no longer any need for the *kalam*, but it was still useful to
study it, for it provided the rational arguments supporting the truth of
Islam. Ibn Khaldun declared that the *kalam* was still a viable path toward
attaining certainty of faith, but he also explicitly mentioned the harm it—
ultimately an un-Islamic "reform" (*bid'a*)—had once caused: the
Mu'tazilites did not put an end to their speculations soon enough, but
attacked even those Muslims who had based their faith simply on the revelation and entirely rejected rationalism. In the waning ninth century, Ibn
Khaldun continued, al-Ash'ari came and attempted to mediate between

Mu'tazilites and Sunnites. Ibn Khaldun recognized that Ibn al-Baqillani's theology was based on a few very simple metaphysical premises which, subordinate only to the basic truths of Islamic faith, essentially signified a development of al-Ash'ari's theories: the created world consisted of individual particles, each of which represented the smallest unit of created being; they were surrounded by empty space, unless they did not somewhere touch another particle of their kind; they were carriers of *accidentes*; an *accidens* could not be the carrier of another *accidens*; it existed only within the span of one "atom" of time.[2] "When the theologians invented the science of the speculative theology [the *kalam*], in order to support the articles of faith with rational evidence, their approach was to use some particular evidence. . . . Thus, they proved the createdness of the world by affirming that accidents . . . are created, that bodies cannot possibly be free from accidents, and that something that cannot be free from created things must itself be created. . . . Then they strengthened that evidence [supporting their assumptions] by inventing basic principles constituting a sort of premise for the evidence. Thus, they affirmed the existence of atomic matter and atomic time and the vacuum. They denied nature and the intellectual combination of quiddities."[3]

It made no sense for Ash'arite Islam to construe facts intellectually or to assume the causal relationship one had observed about two or more facts to be actually existing and to make inferences from this. Only what existed at a certain moment in time was a "thing," and only statements about a "thing" were appropriate and meaningful. Ibn Khaldun continued by saying that the Ash'arites had postulated the exchangeability of proof and what was being proven, for faith would have to be wrong if the arguments supporting it were false. In Ibn Khaldun's brief outline of the history of Islamic theology, the discussion of Ibn al-Baqillani was followed by a look at al-Juwayni, the scholar from Nishapur. He, Ibn Khaldun said, gave us the *Book of Instruction*, a comprehensive description of Ash'arite ideas that was used as a textbook. "After that, the science of logic spread in Islam. . . . [People] made a distinction between it and the philosophical sciences, in that [they stated that] logic was merely a norm and yardstick for arguments and served to probe the arguments of the [philosophical sciences] as well as [those of] all other [disciplines]. [Scholars,] then, studied the basic premises the earlier theologians had established. . . .

Many of these [older arguments] were derived from philosophical discussions of physics and metaphysics. When they probed them with the yardstick of logic, it showed that they were applicable [only] to those [other disciplines and not to theology, but] they did not believe that if the arguments were wrong, the thing proven [by the arguments] was also wrong, as had been the opinion of the Judge [Ibn al-Baqillani]. . . . [The approach of recent scholars] often included refutation of the philosophers where the [opinions of the] latter differed from the articles of faith. They considered the (philosophers) enemies of the articles of faith, because, in most respects, there is a relationship between the opinions of the innovators and the opinions of the philosophers."

In a few words Ibn Khaldun described the fundamental change theology underwent in the eleventh century, when it came under the influence of philosophy (which had already been Islamized). It turned out that the line of argument that had become standard since the waning ninth century—guiding students from epistemology and the explanation of the createdness of the world to an outline of the divine law—turned out to be no longer tenable. According to Ibn Khaldun, it was the philosophical tradition that had unhinged Mu'tazilite theology which bore sole responsibility for this. However, we have seen that even al-Juwayni had had doubts about whether the Ash'arite school would reach its goal of establishing ultimate certainty of faith. In a theological monograph dedicated to Nizam al-Mulk, he had attempted to distance himself from the traditional way of explaining Islamic theology (which al-Ash'ari, among others, had followed as well): proof that the world was created; then the inference that it could only be the work of *one* Creator. Instead, the discussion was now ruled by the logical categories of necessity, possibility, and impossibility: the possible needed a Creator so it could enter into existence, and one had to ascribe to it the necessity of being so that no *regressus in infinitum* would occur.[4]

What caused the change was probably self-doubt in tandem with the knowledge of the new—the philosophical—tradition. Ibn Khaldun indicated that he could not praise it without qualification. He considered the method—or, as he called it, the norms of logic—to be useful; they revealed the weaknesses of the old theology. Physics and metaphysics were useless as a basis for proving theological doctrines; but it also turned out that the logic of philosophy could not be brought into perfect agreement with them. However, if logic and its methods of proof were insufficient, this did not necessarily mean that the pertinent doctrine was not true. The influence of philosophy strengthened and deepened the realization that had been closed to Ibn al-Baqillani and was not made until al-Juwayni: that rationalism and revelation could not be brought into perfect agreement with each other. The influence of philosophy inevitably led to the question of what counted more: philosophy or the revelation. After all the Ash'arite *mutakallimun*'s efforts to preserve God and the content of His speech as the most important element, the answer could no longer be uncertain.

That philosophy and the revelation are rivals that cannot coexist as equals, but try to dominate the other, is a basic fact of the intellectual history of Islam. The philosophical interpretations of existence must not be examined and viewed as imperfect but as absolutely serious attempts to get to the truths of the revelation even before they were revealed (attempts that were possible in Christianity as far back as the second century). Justinus Martyr (executed around 165) had recognized in Jesus Christ the personification of divine reason, of "logos," which had now been given to humankind in its entirety; yet, even before Christ, God had given the various peoples fragments of the ultimate truth. Plato's theories were largely in agreement with Christianity: all human beings "who have lived according to reason" must have been Christians.[5] What a difference to Islam! The relationship between the revelation and ancient philosophy was not even an issue for Muhammad. He had to see to it that he was recognized, especially in Medina, as the last link in the chain of prophets and that people believed that he preached to God's creatures His unadulterated, never-changing message. Within the construct of Islam's concept of history, which began with the *hijra*, the clear demarcation between Quraysh-Meccan paganism and Medinese piousness, any tradition that was not derived from a revelation was not only considered flawed yet nonetheless valuable to a certain degree, but downright false. From the tenth century on, the Aristotelian and Neoplatonic tradition was to have an enormous impact on Islamic scholars, but only under two aspects: either confined to logic, as a tool that was separated from the intellectual context in which it had been developed—or as a construct made of statements that could be traced back to the revelation.

Ibn Khaldun explained that the "modern" *mutakallimun* adopted the first point of view. They used logic in order to fix the flaws of Ash'arite theology, but at the same time to prove the validity of the content of the philosophical tradition. We will discuss this in more detail in a different context. Averroes (1126–98), the commentator of Aristotle's works, tried to defend his life's work from the second point of view. Around 1180 he wrote a short treatise entitled "The Last Word and Explanation of the Connection between the Revealed Law and Philosophy." At the beginning of his examination, Averroes adopted the point of view the Ash'arites had also shared: that the revelation itself required a rational corroboration of its doctrines. Since this tremendous task could not be undertaken from scratch by every human being, one must needs study the ancients' writings. Those who denied the astute and—according to the Sharia's rules—innocent believers this right, kept them from truly recognizing God. However, if the law called on us to do this, which one could naturally not expect unsuitable men to undertake, then speculation that employed syllogisms could not lead to results that were not covered by that law. Averroes, a legal scholar himself, referred to parallels in the scholarly field of the Sharia[6]; by using syllogisms one could find something in that field, too, which was lacking in the extant sources. "And if the Sharia does make a statement (relating its findings), this statement can be either in agreement with the result that was achieved, or it can contradict it. If there is agreement, there is nothing to add. If there is a contradiction, however, then one must attempt to interpret (*ta'wil*) (the text of the Sharia). 'Interpretation' means the transformation of the actual meaning of a phrase into a metaphorical meaning," without however violating the rules of Arab rhetoric.

Averroes asked, if a legal scholar had to proceed in that manner, how much more so did someone who was knowledgeable in pure, non-purpose-oriented syllogism? The legal scholar, he argued, always had to accept that his analogies were only probably correct; yet the theological scholar obtained certainty! Whenever the conclusion of a logical inference contradicted the tradition, the text *must* allow an interpretation, Averroes declared categorically. "How certain of this are those who have practiced it and tested it, those, in other words, who have striven for the unification of what reason has recognized and tradition!" Everyone, Ash'arites and Hanbalites, had interpreted the revelation in this manner. God had imbued the holy texts with an exoteric and an esoteric meaning because human beings had such different dispositions; in order for some people really to believe they needed to do mental work; they had to struggle with contradictions in order finally, after finding the correct interpretation, to sense an even increased certainty.[7] Yet that which "reason has recognized" developed long before the influence of the Koran. Since it was in accordance with the revelation—after it had been interpreted accordingly—Averroes elevated its rank, in a second step of reasoning, so to speak, to that of an object worthy of Muslim scholarship.

The early Ash'arites had made the question of whether the world was eternal or created in time the point of departure from where they started their theology. This plainly illustrates how precarious Averroes's theory became when it was to be proven by applying it to concrete issues. He stated that the debate between the "ancient philosophers" and the Ash'arites was about nothing but terminology; for they all agreed that there were three kinds of beings, two that were clearly distinct from one another, and a third one in between. There was also agreement on what the two distinct beings should be called. One comprised things that were generated from something else, from matter and as the consequence of a cause, with the factor of time present even before their creation. These were the bodies, whose process of becoming was perceived by the senses. Philosophers like the Ash'arites called them "created in time" (*muhdath*). The kind of being that was clearly distinct from this one was the eternal God, who caused everything to be and who preserved it. He did not come into being from and was not caused by something; He was not preceded by time. The middle kind of being, however, the one that was between these two, "did not come into existence from something else, and neither was it preceded by time, but it was generated by a cause—by the one who brings everything about. This [third] kind is the world as a whole." The Ash'arites would confirm that the vast number of phenomena around us were created by God, and God, the Creator, had been before these phenomena. He had also been before the beginning of time, which had been created by Him as well, along with the world. Yet what about the special status of the "world as a whole"? After all, Ash'arite theology, and even the entire early *kalam*, did not distinguish between it and the individual phenomena, but—not least in its battle against the "natural philosophers"—saw both of them together as a single entity, as that which was created.

In maintaining that "everyone" agreed on the "three-ness" of everything that existed, Averroes imputed to the Ash'arites a stand they had never taken. He substantiated his thesis as follows: "The *mutakallimun* concede that nothing precedes time; or this is what necessarily follows [from their theories], for according to them, time is dependent on the [existence of] movements and bodies; they further agree with the ancients on future time being infinite and future being as well." This was true inasmuch as, in Ash'arite understanding, paradise and hell lasted forever. What was controversial, Averroes continued, was only the past, which, as Plato believed as well, was not without a beginning, while Aristotle held that it had existed forever. Those who recognized in that third kind of being a preponderance of the beginningless eternal, called it eternal, and vice versa. Therefore the *mutakallimun* were wrong when they forced the "world as whole"[8] into the first category of being.

These explanations were hardly apt to convince an Ash'arite that he would find in philosophy a worthwhile field of activity. On the contrary, everything that appeared finally to have been overcome in the ninth and tenth centuries now reappeared again! The remark that Ash'arites had practiced exegesis as well because the revelation, too, contained nothing about a God who had existed next to the absolute nothing before creation,[9] hardly did Averroes any good. From his point of view, Averroes was right, but he lost sight of the intellectual-historical conditions that shaped the goals of early rationalism: the rejection of any world view that might question the one personal Creator-God whom Muhammad had proclaimed. Furthermore, in order to embed the philosophical heritage of antiquity in Islamic theology, Averroes fell back on the difference between the exoteric meaning of the revelation and its esoteric meaning, which was accessible to only a few.[10] This reminded his audience, whom his treatise was meant to win over to his side rather than repel, of certain facts that were bound to be detrimental to his cause.

2. A Glance at the Intellectual History of Islam during the High Middle Ages

In the Islamic world the eleventh century was a time of political and intellectual fermentation and of a profound transformation; urban Islamic culture, whose rise coincided with the victory of the Hashimiyya movement, began to decline the moment it had the opportunity to conclude fully its development: Islam appeared to be a construct of doctrines put together with rational arguments. The doctrine's content was derived from the word of God and the norm-setting example of the Prophet. In the daily rites and the Sharia, which regulated peoples' entire lives, Islam manifested itself to all believers as a powerful reality on which they had to and were allowed to count in order ultimately to obtain salvation. It was preserved, interpreted, and applied to the vicissitudes of life by a social stratum of scholars that was connected with the wielders of political and military power in a complex, albeit not conflict-free, way.[11] It was Nizam al-Mulk's great vision to make this state of (Sunni) Islam permanent by turning it into a political goal of the whole empire. The sultanate was supposed to make the support and victory of Sunnism its own concern; it was supposed to fight other religious movements and take care of the training of scholars who were to fight this battle and simultaneously consolidate the Sunni Muslims' ties to the Sharia's norms.

Yet those in power, on whom Nizam al-Mulk relied for that purpose, could not be bound by these goals forever. Still firmly rooted in inner-Asian nomadism, instead of fulfilling Nizam al-Mulk's desires and preserving peace, they turned their weapons against each other in endless conflicts. This was the beginning of several centuries of political unrest, in whose wake the very foundation of the urban elites was impaired and in some parts of the Islamic world even destroyed. Furthermore, deep rifts developed among Sunni scholars that in various ways overlapped and intersected with the political powers that be. Ash'arite rationalism was by no means uncontroversial even within Sunnism. Some regarded it as a dangerously far-reaching concession to the Mu'tazilites, who once had persecuted Ahmad ibn Hanbal and other *sunna* experts. It was said that in the battle with his inquisitors Ahmad himself, who was vividly remembered especially in Baghdad, had expressly refused to argue on the level of the *kalam*.[12] Was Ash'arism not pure *kalam* as well? In Baghdad in the mid-eleventh century, there occurred several acts of violence against Sunnites who were known to practice theology according to al-Ash'ari. Al-Juwayni made derogatory remarks about those inner-Sunni enemies, whom he charged with adhering to offensively naive anthropomorphist ideas; furthermore, he criticized them for not distinguishing between the uncreated-eternal Koran, which as a nontemporal speech in the form of a "meaningful quality" was an inseparable part of the Creator, and its representation in this world in the form of created sounds or letters. By contrast, they believed that it contained a fragment of the divine being within the created world, and ascribed to the written or recited text of the Koran magic effects.[13] This was an inkling of Islam's world view of the late Middle Ages, which was to reassemble the cosmos to a single entity after the Ash'arites had split it into individual atoms without the capacity to form a whole of their own accord. To be sure, al-Juwayni contemptuously called his opponents "blabbermouths"—which was the very term the Mu'tazilites had used for the Sunnites during the inquisition.

The threat for Sunnism and its political order posed by the Sevener Shia and the Fatimid agents, respectively, was far from under control in the eleventh century. While controversies about the succession to the throne weakened the caliphate in Cairo, its propaganda agents operated successfully in the Seljuq sultanate. The man who was feared the most was Hasan-i Sabbah from Qum, who since 1071 held a high office within the Isma'ilite propaganda machine in Iran. In 1076 he went to Cairo for three years to receive training. Back in Iran, he conquered the eyrie of Alamut for his country in 1090. His agents, among them assassins, spread fear and terror, infesting even the Seljuq dynasty with insecurity and suspicion. Nizam al-Mulk's murder in 1092 was allegedly their doing, and perhaps it was carried out with the secret permission of Sultan Malikshah, who had long since been in a feud with his vizier.[14]

Nizam al-Mulk had added to his handbook on political science a chapter on the Sevener Shia's activities,[15] which implies just how seriously he took it. If toward the end of the tenth century it seemed as if its momentum was getting lost,[16] it now became clear that this hope had been treacherous. In his textbook on sects and true Sunni faith, Shahfur Tahir wrote extensively on "the movement of the esoteric meaning" (*batiniyya*) and described the methods of its propaganda agents. Everything he said indicates that his understanding of the theories of the Sevener Shia was somewhat simple; he saw in them everything the Sunnites abhorred, an odd mixture of the views of the dualists and the "natural philosophers." The Sharia's authorities, he said, had tried to interpret that movement allegorically: ritual obligations referred to the religious veneration of the Shiite imams, and the prohibitions discreetly forbade the reverence of Abu Bakr, 'Umar, and of all the other enemies of the "esoteric meaning." They understood the angels to be their secret agents, the Sunni scholars were devils, "and (the Sevener Shiites) called everyone who agreed with their (evil) innovation 'believers,' and their opponents 'asses' or 'movement of the exoteric meaning.'"[17]

The polemic treatise al-Ghazali (d. 1111) devoted to the "movement of the esoteric meaning" is much more profound. He, too, charges it with interpreting the meaning of the law, which was comprehensible to everyone, in the manner Shahfur had indicated; according to al-Ghazali they had to proceed in that manner, otherwise it would become immediately clear that they—unbelievers who they really were—were categorically calling God's message a lie. In order not to risk life and limb, they chose to recognize the Sharia, but to ascribe to it a new meaning. They declared "lechery" to be a betrayal of one's inner knowledge to someone uninitiated; "ritual purity" was achieved by those who abandoned all other beliefs and paid reverence only to the imam; "fasting" meant exercising the arcane discipline. In their view, the Muslims' eschatological beliefs, the fire of hell and the chains fettering the condemned meant the Sharia's rules, which were forced only on those who were lacking in "esoteric knowledge." Sura 47, verse 15 promised that rivers of milk flow in paradise; it was "esoteric knowledge" on which true believers fed. "And rivers of wine"—exoteric knowledge; "rivers, too, of honey purified"— the "esoteric knowledge" originating from the imams. Al-Ghazali also stated that the Sevener Shiites considered the Prophet's miracles to be nothing but allegories: the deluge was the flood of true knowledge in which all Sunnites drowned, and Noah's Ark was the amulet that protected everyone who followed the imams' calling.[18]

The battle against the "movement of the esoteric meaning" created a strange situation for the Sunni *mutakallimun*. Fighting that battle, they had to reject categorically the arbitrary allegories which the Sevener Shiites called "interpretations"; for in Sunnism, the center of life was in the literal understanding of what had been passed on of the Prophet's example. At the same time, however, the *mutakallimun* also had to do "exegesis," not only to classify any new legal problem among the unalterable categories of statements in the Koran and the *hadith*, but also to resolve the theological controversy over what the *visio beatifica* was and how it was to take place. It is worth noting that the panacea that al-Ghazali fervently wished would make believers immune to the Sevener Shia's temptations was no longer the rational teachings on the content of Sunni faith, but pious self-moderation, which reformed the heart, the seat of reason, and restrained the instinctive soul. Rational use of the intellect suggested renouncing the fleeting pleasures of this world—for the sake of obtaining the eternal joys of the next world. Those who did not understand that would leave this world moaning and full of repentance.[19] It almost seems as if under the painful impression of the futility of rationally defending its own faith and rationally striving for ultimate certainty, Sunnism's early perspective on the world and the Muslims' task in it had returned—with all its skepticism of man's responsibility for applying his faculty of reason.

In the eleventh century Sharia Islam reached its conclusion. It now consisted of a sophisticated mechanism of procedures through which any phenomenon of everyday life or the cult could be traced back to the Koran or the *sunna*. Not only were there the institutions of jurisprudence, culminating in the office of the Qadi, but also the Muftis, the rulers' consultants, who used these very sources to decide which action was Islamic and which was not; and in cases of doubt, ordinary persons, too, could and should seek and follow their advice. The Sharia had become the unifying center of all Sunni Muslims. Sufism's ascetically inclined piousness surely played an important part in this outcome.[20] What its eminent representatives had preached and ostentatiously lived since the eighth century, now seemed to have become common knowledge. At precisely that moment, when all Sunni endeavors were successful—the moment Nizam al-Mulk tried to make last through his policies—Sufism began to look for other goals. Life as the fulfillment of the Sharia and more was losing its attraction.

There were those who wanted to unite with God not by submitting to His law, that is to say, by accepting and appropriating something outside of themselves, but who felt the divine radiate in themselves and lived an Islamic way of life from that experience as their starting point. They were still considered odd, and they certainly knew they were outsiders. Abu Sa'id ibn abi l-Khair (d. 1049) embodied this new type of Sufi in many respects. His piousness was not characterized by an oppressive scrupulousness, but by his desire to remain happy. He did not consider God the petty judge whose harshness should make the believer despair; His mercy outweighed His anger. Even in this world one should think of God with joy and not fear. "Know, o Muslims, that you will not be without burden! If you carry the burden of (the) reality (God has imposed on you), you will find peace and joy in this world, and you will find it in the future, too. Otherwise the wrong burden is placed on your shoulders, whereby you will find peace and joy neither in this world nor in the next."[21] Music, and not the repetition of the minutest details of the Sharia or fearfully pondering about possible misdemeanors, appeared to Abu Sa'id as the suitable means to unlock the Sufis' hearts to let in the reality of God.

For Najm ad-Din Kubra (d. 1221) the goal of Sufism was letting go of one's personality and the appearance of the personal God. Reaching this goal did not necessarily entail strictly following the law. "At first the qualities of your personality, reprehensible as well as commendable ones, will unbecome," he pronounced. At the first inkling of God's appearance inside the Sufi, his obligation toward the revealed law became immaterial. "At first you are covered by . . . the qualities . . . (of) God, by the qualities of both sublimeness and friendliness. Now there no longer is a person outside of His person. And thus you will now find realized the prophecy: Whose is the Kingdom today? God's, the One, the Omnipotent (sura 40, verse 16)! On the level of the revelation of one's nature, 'God' means 'the One' because 'One' in no way tolerates a second, other, likewise existing one besides Himself. . . . 'Omnipotent' means 'One' because He conquers the denizens of isolation through His oneness. . . ."[22] God's conquest of the Sufi's ego lets the latter participate in divine being; the huge ontological distance between the Creator and the creature, which the *kalam* set out to justify and explain to all Muslims, was now eliminated in moments of supreme expectation of salvation.

Some precursors of this kind of Sufism are documented even for the tenth century; yet something was lacking in their lives that distinguished their successors in the high and late Middle Ages: leaving the sphere of life of the ordinary Sunni Muslims, the later Sufis' spirituality established a space of devotion to God that was not accessible to everyone—a space *next to* the everyday, one that was organized after Muhammad's model and the rites. The Sufis grew together, forming religious orders that cultivated rites to prepare for the experience of the mystical union, rites that were different than the ordinary ones. Disciples would gather around their masters, who took on an air of sanctity and were revered as teachers of the right path toward the direct experience of God. Rulers as well as ordinary people began to recognize in them mediators of a relationship with God that secured salvation. These holy men, whether or not educated in law, rose to become powerful rivals of the legal scholars. In the late and high Middle Ages, there were *two* paths along which Muslims could gain entry into paradise: as before, they could take the path the Sharia had shown them, but they could also choose the one outside of scholarship, which promised them direct contact with the One in the here and now. The second path became increasingly attractive in the thirteenth and fourteenth centuries, an era of disastrous crises and unfathomable threats to survival, but even then adept and persistent defenders of the Sharia spoke up.[23]

Let us summarize the facts that are indispensable for an understanding of the relationship between the theology and philosophy of medieval Islam. Ash'arism—the Sunni *kalam*—was suspected of undermining Sunni piousness and turning into a kind of Mu'tazila itself. Its opponents had attacked the Mu'tazila not least because it was allegedly unable to attain certainty of salvation; on the contrary, it was accused of unintentionally carrying into Islam the ideas of the enemy, which it was supposed to invalidate. At the end of his polemic against the "movement of the esoteric meaning," al-Ghazali pleaded, not in favor of the teachings of the Sunni *kalam*, but of the ethical beliefs all Sunni persuasions had in common; the faculty of reason did not seem to be up to the task of rejecting the Sevener Shia's "interpretations." Sufism, which had advanced the development of a Sunni theology at the turn of the tenth century, underwent a fundamental transformation. The direct experience of God, without first studying the law and the ways it can be applied to everyday life, became the highest goal. Clearly, the intellectual climate was no longer favorable for a productive study of the philosophical tradition on the part of Sunni scholars. It is equally obvious that Averroes's phrase about the "esoteric meaning" of the revelation, laid bare by philosophy, led to reservation rather than enthusiasm in regard to outside ideas. Since the late eleventh century, professing Ash'arism was severely criticized among Sunni circles; but even stronger was evidently a rejection of a field of scholarship whose goals and methods seemed to be in agreement with the feared and hated Sevener Shia. Only in the Iran of the Mongol period (c. 1260–1335) was it considered an honor if people said about a scholar that he had gained prominence in the fields "of belief *and* of Greek thought." Yet religious and social conditions there were entirely different from those in Syria or Egypt; the old educated urban class, which had produced the representatives of Sharia scholarship, had been expelled or eradicated in disastrous wars; the Mongol rulers, who at first were not yet Islamized and later on rather reserved toward Sunnism,[24] loved astronomy, natural philosophy, astrology, and similar "Greek" sciences. They attracted the few experts in these areas from all Islamic territories.[25]

3. Islamic Philosophy

Typically the history of the Muslims' acquisition of ancient sciences, including philosophy, begins with the "House of Wisdom," an institution whose task it was to produce translations into Arabic. Initially not the Greek originals were used but the existing Syrian versions. Yet Hunain ibn Ishaq (809–73), the most eminent and conscientious conveyor of the wisdom of antiquity, acquired some knowledge of Greek. Before translating a work, he would compile several manuscripts and compare the different text versions. His main focus was on Aristotle, whose works were almost completely translated already, as well as on Galen; Hunain ibn Ishaq alone is supposed to have edited and translated into Arabic one hundred twenty-nine of the latter's treatises.[26] In all of this we must always keep in mind that all philosophical and scientific sources of antiquity were not available to men like Hunain ibn Ishaq, but that they knew them in their late Hellenistic, abbreviated versions and interpretations. Still, we owe them the knowledge of some works whose original texts have been lost. The Muslims received some of the ancient heritage not only via the Baghdad "House of Wisdom," but also via Alexandria and Harran. It seems, however, that philosophy was mainly cultivated in Baghdad.[27]

Apart from writings that had been used in late Hellenistic schools, there were doxographic works that have to be regarded as a consequence of early Islam's grappling with ancient philosophy. For instance, a treatise probably from the ninth century that was ascribed to Ammonios Hermeneiou contained quotes attributed to (and partly documented in the works of) numerous ancient authors. These quotes, however, had not been compiled by the unidentified Arab author, but probably by the Father of the Church Hippolytus (d. A.D. 235). The Arab author did not edit these fragments with the intention of illustrating the various lines of Greek thought, but fit them into the mold of the late ancient, Neoplatonic *weltanschauung* that also shaped early Islamic philosophy.[28]

In its choice of words and style, this text resembles that of al-Kindi (d. 873),[29] who has been called the first philosopher of Islam and even *the* "philosopher of the Arabs." Al-Kindi cultivated relations with the caliphs al-Ma'mun and al-Mu'tasim, and as a theologian is considered to have held Mu'tazilite views. Yet he deviated from generally accepted basic concepts of Islam in essential issues, and his writings already reveal those philosophical trains of thought which were to create a serious conflict between that field and theology. On the basis of comparisons with other religions, al-Kindi declared he had reached the conclusion that the world was the work of one eternal and homogeneous cause. This cause could be identified as God. With this view, he was in sharp contrast to the Islamic revelation, which talks about a personal Creator-God who through an arbitrary act caused the world to exist at a point in time chosen by Him. A cause, on the other hand, always has to have an effect and is not subjected to His inscrutable ways. In other words, according to al-Kindi, the world was the work of God but His acts could be equated with a cause. This supreme cause was passed down through many steps. Everything that happened in the world revealed a consistent causality; for example, the constellation of stars and planets let us predict the future. The divine spirit and the material world emanating from it were held together by the

world soul. Every human being's soul was to a certain degree an emanation of and took part in this world soul. The human soul was a simple,
immortal substance; it had been thrown into this material world and
longed to be delivered from it. This clearly indicates that the ancient tradition al-Kindi followed was influenced by Gnostic motifs.

The world in which we live, the world of growth and decay, was fick-
le and, therefore, calamitous. Human beings obtained salvation by lifting
themselves into the sphere of reason, the fear of God, and of science. Yet,
if we pursued material goods, we wanted something that did not really
exist. This, too, was no doubt a Gnostic idea; the transient world was
devalued. Just like everything we could learn could be divided into spiritual and sensual, so our knowledge, too, was essentially twofold. It could
be based on the senses, which perceived only individual things or material forms; but it could also originate from the spiritual, the general. As
early a philosopher as al-Kindi held a theory of the intellect (*'aql*) that
was to be characteristic of later Islamic philosophy. Al-Kindi distinguished four kinds of intellect: one, the intellect that was always active,
the cause and nature of everything spiritual in the world, the first created
spirit; two, the spirit as a rational disposition or capacity of the human
soul; three, the spirit as the appearance or true property of the soul, which
could apply it at any given moment like a writer does his craft; and finally, four, the spirit as actor which transferred everything the soul carried
within itself into external reality.[30]

In al-Kindi's work, all actions seemed to be man's own deeds, while he
ascribed the transference of capacity into appearance, or the realization of
the potential, to the first cause, the eternally working spirit. We recognize
that, in this theory, the created human being partook indirectly, via several steps, in the divine spirit. The latter was the eternally active intellect
that was, in other words, in its essence identical with God; it was the first
cause of everything that existed. We can clearly see that in this theory of
the intellect the basic truth of Islam's revelation—that God created the
world and resided beyond it, being the entirely other—was glossed over.
God turned into an impersonal, inspiring, activating force. The individual
creatures partook in it in a certain way. Al-Kindi tried to cover up this fundamental contradiction to Islamic theology by using a terminology that
was validated by the revelation. For instance, for the supreme power

which Neoplatonism called the one from which the entire cosmos emanated, he used the term "the One and True" (*al-wahid al-haqq*), which was also a common term for the God of Islam. Particularly in connection with Sufism it referred to God as the supreme truth.

Yet this was not the only regard in which this philosopher was in distinct opposition to basic Islamic beliefs. Al-Kindi taught that human beings were able to increase gradually their knowledge of the world by way of the four kinds of intellect. The knowledge human beings could acquire of their own accord was gained through hard work following certain rules. The prophets, on the other hand, received divine knowledge through inspiration; this knowledge was so condensed that the philosophers had to do a tremendous amount of research to explain all aspects of their knowledge.[31] Yet the philosophers did not depend on these revelations; rather, it was their goal to obtain the truth and recognize each thing's nature independently. This was possible once the cause of its existence and its life span had been recognized, because everything that existed had its own particular truth, its unmistakable nature. The truth was found in the things of this world, it did not need to be imposed on it or inscribed in it from outside, by God. Philosophy decidedly questioned the revelation's claim to universal validity, for it was philosophy and not the Prophet's speech that advanced toward the "knowledge of the first truth that is the cause of every truth."

Al-Kindi saw four causes: matter; form; the cause that was active and initiated all movement; and the one that concluded everything, subjecting every thing to its destination. The knowledge of matter, form, and final cause yielded a definition of every thing that was sufficient to determine its truth.[32] Al-Kindi practiced the kind of philosophy in the Aristotelian tradition, which took its point of departure from the facts of the perceivable world. As al-Ash'ari correctly noted,[33] this philosophy had its parallels in the Mu'tazilite inference from the "visible" to the "unseen," and the circles around al-Ma'mun and al-Mu'tasim seem to have regarded al-Kindi as a brother in spirit. Still, the answer to the question about the radical differences in the goals of Mu'tazilite and philosophical arguments invalidates that equation. The Mu'tazilites needed a rationally comprehensible world with organic traits in order to connect it with the personal Creator-God in a way that let them also conceive of God as the just judge;

therefore the innerworldly events had to be deciphered more and more accurately so that God's justice could be increasingly understood. The Murjiite al-Maturidi as well as al-Ash'ari and his students declared that undertaking illusory; they sensed that it could misfire and turn into an attack on the majesty of the sovereign One. In the Aristotelian al-Kindi's view, the nature of all things that he recognized was initially entirely independent; it did not need to corroborate the Creator's justice. For this very reason al-Kindi, whose intellectual cosmos was defined by the message of a personal God who promulgated laws, eventually did seek to justify his philosophy by the standard of the rules of reasoning which Islam had established. Al-Kindi had no other choice than—comparable to Justinus Martyr—to praise the great philosophers of the eras preceding the revelation: while the theological aspects of their works did not anticipate the truth as pronounced by God, they did prepare the ground for it. To be sure, no matter how often al-Kindi, the philosopher, may have pointed out the pure intentions of his thoughts, his explanation to the effect that it was the goal of philosophy to acquire the entire knowledge the reliable messengers of God had conveyed to humankind[34] could hardly invalidate the Muslim objection that this was precisely why his field of scholarship was so reprehensibly pretentious. *All* knowledge, al-Ash'ari and his school would declare from the tenth century on, was gained through instruction; all knowledge germinating in man was directly related to God.

The years spanning the ninth to the eleventh centuries, the climax of theological rationalism when it was respected even among the top strata of society, was still relatively favorably inclined toward philosophy; in general these centuries exhibited a readiness to acknowledge the achievements of non-Islamic peoples and to abstain from narrowing the history of humankind before Muhammad to a history of the prophets' proclamation of God's ever-same words from Adam on.[35] With the victory of Sunnism, but also through Ash'arite theology (which had sprouted from its own soil), such openness gradually disappeared. Still, the ideas of philosophy, albeit suppressed and denounced as counter-Islamic, lived on almost clandestinely in theology.

Al-Farabi (d. 950), a philosopher from Turkestan who in 942 accepted an appointment to the court of the Hamdanid Sayf ad-Daula in Aleppo, was reverently referred to in the philosophical writings of medieval

Arabia as the "second teacher"—after Aristotle, the first teacher. From the eleventh century on, al-Farabi's metaphysics strongly influenced theology, which, however, was not expressly acknowledged by theologians. Al-Farabi divided everything that existed into a necessary and a possible being. In order to become real, the possible being needed a cause. If the sequence of causes was not to continue ad infinitum, a necessary being must be posited which was self-sufficient, without the need for a cause. Al-Farabi conceived of it as something immutable, as an absolute spirit, as kindness and beauty that transcended everything, as pure reflection, at once thinking and being thought. This last, necessary being could not be proven, since it was proof and original cause of all things in itself; it was God. Human beings tried to give this supreme being the most beautiful names they knew; yet these names were but utterly imperfect, because they stemmed from the possible being of our own world. They should have been understood only metaphorically, as a weak reflection of the reality of that necessary being.[36] Areas where ideas of the Mu'tazilites and their predecessors, the Jahmites, on the one hand, and the philosophers, on the other, overlapped were not all that rare, but in evaluating these analogies we must not forget their different intentions.

We were unable to comprehend God properly. Yet we were more able to recognize the various steps in which beings emanated from Him. The cosmos originated in Him, the only One, for His all-comprehensive knowledge was the supreme power. The world came into being by recognizing itself. Not an omnipotent Creator-will, but (self-)realization of the necessary was the cause of all things. From the beginning, God contained the forms or models of things, and His image emanated from Him in all eternity—the second cosmos or the first created spirit, which moved the outer celestial sphere. The eight spirits of the spheres, which were perfect in their own way and created the celestial bodies, followed it, one after the other. These nine spirits, called heavenly angels, together formed the second step of being. On the third step was reason, which was at work in humankind and connected heaven and earth. The fourth step was occupied by the soul. Both reason and soul did not form unities remaining all by themselves, but multiplied according to the multiplicity of human beings. As beings of the fifth and sixth order, finally, form and matter appeared, which concluded the sequence of being. The first three steps,

God, spirits of the spheres, and active reason, remained spirits proper; the next three steps, however, soul, form, and matter, even though they were not corporeal, related to the corporeal. Corresponding to the steps of the spiritual, the corporeal, which emanated from the spiritual, had six steps: celestial bodies, human bodies, animal bodies, plant bodies, minerals, and elements.[37]

All these theories were, of course, not purely Aristotelian—they were Neoplatonic: there was no creation, only the everlasting emanation of the world; the strict division into this world and the next was eliminated. Thus reflecting on possible and necessary being led to assuming an original point of departure for everything that existed. This point of departure, however, was not a historical creation, but was perfection without a cause. The world turned out to be a transtemporal process. At the same time it formed a construct consisting of various strata of being, the supreme one of which was without underlying condition; the further one moved down the steps, the more complex was the conditionality of being. In Islamic theology, on the other hand, which contrasts everything that was created to a Creator, such a hierarchy of being was unthinkable. To the hierarchy of being corresponds the cognitive process al-Farabi described: lower forms strove toward higher forms; the spirit above us, which gave everything on earth its form, tried to reconnect the individual parts that were separated. It gathered the earthly forms in human beings, who consequently combined in themselves in an ideal way the diversity of the entire world perceivable by the senses. This was the basis of the human capacity for cognition, which went beyond the recognition of individual phenomena. In that respect, the human spirit resembled the lowest spirit of the spheres; it was the goal and *summum bonum* of the human spirit to blend with it in order to be closer to God.[38] The ideal human society was organized like the cosmos; al-Farabi explained this in a book on the ideal state. At its top was the supreme leader whose sole task was to give orders. Underneath him were several ranks whose holders, on the one hand, received orders, but, on the other, passed them on to the next lower ranks, all the way down to the lowest rank, whose holders only received orders. The ruler of the ideal state was comparable to a philosopher, or a prophet; realizations flowed into him that emanated from the supreme being in several steps.[39] This theory has on occasion been misunderstood as a reflection of the Shiite concept of the imamate. The Shiites, too, believed that their leader partook in a suprahuman knowledge because he was related to Muhammad and certain traits of prophetship could be inherited. Actually, however, al-Farabi came from somewhere else. Muhammad had been elected to be the recipient of the revelation in a singular act; but the rise to the position of ruler of the ideal state had nothing to do with being elected by the impersonal supreme being. That men became heads of state during their lifetime was, in al-Farabi's mind, *one* aspect of the multifaceted supra-historical process of being the world represented.

Al-Farabi could not do the impossible either and organically connect ancient philosophy and Islamic theology. His treatises contain frequent allusions to the language of the *mutakallimun*, and some of the issues he discussed document his efforts to utilize philosophy for the *kalam* or to show the thematic parallels between the two. For instance, he discussed in detail the question of why the one God, the necessary being, could have no companions. The One, he argued, was perfect because He alone possessed supreme being; having two beings with a supreme being each was a contradiction in itself. "Only that is perfectly magnificent next to which there is nothing as magnificent. Only that is perfectly graceful besides which there is nothing that has its kind of gracefulness. Likewise, only that has perfect substance of which we can say: Nothing can exist beside it that is of the same substance. The same is true of all perfect bodies. Nothing of their kind exists besides them. This is also true, for example, of the sun, the moon, and the other stars. If, therefore, the first one, God, possesses supreme being, He must be the only one possessing it. It exists only in this being and is in that respect One."[40]

All attempts to incorporate the philosophical tradition into a way of thinking that was based on Islam failed. Playing with philosophy could be an enjoyable pastime, but even as early as the tenth century the general opinion among the educated was that no faithful Muslim and faithful follower of the Sharia could practice it seriously. A collection of evening conversations that took place among a vizier's social gathering has preserved for us relatively new opinions on a Neoplatonically inspired explanation of the cosmos and the history of humankind, the so-called "Writings of the Pure Brothers."[41] The leading speaker was Abu Sulaiman al-Mantiqi (d. c. 1001), who in a different context was introduced as a Muslim dilettante of philosophy (*mutafalsif*).[42] Abu Sulaiman, enough of an authority to have written an overview of Greek philosophy,[43] stressed at the very beginning of his arguments the futility of all efforts to reconcile the ancients' wisdom—astronomy, mathematics, natural sciences, music, and logic—and the Sharia. The revelation, he pointed out, had come directly from God, it was validated by miracles, and, therefore, in all respects superior to philosophy. The kind of speculation that dealt with the examination of everyday occurrences could not possibly generate the sort of firm knowledge that was now, thanks to Muhammad's appointment as Prophet, finally accessible. It was possible to assess of what little use that obsolete knowledge was by remembering that during the religious battle among Muslims it had never been philosophers who had been asked for advice. They would have to realize finally that reason, a gift from God, did not possess the powerful capacities ascribed to it; the knowledge of the revelation touched deeper layers, and prophets should be held in higher esteem than philosophers. Besides, the followers of philosophy were accused of regarding the Sharia as a source of knowledge accessible to everyone; philosophy on the other hand, which probed inner meaning, was open to only a small esoteric circle. Even this early we are confronted with arguments Averroes would use two hundred years later to defend his field of scholarship.[44] Why then, Abu Sulaiman asked, did philosophers promote their ideas if they were meant for only a very few people? Islam, according to which all human beings were at the same distance from God as the source of all knowledge, did not permit its followers to adopt manmade theories![45]

Still, philosophy did remain attractive to a number of Muslim scholars. After all, it provided intellectual tools that were tempting to apply. Just as al-Ash'ari had tried to put the Mu'tazilites' method of theological speculation into the service of the *sunna*, so some representatives of the eleventh century hoped to apply logic to the continued analysis of the Koran and the *hadith*. The Andalusian Ibn Hazm (d. 1064), disgusted by the unfounded interpretations with which the contemporary legal scholars besmirched their sacrosanct sources, devoted himself to a detailed study of philosophy. He hardly liked the *content* of philosophical knowledge. What concerned him deeply were the discovery and preservation of the real meaning of the Koran and the *hadith*. He believed that these were best pursued by way of logic, which was a constant, unadulterated meta-language, no matter what language the logician spoke. In view of this realization, Ibn Hazm dared take the bold step of denying the supremacy of Arabic, the language of the revelation. All languages, he postulated, were equal in their ways of expressing things, since they all preserved the terms—and concepts—God had once taught Adam. Yet, in order to understand a text, one depended on a careful analysis of the language of that text, and on nothing else. There was no interpretation that could discover some "esoteric meaning." Sometimes it was possible to discover a metaphoric expression that was justified because to our mind, every thing in this world formed an extremely complex web of relationships. Yet a metaphor, too, expressed a clear, "extrinsic" meaning (that is to say, meaning that was accessible without esoteric knowledge)—which was its only meaning.[46]

Al-Ghazali (d. 1111), a student of al-Juwayni in Ash'arite theology, also studied philosophy intensively. As he himself admitted, toward the late 1080s—he was meanwhile living in Baghdad—he was beset by grave inner doubts. As even al-Juwayni had sensed, Ash'arite theology did not meet the expectations that had been put into it: it was not able to provide ultimate certainty of faith. In his despair, al-Ghazali plunged into philosophy. The fruits of his studies were several treatises in which he explained the goals and methods of that field of scholarship.[47] Yet he did not find inner peace; pretending that he planned to make a pilgrimage to Mecca in 1095, he vacated his post as professor at the University of Baghdad, which had been founded by Nizam al-Mulk. For several years, he lived as a recluse, until he resumed his teaching activities in 1105, at first in Baghdad, and then in Nishapur. In his *Savior from Error*, a brief autobiographical work, he confessed that none of the methods of gaining knowledge had satisfied him, not even philosophy, which—following al-Farabi's example—was expected to gain unshakable knowledge by way of the categories of "necessary" and "possible." True knowledge, he argued, could be compared to a beam of light God shone into a human being's heart—in other words, it was a gift of mercy. The dignity of reason consisted of nothing but compelling human beings to be unconditionally obedient to God.[48]

4. Re-establishing All Creatures' Power of Being

In contrast to Christianity, in Islam God never descends to the onto-logical level of human beings. Allah, the Creator and ruler of the world, does not get involved in it ontologically, but demands that His laws be obeyed as a prerequisite for possibly attaining salvation in the next world. If the message that Allah was the entirely other was to make sense, there must be an essential difference between being in the "visible" and being in the "unseen." If the difference between these two ontological domains was to be taken seriously, it was inappropriate to make inferences from actions in this world to their assessment in the next. On the one hand, human beings were obliged to seek salvation independently in this world, according to criteria of this world; on the other, they were called upon to confirm Allah's radical otherness, which presupposed His unpredictability.

The gap between the two was unbridgeable. The Mu'tazilites had tried to establish a connection, but to no avail. The Ash'arites abandoned attempts in that direction and clearly based their ontology on God's otherness and unpredictability. Creatures possessed a being that was given them only by God, and it did not imply that they had any control over a certain period of time; rather, control was renewed by God from moment to moment—or it was not, entirely according to His inscrutable ways. It was in Allah alone that all earthly creatures, all earthly events had their common point of reference: this statement succinctly summarizes all Ash'arite metaphysics—with these premises, physics was a futile field anyway. The terms human beings employed to follow God's instructions and talk about the One were but empty words.

The Ash'arite school believed it had definitively understood and explained the Creator-God's otherness; but some of their farsighted members realized that their theology had deprived human beings of all their power. How, after all, should it be possible for that bundle of particles that was held together only by God's inscrutable will to obey the laws imposed on them, and thus potentially attain salvation? Referring to sura 7, verse 171, which mentions that the paradise dwellers were selected even before creation, was no comfort but rather increased that discomfiting sense of being helplessly exposed to a tyrannical God. It required a decisive intellectual sacrifice to follow zealously the entire Sharia down to the last detail, in order to show one's fellow human beings that one was among the elected. And was it not precisely that kind of painstakingly following the Sharia that Sufism, striving toward ethical refinement, condemned as vain and meaningless? The time had come for Sufism and Sunnism to separate; scrupulously following the law ultimately did not bring the believer closer to the ambitious goal of attaining salvation by surrendering the self in the act of uniting with God.

It did not go unnoticed that the loss of human power, if thought to its logical conclusion, made the laws God demanded to be followed look absurd. Al-Juwayni courageously and quite openly declared that God demanded something of His creatures with which they were not able to comply—a stark contrast to the Koranic promise that He "charges no soul save to its capacity" (sura 2, verse 286).[49] How confusing—and even dangerous—Ash'arite theology was for a religion that recognized as the center of its existence an all-comprehensive and God-given law! We now understand that this school had its enemies in the eleventh century, even within Sunnism.[50] After his rejection of rationalism, al-Ghazali would have liked to keep ordinary people away from all speculation and urgently recommended that the Prophet's glorified way of life be emulated quite unintellectually.[51] That was the goal to which he devoted his voluminous main opus, *The Revival of the Religious Sciences*.

Let us skip a century and take a look at the theologian Fakhr ad-Din ar-Razi (d. 1209). He called himself an Ash'arite, which, during that time, was a dangerous minority position to hold, comparable to that of being a Mu'tazilite two hundred years earlier. The great majority of people never warmed up to the theological foundation of the relationship between human beings and God that was manifested in the rites and the emulation of the Prophet. This could have become popular only if certain political claims had been connected to it. Now, in the twelfth century, the few who practiced rationalist—that is to say, largely Ash'arite—theology were considered troublemakers who dared criticize the Prophet's *sunna*. Frequently the authorities were asked to proceed against them. Among the most significant works Fakhr ad-Din ar-Razi left us is his lengthy Koran commentary, which, owing to its numerous and long excursuses on the most varied topics, is a veritable treasure on the intellectual and social history of Islam in the Middle Ages.

Ar-Razi permitted himself to write an excursus on sura 17, verse 87: "They will question thee concerning the Spirit. Say: 'The Spirit is of the bidding of my Lord (*ar-ruh min amr rabbi*). You have been given of knowledge nothing except a little.'" This passage mentions God's *amr*, a term that is difficult to interpret; a literal translation—"order" or "business"—is inappropriate, for what is meant is not one or several concrete instructions God gave for certain occasions, but a nonmaterial medium incessantly originating from Him outside of all time and historicity. It must be understood as the carrier of God's constant dispensation of Providence that brought order into creation, guiding it toward the cosmos. In the Koran the angels sometimes appear as personified carriers of this medium, sometimes the medium stands for itself.[52] Here, in sura 17, the word *ruh* is related to *amr*: the "Spirit" is part or an aspect of the dispensation of Providence. The concept of Providence was not the Prophet's intellectual property; we also find it in the word of one of Muhammad's contemporaries, the poet Umayya ibn abi s-Salt, in whose poetry there are allusions to additional important motifs of the Koranic revelation. That is the reason why the Prophet, who failed to win him over to his side, was angry at him. In short, Providence was something that belonged only to God, which despite His intrinsic ontological separation from this world could always be present in it.

The Islamic theologians kept looking for a third concept that could better connect the world and its Creator; at the same time, insofar as the dispensation of Providence was not supposed to be immediately directed at human beings, this concept was meant to leave them with a vestige of the freedom to act and of their responsibility for themselves. Sufyan ibn Uyayna found this third concept in "God's speech," and Ibn Qutayba, in a medium of fine substance. Neither did al-Maturidi make everything that happened in God's creation dependent on an arbitrary act of God; rather, he assumed that there were "natures" with which human beings had to deal. In Averroes's positing of a "world as a whole" we discover a similar idea, which was powerfully supported by insights from the study of the ancient traditions.[53] Ultimately, however, the strict ontological separation into Creator and creatures always prevailed.

Sura 17, verse 87, gave ar-Razi occasion to elaborate on the question of who human beings really were. He began by going back to verse 86, which states that "every man works according to his own manner" (kul-lun ya'malu 'ala shakilati-hi). That, he explained, meant nothing but that there was a connection between the spirit of a human being and the acts originating from that spirit. Yet what was this spirit? An answer to this question, ar-Razi stated, required four different analyses. First one had to deal with the spirit's quiddity and explain whether or not it was spatial—in other words, a body—or whether or not it subsisted in a body; then one had to clarify the question of whether it was without beginning and eternal, or whether it was contingent; next came the question of whether or not it continued to exist after the body died; and finally, one would need to know what bliss or damnation might mean in relation to the spirit. Here we have to confine ourselves to the first two issues, for it is especially the rather extensive analysis of the quiddity (mahiyya) that shows us how far ar-Razi, the Ash'arite, had ventured to stray from the basic positions his school had supported in the eleventh century, which he had done despite his continued use of essential terms from the standard Ash'arite vocabulary.

Was the spirit a body in itself but present within our body, borne from the four known humores, or was it the combination of their ingredients itself? Did it subsist as an accidens in our body's substance, or was it something entirely different? Sura 17, verse 87, ar-Razi claimed, proved that the latter was the case; the spirit was part of the dispensation of divine Providence, of the Creator's never-ceasing word, "Be! And it is!" So it was this alone, and not the humores, that generated everything! The spirit visited the body, giving it life; its quiddity was ultimately unfathomable, but that was true for many things. Sour honey had the quality of interrupting bile flow; it was impossible to answer the question of what that quality really consisted of.[54]

With this, ar-Razi had already abandoned the basic Ash'arite concept of man. The Ash'arites had regarded "being alive" as no more than an accidens that God assigned to a substance at a certain moment in time. There was no third element besides substance and accidens. Ar-Razi once again implied this view when he stressed that the mutakallimun believed that a human being's appearance as it could be perceived by the senses constituted his or her totality.[55] In short, for ar-Razi sura 17, verse 87, was written proof of the fallacy of this thesis, which had been his motivation for the extensive excursus on the nature of human beings to begin with.

Yet as ar-Razi briefly explained in a handbooklike textbook on the history of Islamic theology and metaphysics, this thesis formed the basis of the early schools' theories until approximately the eleventh century. In the meantime, however, it had been proven incorrect, for the new concept of man was more complex, precisely because it gave more consideration to what can be perceived by our senses. As we shall see, this entailed a significant ontological revaluation of creation and was, therefore, more plausible, as human beings do experience a certain degree of continuity within themselves. The about-face toward the self, toward ego consciousness, marks the decisive step beyond Ash'arism. If human beings were more than particles of matter that could be perceived by the senses, what were they? At first ar-Razi explained that all human beings possessed ego consciousness, a sense of identity that was independent of their physical state. They could grow, gain or lose weight, and even lose some limbs, but none of this either decreased or increased their sense of self.[56] According to ar-Razi, this sense of self, which was apparently not affected by changes of the body, was not only a merely spontaneous and self-sufficient sense of existence, but rather also exhibited impulses without any involvement of the body; the self could be angry or glad without the limbs necessarily being felt, let alone moved.

If it were his or her ego consciousness with its apparently quite individual traits that made up a human being, its relationship with the spirit (which was part of Providence) needed some clarification—in short, the discussion had to go back to where it started. Pure individuality of nonmaterial existence, which constituted human beings, could hardly be thought of as part of divine Providence flowing through creation. Consequently, ar-Razi was impressed by the notion that human beings were bodies of a fine substance that pervaded the perceivable, coarse body like "the element of the fire does coal or sesame oil does sesame seed." Ultimately, however, he had to reject this notion—unless the fluid of fine substance was identified with the spirit. After all, some proponents of the theory under discussion described the spirit as a mass of fine, celestial little bodies of light that were comparable to the nature of sun beams, which were also indissoluble and indivisible.

Yet, according to ar-Razi, only those thinkers had found the truth who recognized the essence of human beings in their *souls*, the individualized form of *ruh*, so to speak, whose connection to the body could be described in two ways. If the essence of a human being was in his or her soul, "human beings are neither in this world nor outside of it, are neither part of it nor separated from it; they are connected with their bodies only inasmuch as they are their rulers, just as God relates to the world only as its ruler. A second group of thinkers believes that when the soul deals with the body, it unites with it, and . . . the totality of body and soul during this unification is what makes a human being. When the moment of death arrives, this unity is destroyed, the soul remains, but the body disintegrates."[57] According to ar-Razi, this theory was supported by undeniable arguments he individually discussed and approved.[58] The human soul was an indivisible totality; in that respect it was juxtaposed to the body, which was composed of various components. Human beings realized this in themselves intuitively, but there were also a number of convincing proofs. Processing sensory impressions, ar-Razi argued, and the impulses to act stemming from them, were so complex that an analysis of only parts of them missed reality; everything happened simultaneously. The realization of the complexity of human behavior destroyed the Ash'arite theory of individual acts of divine Providence and their results having to occur in a *temporal* sequence; this marked a significant step toward an organic concept of being.

Seen from a different angle, the example of ar-Razi illustrates that old Ash'arite metaphysics and the concept of human beings as organisms were mutually exclusive. Since human beings were seen as whole entities, each particle would have to contain the *accidentes* "life," "knowledge," or "capacity to act." This, however, would split their totality into an infinite number of different parts, which was contradicted by ego consciousness. Furthermore, such independent particles could never be made to act in unison.[59] Or, one single quality, such as "being alive," would have to pertain to many particles simultaneously, which in turn, as ar-Razi tried to show, would split up the total entity into a multitude of individually acting components. The concept of self-organization, which even in modern science is still very new, did not yet exist so something had to be found that could put the particles together so that they could form an organism.

According to the concept of the hierarchy of all being, this "something" had to be superior to the being within matter just as God was ontologically superior to His creatures. This implicit tendency within Islamic theological reasoning suggests that an organizer needed to be found within an immaterial soul not subject to the process of growth and decay, as opposed to a soul that did not come into being through the interplay of the *humores* in the individual body, as some natural philosophers believed. What put the particles together so that they formed a body did not entirely belong to them so that it did not suffer their inescapable fate, but survived their death. For ar-Razi as well as for other Islamic thinkers, the soul's ontological otherness and its independence of the body, as it were, were manifested by the fact that the very neglect and even suppression of one's physical needs fully developed the soul's capacities. It was, however, yet another quality that enabled the soul to act as organizer: the capacity to gather knowledge. A piece of wax, for instance, which was pressed into the shape of a triangle, lost this shape as soon as it was pressed into another shape. How different the soul was! The more "intelligible forms" were impressed into it, the more easily it took on and processed additional forms. This was how human understanding and insight, the particles ruled and organized by the soul, were generated.[60]

We need not stress again that Ash'arite metaphysics, which conceived of "knowledge" as the *accidens* God assigned to a particle at a certain moment in time, did not force itself to accept an understanding of such a process of gathering information. However, this process was indispensable for a concept of human beings as organisms to which the power of being was inherent. How did this idea enter Ash'arite thought, and where did it originate? Of the lesser known men among those who "affirmed a spiritual resurrection (*ma'ad*) of the soul," ar-Razi named al-Ghazali, and one can easily show that ar-Razi's discussion of the soul and human beings in his commentary on sura 17, verse 87, was in many ways derived from the latter's work, *The Inner Dissonance of [the Teachings of] the Philosophers*.[61]

The reference to al-Ghazali contains a number of problems. How can one explain that ar-Razi called al-Ghazali, an Ash'arite, a proponent of theories whose unprovability the above-mentioned work tried to establish? Even a number of medieval authors noticed the ambiguity of al-

Ghazali's way of reasoning. That was why Ibn Tufayl, Averroes's teacher, accused al-Ghazali of intellectual dishonesty, and Averroes himself noted wryly: "He is an Ash'arite among the Ash'arites, a Sufi among the Sufis, and a philosopher among the philosophers."[62]

This impression seems to have been created by al-Ghazali's intellectual development, which was marked by a decisive turning point. Around the middle of the eleventh century, when he was still a young man, he seems to have been deeply impressed by the different ways of thinking that were steeped in the ancient philosophical tradition. Compared to Ash'arism's rather thin metaphysics, these ways of thinking appeared to be far advanced. In his treatise *The Philosophers' Goals*, he gave an overview of these ways of thinking, which influenced his own thought processes more than he wanted to admit. There was one thing, however, that philosophy could not accomplish: it could not make the truth of Islam's path to salvation a certainty. Philosophy was useless in that respect, which was profoundly disappointing to al-Ghazali. Consequently *The Philosophers' Goals* was distributed with a preface in which the author distanced himself from its contents, since, he stated, philosophy rested in part on flawed presuppositions. This was precisely what he was trying to prove in a book he was working on at the time, entitled *The Inner Dissonance of [the Teachings of] the Philosophers*. In that work he elaborated on the issue under discussion: "Now we want to disprove by way of reason the [philosophers'] claim that the soul is a substance subsisting in itself—not as someone who declares that God is incapable of creating something of this kind, or as someone who thinks that the Sharia prescribed the opposite. Rather we want to illustrate in our description of the events of the Last Day that the Sharia confirms [the possibility that there is such a soul]. Yet we reject the [philosophers'] claim to have *pure, rational proof* of this, which they say is why they can do without the Sharia in this matter."[63] This was followed by reflections on which the above-mentioned arguments of ar-Razi depended in many ways.

Al-Ghazali tried to fend off the danger for the Sharia that in his opinion was caused by philosophy not altogether rejecting philosophical and natural-philosophical insights, but ultimately declaring them irrelevant: if it were proven that the world was created by God, then it did not matter how it was constituted.[64] Since al-Ghazali's goal in his *Inner Dissonance*

of [the Teachings of] the Philosophers was admittedly purely destructive[65]—the philosophers had no conclusive proof of their theses—he
reserved the right to advance, as the need arose, to the most different, and
even contradictory, views of the Islamic faith.

What al-Ghazali had conceived of and executed negatively—as a plan
to describe flaws—was turned around by ar-Razi. The philosophers did
not base themselves on the Sharia, even though their theories were in
agreement with it. This lack of making their agreement explicit rendered
their theories irrelevant: that had been al-Ghazali's reasoning. Ar-Razi, on
the other hand, argued as follows: the philosophers' theories were not
incorrect, only the philosophers failed to give them a sufficient foundation both in reason and in the tradition. This omission needed to be recti-
fied. Providing a basis in reason could be done with the help of the
philosophers' arguments, with the assistance of Ash'arite ways of reasoning, but with a different aim. In other words, ar-Razi used Ash'arism's
theory of substance and *accidentes* to prove that the organizing soul *must*
be a third element that differed from substance and *accidens*. Initially,
however, that theory's purpose had been precisely the negation of that
possibility! What was decisive was that reasoning occurred by way of the
revelation; ar-Razi accomplished this by connecting this topic with sura
17, verse 87, as well as with additional passages from the revelation and
the *hadith*.

This presents a new issue: the reception of patterns of philosophical
thought by Islamic theologians of the high Middle Ages, and the consequences of that pattern. When we look at the content of ar-Razi's discussion, it looks as if philosophy had won: the Ash'arite adopted the concept
of human beings as individual organisms. Yet if we look beyond al-
Ghazali, back into the past, if we look where he came from, this assessment needs to be substantially revised. In the passages of interest to us,
al-Ghazali was grounded in Avicenna's *Remarks and Admonitions*, which
was still a long way from all the Ash'arite terminology used by al-Ghazali
and, later on, ar-Razi in their discussion of body and soul. Avicenna introduced his reflections as follows: "Turn back toward yourself—to your
soul—and, if you are healthy or otherwise able to comprehend something
correctly, ask yourself: Can you ignore the existence of your self (in such
a state) and *not* affirm it, or your soul? . . . (If you think of your self in a

healthy state) and one assumes that it has altogether been put into such a position so as not to recognize its parts and its limbs not touching one another but being extended and suspended in clear air for a certain amount of time (so that nothing touches them), then you will notice that it ignores everything except the existence of its identity."[66]

The knowledge of the self, of the soul, preceded all other knowledge; it was not imputed by God but was directly available. It seems in Avicenna's work as if the beginning of all knowledge was seated in pure ego consciousness, and as if everything recognized by the ego had to pass through the recognizing person's self, through which process it was subjectively distorted. Actually, however, Avicenna did not go that far; he shied away from the ultimate conclusion, for studying al-Farabi's works had made him adopt the Neoplatonic theories of emanation, where recognition was a supra-personal process through which it was passed on from the higher levels of existence to the lower levels. This brings us close to the Koranic *amr* with which ar-Razi justified the theory of the soul as a third element next to substance and *accidens*. In early Ash'arite theology the unity of a being—an identity and individuality—was reserved for God alone. Avicenna's concept of an individual, indestructible self, of a soul that every human being possessed, penetrated Ash'arite theology via al-Ghazali, which led to an astounding ontological revaluation of creatures. Yet despite their enhanced status, they were not entirely delivered from their dependency on supra-personal being: they continued to hold on to the active intellect of al-Farabi's system of emanation, the Koranic Creator-God's *amr*. Only the philosopher Abu l-Barakat al-Baghdadi (d. 1164) was ready to sever these connections. He took Avicenna to his logical conclusion and found the soul to be a totally homogeneous, individual entity; hence for him, all recognition was a process ruled solely from that soul.[67]

Abu l-Barakat al-Baghdadi continued along the way toward the individual as shown by Avicenna. It seems that hardly anyone followed him. On the other hand, there were a great deal more Muslim thinkers who made the impulse obtained from the early eleventh-century philosopher bear fruit in quite a different way. If divine Providence worked directly in us, His creatures, then part of God's being was within us. Seen against the backdrop of Ash'arism's separation between the Creator's ontological omnipotence and the creature's ontological impotence, this could only mean that among the transient, polymorphic, sensorialy perceivable surface of phenomena in this world was hidden a core of the only true, immutable divine being. God Himself was in everything that was identified as His creation. Misled by the inconstancy of its phenomena, creation was seen as different from Him, but God was ever-present in it, and always in and around us.

Ibn al-'Arabi (d. 1240), who came from Andalusia and later lived in Mecca, Anatolia, and Syria, was the most influential proponent of this new Islamic theology. In 1190 in Cordoba he had a grand vision in which all prophets, from Adam to Muhammad, appeared to him. Through this vision he came to realize that it was this theology that was going to conclude Islam's message and make the promise of salvation an absolute certainty. One of the prophets pointed out sura 11, verse 59, to Ibn al-'Arabi: "There is no creature that crawls, but He takes it by the forelock. Surely my Lord is on a straight path." When the visionary heard these words, he was overcome with unfathomable joy. Then Muhammad joined them and assured him that God was the essence of hearing and the senses of the face, the hands, feet, and tongue; He was the essence of the senses! Had Avicenna believed that ego consciousness was before all perception and cognition, which digested what was perceived, its place was now taken by the divine being; it shone from the deepest ground of the ego.

Ibn al-'Arabi explained that in his vision Muhammad had contented himself with naming the senses; they still had to be described in everyday terms, but for precisely that reason depicted the real, divine being imperfectly; for to the divine being corresponded much more the spiritual forces that resisted any definition. Defining, the procedure of penetrating reality according to the capacity of human language, always meant establishing boundaries around the supreme being. Thus the Koran declared that, after completing His creation, God had sat down on His throne—in other words, had separated Himself from nature. Yet in the Koran God had also explained that He was in heaven and on earth, in every place where we were, "and finally He told us that *He* was *our* essence." Ibn al-'Arabi boldly concluded this from sura 42, verse 9: "Like Him there is naught." If there was nothing like Him, then there was only Him! Therefore, He was every thing. Every thing had its boundaries, but only seemingly so, it was the way we comprehended things. Under the confusing boundaries was hidden the one substance that existed: God.[68]

In other words, after creation had been ontologically devalued, it was now enormously revalued: everything was part of divine being! If one recognized their original source, all the phenomena of the world accessible to our senses formed only a seeming, but not an essential surface. Yet that surface was by no means dismissed as worthless it simply was understood as the One's necessary complement. Cause and effect, God and creation were no longer thought of in a temporal sequence, as in Ash'arism; they were the two sides of the one being there was, and they were always simultaneously present. Creation was not the artifact of a master, it constituted the One's dynamic self-development.[69]

If the object of human cognition and comprehension was but the nonessential surface phenomena of the process of divine being, what use then was all that scholarship, which was dependent on these concepts? What, for instance, was jurisprudence good for, which had to define and judge human actions according to their external manifestations, following criteria that themselves were derived from a body of texts via definitions—texts that, albeit originating from or inspired by God, were tailored for human reason? In light of Ibn al-'Arabi's message of salvation, Sharia Islam, with all its offices and institutions, the Qadis, the Muftis, the countless notaries and scribes, appeared to be disconcertingly confusing, and even "fraudulent" and "deceptive."[70] One did not get close to the One by strictly observing the letter of the law; true faith could be gained only by submitting to the leadership of a seer, a saint who pierced the make-believe mantle the Sharia dealt with. What happened under the surface of the perceivable world could not be explained by way of definitions, it could only be beheld in images; and those who could behold it, who could experience and sense those spiritual forces behind the perception of which Ibn al-'Arabi spoke in the description of his vision, would also influence them, no matter how little: they were in any case the right people to lead the believers toward salvation.[71]

And so the theology of the "oneness of being" (*wahdat al-wujud*), taught by Ibn al-'Arabi and like-minded thinkers, contained not only a challenge for the administrators of Sharia Islam, but also a strong impulse for turning toward magic. Until then magic had been branded as the condescending and anti-Islamic attempt to interfere with God's work. The theologians had dealt with it only defensively: in the Koran we read that Moses had vanquished the Pharaonic magicians with the help of God, and God's miracles served as proof that Moses was His prophet; God was the only cause, and human beings could neither fathom nor, much less, influence Him. However, Fakhr ad-Din ar-Razi, who was extremely knowledgeable in magic, explained its successes—which in his opinion could not be doubted—as a result of the increased knowledge the magicians had of "God's habit." As an Ash'arite, he tried to fend off the "philosophers, astrologers, and Sabians" and hold on to the concept of God as the source of all miracles. If a magician produced something that ran counter to the nature of things, he argued, then God must have changed His habit at every moment.[72] This was a kind of withdrawal, which could not stop the victory of the magic way of seeing the world (a *weltanschauung* that resembled the theory of the oneness of being). As we shall see,[73] Sharia Islam could hold its own not by rejecting this view, but by incorporating and thus taming it.

5. Islamic Theology in the High and Late Middle Ages

We have seen that the influence of ancient philosophical tradition had initiated a process of ontological revaluation of creation. This process left numerous traces in the theological literature of the high and waning Middle Ages, traces that have been observed and analyzed extremely insufficiently so far. For example, in his discussion of the "philosophers" in an overview of the *kalam*, the Ash'arite ash-Shahrastani (d. 1153)[74] tried to prove that God was the *one* starting point of all human actions. He relied not only on known Ash'arite theories, but also incorporated in his reflections the individual's experiences: human beings did have the ability to perform certain actions, but—and here ash-Shahrastani turned the argument of human ego consciousness against the "philosophers"—they also never ceased to sense that they depended on outside help. Neither did they ever cease to sense that their actions did not wholly belong to them: their tongues formed sounds, but only certain sounds, and not others; they moved their hands and fingers, yet if they tried to move only one limb but not those connected with it, they failed. The "philosophers," however, claimed that the ability to act implied the ability to perform a certain action or its opposite.[75]

Much more important than such individual responses to certain intellectual impulses was the fact that the adoption of basic concepts of philosophy led the *kalam* out of the cul-de-sac in which it had got caught in the eleventh century. In Mu'tazilite and early Ash'arite theology it had been standard to explain the otherness of the divine being with the ontological contradiction between "created" and "uncreated," between world and Creator. Ash'arism had taken this juxtaposition to its extreme: everything human beings found in this world, and every action they committed, had been created by God; only the One was uncreated. In looking back at the history of the *kalam,*[76] Fakhr ad-Din ar-Razi called this kind of theology the Method of the Ancients. He contrasted it with the Method of the Moderns, who divided being into necessary and possible being. In the theological work dedicated to Vizier Nizam al-Mulk, Al-Juwayni had for the first time brought these categories, introduced to Islamic thought by al-Farabi, to life within the context of Ash'arite theology.[77]

In assessing the consequences of adopting these ideas, we have to recall that the Ash'arites, too, had taught that knowledge was by no means generated by reason processing sensory impressions or the facts accessible to it; rather, it could be found in the one who knew the moment God gave him the relevant *accidens*. Since no creature could either make or keep God from doing so, the possession of knowledge perforce occurred in the pertinent substratum: all knowledge was necessary and thus entirely independent of the knowing person's previous intellectual activity.[78] At most, that He first created in a person intellectual activity and then its result, could be ascribed to a habit of God. Al-Juwayni and the Ash'arites before him knew that it was the Muslims' duty to get a clear picture of the rational foundations of faith. Yet like the Sharia's other obligations, this too was ultimately an "intolerable burden" that, owing to man's lack of power of being, could not be met unless God had destined him to meet them. In Ash'arite view, the creature's ontological state never implied the duty to penetrate the truths of faith rationally; this duty followed only from the traditions establishing it.

Ar-Razi obviously adopted this concept in his overview, as it served the religious justification of all theology. He regarded as a mere exchange of sophistries the battle over whether that obligation only covered the struggle for knowledge or knowledge itself. The correct application of the rules of "speculation," he instructed his readers, necessarily generated knowledge, not solely according to God's habit, but not as a product of the "speculating" creature either. "For everyone who knows that the world undergoes change and that anything transient is possible, cannot *not* know that the world is possible, as long as he is mentally (*dhihn*) aware of these two pieces of knowledge. The knowledge of this impossibility is (likewise) inevitable. Yet the knowledge of this impossibility is not generated because knowledge in itself is (ontologically) possible and, therefore, subject to *God's* determining power. Thus it can occur only through *His* power."[79]

This passage makes clear two things: ar-Razi did not abandon the old Ash'arite theory that everything happening in creation was effected by God; possible being was what was caused by necessary being, by God. The domain of nondivine being, once characterized as "created" and seemingly accounted for in its entirety by the concepts of substance and *accidens*, here defined the category "possible"; yet it was complemented by a domain of mental processes in which the creature, too, could perforce reach certain conclusions. As "having knowledge," knowledge was still only possible and therefore effected by God; in regard to creatures, this was true for any kind of being. Yet the *content* of knowledge must be separated from "having knowledge"; the content could certainly result from necessary conclusions.

It is obvious that introducing a domain of mental processes did not all at once eliminate the difficulties of Ash'arite theology. But borrowing this concept from Avicenna[80] made it at least possible to continue working on a rational cognition of God. In his *Eastern Debates*, his great examination of Avicenna's thought, ar-Razi revealed that the concepts that were situated in the mental domain could ultimately not be brought into agreement with Ash'arite ontology. How could an Ash'arite affirm "mental existence"? Everything to which was ascribed a positively stated quality must exist, for saying that something had a quality implied the thing's existence. That was the inevitable consequence of Ash'arite ontology, in which, as we may recall, everything that *existed* was a thing, and not merely everything that was known, as in Mu'tazilite thought. Ar-Razi felt compelled to secure "mental existence" within the area of existing things; he tried to do this by extending the content of the term "being" (*wujud*) to the "affirmability" (*thubut*) of a thing; in the mental domain this could exist independently of the world of things (*al-kharij*).[81] This was not a return to Mu'tazilite thought; for the Mu'tazilites considered what was "known" to be a thing—not necessarily existing presently, but certainly at a former time or in the future. Thus the Mu'tazilites' "known" thing was the basic element of the course of the world from creation to the Last Day. In contrast, ar-Razi's "affirmability" of an essence did not assign to it a place in history, but let the world of things and mental concepts exist next to each other, outside of time, but relating to one another.

Yet, even if ontology were reduced to the original Islamic question regarding the distinction between Creator and creature, the terms adopted from the philosophers—"necessary" and "possible"—proved to be tricky; for what necessarily existed—God—existed alongside that which possibly existed. Ar-Razi was afraid that "necessary" and "possible" did not distinguish clearly enough between the two areas of being, the eternal one that had no beginning, and the one created in time. Therefore, he insisted that "existing" produced a common denominator only nominally, but not factually. For one could argue that, as soon as the possible being was caused by the necessary being, it was necessarily brought into existence and could therefore also be called necessary. One must distinguish between being that was necessary in itself and being that was necessary because of an outside cause. Furthermore, ar-Razi added, one could point out that "necessary" was not an affirmable quality of an essence.[82]

These are only some of the intellectual devices ar-Razi used to fend off the threatening (and, as we have seen, frequently made) inference from the theory of possible and necessary being: the theology of the oneness of being (*wahdat al-wujud*).

What did theology learn from its encounter with philosophy? There was a conscious avoidance of philosophical concepts of explaining the world; for the world in the Aristotelian mold, which evolved according to its own inherent laws, could hardly be reconciled with the idea of the Creator-God. Furthermore, openly confirming that the world was eternal would have fostered the suspicion—insufferable for a Muslim!—that human speculation was taken more seriously than God's unalterable word. As was recently discovered,[83] despite these fundamental reservations, during his study of philosophy, al-Ghazali was in many ways influenced by Avicenna, an influence he could not shed even in his late works.

Ash'arite theology had wanted to acknowledge the ontological status of being for everything that existed. Accordingly, God's "qualities of meaning,"[84] the most significant of which was "creating" (khaliq), could be stated only when they manifested themselves. This had been necessary because otherwise, they would have constituted an eternal, special area within God's uniform fullness of being, which would have cast doubt on the theory of God's oneness. The Ash'arite approach avoided that difficulty, but left itself vulnerable to the following argument: Had God not been a Creator-God from the beginning of time, and if so, why did He become a Creator only when he began His work? Al-Ghazali solved that problem by pointing out that khaliq did not necessarily mean "presently creating," but could also refer to His ability, His knowledge in that area, or His intention to create something. "Creating" was a possible predicate of God, independent of whether and when it was actualized.

This adoption of Avicenna's logic (which can ultimately be traced back to Aristotle) was not without consequences. In a treatise on God's most beautiful names—otherwise an object of edifying contemplation that was based on God as the supreme, true being (al-haqq)—al-Ghazali described the created world as a cosmos in which all events appeared as a web of complex causes and effects. To be sure, God still gave the initial, decisive impulse, but what was happening before the eyes of the observer was not a charade of arbitrary measures that attained some kind of permanence only through "God's habit." It was the actualization of the Creator's intent, whose goal it was to form a whole. Thus God's names included that of "the shaper" (al-musauwir), which according to al-Ghazali meant that God brought the shapes of the created things into the best possible order.[85] God knew the shapes; this knowledge was part of Him, and not present only when He was creating something. From this followed that the continuity of being, which we perceived in us and around us, was more than a mere "habit"; it was proof that the Creator proceeded according to a plan.[86] God's determination (qadar) was the realization of His plan, according to which He created the individual beings, one after the other, in the substrata of this world."[87]

Al-Ghazali did not intend to replace Ash'arite metaphysics by one à la Avicenna.[88] On the contrary! In view of the attraction philosophical theories held, he was intent on proving that they were not superior to theology. Al-Ghazali was convinced that in describing creation and God, both reached the same conclusions; if he had believed in the primacy of philosophy over theology, he should not have written a work such as *The Inner Dissonance of [the Teachings of] the Philosophers*. Hence he was inspired by a notion that we frequently see in Islam's intellectual history: the notion that everything human beings can possibly know is already contained in the Koran and the *hadith*; only naive people can be made to believe that there is knowledge beyond them. In order to prevent such misunderstanding, which undermined faith, al-Ghazali urgently warned in a short treatise written toward the end of his life against allowing the uneducated entry into the realm of the *kalam*.[89]

Al-Ghazali had to make numerous references to Avicenna to demonstrate that theology and philosophy were equally valid. He left to the generations after him a highly explosive legacy that already contained the outlines of the main ideas of the theological work of the high and late Middle Ages that were summarized above. The created world no longer consisted solely of matter and its *accidentes*, as it had for the early Ash'arites; rather, it had two different aspects: a physical and a spiritual one. The domain of the spiritual, the "world of the unseen," contained the angels, which in Avicenna's universe were the individual intelligences and souls.[90] As already mentioned, everything that was created was the product of God's creative will; in that respect it possessed necessary being. We have seen what difficulties this statement entailed for Fakhr ad-Din ar-Razi. Al-Ghazali did not yet reflect on the ontological problems of this statement; instead, he neutralized it by arguing that the necessary shaping of everything that existed according to God's will was proof of His justice. Therefore, the world was the best of all possible worlds, and it was nothing less than the result of a Creator making arbitrary decisions.[91] What God wanted was just; it was also necessary insofar as it was impossible to think that God should want anything for anything other than what He really wanted. His endeavors were characterized by what was impossible to reach for human beings: absolute lack of bias. God's intentions were entirely objective because, in creating the world, He had no subjective interests and would by definition never have any.[92]

To reach his goal, al-Ghazali felt compelled to prove that Ash'arite and Avicennian metaphysics were in agreement. In order to explain the unbridgeable ontological gap between creature and Creator, he no longer used the concept of substance and *accidentes* that the Mu'tazilites had developed and the Ash'arites had adopted in a simplified form; instead, he transferred the discussion onto an ethical level—a solution to his dilemma, which sprang from his desire for harmony and in that sense surely was an expression of his personality. This is suggested by his confession, *The Savior from Error*, and especially by his *Revival of the Sciences of Religion*, which praised right acting in agreement with the traditions as the most beautiful expression of one's certainty of faith.

Fakhr ad-Din ar-Razi did not allow himself to evade the issue in this way. In his *Eastern Debates* he discussed Avicenna's metaphysics, without, however, finding satisfactory solutions. That large parts of the Aristotelian-Neoplatonic way of explaining the world could be brought into agreement with Islam's holy texts had become a certainty to him. In our description of the ontological revaluation of human beings through the introduction of the soul as part of God's determination, we noted that the quote from sura 17, verse 87, served the purpose of defending Ash'arism's foreign concepts as Islamic concepts. In a treatise devoted specifically to the power of the soul, ar-Razi explained how the individual can succeed in gaining increasingly clear and perfect insight into the domain of the unseen. Here, too, he was not short of quotes from the Koran and the *hadith*,[93] just as if the central topics of Islamic theology's main ideas of the late Middle Ages with their Avicennian slant had been valid since the days of Muhammad.

The "inner contradictions" of philosophical ideas which al-Ghazali demonstrated in order to take away the luster of pre-Islamic wisdom had to disappear from the theological debate on philosophy as soon as it had been proven that theology and philosophy were equally valid. Naturally, this was not possible in every respect, and whenever there was an unsolvable contradiction between the two—for instance, regarding the philosophical theory that the world was eternal—the revelation had to serve as the touchstone for what was right and what was wrong. That was the basic idea from which a certain Ala ad-Din at-Tusi (c. 1414–82) started out at the order of the Ottoman Sultan Mehmed II (r. 1444–46 and 1451–81), the conqueror of Constantinople, to weigh the teachings of theologians and philosophers against one another and to explain where they were right and where they were wrong. His conclusion was that not everything the philosophers taught should be condemned. Entirely correct was the statement about the life of the spirit, the soul, after death; furthermore, that the pleasures of the mind were nobler than those of the body. Several philosophical concepts, at-Tusi stated, did seem to be probable, such as the idea that when human beings were created, they were joined by a soul. The revelation did not support the argument that there was a causal connection between the many different phenomena of possible being, but believing that there was, did not make one an unbeliever. Only those abandoned true faith who were convinced that the world was eternal, claimed that God did not have an arbitrary will and did not have prior knowledge of all creatures' actions, and finally, and above all, those who denied that there was a physical resurrection.[94] It will be the task of future scholarship to determine how and under what circumstances the partial blending of theology and philosophy, which has apparently been generally approved by scholars, came about; particular attention will also have to be paid to the question of how the two ways of viewing the world, which were so different in their ways of thinking, were forced together at the seams.

CHAPTER VII

Islam and Gnosis

1. Prophetic Message and Gnostic Weltanschauung

Islam is a prophetic universal religion. Appointed in a society with a tribal organization and with an ethic code grounded in the solidarity among clan members, even in the earliest revelations Muhammad addressed people as individuals, warning them of the Day of Judgment. Those who wanted to prevail must not rely on the aid of their kin; they were going to be all by themselves and, as God's creatures, would have sole responsibility before their Creator for every deed they had committed or omitted here on earth. We have seen how this message blended with the Quraysh's quest for power in its own peculiar way, and how the Prophet's expulsion from his hometown led him and his followers to find their identity as the community of the "believers," which, during the first decades after Muhammad's death, was expanded into the community of "Muslims."

We have ignored a significant aspect in our discussion: the development of Islam within the world of late antiquity, in an era whose intellectual life was molded by Gnostic concepts that transcended the boundaries of all Christian—as well as other religious persuasions; in Manichaeism, Gnosticism itself appeared as a prophetic universal religion. The theology of Islam must somehow be related to Gnostic ideas, and by outlining the relationship between the two, we are casting light on the topics of Islamic theology which are recognized as important, but which we have excluded from our analysis up until now. Let us first try to summarize the basic ideas of Gnostic religiosity.

The Gnostics viewed the world as the work of a satanic demiurg; therefore, it was evil through and through, and human beings were in its clutches and themselves part of the evil into which they had been thrown. The evil in *this* world was juxtaposed by the good in the *next* world, to which human beings had no access; it was out of reach and entirely transcendent. Yet, at the same time, there was speculation about human beings having within themselves a tiny spark of that transcendent good. After an act of mixing together, which took place at the beginning of the world, "life"—in Gnosticism often equated with good—was locked inside this world of evil and darkness, to which this "life" was ultimately entirely foreign.[1] Thus human beings, who were imprisoned in this world, were in an utterly threatening and calamitous situation. Beyond the celestial spheres was the domain of the good, but we were locked out of it; we were lost in this world, the domain of our being, which in all its impulses and desires was exposed to the force of the stars. "All of human earthly and physical relations are 'in and of this world'; juxtaposed to them is 'that' world, the world outside the world in which life resides. Yet, if those worlds of light and of life speak of this world, it is called 'that world' from that perspective. The addition of the demonstrative pronoun as a requisite determinant to the term 'world' is a . . . fundamental verbal symbol of the Gnosis that is closely connected with the original concept of the foreign and of foreign life."[2]

The Gnostics no longer experienced the stars and planets as carriers of positive forces forming a meaningful whole, as the Stoics had. Rather, they appeared to them as the tyrannical border guards of this world, which was utterly distant from God; "the cosmos becomes a prison; its order, which is imposed by the stars, means being separated from God—and thus, in forming a realm of hermetic, divine laws, they represent the antidivine principle itself."[3] A frequent topic in ancient Arabic poetry was the tyranny of days, of time; on occasion they may have been clement toward human beings, but that clemency was always transitory: in reality they pushed man relentlessly into the abyss. Life ended in senseless destruction, which could be neither avoided nor postponed.[4] The life of human beings was overshadowed by deep insecurity and unconquerable fear; the world could not offer them refuge. It was reinterpreted as a realm of darkness from which people had to escape. Salvation from disaster meant being released from one's entanglement in the affairs of the world. From that perspective the soul was perceived as something that kept human beings from conquering the world and chained them to the "hated, hostile cosmos"[5]; it never stopped urging people to surrender to the world and leading them to stray from the path of salvation that was meant to lead them out of this evil world so they could attain true life. "Yet I claim not that my soul was innocent—surely the soul of man incites to evil," Joseph told Potiphar in the Koran (sura 12, verse 53) when it turned out that the latter's wife had tried to seduce the handsome lad. In sura 79, verse 40, the believers are assured, "But as for him who feared the Station of his Lord[6] and forbade the soul its caprice, surely Paradise shall be the refuge." In other words, the soul as a place where destructive forces are condensed whose power is difficult, if not impossible, to overcome—this thought, which Gnosticism fostered, was familiar to the Prophet.

All Gnostic systems shared the belief that a tiny divine spark glowed in human beings, who were thrown into this abominable world—a spark that was testimony to that infinitely distant world of salvation, which the evil spheres kept us from reaching. Gnostic myths attempted to explain in different, often somewhat confusing, ways how this spark fell into the domain of the anti-divine. The process of pulling the divine light into our realm of darkness was just as complex as the gathering, separating, and finally saving of that substance of salvation. In any case, the path to salvation began with human beings recognizing their calamitous situation in this world; they must realize that they were caught in darkness! This was the first step toward salvation. The Gnosis led them toward the path of saving themselves, along which they must have walked a certain distance before possibly receiving some help.

The good Lord, whose paradisiacal sphere of light the Gnostics yearned to enter, was entirely outside of the cosmos. All human predicaments were utterly foreign to Him. One could describe Him only negatively, for His nature was radically different from this evil world: "The true God, the father of the universe, the Holy Ghost, the invisible one who is above the cosmos, who exists in His immortality by being in the pure light, which eyes will never see: we must not think of Him, the spirit, as if of a god or that He has a specific nature. For He is more magnificent than the gods, an empire over which no one rules but Him. For no one is above Him, and neither does He need the gods; nor does He need life, for He is eternal. He does not need anything, for He cannot be completed, since He did not need to be completed, as He is always absolutely complete. He is light. He has no limits, for there is no one before Him to limit Him. He is never judged, for there is no one before Him to judge Him. . . .

He is neither tall nor small. He has no measure, for He is not a creature: no one can fathom Him. He is like nothing whatever that exists, but something that is more magnificent than that. Not as if He were magnificent (in Himself), but because He is Himself, He does not belong to one eon. He does not possess time, for those who belong to an eon were formed by others. . . . He, who only desires Himself, in the perfection of light comprehends pure light. The limitless dimension, the eternal one, the distributor of eternity; light, the distributor of light; life, the distributor of life; the blissful one, the distributor of bliss; knowledge, the distributor of knowledge; the one who is always good, who always distributes good and accomplishes good; not, in short, that He has it, but that He distributes it as well—mercy that has mercy; forgiveness that forgives; infinite light— what shall I tell you about Him, the unfathomable one?"[7] This is how a Gnostic papyrus described God, who was wholly from the other world, outside of the cosmos. Like the Allah of the Koran, he was radically different from manmade idols; He was not limited by time and space, a concept that was to become significant in Islamic theology as well. "Like Him there is naught," sura 42, verse 9, says about Allah; we have seen that Muslim theologians struggled to interpret this sentence. Yet they had to do so under entirely different circumstances than the Gnostics. The father of the universe, the true God whom the author of the papyrus celebrated so exuberantly, gave us light, life, everything that was good, mercy, and forgiveness; yet all this happened only inasmuch as He was light, the one medium in which His power unfolded. Allah's power, on the other hand, was extended purposefully to this world to preserve it—in fact, this world existed only because of Him.

A product of its time, the Prophet Muhammad's message was closely related to the Gnostic understanding of attaining salvation and of the world; we have to see it as a serious attempt to overcome Gnosticism. The Prophet adopted the strict separation between this world and the next; rigidified into a *topos* we can perhaps no longer understand adequately, the Gnostic structure of the universe is ever-present in the Koran's descriptions of paradise: the believers are taken to gardens "underneath which"[8] rivers flow; Mandaean literature states repeatedly that at the bottom, paradise is separated from this world by a body of water[9]; in other Gnostic cosmologies Leviathan lives in this border area, which separates this world immediately behind its seventh sphere from paradise, the here-after.[10] In the Koran, however, the calamitous separation between this world and the next has become a meaningful relationship between the two domains, showing us the path of salvation. In sura 95, verses 4–7, there seems to be a vague echo of the concept of the world as a prison into which human beings are thrown, without them being able to understand the meaning of this: "We indeed created Man in the fairest stature, then We restored him the lowest of the low— save those who believe, and do righteous deeds; they shall have a wage unfailing." In the Koran's con-cept, however, the fact that human beings were put into this world no longer spells doom for them, because faith and good deeds are justly rec-ompensed. Law-abiding actions in this world, and with the things of this world, are the path toward bliss in the next world; it is not the rejection of this world as the realm of darkness that leads to salvation. Instead, human beings are to prove themselves in this world, which now can no longer be understood as the work of an evil demiurg but as a kind Creator-God's gift of grace—a gift of grace precisely because it has become a realm in which human beings can take responsibility for saving themselves from the fires of hell.

Islamic theology had to explain why God was the wholly other, the One entirely of the next world, but not in the sense of Gnosticism's good Lord who was entirely outside of the cosmos that He did not even create. Thus the concept of God's total otherness, of His being entirely of the next world, was something that was passed on to the Muslims, who, how-ever, saw it in a different context: the wholly other was Himself the Creator of this world, which He ruled and tirelessly preserved. The tyran-ny of the stars and of destructive time was overcome[11]; God alone had the power of determination, and insofar as this world and the laws imposed on human beings in it were the result of the One's determination, the world, and man's life in it, had meaning. Gnosticism's inactive God, who was entirely of the other world, became the Koran's and Islamic theolo-gy's Creator-God who was entirely of the other world and ruled every-thing. He deprived the "soul, always commanding evil," of its power; it too was dependent on Him—it could do damage not always and inevitably, but only if He allowed it to. Joseph "would have taken her, but that he saw the proof of his Lord," we read in sura 12, verse 24. The struggle between—instinctual—soul and reason—which determined all of human life was not the duel between two independent forces, but the trial God had planned for His creatures, a trial that took place under his untiring direction.

Islam juxtaposed to Gnosticism's pessimistic view of the world a thoroughly optimistic concept of human beings and their possibilities for attaining salvation. Escape from the world, in all its varieties, was expressly rejected; an asceticism that imposed the burden of securing one's subsistence onto others, was considered indecent. The believers the Koran portrayed went about their everyday business without interference. There must not be a division into the mass of the *auditores* and the few *electi* as the Gnostic religion of Manichaeism knew it. A tenth-century treatise examining the relationship between Islam and other religions emphasized this strongly.[12] Basic traits of Islam can be interpreted as a defense against Gnostic religiosity. Yet Islamic theologians were certainly aware that the Prophetic message alone was not a defense against this; its anti-Gnostic traits needed to be distilled and extracted, for that *weltanschauung* would endure for a long time and was so adaptable that at times it even managed to put on an Islamic garb.

2. Gnosis and Early Islamic Theology

We have discussed Ibn al-Muqaffa' as a proponent of the caliphate as the institution with legislative responsibility.[13] But this was not the only regard in which he transferred ideas from his native Iranian tradition to his new field of activity, which was dominated by Islam. He is said to have wanted to replace the word "Allah" in the ever-present formula "in the name of Allah, the compassionate, the merciful" with the term "light." This would have been perfectly in line with the Gnostic concept of the nature of the good Lord outside of the cosmos that is described in the papyrus quoted above, for, as we have seen, it is divine light itself that is "mercy that has mercy." Ibn al-Muqaffa''s proposal indicates the closeness between the wording in the standard Islamic formula and Gnostic ideas, just as it points to the serious possibility of misinterpreting Islam gnostically. The Arabic term for "the compassionate" also refers to a qual-

ity, and "the merciful" to its realization. Yet, if this is connected to a personal creator and ruler of the world, then the meaning is totally different
than it is in its Gnostic context, and, to a Muslim, exchanging "Allah" for
"light" sounds like blasphemy. We can, however, see why early Islamic
rationalism could be enticed to "deflate" the concept of God—precisely
to take the target away from Gnosticism's attacks on Allah, the Creator;
and we also begin to understand why the God of the Koran, who is vividly described as someone whom His creatures perceived as an actor, prevailed against a pale construct of God: He formed the indispensable core
of Islam's message.

Ibn al-Muqaffa' attempted to devalue the Creator-God who was
praised throughout the Koran, which was also an indication of typically
Gnostic religiosity. As Creator, Allah could not resemble that sublime
God who existed beyond and without direct contact with this world. Ibn
al-Muqaffa''s criticism was also directed against the Islamic concept of
Allah as someone who assigned even illness and disaster to man.
According to Gnostic belief, these were consequences of the evil darkness that chained human beings to the dungeon of this world; it was utterly impossible that the good God of light, who was entirely of this world,
should be responsible for them. All of a sudden we begin to see the background of Islamic thinkers' struggle with God's *qadar*; as polemicists put
it, the Qadarites were the "sorcerers of this community,"[14] not only
because they postulated that God *and* human beings were (*two*) independent actors, but also because they turned all their attention to analyzing
the circumstances surrounding an action and its preconditions within
man. This entailed the danger of losing sight of Allah as the Creator,
which seemed to demote Him to an idle God. We may see early Islam's
increasing tendency to view everything that happened in this world,
including all human impulses, as the result of divine determination, also
as an attempt to stave off Gnostic theories. In addition, we can now see
how the Mu'tazilites' thesis that God only wanted what was best (*al-
aslah*) was apt to calm down their opponents within Islam: those who
tried to save the theory of human beings' responsibility for themselves in
this manner came dangerously close to the theory of the "good Lord" who
was entirely of the next world, in other words, to a Gnostic-dualistic way
of viewing the world. In the inner-Islamic battle among theologians, the

suspicion of having Gnostic tendencies was an insinuation that denigrated one's opponent; that it was voiced so frequently indicates how difficult it was to justify the Koranic concept of man against the backdrop of a deeply pessimistic perspective on this world, a concept according to which human beings were called upon to take responsibility for recognizing their own, God-given abilities and potentials.[15]

In Ibn al-Muqaffa', Allah has the traits of an evil demon. "Allah battles human beings; He boasts of His victories and the destruction of cities, He interferes in battles on the Muslims' behalf and gains victories that in reality are possible only with horses and swords, He sits on a throne from which He can step down. He has all the affects that are praised in human beings—grief, sadness, anger, change of mind." Ibn al-Muqaffa' furthermore criticized Islam's theory of the world's creation out of nothing. Dualism, he said, rigorously negated such a view, as the two principles of light and darkness were considered to be eternal. Therefore, creation out of nothing was inconceivable, and consequently it did not happen. Again we can see to what extent one of the core topics of Islamic theory can also be regarded as a reflection of its battle against Gnostic concepts. It almost seems as if Muslim theologians had let themselves be driven into the cul-de-sac of eleventh-century Ash'arite metaphysics, so much were they afraid of Gnostic speculations on the nature of this world, speculations that in the theory of the eternity of the world were also in agreement with ancient philosophical traditions. The vicinity of the two may have increased the Muslim theologians' defense against "Aristotle." And so, for Ibn al-Muqaffa', who was grounded in Gnostic tradition, Islam turned out to be the worst of all present and past religions because it rested on the oppression of peoples, on victories by the sword. It used human stupidity and continued to foster it. Living entirely in this world, it did not try to overcome it, but adapted to its lack of discipline.[16]

It appears that Ibn al-Muqaffa' did not utter his polemical remarks against Islam only because he wanted to disprove this new religion. Perhaps he intended to combine the politically victorious faith with Manichaeic or other Gnostic principles in order to purify it. In that case his criticism of Islam would be an indication of Gnosticism's much-documented attempts to appropriate foreign religions. As the Muslim concept of God appears in the Koran, Ibn al-Muqaffa' did not consider it to be the

original concept but viewed it as adulterated and humanized. He juxtaposed to it his own concept of God, which he obviously regarded as the
only correct one and therefore the one that had been originally intended.[17]

Abu 'Isa al-Warraq's (d. 861) life proves that the Muslim theologians'
worry about the attraction Gnosticism held was not unfounded. He was a
contemporary of the Mu'tazila's zenith in Mesopotamia, and initially he
probably leaned toward it, too. Yet the Mu'tazilites in Baghdad expelled
him from their midst for holding heretic views. For a while Abu 'Isa flirted with Shiism, and finally he allegedly turned toward Manichaeism.[18]
This is documented by his description of the myth of the deliverance of
the particles of light that were spread into this world. It is the only reason
the "light king" orders the building of the present world. Angels carry out
his order; the stars are created so that a procedure can be established by
which light can be extracted from the world. Numerous particles of light
now rise up along the "pillar of magnificence," along with eulogies, sanc-
tifications, the good word, and pious deeds. The particles of darkness, on
the other hand, sink down, until eventually the mixture has been separated. This, the myth states, is what resurrection and second coming means.
In other words, what is taking place here is a combination of the
Manichaeic process of deliverance and Islamic eschatology. Finally there
is only a little bit of light left, which, however, is so entangled with matter that the stars cannot tear it away. The two angels that hold the world
from above and below let heaven and earth break apart. Then the world is
ablaze, and the last vestige of light is liberated. Darkness, which now
yearns for the light that was wrested away from it, is pressed hard by
armies that finally push it into a specially prepared grave that is sealed by
huge rocks. This marks the end of the process of deliverance.[19] From
everything we know, the Manichaean myths of cosmogony and deliverance were actually much more complicated. It appears that Abu 'Isa al-
Warraq left out details that to his Islamic compatriots would have seemed
offensive. Apparently he revised and simplified the Manichaean theories
for his audience.

We have a source from al-Khayyat, a Baghdad Mu'tazilite, from
around 900, which disproves important Manichaean theories. "Recognize
that the Manichaeans believe that honesty and lying are two different,
mutually exclusive things. Honesty is good, it comes from light; lies are

the evil which is darkness. Ibrahim an-Nazzam[20] posed a question to them that compelled them to admit that someone lies at one time but another time speaks the truth. For he wanted to force them to state that one single actor sometimes commits two different things, good and evil, truth and lie. This, after all, would have implied a refutation of their theory of the beginningless eternity of two principles, of good and evil. This was a famous debate. He asked them how matters stood with someone who lies: was he not a liar then? They replied it was the darkness. He then asked what happened if that liar regretted having lied and said, 'I have lied and therefore done evil.' Who then was it who said, 'I have lied'? This confused them and they did not know what to say. But Ibrahim an-Nazzam continued, 'If you maintain that light made this last statement, "I have lied and therefore done evil!"—then light has lied, for (in your opinion) it was not light that uttered the lie but darkness. And so evil would have been committed by light, which disproves your opinion.'" Al-Khayyat explained that even if the line of argument had been reversed, Ibrahim an-Nazzam would have disproved the theory of the two basic principles, since in that case darkness would have spoken the truth. So while Ibrahim an-Nazzam emphasized that a human being could commit both good and bad deeds, the Manichaeans wanted to argue that one species could perform only one single action, fire could only heat up, and ice only cool down.[21]

Manichaeism appeared to be a religion that undermined the idea of human responsibility for oneself, the theory of the freedom of choice. Therefore, Islamic theology had to put the Koran's emphasis on man's duty to make a decision to commit good deeds in the center of its dispute with the Gnosis. On their balance sheets presented to them in the next world, human beings collected good and bad deeds, according to their behavior, for which they were solely responsible; this behavior could not be explained by the density of light particles in them. This would be nothing but an external force; but God gave this world to human beings with a usufruct, which is why they owed Him gratitude and obedience to the law.

We have already seen how the Sunnis' objection to this Mu'tazilite interpretation of the revelation used the suspicion of dualist tendencies, and how in view of the extent of divine and human determination of actions—vehemently debated since the Umayyad period—led to the negation of any freedom of choice on the part of the creatures. Thus this reveals the entire dilemma of Muslim theologians' attacks against Gnosticism: they really had to insist on human beings' potential to take responsibility for their own actions in and with creation and reject Gnosticism's interpretation of the world as a system of insuperable forces. Aside from the experience of God's omnipotence, this was in conflict with wanting to avoid the appearance of sharing dualistic views. The only way out was a system of different constraints—the Ash'arite system with its Creator and Lord who was the only one equipped with the power of being, and who arbitrarily ruled over His completely powerless creatures. Several modifications of Aristotelian philosophy taught the Ash'arites to view the world as a cosmos designed by God. This rescinded to some extent the new turn Islamic theology had taken and returned to creation a certain degree of power of being—a development recognizable since the late eleventh century that became possible not least because only vestiges of Gnostic and dualistic religions survived in territories ruled by Islam,[22] and furthermore, because a powerful Islamic orthodoxy developed which had tended either to annex or destroy foreign ideas rather than embark on the adventure of dealing with them intellectually.[23]

3. Gnosis within Islam

Gnostic ideas infiltrated Islamic intellectual life in connection with other traditions of late antiquity from the early Middle Ages on. This is richly documented, although one can hardly speak of a truly Gnostic revision of Islam's central message. Sufism adopted in a modified way the theory of a preexistent substance of light that was conceived of as the carrier of salutary divine being. However, Allah always remained the one God *and* Creator and preserver of this world; creation was never declared an anti-divine process. The Gnostic concept of the evil of the instinctive soul, on the other hand, which was alluded to in the Joseph sura, became a *topos* that Sufism liked to use in support of asceticism or practices aimed at subduing the self. Still, the backdrop against which the speculation on possibilities of purifying the self took place—for instance, in the work of Fakhr ad-Din ar-Razi or Ibn al-'Arabi—can hardly be called Gnostic. Rather, the point was to deliver the soul or the self from its entanglement in the extrinsic reality of this world, which was perceived through the senses, so that the ascetic could recognize under the surface phenomena the workings of the one being. Human beings needed not be delivered from the prison of this world, only from the chimera of their sensory perceptions and the way they were processed intellectually: then they would realize that the salvation of the next world was present even in the midst of the confusion of this world. These doctrines can hardly be called Gnostic; Ibn al-'Arabi saw in them—correctly, I believe—a sort of perfecting of the Prophet's message.[24]

If we turn back to the tenth century, we discover ideas whose Gnostic influence was much more distinct. Telling proof of this are the writings of the so-called "Pure Brothers of Basra," a cosmological collection in which Islamic views were combined with Gnostic ideas. Even this work's division of human beings into those who know and those who are ignorant may serve as evidence of the influence of Gnosticism. As we shall see, this theoretical device can also be detected in certain Shiite movements of that time, and later again in philosophers such as Averroes. Here it is difficult to decide to what extent the one element of Gnosticism—the division into *auditores* and *electi*—may be viewed as indicative of the appropriation of essential traits of this philosophy. As far as Averroes is concerned, we can safely say that this did not happen, and as for the "Pure Brothers," too, Gnosticism was only one of many ingredients. We can demonstrate this in the example of Islam's revision of the theory of the soul in need of salvation: "Not every soul that descends into the world of growth and decay is imprisoned in it, just as not everyone who enters a prison is locked inside it. Sometimes someone enters a prison in order to free the prisoners, just as someone may enter the land of the Rhomaeans in order to free the imprisoned Muslims. The souls of the prophets descend into the world of growth and decay in order to free the souls that are locked inside the prison of nature, drown in the sea of Hyle, and are chained to physical desires." This reveals the familiar Gnostic myth of the redeemed redeemer as it was preached, for instance, by the Manichaeans. The comparison with the redemption of Muslim prisoners—clearly an allusion to the heavy losses during the wars against Byzantium[25]—is probably based on sura 17, verse 73, which is typically interpreted to the effect that one day the Muslims will gather behind their Prophet and walk up to God. "Just like the prisoner escapes and is saved if he follows him who enters the prison in order to free him, so the one who follows the prophets in their laws, statutes, and on their way, escapes the world of growth and decay. He will be saved and will escape, even if this should take a long time. Of the Prophet it is said that he remarked, 'There is no God besides Allah.' The majestic God's speech says the same thing (sura 19, verses 71–72): 'Not one of you there is, but he shall go down to it; that for thy Lord is a thing decreed, determined. Then We shall deliver those who were god-fearing; and the evildoers We shall leave there, hobbling on their knees.'"[26]

Even earlier, the "Pure Brothers" had viewed this world and the next as directly relating rather than being in hostile opposition to one another as the Gnostics had taught; one could not be comprehended or exist without the other. "In reality, knowledge of the other world consists in knowledge of this world, for both belong to the species of that which is relative." Those who recognized this world at the same time recognized the other world, for both were intertwined. This world was the first object of our perception and thus also the first object of our knowledge. We perceived the state of our bodies and of the other members of our species "before we recognize our souls, see their world, recognize the members of their species, and enjoy the intelligible things among them. For all of that does not occur within our souls until they have separated from their bodies, just as we do not have sensory perception until our bodies have been born. For the soul's separation from the body is its birth, just as the separation of the fetal body from the mother's womb is the birth of the body."[27] This quote reminds us of Avicenna, who deduced from the ego's self-realization the individual's power of being, which was probably the decisive impulse toward the revaluation of the creatures' power of being. To be sure, the process of recognition in this passage, and even more so its further development by Avicenna, were certainly outside the boundaries of Gnostic religiosity in that this world had positive traits inasmuch as it was the first object of perception, the first indispensable step toward further development.

Once separated, the souls left the material world, the house of death, and returned to the immaterial world, the house of life. "God threatened the unbelievers to resurrect their bodies in order to confront them with their lies and pay them back for their evil deeds. He promised the believers to resurrect their souls and their spirits in order to pay them back for their good deeds and reward them for their actions. Therefore, may you, o my brother, not belong to those who may expect the resurrection of their bodies. Rather, endeavor to belong to those who expect the resurrection of the souls and hope for their lives and that they may reach their spiritual world in the house where true life is, where they shall live well for ever and ever, with the prophets, the truly righteous, the martyrs, and the pious. What good companions they are!"[28]

Once again we have approached the issue of Avicenna's influence on the development of Ash'arite theology, but via a different route than the one we followed in the last chapter. Were certain elements of his ideas also influenced by the Gnostic tradition? In his memoirs he wrote that his father had been recruited for the Isma'ilite Shia. Owing to his father's and his brother's instruction by Shiite agents he, Avicenna, had learned about their theories of the soul and the intellect, without, however, approving of any of this deep inside. Attempts to win him over to the Isma'iliyya had been in vain. Thereupon his father had him instructed by a greengrocer with knowledge in arithmetic, and later on hired a house teacher of philosophy who apparently did not lean toward the Isma'iliyya.[29] In any case, Avicenna was quite familiar with the faith of the Isma'ilite Shia, which—as we shall presently see—had definite Gnostic elements, even if he distanced himself from it in his memoirs. It would require a detailed analysis of his numerous works to decide how distant he actually remained to the Isma'ilite theories that those agents once taught his father and his brother.[30] There is at least the possibility that Gnostic ideas, too, had their share in shaping Islamic theology during the high and late Middle Ages, a theology whose most thrilling and—in the blending of this world and the next—most decisive rejection of Gnosticism consisted of the doctrine of the oneness of being.

The strange mixture of Islamic, Gnostic, and philosophical elements in the writings of the "Pure Brothers of Basra" was considered so characteristic of the Isma'iliyya that for a long time it was assumed that the author of that collection was an Isma'ilite Shiite.[31] Indeed, the Isma'iliyya of the tenth century was the reservoir into which Gnostic redemption myths and cosmological ideas flowed that were partly present in earlier branches of the radical Shia but were now interwoven with the philosophical traditions of late antiquity and therefore elevated to a more sophisticated level of reflection.

The early Shiite sects' Gnostic theories of redemption divided the course of the world into seven cycles on each of whose beginning is one Adam. "The first Adam and his offspring lived on earth for fifty-thousand-years living and dying and one following the other, and their spirits migrating from one person to the next. [The followers of a certain 'Abdallah ibn Harb, d. after 750] maintained that this happened according to the difference between the obedient and the sinners. And every time fifty-thousand years had passed, the obedient became angels and were lifted to the heaven of this world, but the rebels became creatures with deformed figures of whom God did not take care, and were placed underneath the earth. They said this confirmed God's word (sura 32, verse 26): 'Is it not a guidance to them, how many generations We destroyed before them in whose dwelling-places they walk? Surely in that are signs; what, will they not hear?' And they maintain that the ants, dung beetles, and roaches running about in their homes are those God let perish in former times, whom God transformed and whose spirits he made enter these clearly visible bodies." Thereupon a second Adam would be born with whom, and with whose offspring, the same thing would happen: the redeemed of the first cycle would make room for the redeemed in the lower heaven and rise into the next higher one; the condemned of the first cycle would be thrown into the next deeper earth by those who followed them. Thus, it would continue until all seven cycles had been completed.[32]

In this myth, 'Ali and the imams assumed the tasks of the redeemer. They appeared as celestial messengers of light who enlightened the souls imprisoned on earth about their calamitous situation. Obedience toward these imams erased the original sin for which the souls were thrown into this material world. Succumbing to the imams could bring deliverance from one's physical existence. This also entailed being freed of the obligation to observe all the details of Islamic law; for, 'Abdallah ibn Harb taught, at the end of the last cycle the cult would come to an end. These views were particularly shocking to other Muslims. They kept accusing the extreme Shiites of promoting lawlessness and suspected them of committing the most abominable deeds. Accusations of this kind spread to the different groups adhering to Gnostic ideas, even if charges were not leveled as openly as among 'Abdallah ibn Harb's followers. The doctrine of the oneness of being also aimed toward the elimination of the Sharia—not, however, at the end of times or under the rule of a redeemer-imam, but here and now.

From the oldest sources on the Isma'ilite Shia, we know that it, too, divided the entire history of the world into seven cycles. Each cycle was assigned to a great prophet. These were the "resolute ones" (*ulu l-'azm*) mentioned but not named in the Koran. The Isma'ilites believed that this group of seven prophets included Adam, Noah, Abraham, Moses, Jesus, Muhammad, and finally the Mahdi, who had not yet appeared; they were also called "speakers" (*nutaqa'*), since each of them had given humankind a revelation. The politically active groups within this Isma'ilite Shia believed that the appearance of the last prophet, the Mahdi, was imminent, and that preparations for his appearance had to be made by fighting a battle.[33] The first six of this group of seven had only been prophets of an extrinsic truth that corresponded to the revelation (*tanzil*). All of those, however, who carried each individual prophet's legacy, always brought the intrinsic truth (*batin*), the correct interpretation (*ta'wil*). Only the last prophet, the Mahdi, would reveal the intrinsic meaning once and for all.

The community's eschatological expectations were directed toward the Mahdi's coming. "Then Gabriel will appear to them on a piebald horse with eyes shining with light and a saddle with light on it; he will carry an armor of light, a helmet of iron, and in his hand he will hold a spear of light. . . . In the tip of the spear is victory, in its center, horror, and in its clamp, triumph; its shaft is made of the light of God's throne. . . ."[34]

As in all Gnostic systems, so in the center of Isma'ilite thought was the salvation of the human soul. Attempts were made to correlate these Gnostic theories to verses in the Koran, which was not always very successful. Sura 25, verse 46, says: "Hast thou not regarded thy Lord, how He has stretched out the shadow? Had He willed, He would have made it still. Then We appointed the sun, to be a guide to it; thereafter We seize it to Ourselves, drawing it gently." An early Isma'ilite text interpreted this passage as follows: "This refers to the completion of all growth and to the rule by the power of the sun and its effect—that the moon receives from it and its light increases on account of it, that it perfects itself by receiving the power of the builder, that it waxes, turns its full face, and after this has been concluded, wanes again by fading and disappearing, until it faces it again and steps into its light. Of itself, however, it has no power by which it would receive its light and brilliance, nor does it have a power through which it would be subjected to fading and disappearing; rather, the sun, when it unites with it, faces it, and steps into its light, releases again all human souls that were created by the assembly of the spheres and the earthly-material forces, and that rose up to it, because they and the intelligible soul of reason attract each other like magnets, with the soul of reason being above the spheres and ruling stars, while the human souls formed through assemblage remain below. Thereupon the sun transports them further into the sphere of Jupiter and Venus, according to the power of their deeds. In the same way, they then either remain in the other spheres or continue to rise up."[35] This description of the rise of the soul has parallels particularly in Manichaeism. The spheres of the moon, the sun, and the planets form a gigantic mechanism for filtering light, which has fallen into this world of matter and darkness.

In the tenth century 'Ubaydallah al-Mahdi (r. 909–34) established the empire of the Fatimids. In the same century the Gnostic legacy within Isma'ilite doctrines was reformed under the influence of Neoplatonic ideas. Neoplatonism exhibited traits that were similar to Gnosticism in that it considered the quality of being in the sub-lunar world to be inferior, as there the emanation of the one being was at work only in its innumerable split-off parts. However, this world was still the emanation of the One, and the process of emanation was neither good nor bad; it occurred with necessity, and in that sense was of neutral value. Therefore this world was not darkness per se; as the paragraphs from the above-quoted writings of the "Pure Brothers" have shown, Gnosticism's condemnation of darkness was mitigated. Furthermore, Neoplatonism now proved to be useful to the Isma'iliyya for religio-political reasons as well. The strict division of world history into a rigid system of cycles within which the location of the present time had to be precisely determined in order to prove that the Mahdi's arrival was imminent, was superfluous—and even troublesome—the moment the successors to the first two Fatimid caliphs, who had let themselves be celebrated as rulers at the end of days, had to legitimize their rule. The adoption of Neoplatonic ideas made it possible to glorify the "imam" in Cairo as someone with superhuman fullness of being,[36] without tying his rule to the course of a certain cycle. The Isma'ilite propaganda agents, who mixed Neoplatonic and Gnostic ideas,[37] were intellectually entirely up to date. And so they helped spread the traditions of late antiquity among Muslims, but for that very reason philosophy, which they made serve their purposes, was discredited in the eyes of many Sunnis.

Al-Ghazali's polemic against the Isma'ilites, in which he called these Shiites the "direction of the esoteric meaning" of the revelation, was written against the backdrop of Isma'ilite assassinations of Sunnite rulers and dignitaries and the foundation of the small assassin state of Alamut.[38] This polemic hardly did justice to the high intellectual level of Isma'ilite theories. Al-Ghazali attacked particularly the imams' claim to have infallible authority in matters of doctrine and to be teaching their followers the only true, allegorical reading (ta'wil) of the Koran; he also tried to disprove the statement that every caliph in Cairo was an "imam" without sin.[39] In al-Ghazali's description, the Isma'ilites' theory of the resurrection and immortality of the soul has much in common with the ideas of the "Pure Brothers"; overall, he characterized the Isma'iliyya as a movement that succumbed to Shiite influence only superficially, but according to their inner goals spread a mixture of dualistic and philosophical set pieces that were meant to create doubts about Sunnism's clear doctrines.[40]

After the end of the Fatimid rule in 1170, the Isma'iliyya regressed into a many-splintered group of sects. Besides the Alawis, who probably did not fully develop their ideas until then,[41] we should mention the Druzes,[42] as well as other splinter groups whose tradition lives on mainly in India today.[43] Many of these sects practice an arcane discipline. Their theories are often bizarre, which is no doubt a consequence of their being esoteric. Let me illustrate this by way of two quotes from Gnostic texts by late Isma'ilites. "The imam's humanness comes from the sublimated psyche of all . . . believers, which entered plants via the stars, and from there, as food, the present imam. He fathers the new imam in a natural but pure act guided by the ruler of the world, while the providence of the first intellect and mediation of the tenth connects this conceived human with the divine temple of light which until then is kept near 'gates.'"[44] "Sura 4, verse 156: '[T]hey did not slay [Jesus], neither crucified him, only a likeness of that was shown to them,' as well as from a poem by Husayn: 'You have not been killed, but limbs appeared for the enemies' eyes which resembled yours': the nonmaterial souls and the sublime temples of light can be neither killed nor crucified nor die at all, but only the physical frames of flesh and blood, which are but an allegory of the nonmaterial temples of light."[45]

Gnosticism was an efficient catalyst for the development of Islamic theology and even the development of the religion itself. In regard to Sunnism, where the vast majority of Muslims found their center of existence from approximately the mid-ninth century on, Gnostic ideas lost their quality as a serious challenge after the end of the Fatimid caliphate. Gnostic religiosity lives on in splinter groups such as the Druzes, who Sunnis have often claimed do not belong to Islam, and the passages just quoted seem to indicate that the Neoplatonic penetration of the Islamic Gnosis was partly reversed in those sectarian movements. The Gnostic metaphor of light lived on in the theory of the oneness of being and similar persuasions, as well as in the Iranian theosophy of the Twelver Shiites during the early seventeenth century.[46] Yet the radical devaluation of the world as a dark dungeon, which is Gnosticism's most prominent characteristic, did not find a home there.

CHAPTER VIII

Islamic Orthodoxy

1. Sunnism as the Religious Creed of the Majority

The various religious persuasions within Islam that had developed during the Umayyad period differed from one another in what they considered to be the essence of right guidance and in their interpretations of Islam's early history. The different branches of Shiism tended increasingly to distinguish 'Ali, his early followers, and his descendants from the rest of the Muslims; the vast majority of Muhammad's companions, who during the first decades after his death had not joined 'Ali's camp, were reviled as sinful and not even considered to be a part of Islam. Later generations were to be guaranteed salvation solely based on their pledge of allegiance to the imam, who was a descendant of 'Ali. Only the Zaydi Shiites repudiated this narrow view and opposed the rejection of the major part of early Islamic history as a chain of antidivine misdeeds[1]; yet once their views gained political influence under Caliph al-Ma'mun (r. 813–33) and his successors, the other Shiite branches could no longer be kept from walking the path of sectarianism either, nor could Sunnism's victory be averted. Not even the two and a half centuries of Fatimid—that is to say, Sevener Shiite—rule over Egypt and parts of Syria and northern Africa could halt this victory. Among intellectuals and sometimes even the politically powerful, the Isma'ilite propaganda agents were not without success, but they were not able to win over the masses to the Shia. On the contrary, thanks to the theological groundwork of such men as al-Ash'ari and al-Juwayni, the tenth and eleventh centuries were marked by the triumph of Sunnism, and, in the area of politics, its explicit claim to political leadership within the Islamic world. The Abbasid caliphs now acted as pioneers of the preservation of the Prophet's *sunna*, and the Saljuqs, forcing their way in from the east, legitimized their sultanate by becoming the Sunni caliphs' agents. Therefore, Shiism remained the faith of a minority. In some areas, however, it was highly influential—for instance, in the capital of Baghdad, where 'Ali's party dominated several districts and, with some frequency, fought battles with the city's inimical Sunnite quarters.[2]

Ahmad ibn Hanbal (d. 855) had tried to replace the Shiites' hatred of the Prophet's companions by the obligation not to say anything bad about them and let the partisan conflict among Muhammad's successors rest. The Prophet's companions had been promoted to guarantors of all aspects of early Islam's way of life, which was to be adopted by way of the *hadith*, in order to prevail on Judgment Day.[3] Sunnism was characterized by a generosity that forgave and embraced everything that had happened in the past—a generosity that was now also extended to 'Ali and his followers: 'Ali, it was now said, had been a heroic fighter for the Prophet and his cousin and father-in-law, and even after the latter's death he had accomplished great things for Islam. Love of 'Ali and the entire family of the Prophet was certainly compatible with Sunnism,[4] except viewing 'Ali as a conveyor of salvation who had bequeathed the only true, authoritative interpretation of the revelation—that was impossible!

Ahmad ibn Hanbal was named as the author of a credo[5] that also illustrates the conditions for the Muslims' entrusting themselves to Sunni generosity. That individual Mu'tazilite and Shiite theories were condemned, is not surprising; but membership in the community of the orthodox required major sacrifices: "All questions of doubt avoided by the (*sunna*) scholars must be detested! Be altogether aware of [impermissible] innovations (*al-bida'*)!"[6] Analyzing doctrines by applying the categories of reason was to be abstained from altogether. We have already seen that in the eleventh century, the Shafiite al-Juwayni got around the prohibition against the practice of theology with the means of human reason—that is to say, rational theology—by declaring that any knowledge someone possessed was "necessary," in other words, given solely by God.[7] "Consult about your faith with no one who supports [impermissible] innovations! Never choose him as your travel companion!"—this was how Ahmad ibn Hanbal reinforced his exhortation about speculation in religious matters. Religious speculation was the first thing orthodox Muslims had to renounce; the second thing consisted of abandoning any millenarian hope such as Shiite movements kept taking advantage of in rebellions against the existing order. After all, millenarianism was out of place in a community that conceived of itself as the realization and perpetuation of the wholesome beginnings. There would be the end of history, an end of antidivine disorder, and the prophesied Mahdi would destroy the satanic enemies directly before the verdict on the Day of Judgment. That was promised, but for those living here and now this promise could not be a justification of revolutionary activities. "After the Prophet, the best human being was Abu Bakr, after Abu Bakr, 'Umar, after 'Umar, 'Uthman, after 'Uthman, 'Ali ibn abi Talib. These, by God, are the rightly guided caliphs! And we attest to the fact that these ten men have entered paradise: Abu Bakr, 'Umar, 'Uthman, 'Ali, Talha, az-Zubayr, Sa'd, Sa'id, 'Abd ar-Rahman ibn Auf, and Abu 'Ubaida; because him whom the Prophet promises paradise, we, too, acknowledge as destined for paradise. . . . Love the people of the *sunna*, no matter what their actions are! May God let us and you die believing in the *sunna* and the harmonious community! May God allow us and you to pursue true knowledge, may God grant us and you that we successfully do what He loves and approves!"[8]

These beliefs paralyzed reason, anxiously sought acceptance of the religious doctrines and the Sharia, and rejected any kind of millenarianism, and it was thus that Sunnism had its first great success on the political stage. Caliph al-Mutawakkil (r. 847–61) allowed the Sunnis to exert their influence at court, a privilege the Mu'tazilites had previously enjoyed. Still, the Abbasid caliph did not become an integral part of Sunnism until the early eleventh century. As far as we can tell from the sources, until that time a clear idea of what orthodoxy was developed mainly among Ahmad ibn Hanbal's students and their students in Baghdad.

Even Ahmad ibn Hanbal, in his discussion of the Mu'tazilite theories concerning God's attributes, had demanded that all statements in the Koran be accepted without being questioned. What God's hands or face were really like, human beings would never fathom so they should not speculate about them. Yet as a tenth-century Hanbalite explained, this prohibition did not extend to the use of reason altogether; on the contrary, on the Day of Judgment the verdict would be rendered according to how much or how little reason the individual possessed. Only in matters of faith was it usually deleterious to follow one's reason.[9] What was important was to protect from all criticism the holy texts, the Koran and the traditions concerning the Prophet, which were now available in collections; for even a cursory reading of these texts revealed how contradictory their statements were and to what extent they sometimes required that reason be abandoned. If one looked at the details, the close connection between this world and the next that was expressed in the revelation could be maintained only by seriously straining faith; if statements about the domain of the "unseen" were as general and abstract as possible—which rationalism aimed at in the metaphysics of that time—then less effort was required. But in that case, what were those texts of the revelation and the *hadith* worth? If their content was not supposed to be a subject of debate, then Ahmad ibn Hanbal's "Without How!" was the only solution. To be sure, it was reasonable only in regard to its aim, the suppression of a religious battle: had this battle really gotten underway, it hardly could have come to a conclusion that was satisfactory to reason, as our lack of knowledge of the "unseen" would have made it impossible to weigh things against each other. Sunnism put its stake in what was considered "Islamic" by as general and informal a consensus as possible,[10] and insisted on binding reason to the content of that "Islam." Refusing to let reason even get close to the contradiction as a means to avoid conflict was not enough; rather, what needed to be accomplished was the development of rational arguments supporting the claim that "Islam," even though it ran counter to reason in some respects, was the highest goal of human knowledge.[11] Reason needed to disempower itself by explaining with rational arguments that believing to be true was better than comprehending.

In a brief outline of Sunni doctrines written in the tenth century, we find the following passage: "Know that in the *sunna* there can be no analogies. Allegories cannot be applied to it, and [in order to recognize it] one must never follow one's own views (*al-ahwa'*)! The only thing of importance is that one believes the traditions about God's messenger, without How and without explanations. Never ask, Why or how? For speculation, argumentation, dialectic debate, and dispute are [evil] innovations which ignite doubts in one's heart, even if [one's statements] express the truth and the [right] *sunna*. And know that speculation about God is also an innovation; it is impermissible and an error. One should say about God only what He has said when He described Himself and what God's messenger told his companions in the Koran. So the magnificent God is One; like Him there is naught; He is the One who sees and hears. Our Lord is the first one, without when, and the last one, without end. He knows what is hidden and secret, He sits up on His throne. His knowledge is everywhere, no place is free of His knowledge. In regard to God's qualities, one must not ask why or how. Only doubters do that. The Koran is the word, the message, and the light of God. Yet what is part of God, is not created." Another passage impresses upon the reader: "Whenever you hear a tradition that is too difficult for your intellect to understand, such as the statement of God's messenger: 'The hearts of the believers are between two fingers of the Merciful,' or 'God descends to the next heaven, He descends on the day of 'Arafa, He descends on the Day of Resurrection,' or: '[Human beings] are thrown into hell until He, the Magnificent One, sets His foot on it,' or God's promise to humankind: 'If you approach me, I hurry toward you,' or: 'God created Adam in His image,' or the statement of God's messenger: 'I beheld my Lord in the most beautiful figure,' or whatever may correspond to traditions like these, then it is your duty to accept this as true, to leave what is meant up to God and to content yourself. Do not interpret any of this arbitrarily; it is necessary to believe in it. He who interprets any of this arbitrarily or rejects it is a Jahmite. . . . For God's messenger has said: 'Think about creation, but do not think about the Creator!' For thinking about the Creator foments doubt in your heart."[12]

Believing to be true guaranteed harmony within the community. We will recall the idea of the "harmonious community" as the only legitimate manifestation of the community established by the Prophet upon God's order. Even back during the Umayyad period, the idea of the "harmonious community" had been so powerful and influential that the kind of active piousness that tried to reach its goal through the performance of bold deeds (*iman*) was softened and largely replaced by the ideal of a piousness of rites (*islam*).[13] In the tenth and eleventh centuries we can observe a similar process in the field of theology. The efforts to explore the content of faith by reason had led to a confusing mass of theories and views that threatened the community's harmony. It became advisable to reflect on the consensus on what Islam was, whether or not this Islam proved to be rationally convincing. The reason it had to be considered true was shown by the quickly evolving theology of Ash'arism in its discussion of the theories of rationalism. The Ash'arites practiced polemics that appeared to be rational; in their opinion, the content of "Islam" in the sense of orthodoxy had already been established, once and for all, in the Koran, the hadith, and their standard interpretations. Therefore the only issue in question was whether Ash'arite polemics were still necessary. Could orthodoxy not do without them? The Sunnis, following Ahmad ibn Hanbal, answered that question in the affirmative. Thus a certain Ibn Batta (d. 997) wrote in a theological work, which he started out by distinguishing Shiites, Kharijites, Mu'tazilites, and other groups from "right" Islam, that Islam was characterized first by adopting (taqlid) the views of the Prophet and his companions without reservation, and second, by leaving up to God those questions of theology that were incompatible with human reason and its categories; and third, orthodoxy meant unconditional submission to all of God's laws.[14]

Orthodox believing to be true was accompanied by the desire to cover up all religious conflicts of the past; what was not supposed to be part of the "harmonious community" could only be individual splinter groups and sects that on account of their small membership alone did not pose a danger to Islam's basic consensus. The Shiites, whom Ibn Batta excluded, broke up into many movements; the Kharijites—also split into several groups—survived as minorities at the fringe of the Islamic world; and the Mu'tazila was for a few educated people. Everything else that could not be labeled as insignificant had to find room under the broad banner of orthodoxy: Ahmad ibn Hanbal granted 'Ali ibn abi Talib and other controversial companions of the Prophet admission to the "harmonious community." This tendency to include all kinds of opinions in orthodoxy was reinforced in the eleventh century. Abd al-Qahir al-Baghdadi (d. 1037) described the foundations of Islamic faith and explained why Sunnism was the only true movement. He found his explanation in early Islamic history as he chose to see it, including among the ancestors of orthodox Islam even some of the Umayyad caliphs during early Sunnism, such as al-Walid I (r. 705–15), who had been criticized for their love of ostentation; due to Sunni zealousness, the same happened to Ja'far as-Sadiq, the sixth Shiite imam, one of the most important authorities of early Shiite theory.[15]

2. Orthodoxy and the Islamic State

We still are lacking a history of the relationship between Islamic rule and Islamic orthodoxy. It would have to begin with the efforts of the Abbasid al-Ma'mun basically to determine from the top what was the right and generally accepted content of Islam, a content that could be explained rationally and was supposedly acceptable to everyone.[16] Thwarting these efforts, the inquisition quite unintentionally supported Sunnism's rise to Islam's majority faction. Even back in the tenth century, Islamic rulers who wanted to appear as administrators of the "right" Islam could do so only as champions of the *sunna*. The antimillenarian and anticonflict character of that religious camp openly offered itself to, if not forced itself upon, the caliphs as an ally. The first to describe this was the Abbasid al-Qadir (r. 991–1031). His long rule was overshadowed by the threat of an attack by the Fatimids, whose secret propaganda agents were active even in Baghdad; it was also overshadowed by the disintegration of the Buyid dynasty, which was from Iran and since the middle of the tenth century was factually in power in Mesopotamia. The capital itself suffered frequent outbursts of the hatred between Sunnis and Shiites, the latter enjoying the Buyid princes' favor.[17]

In this unfortunate situation al-Qadir gave the Sunnis his full, unqualified support. An obvious sign of this policy was a Sunni doctrine published under the name of Qadiriyya, which was expressly confirmed in 1034 by al-Qa'im (r. 1031–75), his son and successor. The Qadiriyya started with a definition of God's oneness: He was the sole Creator and preserver of the world; from our perspective, we human beings could not comprehend His omnipotent nature. All qualities God attributed to Himself in the Koran and the qualities in the Prophet's description of Him must be understood as real not metaphorically. This was clearly an antithesis to Jahmite and Mu'tazilite views. The statement that human beings could not deduce their fate in the next world from indications in this world points in the same direction. The Qadiriyya also took a stand on early Islamic history: all of Muhammad's companions, including of course 'Ali, were to be lovingly revered.

Many parts of the Qadiriyya reflect the theological debate that took place before the turn of the millennium. One passage explicitly states that

God created light *and* darkness. This was directed against dualistic doctrines, and particularly against the Mu'tazila, which had claimed that darkness was nothing but the absence of light. This would have meant that a large part of what we perceive could be interpreted as the mere nonexistence of another thing or fact; for instance, the evil that human beings commit could be conceived of as a lack of good. In the Mu'tazila's view, God always created what was good and helpful to human beings. The Sunnites, on the other hand, insisted that both good and bad came from God; that was the only way the appearance of dualistic views could be avoided. Another argument that was directed against the Mu'tazila was the relatively detailed explanation of the uncreatedness of God's word. Whether it was recited, known by heart, written down, or heard, God's word itself always remained uncreated. Those who believed anything else, this warning said, were to be outlawed. Even when human beings uttered or wrote down God's word, it remained in its essence uncreated and eternal. This was in agreement with Ash'arism's teachings. The same holds true for the definition of faith, which in the Hanbalite view simply meant observing the Sharia's doctrines (*din*), as established by law, and in holding on to the community. The Ash'arites, on the other hand, stated that this alone did not sufficiently establish faith, which went far beyond that. Accordingly, the Qadiriyya acknowledged the formal proof of faith, which was furnished by one's participation in ritual prayer; but it also stressed that there was no limit to the number of actions of faith. As long as a human being lived, his or her belief was connected to right action. In the Qadiriyya's words, faith covered the spectrum from professing the one God to removing dirt from a road. In addition, we find in the Qadiriyya the foundations of a Sunni ethic that is based on the virtues of modesty and humility (*haya'*) and of persistent patience (*sabr*): one had to surrender to everything God had predestined.[18]

Whenever al-Qadir and his successor referred to Sunnism, that persuasion may have seemed to them like a homogeneous entity. This changed from the mid-eleventh century on. The Ash'arites gained more and more enemies. After all, they practiced *kalam*, and had not Ahmad ibn Hanbal criticized that very *kalam* as an expression of the arrogance of the human mind? 'Abdallah al-Harawi (d. 1088), a Sunni with Hanbalite tendencies, attacked the Ash'arites downright furiously; he believed he recognized in them not defenders of *sunna* piousness but one of the many reprehensible movements of rationalist theology from which Islam had had to suffer for centuries.[19] In Baghdad tensions within Sunnism became noticeable and, for the first time, erupted in excesses against Ash'arites in 1068. And yet, just during that time there would have been the chance to make the *sunna* the "state religion." The Saljuqs, who leaned toward the Sunnis, had replaced the Buyids in positions of political power; the caliph had formally promoted them to his agents with unlimited authority. Nizam al-Mulk, the energetic vizier of the Saljuq great-sultans Alp Arslan (r. 1063–1072) and Malikshah (r. 1072–92) emphatically supported Sunnism, founded universities of law and theology, as well as new Friday mosques when this proved convenient for appointing preachers faithful to them. Yet he would not let himself be involved in the Sunnis' debate on Ash'arism[20]; deciding that argument in favor of one of the opponents, even if he had been in a position to do so, would in the long run have frustrated Nizam al-Mulk's efforts. And so the conflict continued to smolder, which helped to push a thorough blending of orthodoxy and political rule into the distant future. The highly acrimonious battles between proponents and opponents of rational Sunni theology continued; increasingly the Ash'arites became a minority persecuted by the Hanbalites. The guardians of the silencing of reason in religious matters did not shy away from denouncing Sunnis who flirted with al-Ash'ari's teachings. They told the rulers these Sunnis were proponents of unbelief, which put their lives in extreme danger.[21] To be sure, the Hanbalites' Sunni enemies were not exactly indulgent either. Their time came in the mid-thirteenth century with the rise of the Mamluk sultanate. The military rulers in Egypt and Syria were not the most zealous fighters for a rigorous application of the Prophet's *sunna*; naturally they were Muslims, but often their Islam was strongly influenced by the hagiolatry that became popular at that time. The living conveyors of a relationship with the world of the unseen were closer to them than Islam's dead Prophet with its incredibly intricate sets of rules that could be traced back to him. Therefore conflicts with the strict proponents of the *sunna* were unavoidable.

The towering figure in the battle for Sunni orthodoxy under the conditions that had changed so radically since the eleventh century was Ibn Taymiyya (d. 1328). In 1293 he became for the first time involved in political matters. A Christian had been accused of offending the Prophet. Ibn Taymiyya took up the matter and whipped up passions. This made him unpopular with the Mamluk rulers, who disliked such zealousness since it forced obligations on them that they wanted to assume only when it was politically convenient. Ibn Taymiyya was thrown in prison. Later, however, the sultans were compelled to take advantage of his oratory power. During al-Malik al-Mansur Lajin's rule (r. 1297–99) he was ordered to incite the Muslims to wage a religious war against the kingdom of Armenia Minor. Ibn Taymiyya finally gained great renown in 1300, during the Iranian Il-Khans' advance against Syria. He distinguished himself once again when he prodded the Muslims into fighting the holy war against the Mongols. In addition, he personally participated in battles against the Shiites in the area of Kasrawan.

Yet fending off external enemies was not the only issue during those turbulent centuries; Ibn Taymiyya's orthodoxy was called into question, and he was accused of anthropomorphism. Ever since the split within Sunnism in the eleventh century, the Ash'arites had kept leveling that charge against their Hanbalite enemies, claiming that Ahmad ibn Hanbal's "Without How!" did not mean one should leave the Koranic statements on God alone, but was aiming at believing the "this-worldly" content of Koranic statements such as "hand of God" to be true. Accusations leveled against Ibn Taymiyya became increasingly serious. Finally, in January 1306, two debates took place at the court of the Mamluk governor of Damascus. Ibn Taymiyya was spared; it was confirmed that his statements were in agreement with the Koran and the *sunna*. Still, the matter was not over. One month later there was another meeting, whose upshot was that he and his harshest enemy, a Shafiite Qadi, were sent to Cairo. There Ibn Taymiyya was again accused of anthropomorphism and arrested. He had to spend almost one and a half years in the capital's citadel. Barely released, he continued his fight what he regarded as impermissible religious reforms. Not until 1308 did he receive permission to return to Damascus.

In 1309 he was arrested again, probably because of his attacks against the theory of the oneness of being. His agitation had antagonized the spiritual mentor of Sultan Baybar II (r. 1309). He was deported to Egypt and placed under house arrest in Alexandria. There he still managed to make contact with pilgrims from Maghreb and promote his ideas. He wrote a refutation of the teachings of Ibn Tumart, the founder of the Almohad movement. Apparently this work was a rejection of millenarian ideas. Unfortunately, it has been lost. His house arrest finally suspended, Ibn Taymiyya went to Cairo, where he wrote his treatise on political government in accordance with the Sharia. In this book he demanded in the uncompromising manner characteristic of him that all of the sultans' measures be in agreement with the Sharia.[22]

In 1313 Ibn Taymiyya returned to Damascus. He received the sinecure of a teacher at a school of law and theology and finally found some rest, propagating his ideas and attracting many students. Yet during those years too he continued his fight for orthodoxy. He did not stop arguing with the Ash'arites and wrote an extensive treatise on the Prophet's *sunna*, a rejection mainly of Shiism. In his old age he still clashed with the political authorities. Ibn Taymiyya had raised objections against certain measures that in his opinion were not in agreement with Islamic law, and in 1321 he was incarcerated in the citadel of Damascus for five months. In mid-1326 he was arrested again. This time he had provoked the authorities' anger through a polemic condemning the cult of gravesites and stating that only the Prophet had the right to intercede with God on behalf of a believer. He penned yet another series of polemic writings in his dungeon; later, however, ink and paper were taken away from him. In 1328 he died while in custody.

Ibn Taymiyya's fight for a pure Sunni faith has four prominent traits: one, he constantly assailed the *kalam*, and in particular logic, which in his opinion should not play a part in matters of faith. Two, he attacked the theory of the oneness of being as it had been popular since Ibn al-'Arabi and others in his wake.[23] Three, as can be deduced from the fact that he wrote a treatise against Ibn Tumart, he pounced on any kind of millenarianism that tried to put the beginning of the epoch of salvation in the present. Four, he naturally fought against Shiites of all colors. The purpose of Ibn Taymiyya making clear distinctions between different ideas and movements, however, was not exclusively to fend them off; what concerned him was not a literal faith that was predefined in all its details and originated in scholarly speculation and instruction by the imam or some Sufi sheik. On the contrary, Ibn Taymiyya tried to regain unqualified

respect for the ancient Islamic principle of rejecting anything that mediated between God and the believers (cf. sura 9, verse 34). He was concerned about regaining a simple and genuine experience of faith as, in his
opinion, the ancients had had a faith that could do without all these artificial aids and the good offices of mediators. He explicitly picked up
where al-Ghazali left off in the description of his conversion in *Savior
from Error*: true knowledge of Islamic faith was like a light one had
received directly from God. Ibn Taymiyya hoped that all believers would
have a similar inner experience. Yet he did want to spare Muslims the path
through the onslaughts of doubt. Al-Ghazali had had to suffer them; but
Ibn Taymiyya was convinced that there was the possibility of directly
acquiring the ancients' unshakable faith, and that it could be found in the
tradition from Islam's earliest times. Ibn Taymiyya presupposed that the
ancients had been fully instructed about all matters of faith so it was a
sign of stupidity to regard as more intelligent and better those who came
after them. He did not even want to let the argument stand that those who
came later had developed more refined and meaningful methods of theology. As far as Ibn Taymiyya was concerned, these refined intellectual
tools were nothing but signs of a weak faith that had spread all around.[24]
Even he made palpable the transformation which the worship of saints
and the theory of the oneness of being had brought about: the goal of Ibn
Taymiyya's orthodoxy was a kind of certainty of faith that could not be
attained by acquiring knowledge of the content of the tradition.

Orthodoxy is not simply the rejection of theories considered false; in
that case it would degenerate into sectarianism. From the ninth century
on, Sunnism had the tendency to incorporate as many forms of Islamic
piousness as possible. Ibn Taymiyya did not strongly support that trait of
Sunnism. In view of the tremendous success of the worship of saints and
the doctrine of the oneness of being in which it was rooted, the reliable
forces of integration had to become active sooner or later. Indeed, they
can be detected as early as the early fourteenth century, during Ibn
Taymiyya's lifetime: al-Qashani (d. c. 1335) wrote a commentary on Ibn
al-'Arabi's *Original Messages of Wisdom*—from a Sunni point of view
the theological standard work on the oneness of being—as well as the
famous poetic description of the Egyptian Ibn al-Farid's (d. 1235) Sufi
experiences, in which work the hierarchy of saints culminated in

Muhammad and the four rightly guided caliphs.[25] The magical practices, too, that are part of this kind of Sufism were accepted and defended among Sunni scholars.[26]

It was not least the piousness of the general populace that helped Sharia Islam stand its ground next to Sufism with its strong influences of the worship of saints and the doctrine of the oneness of being. It even prevailed as the dominant element of an orthodoxy that *also* integrated the spiritual aspect of religion, the area where saints played their roles. In a didactic poem written in Anatolia at the time, we read that the world was ruled from three thrones created by God. The men on these thrones, the ruler, the Sharia scholar, and the saint, organized the world on behalf of God—ruler, scholar, and saint were indispensable for its continued existence. From the first throne human beings were ruled by the sultan, now with fairness and clemency, now giving free rein to the force of his anger. From the second throne human beings were instructed by the scholar versed in the Sharia and the proper performance of the rites. The third throne was reserved for the saints; they purified the human heart; that was why God gave the saints power over the unseen—they established direct contact with the One.[27] The orthodox Muslim's life took place in a triad consisting of the ruler's power, the performance of rites, and the instruction of the heart.

This triad was most lastingly and harmoniously realized in the Ottoman Empire, whose Anatolian founders breathed the very spirit expressed by the didactic poem just mentioned. Orthodoxy without including the saints—the orthodoxy of an Ibn Taymiyya—did not gain the upper hand there, precisely because of where the Ottomans came from. Even when many members of the Syrian-Egyptian stratum of Sharia scholars joined the Ottomans in the fifteenth century, this did not destroy the symbiosis between saints and experts of the law. On the contrary, the balance between the two ways of thinking, which had been achieved among the common people, was now duplicated on the higher level of theory of law, theology, and philosophy.

We have already heard in a different context about 'Ala' ad-Din at-Tusi's efforts in that direction: Sunni orthodoxy defined the limits within which philosophy could be practiced.[28] Yet the influence of this balance between the two ways of thinking can be shown not only in theoretical treatises but also in the biographies of that era. Prince Bayazid, a son of Mehmed the Conqueror (r. 1444–46 and 1451–81), was governor of Amasya when he was young. There he cultivated the friendship of a certain Mu'ayyad-zade. For unknown reasons Mehmed ordered his son to kill that companion; yet even before he held the sultan's decree in his hand, he had given his friend some items he needed for his survival and sent him abroad. Mu'ayyad-zade went to Shiras, where he studied Koran interpretation and the *hadith*, but also gained familiarity with the "sciences of reason," theology and metaphysics. When he heard that his sponsor had ascended to the throne, he returned to Anatolia; soon afterward Bayazid II (r. 1481–1512) made him director of a number of schools of law and theology in Constantinople, later promoted him to Qadi of Edirne, and eventually even to military judge of Rumelia, the European part of the empire. His Ottoman biographer praised him because he had perfectly mastered the sciences based on tradition *and* rational inferences.[29] The life and work of Mu'ayyad-zade—we have, for instance, a collection of *fatwahs* and a treatise on various issues of Islamic law by him, plus his commentary on a fourteenth-century *kalam* work—would offer a good starting point for an analysis of orthodoxy in the Ottoman Empire, with which we can deal here only very briefly.

The establishment of a hierarchy of legal scholars (*'ulama'*) under the Ottomans, which up to that point was unparalleled in the Islamic world, expressed a profound blending of orthodoxy and political power. At the top of that hierarchy were the military judges of Rumelia and Anatolia as well as the Mufti of Constantinople, who bore the title "Sheik al-Islam."[30] This hierarchy of scholars was intricately intertwined with the Sufi orders, where the "instruction of the heart" was tended to, in particular those orders that knew how to appear Sunnite—such as the Khalwatiyya, but especially also the Naqhbandiyya, whose influence reached its climax in the eighteenth century.[31]

3. Shiite Orthodoxy

The tenth century was a time of profound transformation for the Shia; in the end two kinds of Shiism were irreconcilably opposed to one another. The first one urged its followers to be politically active, fueling their fighting spirit with the promise that the arrival of the ruler of the eschaton was imminent. The second one was prepared for a long wait and, for the time being, took on the task of cultivating the traditions of the imams in the non-Shiite "state of untruth." It would continue to do so until the twelfth in that series of imams, Muhammad al-Muntazar, who had been carried off in 874, would at an unpredictable point in time return and destroy everything that was against God. The believers who were ready to fight here and now for the Mahdi, whose imminent arrival they were hoping for, gathered in the so-called Sevener Shia, whose by far most influential institution was the Fatimid caliphate. Established at the beginning of the tenth century in what is today Tunisia, it transferred its center to Cairo in 969; it lasted until 1171. As we have already seen, it was a threat to the Abbasids in Iraq, but in the long run was no competition for them in the fight for supremacy in the Near East: the Fatimids did not succeed in suppressing their followers' chiliastic zeal, which had brought them to power—certainly not to the degree that once the caliphate was established, they would be able to extend their influence without interference. On the contrary, inner conflicts concerning the question of which caliph was the real savior weakened the Fatimids and split their followers a number of times.[32] The idea of individual responsibility for one's salvation remained so much alive that, throughout their history, the Fatimid caliphs were unable to create a society that was based mainly on Shiite orthodoxy. During the Umayyad rule, there had been conflicts between "faith" and "Islam," in the wake of which piousness based on the rites and the traditions had become the characteristic sign of the religion that Muhammad had established. This conflict was now repeated in the tenth century within Shiism.

Like the Sevener Shiites, the Twelver Shiites were convinced that there must be a living imam who would guarantee salvation to all those declaring their loyalty to him. In the ninth century the Twelvers' imams claimed authority in matters of doctrine, which allowed them to proceed against renegades within their own ranks. The Twelver Shiites' period of the "lesser occultation" began in 874. It was said that the last imam was removed from the midst of his followers on earth because those in office in the "state of untruth" had persecuted him so tenaciously and cruelly that he had had to fear for his life. The "lesser occultation," which was followed by the "greater occultation" beginning in 941 and lasting to this day, made clear that the Twelver Shia had stopped believing that the end of time was near. Around the same time the conflict with the Isma'ilites began. While the latter tried to enforce the rule of the Mahdi, weapon in hand, the Twelver Shia taught that one's true faith should be concealed in a hostile community, for one lived in a state of truce with that malevolent community. Two fragments of a speech attributed to 'Ali ibn abi Talib defended that view: God would always leave something on earth that would safeguard the continuity of the order He had established; even if the imam had been removed during the era of the truce, this did not mean that the knowledge that had been passed on to the believers had disappeared. Rather, the ways of conduct taught by the imams lived on in the hearts of the believers and determined their actions. Only if there were no longer any upholders of that knowledge would evil have been victorious. Yet it would never come to that. It was "the true Shiites who follow the leaders of the faith, the rightly guiding imams, who comply with their rules of conduct, and who emulate their example. . . . It is they who follow the scholars and accompany the people of this world in obedience to God and His friend, and who exercise caution with regard to their faith and fear their enemies. Their spirit is connected to the supreme place. (The Shiite) scholars and their followers are deaf and mute in the state of untruth, and expect the state of truth. God will make the truth in His words prevail and extinguish their untruth! Blessed are those whose faith endures in the state of truce! How I yearn to behold them when their state of truth has arrived! God will unite us with them in paradise, and with their pious fathers, wives, and offspring!"[33]

The Isma'ilite scholars had inherited the knowledge the imams had taught. The Twelver Shia's tradition developed from the ninth century on, comparable to the Sunnite tradition one century before. Convinced that one could live in the state of untruth and keep a truce with its leaders, the Twelver Shiites rejected radical millenarianism. Yet even within this group sometimes the belief surfaced that the end of time was near. The scholars, however, the guarantors of quietist orthodoxy, tried to suppress such developments. They insisted that giving any thought to the date of the Mahdi's arrival was taboo.

One example of the Isma'ilite scholars' battle against millenarianism was the early history of the Safavids. Sheik Isma'il (r. 1501–24), the founder of the Safavid state, had believed himself to be the incarnation of the expected Mahdi. He celebrated himself in poems as God's secret, as one of the twelve imams, and even dared say: "Prophetship is with me, . . . I am the elected Muhammad's successor." Yet apparently the poems in which he expressed these thoughts were edited by scholars. The earlier his manuscripts, the less frequent are their allusions to Isma'il's Mahdiship.[34] The rise of the Safavids gave the Shiite scholars for the first time the opportunity to implement their ideas of Shiite orthodoxy in cooperation with a ruler. Incidentally, they always viewed themselves as to a certain degree being in opposition to the powers that be. As far as the Sunnites were concerned, for the simple reason that the rule of Sunni sultans was an actual reality, it was legitimate—as long as the Sunni scholars could see to it that their legal opinions made sure that power was exercised in formal agreement with the Sharia. This was different in Shiism. The Shiite scholars remained convinced that even the Safavids' power was ultimately illegitimate; for only the expected twelfth imam could be a legitimate ruler. Thus they always kept a certain distance to worldly power. They could, for example, tie the Shiite believers more closely to themselves than the Sunni scholars had been able to. The task the Shiite scholars had to perform was, similar to that of Sunni scholars, to preserve the tradition and see after its correct application. Yet the believers were obligated to a more comprehensive and profound loyalty to the scholars than they were in Sunnism, for this loyalty was also determined by the emphasis on the imams' responsibility for salvation before the era of occultation.

Incidentally, Shiite orthodoxy also struggled with the issue of the extent to which the right doctrines could be preserved simply by constantly reading and studying the traditions, or whether a rational theology was not necessary after all to corroborate those doctrines. In regard to Sunnism, this conflict ended with the defeat of Ash'arism, the theology employing rational arguments. As soon as the Safavid state was consolidated, the "traditionists," called Akhbariyyun, also gained the upper hand in the Twelver Shia. Their opponents, the Usuliyyun, were unable to exert more influence until the second half of the eighteenth century.[35]

CHAPTER IX

Islam as Ideology

1. Islam Is Knowledge

There is a general consensus that Napoleon's landing in Egypt marks the beginning of the modern period in the Islamic world. In 1798 a militarily, economically, and technically superior and rapidly expanding foreign power invaded a living space that had been firmly structured since the days of old. From a Muslim point of view, until then this power had been faithless and therefore seemed inferior, but now it forced its laws onto the believers, at least on the surface. The Egyptian Mamluk regime, which had been under more or less relaxed Ottoman sovereignty since the beginning of the sixteenth century, collapsed. A new, strong man rose during the time of confusion that followed the French's inglorious retreat: Muhammad 'Ali (r. 1805–48), an Albanian from Kavalla in what is today Greece, who had proven himself for the first time in the Ottoman army. At a suitable opportunity he had the leading Mamluks murdered with ruthless brutality,[1] but he also recklessly pressured the notables in Cairo and the city's population, which had hoped he would restore public order—all in pursuit of his political aim: to seize power. Countless despots had sought power before him, but 'Ali's means were new to the Islamic world.

Muhammad 'Ali believed he would be most successful if he put together a new army that was loyal only to him. This became his primary objective and he was assisted in this by a large number of European experts who came to Egypt to advise him. Muhammad 'Ali used state capitalist methods to exploit the entire country for the purpose of assembling his army. When he temporarily expanded his rule to Syria in the 1830s, he was again mainly concerned with measures that exploited the conquered territory for the maintenance of his army. That Muhammad 'Ali concentrated so exclusively on the military sector and secured the abilities of European experts was not that unusual for an Islamic ruler of that time.

After the bitter experiences during the eighteenth century, especially in Russia, the Ottoman sultanate itself initiated military reforms modeled after Western examples; yet after the radical upheaval in Constantinople, there was no opportunity for a new beginning as there was in Egypt. In that respect the situation was more favorable to Muhammad 'Ali; he could take control of his country's entire economy inasmuch as it was able to come up with the moneys and goods he needed for his army. The fact that his battalions thoroughly defeated the Ottoman army in 1839 and came dangerously close to Constantinople seemed to affirm his policy of Egypt's forcible westernization. Furthermore, Muhammad 'Ali also tried gradually to become independent of his foreign experts. He sent four gifted young men to study in France. One of them, at-Tahtawi, wrote a long report about his stay in Paris in which he enthusiastically described the achievements of Western civilization and remarked bluntly on the embarrassing state in which his home country was. To be sure, he also realized that simply imitating technological innovations would not be enough; he supported the introduction of a political system comparable to that in France.[2] If most members of society were excluded from the modernization and transformation of the country, a lasting success was impossible, and reforms would only expand the ruler's power.

Indeed, as far as the vast majority of the population was concerned, Muhammad 'Ali's goals had remained strange and incomprehensible; most people had to carry an ever heavier burden. They witnessed the creation of a world of glitter that was inaccessible to them, populated primarily by foreigners. In his memoirs, Muhammad 'Abduh (1849–1905), one of the outstanding figures of Islam during the late nineteenth century, expressed with great passion the helpless anger this state of affairs generated. Muhammad 'Ali, he wrote, had considered all of Egypt as his private property and crushed any sign of independence among the population. "And what did he do then? He greedily wanted to become a ruler independent of the Ottoman sultan. To reach this goal, he secured the assistance of Europeans! He treated them extremely courteously and helped them get more privileges than had been agreed upon between them and the High Gate. In the end just about any European scoundrel who previously did not know how to feed himself from one day to the next became a king in our country, who could do whatever he wanted without being accountable for anything. Thanks to the ruler's power the natives had to humiliate themselves before the foreigners; the foreigners enjoyed those rights of which the natives had been deprived, and the Egyptians became frightened strangers in their own country." The Islamic foundation they had inherited, on the other hand, had been totally neglected; Muhammad 'Ali did not in the least deal with the language reform that was so desperately needed, nor with the creation of a school system grounded in the country's own tradition. And Islamic faith, the pillar of the sultanate? In nothing he did, 'Abduh complains, did Muhammad 'Ali pay his respect to religion. Still, some might say that the despot expelled the Wahhabites from the holy places of Islam; but 'Abduh remarked that this certainly did not happen in order to lead those who had gone overboard on some religious issues back to the right middle course, but only to reach a power-political aim: to expand the ruler's influence onto the Arabian peninsula, to the detriment of the Ottoman Empire.[3]

Muhammad 'Abduh criticized the fast modernization of Egypt, which was triggered by France's attack, as utterly superficial and having no organic connection whatever with the gradually developed Islamic culture. This criticism was certainly justified. Muhammad 'Ali's policies, continued by his successor, ruined the country. This is not the place to retell this often told story[4]; may the remark suffice that these events were always analyzed with the question in mind of why Muhammad 'Ali's attempt at modernization—an attempt imposed from above, and by force—was doomed to fail. It is automatically assumed that France's technological rationality could not be implanted into Islam's quite different rationality. But in what sense Islam is so different is an issue that has so far been insufficiently examined, if at all. It is, however, key for any discussion of what Islamic theology might be under the influence of a superimposed foreign civilization that, as no Muslim denies, makes life easier. We shall discuss it in the next few pages by looking at some writings by Ibn 'Abidin (1784–1836) from Damascus, a man with a strict, classical Islamic education who lived apart from the main political events in Egypt and can serve as a witness to the *weltanschauung* of the major part of the population, which had not yet come in contact with Europe.

Ibn 'Abidin was born to parents who traced their family back to Hasayn ibn Ali ibn abi Talib.[5] As was usual in scholars' families, he began to study as a child, starting out by learning the Koran by heart and then penetrating the voluminous scholarly literature on the interpretation of the Holy Book. Soon Arabic grammar and Shafiite law were added. Later he switched to a Hanafite teacher and was instructed in the "sciences of reason"; he now also worked his way through the large compendia of the Hanafiyya's sixteenth-century law. The Hanafiyya was the predominant school in the Ottoman Empire, and eventually Ibn 'Abidin joined it. In addition, he was accepted by the Naqshbandiyya order and wrote a treatise in which he defended Shaykh Khalid, a prominent member of that Sufi association, against certain charges. The worst of the accusations was that his attitude—he claimed he could see into the future—violated the Sharia.[6] Working in Damascus as a teacher, Ibn 'Abidin enjoyed great respect. He was buried there next to the famous Hanafite jurist al-Haskafi (d. 1677), "and pilgrims traveled to his grave to pray for the fulfillment of wishes."[7]

During his studies of Hanafite law, Ibn 'Abidin had reproduced part of a much-studied legal opinion by Hamid ibn Muhammad al-Qastamuni (d. 1577).[8] He had touched on the question of how someone who had talked derogatorily about the Prophet Muhammad should be punished. Since the high Middle Ages, members of the other law schools had pleaded for the death sentence for the guilty. Yet the Hanafite tradition did not justify this sentence; rather, the perpetrator should be given the chance to meditate on his deed and repent, which could avert the execution. Ibn 'Abidin admitted that he was disgusted by such clemency, "but reason has no room for its own rules when the tradition is clear and unequivocal."[9] Under pressure from Sultan Süleyman II (r. 1520–66), the Hanafite law school had to get closer to the somewhat stricter opinion of its competitors in the sixteenth century[10]; fortunately, the justification for this had been found in the writings of al-Bazzazi, an early-fifteenth-century Hanafite.[11] Ibn 'Abidin, dissatisfied with this development because it circumvented ancient Hanafite tradition, had become involved in a learned debate with the Mufti of Homs on this issue. He presented his view, which differed from the opinions of Sultan Süleyman and al-Bazzazi, in a treatise that illuminates his understanding of knowledge and science.

According to Ibn 'Abidin, there were two different ways of assessing the legal implications of insulting the Prophet. The offense could be viewed as an instigation to unbelief and thus to overturning the Islamic order; then it would have to be punished by death, like all rebellions, as it was suggested in sura 5, verse 36. Yet the offense could also be interpreted as a renegation of Islam; in that case, the offender would have to be urged to repent and reaccept Islam before he could be sentenced; if he complied, his life was saved. As Ibn 'Abidin explained, both views could be substantiated by legal arguments. Yet as far as he was concerned, that was not decisive (in the true meaning of the word). Only Abu Hanifa's opinion, *as it had been passed on to us*, that the offender was a renegade, must serve as the basis for any further reflection. Yet what about the teachings of the great Hanafite jurists of the fifteenth and sixteenth centuries, who had followed al-Bazzazi and, therefore, pleaded for the death sentence? For Ibn 'Abidin, that was the crucial question![12] Perhaps those jurists let themselves be blinded by considerations of pragmatism or the validity of the lines of legal argument of the other law schools. A careful and conscientious scholar, however, must not be influenced by any of this. He first had to examine the forefathers' views! In Ibn 'Abidin's opinion—which expressed the standard view of his school—these were Abu Hanifa, and then his students Abu Yusuf and Ash-Shaybani, plus a few prominent authors of the next generation. The prominent Hanafites of the various epochs did not carry the same weight; the later ones had some degree of influence only under certain conditions, particularly if none of the elders' opinions had been documented. At the time when Ibn 'Abidin was writing, there were only people who passed on traditions; no one could claim to be forming his decision independently any longer.[13]

Ibn 'Abidin characterized the long-completed work of the first generations following the Hanafite school's founding fathers as "interpretation by quotation, derivation (of legal maxims)," and then "considering and (possibly) correcting" the results.[14] That, however, meant nothing else than that absolutely all new legal knowledge could be found in the works of the ancestors, and only there! It was the task of Muslim scholars to hold on to the level of knowledge that had once been obtained, even if it had not been entirely explained. Therefore, all scholars of former generations were to be esteemed more highly than those of the present generation; for all former generations were closer than the current generation to the one and perfect knowledge the ancients had possessed. Thus even a man like al-Bazzazi deserved the greatest respect, and he should not be criticized perfunctorily. "It is part of the sublime God's mercy that He has protected the Sharia through spokesmen who preserve and explicate it, and that He instructed (them) to explain it openly, forbade them to keep it secret, and did not grant them any flattery or leniency. The scholars constantly corrected one another, even when they were talking about their own fathers, teachers, or someone who was older or the same age as they were. . . . God kept only His book (the Koran) unassailable. The errors a scholar makes are in part spelling mistakes, and in part they come from combining two different legal assessments or something of that kind. Yet none of this decreases the scholars' rank, and by no means does it lead to distrust toward them. . . . Usually one of them makes a mistake, and the one who comes after him sustains this mistake. . . ."[15]

That is how it apparently happened in the case of the verdict on the man who had insulted the Prophet. Ignoring by mistake the tradition going back to Abu Hanifa, al-Bazzazi used inappropriate arguments, and others, relying on his authority, adopted his solution. Yet saying "I followed al-Bazzazi!" on the Day of Judgment would not help a scholar; al-Bazzazi lived too late to be considered one of the people who "weighed things," let alone one of the ancestors who were able to come to a decision independently (*mujtahidun*)![16] For men like Ibn 'Abidin, scholarly activity could only mean to examine, one by one, the handbooks from the early and late Middle Ages and the Ottoman period that were still extant, in order to detect mistakes such as the one al-Bazzazi had made. Ibn 'Abidin reported proudly that he had several times succeeded in doing so.[17]

Early Islam developed a concept in which "knowledge" was a treasure of information given to human beings once and for all; this concept found its literary expression in the genre of the *hadith* and then also influenced the concept of scholarly activity and activities in which reason was used in general. As we can see in hindsight, it furthermore also determined the development of Islamic orthodoxy: if the entire knowledge available to human beings already exists, any millenarian hope is destroyed, for it is simply impossible to believe that the God-given *conditio humana* can be surpassed. God "taught Adam their names, all of them" (sura 2, verse 29); human beings were obliged to pass them on unadulterated. The knowledge God had taught Adam was the only one that counted; anything beyond this knowledge was ultimately insignificant—al-Ghazali had illustrated that in the example of the sometimes abstract mathematics developed in antiquity, and in his outline of the parts of philosophy that had to be compatible with true faith, 'Ala' ad-Din at-Tusi explained the same thing four centuries after him. Only the knowledge that contained Islam as an order of faith, society, and political rule was important, necessary, and real knowledge; human beings were equipped with reason only for the purpose of saving it from being tainted or of cleansing it from perhaps already present contamination. Therefore, reform and innovation could never mean to revisit what was inherited with regard to new developments and events the ancients could not have predicted, or to let oneself be guided by the spirit of one's inheritance whenever necessary, and to use it for interpreting and processing the unexpected. Rather, reform meant revealing the content of already existing knowledge—of the Muslims' *conditio humana*, in which al-Ghazali had recognized the best and most just of all possible worlds. The better this revelation would succeed, the more Islam would triumph, simply because Islam was the best way human beings could live together—it was the way God wanted it (sura 3, verse 110)—because it was also the entire knowledge of the perfectly just cosmos, of God's creation, that was accessible to human beings.[18]

All of the Islamic reform movements we will discuss in the next subchapter are rooted in these ideas; hence they fit snugly into the centuries-long development of Islamic orthodoxy. By no means can they be explained primarily as a response to the "Western challenge." This challenge certainly acted as a catalyst from the mid-nineteenth century on, but it was not the reason for what has become characteristic of present-day Islam: the increasing prominence of its ideological component.

Al-Ghazali and 'Ala' ad-Din at-Tusi—to limit ourselves to these two—measured the achievements of a foreign culture by their compatibility with Islam, with the unchanging, God-given knowledge. From the Muslims' perspective, a foreign culture has no value in itself, as its way of seeing the world is wrong or at least inadequate. If a foreign culture has produced anything of significance, this significance consists only of it being—inadvertently—in agreement with part of the real "knowledge," which is accessible only to Muslims. There is no process of civilization in which all peoples and cultures participate in different ways—sometimes as inspiring leaders, and sometimes by receptively and appropriately developing it. Hence European civilization, whose breathtaking rise since the waning eighteenth century has threatened the Islamic world, is not perceived as something that should be examined as an autonomous phenomenon in order to integrate it creatively into Islam's own culture whenever and wherever possible. European superiority in the areas of science, technology, economics, and politics can be explained only by believing that the West took certain parts of the unchangeable treasure of knowledge and purged them of all distortions—more so than the Muslims are able to at this time. What comes to mind in this connection is that in the Middle Ages Latin Europe had borrowed from Islam the basics of what had led to its apex—and that in the nineteenth century, the Muslims would have needed only to copy the achievements that seemed useful in order to stand up to the West. In light of these ideas, copying new developments, particularly in the area of technology, turns out to be merely a transplant of achievements of civilization to their place of origin.[19]

In contemporary Islamic literature, this view of things is very popular, and hardly anyone dares question it. It is the main reason why the whole world of technology with its effects that profoundly shake up religiosity has not become a theological problem of the first order, and why it is hardly ever even seriously discussed. Usually we hear the smug remark that as the religion that is based on human reason, Islam simply has no difficulties with science and technology, but in view of the disputes over the question of where the border is between divine and human determination of actions, and of the tendency of Islamic theology to draw this border very much in favor of God, this is a rather implausible claim. Islamic theology's peculiar silence about a radical challenge to its basic beliefs can be explained as follows: without further questions, all "useful" products of Western civilization are declared part of the stock of unchangeable knowledge that jurists such as Ibn 'Abidin tried to make accessible in an uncontaminated form; thus these products are legitimized within the framework of Islamic orthodoxy and identified as Islam's "property." Hence the only way out of the decline of their culture and power, which the Muslims of the nineteenth and twentieth centuries could not possibly ignore, is in completely revealing the God-given treasure of knowledge already mentioned. This transforms the content of this knowledge—Islam in an ideal sense—into an ideology from which advice and guidance can supposedly be gained in all questions and vagaries of modern life.

2. Reform in the Spirit of Orthodoxy

As we have seen, the so-called reform movements of the nineteenth century may be interpreted as a continuation of the battle for orthodoxy that had been fought since the early Middle Ages. If we look at Sunnism, we can make out two different interpretations of what established orthodoxy: one more inclusive interpretation, which grew out of the history of thought in the Ottoman Empire; it tolerated philosophy as well as the worship of saints to the extent that they did not violate the Koran or the *sunna*; and a more exclusive, narrow interpretation, which considered valid only the two specifically Islamic sources. Ibn 'Abidin leaned toward the former interpretation. He was a member of the Naqshbandiyya order, an association whose Sufi ideals were rooted in *sunna* piousness.[20] He described the hierarchy of saints, at whose top was Muhammad, in a short treatise in which he leaned on the preliminary work of an early-fourteenth-century scholar, 'Abd ar-Razzaq al-Qashani, who even back then strove toward a balance between Ibn 'Arabi's spirituality and Sunnism.[21] In another short essay Ibn 'Abidin focused on a defense[22] of the activities of the Naqshbandi leader Shaykh Khalid (d. 1827),[23] who spent the last years of his politically very active life in Damascus.

Ibn 'Abidin himself was not yet a reformer of Islam. He had no doubt that the unchangeable and perfect knowledge given to the Muslims by God could and should be acquired, comprehended, and, if necessary, purified of misinterpretations through a study of the commentaries on and annotations to the real sources, the Koran and the *hadith*. In other words, the products of scholarly diligence that had piled up over the course of many centuries were the indispensable means for the acquisition of that knowledge. The innovators, on the other hand, viewed them as an obstacle that was difficult to overcome and distracted from what was essential those who sought access to real knowledge; this did not affect the view *that* that knowledge was comprehensive and unsurpassable.

Let us briefly look at the life's work of Muhammad ibn 'Ali as-Sanusi (1787–1859), which may serve as an example of reform movements originating in the more inclusive kind of orthodoxy that was inspired by Sufi spirituality. As-Sanusi was born near Mustaganim near Oran and educated mainly in Fez in the sciences of Islamic faith. He quickly established close connections with several Sufu orders. Early on he was himself rumored to be a holy scholar. As a mature man he felt the desire to visit the cities of the Hijaz. His first pilgrimage took place in 1815, and his second, in 1826, took him to Mecca. He had spent the year 1824 in Cairo continuing his studies at the University of al-Azhar, the most reputable school in the Islamic world. Yet what the scholars there had had to offer must have deeply disappointed him. As in former years, they still cultivated the huge volume of commentaries and metacommentaries, amassed over centuries, while as-Sanusi was looking for his own access to the sources, freed of the jungle of didactic scholarship. He had promoted his ideas and, as could be expected, incurred the displeasure of the representatives of conventional instruction. After his arrival in Mecca he made friends with Ahmad ibn Idris al-Fasi, the founder of a Sufi brotherhood. Al-Fasi, some thirty years older than as-Sanusi, was also from Maghreb, but had left his home as early as 1798 and since then lived in the Hijaz. Muhammad ibn 'Ali as-Sanusi, who was displeased with the scholarly literature that had superimposed itself on the original Islam and kept growing rampantly, found in Ahmad ibn Idris a brother in spirit: for Ahmad, Sufism's supreme goal was not the mystical union with God, which he considered impossible to achieve, but the spiritual union with the Prophet. This replaced the belief—which is often hard to distinguish from magic—that it was possible to influence directly the domain of the unseen by an effort to bring Muhammad's life and work to life, as the works of al-Qashani and those leaning on him had suggested to the believers. Becoming engrossed in what life was like during the early history of Islam now became the focus in lieu of the theology of the "oneness of being," which was degenerating into speculations that were difficult to understand and could ultimately no longer be controlled by reason.

Ahmad ibn Idris and Muhammad ibn 'Ali as-Sanusi's thoughts went in a similar direction; so it is not surprising that they found each other, just as it is not a surprise that they made enemies in the more conservative circles. They withdrew into the mountain area of Asir, where Ahmad died in 1836. Later on as-Sanusi returned to northern Africa, where he established a Sufi order in what is today Libya. How much his success irked the circles devoted to antiquated scholarship is indicated by the *fatwah* issued against him in 1843 at the University of al-Azhar. The critical events specified in the *fatwah* had happened almost twenty years before.[24] As-Sanusi was accused of having intentionally failed to attend the Friday services and the prayers led by an imam—which, should the accusations be true, may have expressed his disrespect for the dignitaries of the University of al-Azhar. The authors of the *fatwah* insinuated that his behavior constituted a haughty violation of the Prophet's *sunna*. They then addressed their real point: the interpretation of the Koran and the *sunna* which as-Sanusi had taught was above criticism, really; but what was reprehensible was that he set out to interpret both sources all by himself, even though the founders of the four law schools had already rendered definitive interpretations. In going back behind the ancestors' achievements and arrogating the right to find the truth (*ijtihad*) all by himself, he had left the firm ground of Sunnism.[25]

As-Sanusi justified his search for direct access to the sources of Islam. Uncritically adopting the conclusions of previous generations, he wrote in a treatise, was dangerous; for in the past mistakes had been made, too. Ibn 'Abidin and many other Islamic legal scholars and theologians had been aware of this as well; but they had believed in the possibility of preserving the entire theoretical construct of prevailing ideas and ridding it of all defects in an endless, laborious, and painstaking process. As-Sanusi did not altogether reject that notion, but insisted that later generations too should be allowed, and even had, to start out their intellectual work with the sources, the Koran and the *sunna*. Then it would turn out which scholarly achievements would remain and which would not. In any event, it was irresponsible to accept blindly a kind of interpretation of the sources that was sanctioned by any law school. The Koran contained the solution to any conceivable problem; if the Prophet, who was divinely inspired, made a remark on how a certain question was answered in the revelation, this remark was obviously binding for all Muslims; but none of the interpretations of any other believer could claim similar authority and was, therefore, subject to revision. Hence a new beginning in the independent search for knowledge was nothing but a return to the conditions of early history. Since what the revelation and the *sunna* determined had not yet been established, one had to rely on one's own intellectual capacities.[26]

Like al-Ghazali before him and Ibn Taymiyya after him,[27] as-Sanusi was concerned with shaping Islamic life from the supposedly spontaneous piousness of the beginning as a starting point. He expressed this quite explicitly toward the end of his treatise: Sufism, aligned with the Prophet, offered the best foundation for this, for those who immersed themselves deeply into spirituality received abundant knowledge, "just like God explained it through the mouth of His Messenger." Knowledge came down in a stream from up above, not as a revelation in words, which required the form of the law or mediation by a prophet.[28]

The most important reform movement adopting the narrow interpretation of orthodoxy was Wahhabism. It was established by Muhammad ibn Abd al-Wahhab (1703-92), a Hanbalite from the area of Nedjd. After pursuing his studies at home and in the Hijaz, Ibn Abd al-Wahhab, still a young man, went to Basra, where he had the opportunity to encounter Islam in all its manifold variations, including Shiism and Sufism. In the 1740s he was again in Nedjd, where he preached to Bedouin princes, trying to ignite in them the fire of the ancestors' strict faith. He found support in the emir dynasty of the Banu Sa'ud; in 1744 he and the ruler of the Bedouins entered into a sworn agreement that obligated them to build an empire in which God's unadulterated word was to rule. This was the birth of the kingdom of the Sa'ud which by the end of the eighteenth century posed a serious threat to the rulers of the Hijaz, the Hasanite sharifs of Mecca. The Ottomans, the lords of the Arabian peninsula, noted this with concern. In 1803 the Wahhabites entered Mecca for the first time, where they immediately put an end to the merry activities that took place there each year during the pilgrimage season. Yet their puritanical, strict interpretation of Islam earned them the reputation of being barbarians. Now the Ottoman Empire felt compelled to interfere. The High Gate ordered one of its vassals in Egypt, Muhammad 'Ali, to test the army he had assembled and wage a battle against the Wahhabites. Muhammad 'Ali complied; between 1811 and 1813 the Wahhabites were expelled from the

Hijaz. During the entire nineteenth century they fought among the Banu Sa'ud for their survival. Under Abd al-Aziz they succeeded in 1901 in reestablishing their rule by conquering ar-Riyyad; since 1925, when the conquest of the Hijaz was completed, their territory has been what is today Saudi Arabia. Yet the impact of Muhammad ibn Abd al-Wahhab's ideas, even back in the nineteenth century, extended much further than his unsuccessful battles may lead one to assume; they fell on fertile ground in the Islamic part of India, and also gained followers in all areas of the Arab world. At this point it is difficult to determine to what degree Wahhabism was responsible for the most prominent reformers of the late nineteenth and early twentieth centuries so clearly adopting the narrow interpretation of Islamic orthodoxy.

Muhammad ibn 'Abd al-Wahhab's understanding of the true nature of Islam was formed by his study of Hanbalite writings, in particular the works of Ibn Taymiyya. That the Arabian peninsula was anything but a bulwark of Islamic strictness, is not only proven by the Wahhabite justification of the war against the holy cities of Islam, whose loose, impious lifestyle,[29] incidentally, is documented even for the waning nineteenth century. In general, we have to see Islam, as it was exercised by the majority of Arabia's population, as a religious practice that was determined more by popular religious customs than by the Koran. As during the time before the Prophet, the cultic worship of trees and holy places blossomed; there were many gravesites to which were ascribed beneficent powers and which people visited to pray for having their everyday needs met. The oldest sources on the appearance of Muhammad ibn 'Abd al-Wahhab paint a lively picture of all these "un-Islamic" goings-on[30]; wherever possible, Muhammad ibn 'Abd al-Wahhab destroyed such places of "unbelief" and tried to advance the Islamization of the Bedouins. He tackled a task in which the Prophet had once failed.[31]

In his statements on the theology of Islam—which naturally were meant not for the Bedouins but the scholars—Ibn 'Abd al-Wahhab stressed that the Koran and the *sunna* constituted the only foundation of faith. Any movement that ignored this principle removed itself from orthodoxy, which was to be regarded as a position of the center, one between all controversial views. As far as God's qualities were concerned, the orthodox believers were "between the Jahmites, who drain the divine predicates of their content, and the anthropomorphists, who compare them with human qualities; in regard to divine action they are in the middle between the persuasion that presumes the freedom of human will, and those who deny it. As for God's threat (of punishment in hell), they are in the middle between the Murjiyya and those proponents of the freedom of will who believe that threat to be true. In regard to faith and religion, they are between the Kharijites and the Mu'tazilites on the one hand and the Murjiites and Jahmites on the other. As for the issue of the companions of God's messenger, they are between the Kharijites and the Shiites."

It is doubtful if this center is more than the simple negation of clear statements. For Muhammad ibn 'Abd al-Wahhab does not seem to have tried to describe the content of this center position in theological terms. He probably would have refused such a request as unreasonable. For, in his way of thinking, everything that was not part of that center—any explicit theological statement, that is to say, any statement that went beyond a quotation from the Koran or the *sunna*—was bound to appear as a deviation, as a sacrilegious "innovation" (*bid'a*). It seems that he was charged with condemning the entire history of Islamic thought, for in a sort of credo he penned in 1768 he defended himself. All these charges, he said, were slanderous: "God knows . . . (that) I did not claim and . . . it did not even occur to me that the writings of the four law schools were null and void, and to proclaim that people have not taken a valid stand for six centuries; that I lay claim on making the law an independent search (*ijtihad*) for myself and am not continuing the work of the scholars of previous generations; that I teach that the difference of scholarly opinions is a punishment; that I declare those to be unbelievers who seek the interference of the pious (with God) . . . ; that I prohibit the pilgrimage to the Prophet's grave, disallow visits to one's parents' and others' graves, declare those to be unbelievers who swear by anything but God; that I declare Ibn al-Farid and Ibn al-Arabi to be unbelievers. . . ."[32] If, for example, Muhammad ibn 'Ali as-Sanusi's theories made the law schools' accomplishments look questionable, then the same holds true for Ibn 'Abd al-Wahhab's aim to build an Islam entirely on the basis of the Koran and the *sunna*. In that case, he must disprove the suspicion that he had declared unbelievers all brothers in faith whose performance of the rites and way of life followed the rules of a law school, as well as all Muslims

who were steeped in Sufi piousness. This would have been the vast majority of all those who professed Islam, and could hardly have been taken as
a "center position." Therefore, Ibn 'Abd al-Wahhab conceded in his credo
that he rejected only the presumptuousness of those saints who, disregarding the power attributable only to God, claimed that they could
achieve something on the supplicants' behalf; but he did not deny that
there were indeed saints.[33]

Yet what was the significance of his, a Hanbalite's, being accused of
claiming for himself the right to an "independent search" for the solution
to matters of law and rites within the context of the Koran and the *sunna*,
but rejecting the law schools? This touches on the crucial point that makes
clear why it was the Hanbalite version of orthodoxy and not any other that
became the basis of reform efforts. Hanbalism had always claimed that it
was able to come to its own conclusions and determine its application of
the Koran and the *sunna* independently; but its understanding of this
intellectual task differed from that of the other law schools. As far as the
Hanbalites were concerned, the "independent search" always had to be
pursued by going back directly to the documents of Islamic faith[34]; the
accomplishments of the scholars after Muhammad were irrelevant for any
interpretation of the Koran and the *sunna*. Ibn Taymiyya had become convinced of this when examining the entire history of Islamic thought; he
wrote down the results of his analysis in a treatise with the programmat-
ic title, *Parallels between What Was Passed On Correctly and What
Untainted Reason Determines.*[35]

In other words, there is perfect agreement between the content of the
revelation Muhammad had received and the content of everything human
beings who apply their faculty of reason correctly can find out about
themselves, the world, and their own destination. An Islamic orthodoxy
that is rooted in this belief was really constantly called upon to use its own
reason as well as the traditions and to determine if the scholars' statements were correct; it no longer looked upon the work of the ancestors as
reluctantly as Ibn 'Abidin had. As far as he was concerned, pure and complete knowledge could be acquired only by laboriously studying the
works of all scholars and conveyors of tradition since the Prophet's death;
to him, reform, the direct appropriation of the revelation and the *sunna*,
would have appeared as a sacrilegious enterprise. Yet as-Sanusi and 'Abd

al-Wahhab—the examples we chose of Muslims who moaned under the vast material that had piled up over the centuries—wanted precisely that, even though they had their own reasons for this and although their religious styles were quite different from one another: as-Sanusi was propelled by a Sufi Muhammad piousness, and Ibn 'Abd al-Wahhab was hoping to make the pure statements of the Koran and the *sunna*—whatever these may be—the foundation of the Islamic community.

From the mid-nineteenth century on, belief that faith and reason were in agreement with one another became the main theme of all intellectual movements that tried to save the Islamic religion and culture from the influence of Western civilization. To be sure, at the end of the last century there were a number of voices in Europe who, considering the decline of the Islamic world to be unavoidable, assumed that religion was the reason for this development. A heated polemical discussion developed between those observers of current events who rashly proclaimed the definitive universal triumph of the Western way of life and thinking and some prominent Muslim scholars who conceded no more than that Islam had been temporarily weakened, but that this development would be reversed once the Muslims had returned to the sources of their faith. The most significant representative of that camp was the aforementioned Egyptian Muhammad 'Abduh, a man not only of letters but also with political drive: as president of the University of al-Azhar he tried to open it up for modern methods of academic instruction and those sciences[36] on which Europe's superiority seemed to rest. His ideas dominated and determined Islam's intellectual life in the twentieth century, which must be understood mainly as a confrontation with the West's challenge. In a polemic in which he compared Christianity and Islam, he maintained that Catholics, the Christian Orthodox, and Protestants all taught that religion surpassed reason by "running counter to (its) conclusions, but one must still believe in it." In contrast, Islam's first principle was to apply reason in order to acquire faith. Muhammad 'Abduh even went as far as to make reason the yardstick for the truth of traditions: "With a few exceptions not worth considering, the Muslims agree that in cases where reason and tradition are in conflict, what reason says is valid. This leaves two options for dealing with the tradition: one, one admits that the tradition is right, but concedes that one does not comprehend it and leaves its content up to

God; two, observing the rules of language, one interprets it in such a way that it coincides with reason. Thanks to this principle, which is based on the Koran, the genuine *sunna*, as well as the Prophet's practices, every conceivable path was paved for reason, and all obstacles in its path were removed so it would have an unlimited area where it could be employed. What would a philosopher's speculations have to achieve to go beyond that? What free space could comprise all speculative thinkers and all those who are involved in the sciences, if not that space? If even that should be too confined for them, neither the earth with its mountain ranges and plains, nor the sky with its stars and (infinite) expanse would give them sufficient space!"[37]

On another occasion 'Abduh wrote that in the *kalam*, the Muslims had managed to define the entirely rational content of the Koran and the *hadith*. Even back in the early Middle Ages logic had been explored in all its variations and had been turned against the enemies of true religion.[38] Great scholars such as al-Ghazali or Fakhr ad-Din ar-Razi had had good reason to declare the study of these sciences a religious duty which would always have to be carried out by a sufficient number of Muslims.[39] "[Is this] not particularly [true] today, when people of the most different religions have come to associate with one another?" There must be no cracks in the house of faith! If once faith was defended with the help of logic, now the Muslims were facing the task of opening up to the "new useful sciences," which were more apt "to protect us from attacks and humiliation." The "new" sciences and the ability to apply them—for instance, building technologically superior weapons—should be acquired for the protection of Islam just as logic once was.[40] The *kalam* was proof, furnished in the Middle Ages, that Islamic faith and reason agreed with one another, and the acquisition of European technology would be the modern proof of the same thing—this, in short, is a summary of 'Abduh's line of reasoning.

That all the knowledge human beings can acquire is precisely what they received from God is an argument 'Abduh deduced from sura 2, verses 29–31: "And He taught Adam the names, all of them; then He presented them unto the angels and said, 'Now tell Me the names of these, if you speak truly.' They said, 'Glory be to Thee! We know not save what Thou hast taught us. Surely Thou art the All-knowing, the All-wise.' He

said, 'Adam, tell them their names.' And when he had told them their
names He said, 'Did I not tell you I know the unseen things of the heavens and earth? And I know what things you reveal, and what you were
hiding.'" Adam, at once the first human being and the first prophet,
received from God knowledge of all things and was made the creator's
deputy on earth; God gave Adam "knowledge of all things—without limitation or specification. . . . Yet true knowledge consists of grasping all
knowable things; the words referring to them are different from language
to language, according to their agreed-upon terminology. . . . Their meaning, however, does not change. God taught Adam about every thing—and
it makes no difference if this knowledge is at Adam's disposal during one
moment or during many moments. God is capable of anything. Yet this
capacity for knowledge has been granted to Adam's entire race. Therefore
(the Koran passage) does not mean that the sons of Adam knew the names
from the first day on. The only necessary proof of the existence of this
ability is that they can know the things through research and logical conclusions. . . . Thus it is our duty to struggle for it, to perfect ourselves
through those sciences for which God has prepared us, but not the angels
and other creatures. Thus God's wisdom is revealed in us."[41]

Human beings' entire possible knowledge has been conveyed to them
by God; it is identical with the full content of the message Adam received.
Human beings may not be clear about the details of this knowledge; in
that case they must use their reason. If they use it correctly, they manage
to close a gap in knowledge, but their own studies will never get them
beyond what God taught Adam. With this we have touched upon the most
comprehensive interpretation of Islamic orthodoxy: in its essence,
Islam—according to 'Abduh the quintessence of all religions[42]—is by its
nature the right knowledge of everything knowable. This unchangeable
treasure of knowledge was distilled in the books of the Koran and the
hadith; if necessary, rational conclusions can illuminate it. It is independent of language and scholarly terminology—hence, it does not matter
what tradition in the history of thought is used to acquire it. The partial
secularization of Arabic,[43] which was a result of Sunni Islam's characteristic belief in the nontemporality and ahistoricity of Adam's message,
now reveals its full meaning. What Ash'arism had striven for[44]—Islam's
delivery from its contingent admixtures, which were the products of its

history—is impelled toward its perfection here, in 'Abduh's orthodox reformism.

3. Islam as Ideology

If the content of the divine message that was transmitted to all the prophets is expanded and generalized to a degree where the right application of reason—'Abduh and his numerous imitators never tried to define what that really means—leads to the message already containing its meaning, then there is no longer any reason to see a theological problem in the rapid changes in the modern world. This is disconcertingly illustrated in 'Abduh's *Treatise on God's Oneness*, which he wrote in the 1880s. 'Abduh himself probably considered this work to be a renewal of the *kalam*, which he often did advocate vigorously, after all. However, this work is anything but that. 'Abduh's terminology is reminiscent of late Ash'arite authors such as Fakhr ad-Din ar-Razi, and even on a content level, he was not able to leave the idea behind that "God's power [is] the origin of everything that is." He even fell back behind the idea of "God's wisdom," which from the waning eleventh century on mitigated the strict doctrine of the discontinuity of everything that was created. This theory attributed to the forces and various matters human beings have to deal with certain effects that could be predicted and utilized.[45]

But clearly, 'Abduh was not concerned about *theological* issues. His treatise dealt with thoughts on Islam's position within the history of humankind, which he frequently discussed in other works of his: "In their society human beings had reached the stage of maturity. . . . Then Islam came and addressed [human] reason and, appealing to the ability to form mental concepts and to understanding, gave reason along with affects and sensations a part in leading human beings to their happiness in this world and the next."[46] We recognize here in a new disguise the charge Muhammad had leveled against the idolaters: if they could muster the willingness to use their reason, they would have to concede that they were led by mere appearances or by their sensations or suppositions when they were attributing power to someone else but the one God. The consideration of what happened in nature was brought to its logical conclusion, which unarguably led to the realization that this world was created and that one God was the origin of everything that was created and of everything that happened in this world. 'Abduh considered all forms of religion before Islam imperfect; they did have a vague idea of the one truth God gave Adam, our forefather, as the ideal type of the human species, but it had not yet been defined; those early representatives of our species were still lacking in intellectual maturity.[47] The stage of maturity was not reached until Muhammad was appointed Prophet: in Islam reason was finally propelled as well as enabled to do the task it was meant to do from the very start—freed of all preconceived notions and conventional errors, to recognize the true nature of the world and of the Creator ruling it. This led to the realization that the content of the revelation, which at least in part could not be understood by former, less perfect generations, and the goals of rational knowledge were identical.

Al-Ghazali and Ibn Taymiyya had demanded that the Muslims reassure themselves of the ancestors' spontaneous religiosity. 'Abduh now augmented this demand by the concept of the gradual development of all living beings from lower forms, which had been popular since the mid-nineteenth century: humankind's development toward higher forms is expressed in its path toward monotheism and its foundation in reason. In the dream of the renewal of the religiosity of the beginnings, we have detected a trait that ran strictly counter to the examination and interpretation of Islam's basic texts that had taken place over several centuries. This trait continued a view that is repeatedly mentioned in the Koran and that substantiated the Prophet's claim to the unadulterated truth of his message: when he spoke, he was directly inspired; in contrast, the followers of the older religions—the Jews and Christians—could refer only to Scriptures whose content was adulterated during the process of being passed on.[48]

Naturally, the statement that only in Islam did reason attain the power to do what it was meant to do is a claim that entirely rests on the assumption that that unchangeable treasure of knowledge exists. How much 'Abduh's way of thinking and that of his students and imitators remained locked inside the concepts that had been standard for more than a thousand years becomes clear when we look at the meaning of an Arabic key word in that debate. "Knowledge" is rendered as 'ilm. 'Ilm contains the entire rules of life and modes of behavior, of the laws, the rites, and all those regulations that comprise the Sharia; in its most general sense, *'ilm* is the knowledge of God and the laws He has imposed on humankind. "Knowledge is good, and after the knowledge of God and His oneness, the best and most important knowledge is the knowledge of the Sharia"[49]; hence *'ilm* is the knowledge that brings salvation, and its acquisition offers human beings a guideline for properly dealing with this world, thus paving their way to bliss in the next world. Human beings cannot alter or expand the content of this knowledge; they receive it by studying the revelation, and the only way along which they can walk is the one at whose end is the realization that the revelation entirely coincides with what they can know with the help of reason. To be sure, Islamic culture, too, is familiar with the desire to interpret the term *'ilm* more widely and to concede that with the human capacity for knowledge it may be possible to go beyond what has already been achieved; but in the end, orthodoxy prevailed in its claim to decide what was and what was not the proper application of reason. However, in Arabic the term *'ilm* is also used for European "science," which led the followers of Islam to ignore how open this science was—a misinterpretation that constitutes the basis of 'Abduh's polemics. Turning his concept of progress and development against the West, he claimed that the Muslims had already reached the end of human history, and no one besides them would ever reach it.

'Abduh did not yet explicitly state that Islam, the unalterable message that Adam once received and which, in the revelation given to Muhammad, —the last one in history—was tailored toward humankind's stage of maturity, contained the solution to all difficulties. That was not claimed until the so-called fundamentalist movements came along, all of which are rooted in the ideas of orthodox reformism.[50] Before dealing with the challenge of Western civilization, the Muslims considered Islam their natural foundation to which could be traced all ways of life as well as all aspects of dealing with others in everyday life, and if new facts surfaced—which could not have happened all too often—these were assessed by that foundation and, if possible, integrated into the time-honored customs. When at the schools of law and theology small water basins with fountains in the middle became fashionable in the sixteenth century, the Hanafite legal scholar Ibn Nujaym (d. 1563) wrote a treatise in which he explained that performing the ritual ablutions there was permissible.[51] This made this innovation a legitimate part of Islamic everyday life. In view of the vast number of entirely unknown devices that could not be produced in the Islamic world—devices that represented a formerly unfathomable and unattainable level of civilization—as well as in view of entirely unknown methods of administering and cultivating land that were imposed on some territories of the Islamic world, it would have been extremely dubious to proceed in the same manner. Therefore, 'Abduh dared take the bold step and declare *all things* altogether as being ultimately the Muslims' own kind.

Probably, without realizing it, he laid the foundation stone for the transformation of Islamic theology into an ideology that has become dominant in various political movements of the twentieth century. The return to "Islam," whatever that may mean from case to case, is now considered the sole panacea for any predicament. That kind of Islam contains not only the possibility of forming a society blessed with the most sophisticated technological luxuries—if only the enemies of true faith are destroyed first—it is also humandkind's most wonderful form of living with each other. The state that is shaped according to that "Islam" combines the advantages of socialism and capitalism without having their disadvantages.[52]

Perusing those ideological books that have flooded the market in the Islamic world removes us far from the theological questions with which the great Islamic thinkers of the Middle Ages and the early modern period wrestled. These titles do not even attempt to find out how convincing those statements are that Muhammad 'Abduh formulated under the impact of the historical situation of the waning nineteenth century. It almost seems as if these positions were defended all the more tenaciously the less they can be substantiated by the actual historical events. When will the intellectual life of the Islamic world, which has been so disastrously ideologized, find its way back to the serious attempts at recognizing God and His plans for this world which the study of the older sources make so fruitful and rewarding? The piousness of a Muhammad ibn 'Ali as-Sanusi, which penetrates the life of the Prophet intellectually and emotionally, thus hoping to gain the strength for dealing with the present—it seems to me that this kind of piousness, whose vast numinosity can also be fathomed by those of a different faith who listen to a recitation of the Koran among a circle of Muslims, may be the most fertile ground on which an Islam that faces reality could grow anew.[53]

Epilogue

1. Summary

Giant steps we have walked through the extensive realm of Islamic theology, and it is to be hoped that these steps were always such that our subject's most essential parts became comprehensible. In organizing the vast material, I have been led by two general aspects, without constantly pointing this out to the reader: the principle of expansion and generalization of the pious devotion (*din*) to the one God and the principle of remembering the beginnings.

The Allah who was worshiped during the annual pilgrimages at the shrine in Mecca had revealed Himself to the Prophet whom He had appointed. He demanded religious services that had permanence and, therefore, must not confine themselves to the short time spans common to the usual seasonal cults. Corresponding to God's power, which even in the early revelation was no longer limited but extended to encompass the entire life of every human being, Muhammad felt compelled to preach about the one Allah and to declare polytheism invalid, even at those places of worship around Mecca that were dedicated to other noumina. The Prophet's expulsion from Mecca meant that he was removed from the place in which the deity was present; the direction of the prayer, introduced out of necessity, had to symbolically take the place of the worshiped God's actual presence at the shrine—Allah became omnipresent, in the true meaning of the word. Yet Muhammad's yearning for his hometown, which determined his policies in Medina, also seems to have been caused by his desire to again encounter God "face to face." The experience of God, which through the expulsion from Mecca necessarily became abstract, deprived the rite of its concrete center; as a result, it liberated human will and unleashed people's power to establish rules that were accepted as divine guidelines and also applied to the community's everyday life beyond the religious cult—an extension of the religious order (*din*) with serious consequences. Yet first the community, in accordance with the political reality, took on the identity of a brothership-in-arms of believers (*al-mu'minun*) bound to God and His Prophet. While the Prophet was still alive, however, it turned out that the rites—the externally recognizable tie of that community—could be performed even by members who did not keep themselves available for Muhammad's battles. This contradiction between a belligerent religiosity and a performance of rites that was tied to a peaceful everyday presented difficulties during the first decades after Muhammad's death. It disappeared only to the degree that, in combination with the principle of remembering the beginnings, a generally accepted concept of the way of life developed that was aligned with the Prophet's message—in other words, to the degree that "Islam" was superimposed on the domain of the rites as a set of norms.

The more life became "Islamic," the more one had to consider how every element of daily life related to God; this was a demand that was expressed even in the Koran (for instance, in sura 38, verse 29). It became necessary to form a general concept of the domain where God exerted His power, and to determine His nature and distinguish it from the specifically human nature, from the essence of a creature. This was accomplished by the *kalam*. As was shown in the example of al-Jahiz, the "Islamizing" of man, that is to say, the transformation of his "pagan" domination by feelings (*jahiliyya*), and the rational interpretation of the world and of God are inseparably intertwined; yet at that time the two could not be brought into agreement with each other, and as we have seen, Muslims still wrestle with that difficulty to this day—a difficulty whose solution would signify the highest conceivable degree of thematic expansion and generalization of the Prophet's message of God.

The Ash'arites confronted the challenge this implied. They loosened the ties between the *mutakallimun*'s speculations and the richly expressive Arabic manner of speaking with its numerous synonyms; by developing a strict and condensed language they stressed the few aspects that supposedly illustrated the relationship between God on the one hand and His creation and human nature on the other. Abstract as these aspects were, they could easily be proven to be the ones the Koran and the *sunna* prescribed. This way the Ash'arites opened theology's door for logic— but as the opponents of logic within Sunnism may have sensed, this took place at the price of "Islam," the comprehensive set of the Sharia's rules that were codified and had been given the Prophet's seal of approval.

Owing to the discontinuity of everything that was created, human beings did not have the power to follow these rules of their own accord: if God alone had all power of being, the law had become meaningless. The development the Ash'arites had set off in the tenth century led to its most radical manifestation in the doctrine of the "oneness of being"; the message of salvation about God's immanence in everything that existed and only appeared to have many different forms deprived the Sharia, the quintessence of Islam, of its plausibility and justification. Independent of all speculation and all individualizing spirituality, the recorded memory of the beginnings, the *hadith* in its quality as the Sharia's richest source of material, is superior to an immediate experience of God, at least as far as the vast majority of people are concerned. The *hadith* was also an obligation, which staved off the danger of undermining Islam. Therefore, orthodoxy prevailed in the long run—not by suppressing the spirituality of the saints, but by integrating it.

We have in this brief summary several times touched on the importance of remembering the beginnings, and indeed, expansion and generalization always have to be considered in connection with this principle. We have remarked that, in the first decades after Muhammad's death, the Medinese community of combatants in faith was transformed into the more inclusive community of "Muslims," and that the rites emerged as the one unifying center. Yet this community alone did not suffice to convey the sense of certainty of salvation that, thanks to the fact that it kept itself constantly available to "God and His messenger," inspired the fighting community of "believers." The loss of this sense was compensated for by remembering the beginnings as people began to imagine them. Thanks to the imam from among Muhammad's descendants and thanks to the stories about the Prophet, the period of the original Medinese community never became history but, then as now, was projected into the present. Imamate and *sunna* thus became surrogate institutions for direct Prophetic right guidance; the "Muslims," too, not only the "believers," were assured of salvation. The Ash'arites struggled hard to make sure that remembering the beginnings did not turn into wild and virtually unrestrained rationalist speculation, which, however inadvertently, also entailed the danger of the memory of the ideal, concrete image of Muhammad and the original community turning into a union with God that ignored the Sharia—the certainty of salvation being obtained while ignoring all laws. The ideal of the ancestors' spontaneous religiosity, which Ibn Taymiyya developed by leaning on al-Ghazali, seemed to show a way out of this cul de sac. Ibn Taymiyya's contemporary 'Abd ar-Razzaq al-Qashani already worked on integrating the theory of the oneness of being into Sunni Muhammad piousness; five hundred years later, the reflections of the Nashbandiyya order and men like Ahmad ibn Idris al-Fasi or Muhammad ibn 'Ali as-Sanusi went in the same direction.

Nineteenth-century orthodoxy combined the two principles of generalization and remembering. The basis of this combination was the concept of an unchangeable treasure of knowledge which had once been given to Adam. This treasure of knowledge was so general and comprehensive that it included everything human beings can know, and those who wanted to take it in its pure form, returned to the beginnings, to the present of the Prophet.

2. The Tasks

The image we have painted of the history of Islamic theology needs to be refined in several places. What has been analyzed are the ninth to the eleventh centuries, but the large time span between the twelfth century and the present has been largely ignored. Virtually all scholarly work is still outstanding in that area, and numerous discoveries are waiting to be made. Within the Arab community, the term "era of decline" has become an established notion for that period; this notion is in the way of a detailed study of that era's literature, with the possible exception of historiographic works. The generally accepted dismissive verdict may to a large degree be corroborated by the influence of orthodoxy as it was described in the last chapter: the vision of a purified Islam that rests only on the Koran and the *sunna* devalues huge areas of Islam's past intellectual life, which then casts on them the suspicion of concealing germs of "unbelief." Yet an examination of that period is also obstructed by the widespread prejudice within Orientalism that from the tenth century on the intellectual life of Islam exhausted itself in reshifting already acquired knowledge by way of compendia, commentaries, and marginalia.

To be sure, the Ash'arite theology of the eleventh century was a cul de sac as well, and there was no "critique of theological reason" to show a way out. But we have observed that a standstill in reflections on God and His relationship with creation was prevented in a different way, and that the late Middle Ages and the early modern times wrestled with the tasks of reconciling this entirely different kind of philosophy, the theory of the oneness of being, with the "Islam of law." Therefore, the view of that era as an infertile period of Islamic intellectual life is untenable, and this realization poses a tremendous task for future research.

However, scholars should not study of the Islamic world of the late Middle Ages and the modern times only in order to search for more profound insights into *Muslim* thinking, but also with a view toward Judaism as well as Oriental and Latin Christianity. The history of the religions of Islam, Christianity, and Judaism should become one single topic: revelation and reason struggle with one another to discover the nature of the human beings who belong to this world and yet are connected to something that transcends it. For long stretches of time within the period we have examined in this book, Muslim thinkers determined the substance of that analysis; if we look at all of this from a higher plane, we begin to detect in the Near East a history of thought that comprises the different religions that had an impact on Latin Europe.

Sources documenting that Oriental Christianity participated in the Jahmite and Mu'tazilite debate on God's attributes date back to the ninth century; it even looks as if an analysis of the pertinent Christian-Arab sources might help us to get to a clearer understanding of inner-Islamic debates.[1] Later on, Islamic theology had a strong impact on the Copts; their theology apparently still contained patterns of thought taken from the

Mu'tazilite *kalam* after they had already been abandoned in Islam. A treatise from the first half of the thirteenth century on *The Oneness [of God], the Trinity, the Incarnation, and on the Truth of the Christian Faith* begins with the claim that the realization of the createdness of all things compels human beings to conclude that there is an eternal Creator-God[2]—almost two hundred years after this line of argument was replaced by the categories of "necessary, possible being" in metaphysics.

We know more about the appropriation of the *kalam* by Oriental Jews than about the intertwinement of Islamic and Christian theology; adopting and processing elements of Islam must have been easier for the Jews anyway, as they did not have to worry about the issue of the trinity, which stands like a wall between Muslims and Christians, a wall that was fortified again and again through hostile misunderstandings on both sides. Da'ud ibn Marwan al-Muqammis, Saadya, Yusuf al-Basir, these three Jewish scholars of the waning ninth to the early eleventh centuries attest to Judaism's openness toward the Islamic *kalam*.[3]

Medieval authors such as the Muslim al-Juwayni (d. 1085) or the Jew Maimonides (d. 1204) realized that there is a connection between the *kalam* of the Mu'tazilite or Ash'arite mold and similar lines of arguments in late antiquity. Both, for instance, mentioned John Philoponus (c. 500) who, in discussing the Aristotelian theory of the eternity of the world after his conversion to Christianity, tried to invalidate it in light of the belief in the Creator-God.[4]

With their similar roots, the three great prophetic religions of revelation—Judaism, Christianity, and Islam—have had to confront the question of how the truth of their salvation relates to rational realizations and categories of thought. The centuries-long struggle for conclusive answers to this question, which in many different ways connects everyday experiences and profound speculations—a struggle that has lasted until this day and will never be decided definitively—is, beyond all particularities, the one common denominator of the histories of the Jewish, Christian, and Muslim religions and thought. If this is true, then it is also true that the efforts, achievements, or errors of Jewish or Muslim thinkers are also part of our Christian history of religion and thought, and vice versa.

The task that is before us and that has been tackled only here and there,[5]

is nothing less than to write a history of the rational interpretation of the religion of revelation. We are still far from being in a position to presume to attempt such a comprehensive view. Much would be gained if the representatives of the three individual fields were more ready to listen to each other without being afraid of letting obvious analogies lead them to questions that probe still deeper. To cite one example, a great deal has been written about Nicholas of Cusa's thoughts on the union of opposites; in the theology of the "oneness of being" and its popularization through

Arabic and Persian poetry in the thirteenth and fourteenth centuries, we discover the recurring idea that the contradictions in the phenomena of this world are abolished in the one, the divine, being.[6] Can we understand Cusa's ideas only from the context of Christian-Latin medieval literature? Is it a concept of being that is contained within the large theme of the conflict between reason and revelation and always surfaces under certain conditions? Might Cusa, who studied Islam intensively, have been inspired by the Islamic theology of the "oneness of being"? We are looking at a vast number of fruitful questions—and may God give us the strength to deal seriously with at least some of them.

Chronology

6th CENTURY

Rise of the Quraysh in Mecca, in association with the cult of Allah performed at the Kaaba; members of other tribes participating in annual pilgrim ceremonies at shrines near Mecca that are dedicated to other deities are accepted into a Quraysh menís association, thus backing the Qurayshís religiopolitical quest for power.

569

Birth of Muhammad; he belongs to the Quraysh clan of the Banu Hashim; on his maternal side he is a distant relative of the Medinese clan of the Banu Adi ibn an-Najjar. He becomes a member of the Quraysh menís association.

C. 610

Muhammad is appointed Prophet by Allah; the "affective" monotheism of the Quraysh and their allies becomes more radical, and is transformed into an absolute monotheism.

622

Muhammad's expulsion from Mecca, "hijra."

622-632

Muhammad in Medina; a community of believers is formed with the purpose of fighting under the command of "God and His Messenger"; first attempts to develop the new religion into a religion of law and rites.

632

Death of the Prophet.

632-661

Rule of the "Refugee" (muhajirun), that group of people who in the wake of Muhammad's expulsion from Mecca had immigrated to Medina, where they had formed the core of the community of "believers." Caliphate of Umar ibn al-Khattab (634-644; official title as ruler: commander of the believers): attempts to curtail the growing influence of the former Quraysh enemies of the Prophet, who had become threatening; introduction of the hijra calendar. First military expeditions to conquer new territories.

First Civil War (656 murder of Caliph Uthman ibn Affan; Ali ibn abi Talib, the Prophetís cousin and son-in-law, becomes prophet); beginnings of Kharijite movement and the Shia, who both regard themselves as the only legitimate heirs to the Medinese fighting community of "believers."

660-750

The Umayyads of Damascus take over the caliphate (members of the Quraysh clan of the Banu Abd Shams, to which aside from Uthma ibn Affan, however, mainly enemies of Muhammad had belonged). Battles between Kharijites and Shiites (Second Civil War, c. 683-690); split of the Kharijia; bellicose "religiosity" becomes more radical, sometimes even anarchistic; begin of a split within the Shia. Caliph Abd al-Malik (685-705) pacifies the empire harshly and with determination; "harmonious community" (jamaëa) as religiopolitical ideal; performance of rites ("Islam") as unifying center of the religion founded by Muhammad.

Beginnings of theology in the discussion about the guilt of the individual factions during the First Civil War, debate of the extent of human and divine determination (Qadarites, Murjiites); idealization of the pious renunciation of getting involved in the sectarian inner-Islamic conflict and lively memories of conditions "in the beginning," which were probably characterized by harmony; attempts to recall the way of life (sunna) of the ancestors, particularly of the Prophet; first seeds of a "Sunnite" Islam.

750-1258

Abbasid caliphate (descendants of Abbas, an uncle of the Prophet).

The center of the empire is moved to Iraq; foundation of Baghdad.

(C. 770-847) Preponderance of rationalist theology (Mutazila); discussion of human and divine qadar becomes more refined and profound; God's "oneness" (tauhid) becomes problematical, not least as the consequence of the effort to fend off Gnostic ideas; development and apex of Islamic atomism. At the same time the hadith develops into the specific literary genre of this persuasion; 818-847 inquisition against the leaders of Sunnism by the caliphs, who had a stake in a uniform faith with a rational foundation and supported rationalism; abolished by Caliph al-Mutawakkil (r. 847-861).

(C. 850-940) Rationalism loses its attraction, disappointment about the inability of rational arguments to reach a general agreement on the main issues of the theological debate (relationship between human and divine determination, assessment of human actions on the Day of Judgment, Godís oneness, and relationship between the nature of the creator and that of creation).

Beginnings of Asharism: revelation and hadith as the sole and authoritative basis of reflecting on theological issues.

(C. 940-1100) Apex of Sunnite rationalism of the Asharite mold: theories concerning the creatureís ontological loss of power and the transhistoricity of God's speech.

(C. 1075-1220) Aristotelian logic penetrates Asharite theology via

Islamic philosophy (especially Avicenna, d. 1038), transformation of its basic way of reasoning; step by step the power of being of everything that was created is restored by falling back on the Koranic concept of divine "providence," which permeates all creation.
1220-1500

Transformation of the political structure of the Islamic world as a consequence of the Mongolian attack: sultanate of the Mamluks (Egypt, Syria 1260-1517); empire of the Il-Khans and its successor states (eastern part of the Islamic world; 1256-1501); (c. 1200-1400) triumph of the theology of the "oneness of being," in combination with the worship of saints; belief in the possibility of using the insight into the domain of the "unseen" to influence the course of the world; law-based Islam in jeopardy.

c. 1280-1918

The Ottoman Empire (c. 1300-1800) The theology of the "oneness of being" is repressed and defused, along with the worship of saints connected to it, by establishing a Muhammad spirituality; attempts to relate the knowlege human beings can possibly gain to an Islamic orthodoxy and to legitimize it to the extent that it concurs with this orthodoxy.
(Since c. 1800) Development of Islamic modernism; wrestling about the "unadulterated" portrayal of Adam and all prophets after him according to the "knowledge" that was passed on to him for good and cannot be augmented through human efforts.

Notes

Preface (pp. ix–xii)

1. All quotations from the Koran in this book are taken from *The Koran Interpreted*, tr. Arthur J. Arberry, New York: Collier Books/Macmillan, 1955.

Chapter I (pp. 1–26)

1. *Badr ad Din az-Zarkashi: al-Burhan fi 'ulum al-qur'an*, ed. Abu l-Fadl Ibrahim, Cairo, 1957, vol. 1, pp. 3–4.
2. Sura 6, verse 38.
3. Tilman Nagel, *Der Koran*, Munich, 1983, pp. 326ff.
4. Toshihiko Izutsu, *God and Man in the Koran: Semantics of the Koranic Weltanschauung*, Tokyo, 1964, pp. 199–229: an extensive analysis of the meaning of the term j*ahilyya* (ignorance) in relation to the Old Arabic and early Islamic concept of man.
5. The discussion on the character of the sources on Muhammad's life has led to quite different views; cf. W. Montgomery Watt: *Muhammad at Mecca,* Oxford, 1953, pp. xff., and Patricia Crone, *Slaves on Horses*, Cambridge, 1980, pp. 3–17.
6. See, e.g., *Encyclopedia of Islam*, 2nd ed., Leiden, 1960ff. (henceforth quoted as *EI2*), see "al-Kinda."
7. See, e.g., in al-Uqaysir in Syria (Rose Klinke-Rosenberger, *Das Götzenbuch des . . . Ibn al-Kalbi*, Winterthur, 1942, pp. 50 and 55).
8. Trade originated as a means to make peaceful contact between people who are not related with each other by blood or marriage; Islamic law still preserves part of this original function of trade: it provides for the *immediate* exchange of goods of equal value or, if possible, even equal similar goods and disapproves of profit-seeking.
9. Altheim/Stiehl, *Die Araber in der alten Welt*, Berlin, 1964–69, vol. 5/i, pp. 358–67.
10. Ibid., p. 385.
11. M. J. Kister, "Mecca and Tamim: Aspects of Their Relations," in *Journal of the Economic and Social History of the Orient*, vol. 8 (1965), pp. 113–63 (p. 126).
12. J. Wellhausen, *Reste arabischen Heidentums*, 3rd ed., Berlin, 1961, pp. 79ff. The fact that today's pilgrims' rites go back to a fusion of two cultural traditions—one Meccan and Quraysh, and one cultivated nearby—serves P. Crone as the ground for her argument that in Quraysh Mecca—at the Kaaba—there were no *pilgrims'* rites before Muhammad (Patricia Crone, *Meccan Trade and the Rise of Islam*, Princeton, 1987, p. 173). Since the author's intention is not to illuminate but to eliminate early Islamic history, she concludes from this that Islam had nothing to do with Quraysh Mecca but developed in close connection with Jewish communities in northwestern Arabia (ibid., pp. 197ff.).
13. Kister, "Mecca and Tamim," p. 138.
14. Ibid., pp. 137ff.

289

15. Al-Humaydi, *Musnad*, ed. Al-Azami, Beirut, n.d., no. 559f. Another Quraysh who, "contrary to all the other Quraysh," ignored that rule: Ibn Hazm, *Jamharat ansab al-'arab*, ed. Harun, Cairo, 1962, p. 76.

16. M. J. Kister, "Labbayka, allahumma, labbayka . . . On a Monotheistic Aspect of Jahiliyya Practice," in *Jerusalem Studies in Arabic and Islam* II (1980), pp. 33–57 (p. 36).

17. W. Montgomery Watt, "Belief in a 'High God' in Pre-Islamic Mecca," in *Journal of Semitic Studies* XVI (1971), pp. 35–40. Sura 12, verses 105–106, says, in the same vein, that the unbelievers passed by the miracles of creation without really taking notice of them; most of them believed in God only by associating other gods with Him.

18. Kister, "Labbayka," p. 39.

19. Cf. the explanations and examples in Helmer Ringgren, "Islam, 'aslama, and Muslim," in *Horae Soederblomianae* II, Uppsala, 1949, pp. 22–25; see also the following chapter, n. 2. In the context I have mentioned, the verb *aslama* also occurs in the following places in the Koran: 2:113; 31:22; 3:20. "To seek the Face of God" (*arada, ibtagah*) means creating a pure relationship with God, which guarantees salvation: 2:272; 13:22; 30:38ff.; 92:20; 6:52; 18:28. In the adverbial phrase *li-wajh Allah* (for Allah's sake, literally: "—in order to strive for—the Face of God") the concrete meaning begins to pale; in the Koran, this phrase occurs only in sura 76, verse 9. On the transitive meaning of *aslama* in the Koran, see Otto Spies, "Islam und Syntagme," in *Oriens Christianus* LVII (1973), p. 19. Baljon ("To Seek the Face of God," in *Acta Orientalia* XXI [1953], pp. 254–66) points out that we find phrases such as "to seek the face of God" in the Old Testament; he rejects the possibility of pertinent phrases in the Koran proving a Jewish influence. However, Baljon is forced to admit that, with one exception, all the pertinent passages in the Koran were written during the Meccan Period (p. 261).

20. The phrase "Lord the Most High" disappeared quickly, as it obviously presupposed the existence of additional "lords"; it can be found only in the early Meccan sura 87, verse 1; in sura 79, verse 24 (also early Meccan) Pharaoh, claiming to be God, says: "I am your Lord, the Most High!" In later passages, God is simply "the All-high" (e.g., 2:257; 22:62; 31:30).

21. On the issue of integrating the Bedouins into the Prophet's community, see T. Nagel, *Staat und Glaubensgemeinschaft im Islam*, Zurich, 1981, vol. 1, pp. 45ff. The Quraysh were well familiar with the early-morning worship of God, which was practiced during the era of the pilgrims. However, they rejected the additional evening prayer that Muhammad introduced. (U. Rubin, "Morning and Evening Prayers in Early Islam," in *Jerusalem Studies in Arabic and Islam* X [1987], pp. 40–64.)

22. Al-Humaydi, *Musnad*, no. 1219.

23. On the God-seekers (*hanifs*), see U. Rubin's comprehensive study, "Hanifiya and Ka'ba," in *Jerusalem Studies in Arabic and Islam* XII (1990), pp. 85–112. In light of the documents presented there, it is not plausible to believe the Kaaba had not been "Abrahamized" until Islam (as maintained by Hawking, ibid., p. 83, probably following Patricia Crone, *Meccan Trade and the Rise of Islam*, pp. 190–91). Ms. Crone quotes documents mentioning the Arabs' "Abrahamization" in the fifth century, but since her source is a man from Gaza, she tries to limit this development to Arabia's northwestern border area—Palestine, the land by the Jordan. In order to maintain this hypothesis, it is necessary to assume that from the fifth to the seventh centuries, the

Hijaz was a part of the Arabian peninsula that was completely isolated from its surroundings, or that, as the author suggests, the area in the Hijaz containing the Kaaba, the place called Mecca, was altogether an invention of the second half of the seventh century.

24. Nagel, *Der Koran*, pp. 34ff.
25. Watt, *Muhammad in Mecca*, pp. 138ff., esp. the text on pp. 145–46.
26. See below, pp. 27ff.
27. Al-Tauhidi, *al-Imta' wal-mu'anasa*, ed. A. Amin and A. az-Zain, Beirut, n.d., vol. 2, p. 81.
28. Ibn Hisham: *as-Sira an-nabawiyya*, eds. as-Saqqa', et al., Cairo, 1355, vol. 2, pp. 156ff. It should be pointed out that in these verses, there are no allusions whatsoever to the agreements between Muhammad and the Aws and Khazraj which were allegedly made *before* the *hijra* and occupy such a prominent place in the story of the Prophet's life. This "mark of honor" of the Medinese helpers is also missing from the poems of Hassan ibn Tabit. Therefore Watt, *Muhammad at Mecca*, pp. 146ff. has good reason to believe that these agreements were made during Muhammad's early days in Medina.
29. The fact that the historical course of events was so different made it necessary to interpret this verse eschatologically (cf. Nagel, *Staat und Glaubensgemeinschaft im Islam*, vol. 1, p. 108). If we read this verse literally, we no longer need to indulge in—due to the lack of sources quite unsatisfactory—speculations as to how Muhammad envisioned his and his followers' future in Medina (Watt, *Muhammad at Mecca*, p. 148).
30. I have analyzed these issues in detail in my book, *Medinensische Einschübe in mekkanischen Suren*, Göttingen, 1995.
31. M. J. Kister, "The Market of the Prophet," in *Journal of the Economic and Social History of the Orient* VIII (1965), pp. 272–76.
32. Examples: sura 74, sura 88, sura 111.
33. Examples: sura 19, sura 20, sura 21.
34. Examples: sura 6, sura 7.
35. Examples: sura 2, sura 5.
36. Most radically argued by John Wansbrough, *Quranic Studies*, Oxford, 1977.
37. An overview of the state of research on the oldest Koran manuscripts: *Grundriß der arabischen Philologie*, vol. 2: Literaturwissenschaft, ed. H. Gätje, Wiesbaden, 1987, p. 112.
38. E.g., in sura 24, verse 1.
39. Arthur Jeffery, *Materials for the History of the Text of the Qur'an*, Leiden, 1937.
40. *EI2*, see al-Kur'an, pp. 413–14.
41. I elaborate on more details in the study mentioned in n. 30.
42. Cf. Nagel, *Der Koran*, pp. 173ff.
43. Cf. *EI2*, see Amr.
44. Cf. Baljon, "The Amr of God in the Koran," in *Acta Orientalia* XXIII (1959), pp. 12–13.
45. Examples in Nagel, *Der Koran*, pp. 178–79.
46. Nagel, "Der Koran als Zeugnis einer Zeitenwende," in *Zeitschrift für Missions- und Religionswissenschaft* LXVII (1983), pp. 97–109.
47. References in Ullmann, *Wörterbuch der klassischen arabischen Sprache*, Wiesbaden, 1970, vol. 1, p. 264.

48. A comprehensive description of the Koran's ethics from a Muslim point of view is offered in M. A. Draz, *La morale du Koran*, Cairo, 1950.

49. Sura 2, verse 30, 6:165; 35:39.

50. Sura 2, verse 34; 7:11; 15:33; 17:61, 20:26. According to Islamic belief, Satan is the first monotheist using rational arguments; he erred because he depended on rational thinking. Keeping this concept in mind, one grasps the power of the Islamic drive to leave behind the rational reasons for monotheism (cf. below, chapters 5 and 6).

51. Cf. sura 2, verses 120 and 145; 5:49; 6:119; 30:29; 38:26.

52. *EI2*, see Ahl al-kitab.

53. Heinrich Speyer, *Die biblischen Erzählungen im Qoran*, Hildesheim, 1961 (reprint), p. 413.

54. T. Nagel, "Muhammads Haltung zu den anderen Religionen," in *Theologische Quartalschrift* 161 (1981), pp. 192–200.

55. Cf. Nagel, "Der Koran als Zeugnis einer Zeitenwende" (see above, n. 46).

56. Form of an oath; brief summary in *EI2*, see al-Kur'an, pp. 421–22.

57. Cf. Nagel, *Der Koran*, pp. 292ff.

58. Cf. below, pp. 44 and 51.

Chapter II (pp. 27–72)

1. Tilman Nagel, *Rechtleitung und Kalifat*, Bonn, 1975, p. 34.

2. See above, ch. 1, n. 19. On the basis of the sources he has compiled, Ringgren falsely concludes that *aslama* and *amana* are largely identical terms (Ringgren, *Islam . . .*, pp. 30–31), which is why he has difficulty explaining the two terms' clearly different meanings in sura 49, verse 14 (p. 31). It is precisely the passages in the Koran quoted by Ringgren which contain the two verbs that document the difference in meaning: ". . . neither shalt thou (i.e., Muhammad) make any to hear, save such as believe in Our signs, and to surrender (literally: turn [their face in prayer] to God)" (sura 27, verse 83): belief is *more* than mere rite!

3. Nagel, *Staat und Glaubensgemeinschaft*, vol. 1, pp. 110ff. That at that early time Islamic-type rulers could assume they could do without authorization from Muhammad is documented in the example of 'Abdallah ibn az-Zubayr, whose background, however, is entirely different (Ja'qubi, *Ta'rikh*, vol. 2, ed. Beirut, 1960, p. 261).

4. Tilman Nagel, *Untersuchungen zur Entstehung des abbasidischen Kalifats*, Bonn, 1972; Moshe Sharon, *Black Banners from the East*, Jerusalem and Leiden, 1983.

5. The question of why the Umayyad caliphate collapsed has been the subject of much discussion among scholars. Hamilton A. R. Gibb ("The Evolution of Government in Early Islam," in *Studia Islamica* II [1955], pp. 1–17) believes that the reason was the different speed partly of the development of an empire expanding and partly of religion as a unifying force. The theory of religious development lagging behind, which shrinks Islam down to the social function its proponents want it to have, seems to underlie the opinion of several mainly English-speaking authors, who view Islam's entire early history as a chimera of the eighth and ninth centuries (cf. chapter 1, nn. 23 and 36). Since the sources contradict this "speculative reconstruction of the evolution of the religion," they have to be declared inventions from a later period

(Michael Cook, *Early Muslim Dogma*, Cambridge, 1981, pp. 154 and 158).

6. See above, pp. 16 f.

7. Text references in Nagel, *Staat und Glaubensgemeinschaft*, vol. 1, pp. 111 and 115–16.

8. Arabic: *ra'iyya*. This term occurs here for the first time in connection with Islam (Nagel, ibid., pp. 116–17).

9. Cf. sura 15, verse 21; 20:40; 23:18; and others.

10. Cf. sura 57, verse 29.

11. Sura 16, verse 75–76.

12. Tilman Nagel, "Vom Qur'an zur Schrift," in *Der Islam* LX (1983), pp. 143–65.

13. For more information on him, see Hans Heinrich Schaeder, "Hasan al-Basri," in *Der Islam* XIV (1925), pp. 42ff.

14. Nagel, *Rechtleitung und Kalifat*, pp. 76ff.; *EI2*, see Hadjdjadj b. Yusuf (vol. 3, p. 40).

15. The text, edited by Hellmut Ritter, can be found in "Studien zur Geschichte der islamischen Frömmigkeit I," in *Der Islam* XXI (1933), pp. 1–83.

16. At-Tabari, *Annalen II*, p. 784; the text as quoted in Josef van Ess, *Zwischen Hadit und Theologie*, Berlin and New York, 1975, p. 183, is misleading.

17. Josef van Ess, *Zwischen Hadit und Theologie*, p. 31.

18. Josef van Ess, *Anfänge muslimischer Theologie*, Beirut, 1977, pp. 177ff; *EI2*, see especially Kadariyya.

19. Dieter Derenk, *Leben und Dichtung des Omaiyadenkalifen al-Walid b. Yazid*, Freiburg, 1974, p. 40.

20. Francesco Gabrieli, *Religious Poetry in Early Islam*, Wiesbaden, 1973, p. 12.

21. Nagel, *Staat und Glaubensgemeinschaft*, vol. 1, pp. 111 and 136–37.

22. Karl-Heinz Pampus, : *Über die Rolle der Harigiya im frühen Islam*, Bonn, 1980; *EI2*, see Hidjra.

23. *EI2*, see Isti'rad (vol. 4, p. 269).

24. Tadeusz Lewicki in *EI2*, see Ibadiyya (vol. 3, p. 649). In a letter to Abd al-Malik, 'Abdallah ibn Ibad speaks of the "Muslims," whom he contrasts with the "infidels" (*al-'Uqud al-fiddiyya*, p. 132).

25. See above, p. 27.

26. Salim ibn Hamd al-Harithi, *Al Uqud al-fiddiyya fi usul al-Ibadiyya*, Dar al-Jaqza al-arabija, c. 1974, pp. 121–38.

27. Cf. ibid., p. 137., ll. 4ff.

28. Ibid., ll. 8ff.

29. Nagel, *Rechtleitung und Kalifat*, pp. 39ff.

30. 'Abdallah ibn Abd al-Hakam, *Sirat Umar ibn Abd al-Aziz*, ed. Ahmad Ubayd, Damascus and Beirut, 1967, p. 84.

31. The Banu Taqif had resisted the Quraysh's quest for power, which had reached its peak with Muhammad's entry into his hometown in 630. On the Shia's earliest development see Heinz Halm, *Shia Islam: From Religion to Revolution*, tr. Allison Brown, Princeton Series on the Middle East, Princeton, 1997.

32. Nagel, *Untersuchungen zur Entstehung des abbasidischen Kalifats*, p. 108.

33. He was related by marriage to the Taqif as well (see above, n. 31), surely also for political purposes (al-Mus'ab ibn 'Abdallah az-Zubayri, *Nasab Quraysh*, ed. Levi-Provencal, Cairo, 1953, p. 44).

34. *EI2*, see Hanifa.

35. Tilman Nagel, *Alexander der Grosse in der frühislamischen Volksliteratur*, Walldorf,

1978, pp. 92ff.

36. The "imamate," the leadership of the *believers' umma*, is religiously defined and, therefore, fundamentally different from the Quraysh's claim to power over the Arabs.

37. At-Tabari, *Annalen I*, p. 2942; cf. Nagel, *Staat und Glaubensgemeinschaft*, pp. 108–109.

38. Nagel, *Rechtleitung und Kalifat*, pp. 185–87, 214–16.

39. Ibid., p. 191.

40. Sura 15, verse 89; for parallel passages see Paret, *Kommentar und Konkordanz*, p. 281. In sura 9, verses 30–31 Jews and Christians are accused of seeking agents of salvation.

41. Nagel, *Rechtleitung und Kalifat*, pp. 194–95.

42. An-Najashi = Qais ibn 'Amr. On him, see Fuat Sezgin, *Geschichte des arabischen Schrifttums*, vol. 2, pp. 307–308.

43. Nagel, *Rechtleitung und Kalifat*, pp. 160–61.

44. Ibid., pp. 164ff.

45. Ibid., pp. 172ff.

46. Ibid., pp. 178ff.

47. Ibid., pp. 378ff. and 398.

48. See above, p. 39.

49. J. van Ess, *Anfänge muslimischer Theologie* discusses the facts of al-Hasan's life.

50. See below, pp. 82 ff.

51. Al-Hasan referred to sura 7, verse 24, and sura 20, verse 56.

52. J. van Ess, *Anfänge*. Arabic text, par. 27; regarding the passage above, see pars. 2, 4, 5, 7, and 17.

53. Nagel, *Rechtleitung und Kalifat*, pp. 73f.

54. Hellmut Ritter has examined al-Hasan al-Basri under the aspect of deepening piousness; cf. above, n. 15.

55. That is the reason why the Koran always warns of splits, e.g., in sura 42, verse 13.

56. Josef van Ess, ed., "Das Kitab al-irga'," in *Arabica* XXI (1974), p. 23 (20–52).

57. Nagel, *Rechtleitung und Kalifat*, p. 258.

58. *EI2*, see 'Abdallah b. 'Umar b. al-Khattab.

59. Abu Nu'aym, *Hilyyat al-auliyya'*, vol. 1, 2nd ed., Beirut, 1967, pp. 292–93.

60. Arabic: *fitan*; the word refers to quarrels that are fought out with arms.

61. Parallel passages in Jorge Aguadé, *Messianismus in der Zeit der frühen Abbasiden*, Tübingen, 1979, p. 74. The text's intention is somewhat distorted there.

62. Al-Bukhari, *Sahih*, I'tisam no. 19 and numerous other references.

63. Ahmad b. Hanbal, *Musnad*, vol. 4, p. 278.

64. Ibid., vol. 1, pp. 18 and 26.

65. Ibid., vol. 1, p. 70 and passim; al-Bukhari, *Sahih*, Fitan no. 2 and numerous additional references.

66. Muslim, *Sahih*, Iman no. 6.

67. Sura 2, verses 2–3; 31:3–5.

68. Sura 8, verses 2–3; additional parallel passages in Rudi Paret, *Kommentar und Konkordanz*, p. 13.

69. See the following chapter.

70. One example: Muslim, *Sahih*, Iman no. 7.

71. These statements are preconceived in the Koran: sura 2, verse 285. The second sura marks the beginning of the community in Medina.

72. M. Hinds, "The Siffin Arbitration Agreement," in *Journal of Semitic Studies* XVII (1972), pp. 100–101 (pp. 93–129). R. B. Serjeant holds that the term is an allusion to Medina's so-called community statutes ("The Sunnah Jami'ah . . . ," in *Bulletin of the School of Oriental and African Studies* XLI [1978], p. 16).

73. J. van Ess, "Das Kitab al-irga'," p. 22, par. 4; the emendation van Ess suggests seems misleading to me, as it destroys the rhetorically effective contrast *raha–bala'*.

74. Salim ibn Hamd al-Hariti, *al-Uqud al-fiddiya*, p. 135.

75. J. van Ess, *Anfänge muslimischer Theologie*, p. 148.

76. Ibid., p. 176.

77. Ibid., p. 163.

78. Ibid., Arabic text, p. 54.

79. See above, p. 40.

80. Parallel passage: sura 23, verses 14ff.

81. J. van Ess, *Zwischen Hadit und Theologie*, p. 1; in the Prophet's *hadith*, predestinarian concepts are also developed from sura 31, verse 34 (cf. Muslim, *Sahih*, Iman no. 7).

82. Nagel, *Rechtleitung und Kalifat*, p. 78.

83. Ibid., pp. 78–79.

84. Muslim, *Sahih*, Hajj no. 19.

85. Nagel, *Rechtleitung und Kalifat*, p. 292.

86. Ibid., pp. 76ff.

Chapter III (pp. 73–92)

1. Josef van Ess, *Anfänge muslimischer Theologie*, Arabic text, pp. 50–51; see above, p. 29ff.

2. Miklos Muranyi, *Die Prophetengenossen in der frühislamischen Geschichte*, Bonn, 1973, pp. 165ff.

3. I.e., Muslims and members of other religious persuasions. The phrase "people of the direction of prayer" once more documents the attempt to make the rites rather than "faith" the unifying center; see above, p. 44 f.

4. Ibn 'Abd al-Hakam, *Sirat 'Umar ibn 'Abd al-'Aziz*, ed. Ahmad 'Ubayd, Damascus and Beirut, 1967, p. 122.

5. On 'Umar II's efforts concerning the "tradition," see Nagel, *Rechtleitung und Kalifat*, p. 77.

6. Tilman Nagel, "Hadit—oder die Vernichtung der Geschichte," in *XXV. Deutscher Orientalistentage Vorträge*, Stuttgart 1994, pp. 718-28..

7. See above, pp. 17 f..

8. Ahmad ibn Hanbal, *Musnad*, vol. 1, pp. 44–45; additional references in van Ess, *Zwischen Hadit und Theologie*, p. 33.

9. The fact that the contents of the Koran and the *hadith* are directed toward entirely different goals, can in no way be explained if one follows the theories of von Wansbrough (or Burton, who views the Koran as Muhammad's "Musnad"; see above, ch. 1, n. 36).

10. Tilman Nagel, *Die Festung des Glaubens*, Munich, 1988, p. 110.

11. See above, p. 69.

12. On him, see below, p. 130.
13. Nagel, *Hadit—oder die Vernichtung der Geschichte.*
14. Ahmad ibn Hanbal, *Musnad*, vol. 4, p. 485; al-Bukhari, *Sahih*, Jizya no. 18. Ibn Sa'd, *Kitab at-tabaqat al-kabir*, ed. E. Mittwoch and E. Sachau, Leiden, 1905–28, vol. 3/ii, p. 39.
15. Al-Bukhari, *Sahih*, ibid.
16. Ahmad ibn Hanbal, *Musnad*, vol. 4, p. 486.
17. Nagel, *Hadit—oder die Vernichtung der Geschichte.*
18. Thirty times for each of the five obligatory daily prayers and one hundred times before going to sleep.
19. Al-Humaydi, *Musnad*, no. 583.
20. Cf. also Ibn abi Hatim, ed., *al-Jarh wat-ta'dil*, vol. 6, Hyderabad and Dekkan, 1952, p. 333.
21. On him, see Ibn Hajar, ed., *Al-Isaba*, vol. 2, Cairo, 1328 h, pp. 351–52, no. 4847; Nagel, *Alexander der Große . . .* , p. 91.
22. He died around 767 h (Ibn Hajar, *Tahdhib at-tahdhib*, vol. 1, p. 398).
23. Ibn Hajar, ed., *Tahdib at-tahdib*, vol. 4, Hyderabad and Dekkan, 1325 h, p. 122.
24. Ibid., vol. 7, pp. 205–206.
25. Nagel, *Hadit . . .* , in n. 16; also by Asim ibn Kulaib, who died in 754, ibid., in n. 20.
26. See above, p. 70.
27. A *sunna* by Abu Bakr et al., which was mentioned in connection with early documentations of the term *sunna*, can of course not claim to be inspired by God.
28. Cf. other descriptions in the *hadith*, e.g., al-Bukhari, "Sahih, Bad al-wahy."
29. On him see Ibn Hajar, *Tahdhib at tahdhib*, vol. 4, pp. 222ff.
30. Al-Humaidi, *Musnad*, no. 740.
31. Ibn Hajar, *Tahdib . . .* , vol. 4, p. 223.
32. On this subject see the monograph by Hans-Peter Raddatz, *Die Stellung und Bedeutung des Sufyan at-Tauri (gest. 778): Ein Beitrag zur Geistesgeschichte des frühen Islam*, Bonn, 1967.
33. Ibn Hajar, *Tahdib . . .*
34. Nagel, *Staat und Glaubensgemeinschaft*, vol. 1, p. 160.
35. Theoretically, the Koran is always supposed to be consulted before the *hadith*; actually, however, the *hadith*, which after all expressed the need for the "Islamization" of an empire that comprised many peoples and countries, contains many more pertinent statements.
36. Al-Humaydi, *Musnad*, nos. 1019–1925 (on the holy war).
37. W. Montgomery Watt, *Muhammad at Medina*, p. 75.
38. Regulation concerning the sacred state.
39. Ibn Hajar, *Tahdhib*, vol. 7, pp. 199–200.
40. Cf. sura 73, vverse 1ff.; further references in Paret, *Kommentar und Konkordanz*, p. 492.
41. Al-Humaydi, *Musnad*, nos. 790–791.
42. That is the reason why the chain of traditionists "grew back" to the Prophet himself, as Josef Schacht observed (*Origins of Muhammadan Jurisprudence*, 3rd ed., Oxford, 1959).—With some delay, there developed a tradition in Shiism which is ascribed to the imams and was close to the Sunni tradition in form and content.
43. Schacht, ibid.; Nagel, *Festung des Glaubens*, pp. 198ff.
44. Nagel, ibid., pp. 214–70.

45. An example: Nagel, *Rechtleitung und Kalifat*, pp. 376ff.
46. Cf. on this Josef van Ess's article on the practice of disputation in Islamic theology in *Revue des Etudes Islamique* XLIV (1976), pp. 23–60; see also Ulrich Rudolph's monograph *Al-Maturidi und die sunnitische Theologie in Samarkand*, chapter 1, 1.3. The idea that the *kalam* originated from Christian theology as a certain art of the theological dispute, should probably be abandoned. Cf. on this subject also Michael Cook, "The Origins of *kalam*," in *Bulletin of the School of Oriental and African Studies*, XLIII (1980), pp. 32–43.
47. On this, see Nagel, *Rechtleitung und Kalifat*, pp. 410ff.
48. Yahya was born in Medina; after a first futile attempt to found the Zaydi imamate in Yemen he succeeded in 897 in Saada (C. van Arendonk, *Les débuts de l'imamat zaydite au Yemen*, Leiden, 1960, pp. 127ff.).
49. For religion would no longer have a foundation; that is to say, if the Qadarites respond to al-Hasan's trick question in the affirmative, they, who after all believe in the revelation, have pulled the rug from under themselves.
50. Cf. van Ess, *Anfänge muslimischer Theologie*, Arabic text, pp. 11–12.
51. Yahya ibn al-Husayn, "Ar-Radd wal-ihtijaj 'ala al-Hasan ibn Muhammad ibn al-Hanafiyyah," in M. Ammara, ed., *Rasa'il al-'adl wat tauhid*, vol. 2, 2nd ed., Cairo and Beirut, 1988, pp. 111–280 (116–20).
52. If man is not able to choose his acts of commission and omission freely, he should at least be able to acquire the acts God has committed through him; that is to say, he should consciously and as a fervent believer feel to be a creature of the God who preserves and directs everything. This now contains the human responsibility for salvation. See below, p. 113 and 157.
53. Ibn al-Baqillani, *Kitab at-tamhid*, ed. McCarthy, Beirut, 1957, p. 286, pars. 487–88.
54. Al-Hasan ibn Muhammad ibn al-Hanafiyya also strove toward a rational evaluation, but it was a rationality that looked at the entire potential breadth of individual human responsibility without overestimating it.
55. Tilman Nagel, "Das Problem der Orthodoxie im frühen Islam," in *Studien zum Minderheitenproblem im Islam*, vol. 1, Bonn, 1973, pp. 7–44.
56. On this subject see I. Guidi, *La lotta tra l'islam e il manicheismo*, Rome, 927, Arabic text, p. 35.
57. Nagel, *Rechtleitung und Kalifat*, pp. 361ff.
58. It was R. Frank's accomplishment to have cleared sweepingly the *mutakallimun* of the suspicion of indulging in moot sophistries (*Akten des 3. Kongresses der Union Européenne d'arabisants et Islamisants*, 1967, pp. 315ff.; *Journal of the American Oriental Society*, LXXXVIII (1968), pp. 295ff.).

Chapter IV (pp. 93–124)

1. Ernst Herzfeld, *Geschichte der Stadt Samarra*, Hamburg, 1948; Helmut Töllner, *Die türkischen Garden am Kalifenhof von Samarra*, Bonn, 1971.
2. A brief summary in German can be found in O. Rescher, *Excerpte und Übersetzungen aus den Schriften des . . . Jahiz aus Basra*, vol. 1, Stuttgart, 1931, pp. 207ff.
3. Non-Arabs who have converted to Islam, thus becoming affiliated with an Arabic tribe; the legal institution of clientage, which had originated in pre-Islamic times but

was still practiced under the Umayyads, was not abolished until the Abbasid period.

4. Ibn Hajar, *al-Isaba*, no. 5636.

5. G. van Vloten (ed.), *Talat rasa'il li-Abi Utman al-Jahiz*, 2nd ed., Leiden, 1968, p. 7.

6. Ibid., p. 21.

7. That is to say, don't name it with coarse directness. Otherwise, however, language—the sounds which in Arabic convention indicate a certain meaning—should be chosen in such a way as to make words and their meaning coincide. Untruthful praise or disparagement do not constitute a sensible use of language.

8. A poet from Basra of Iranian descent (715–83).

9. Van Vloten, op. cit., pp. 22–24.

10. Ibid., p. 22.

11. Muslim, *Sahih*, Jana'iz no. 6; al-Bayhaqui, *Sunan*, vol. 7, p. 289.

12. The eminently telling questions arising from this have hardly been asked, let alone comprehensively addressed.

13. Cf. Abdallah ibn al-Muqaffa's report on the Khurasanian army's corps spirit (Tilman Nagel, *Untersuchungen zur Entstehung des abbasidischen Kalifats*, Bonn, 1972, p. 160).

14. Abu Muslim, the ingenious organizer of the Hashimiyya army, a lord of uncertain origin, was tricked and murdered, because he had been suspected of striving (initially via Iran?) for power himself (Sabatino Moscati, "Studi su Abu Muslim III," in *Academia dei Lincei*, Rome: Rendiconti, 1950, pp. 89–105).

15. Nagel, *Staat und Glaubensgemeinschaft*, vol. 1, pp. 161–62.

16. Speech by the first Abbasid Caliph as-Saffah and his uncle on the occasion of his accession to the throne (at-Tabari, *Annalen*, series 3, pp. 29ff.)

17. Nagel, *Rechtleitung und Kalifat*, pp. 297ff.

18. Ibid., pp. 242ff. and 104ff.

19. Ibid., pp. 400ff.

20. Josef van Ess, *Theologie und Gesellschaft im 2. und 3. Jahrhundert Hidschra*, vol. 2, Berlin and New York, 199, p. 39ff.

21. Pertinent passages in the Koran: sura 4:58, or sura 58:1 (hearing and seeing everything); sura 16:75–76 (slave-lord parable).

22. Sura 42:11.

23. *EI2*, see Ibn Dirham.

24. Josef van Ess, *Theologie und Gesellschaft*. vol. 2, p. 21.

25. Richard Frank, "The Neo-Platonism of Jahm ibn Safwan," in *Le Muséon* LXXVII (1965), pp. 395–424 (pp. 395–96).

26. Ad-Darimi, *'Uthman ibn Sa'id: ar-Radd 'ala l-Jahmiyya*, ed. Gösta Vitestam, Leiden and Lund, 1960, p. 19.

27. Ibid., pp. 26ff.

28. Cf. ibid., p. 42.

29. Sura 2:115.

30. Ad-Darimi, *'Uthman ibn Sa'id*, Introduction, p. 21; A. S. Tritton, *Muslim Theology*, London, 1947, p. 63; cf. also A. J. Wensinck, *The Muslim Creed*, Cambridge, 1932, pp. 91–92 (presentation of Jahmite teachings from al-Ashari's perspective).

31. Ibn Taymiyya, *Majmuat ar-rasail wal-masail*, 5 parts in 2 vols., vol. 1, Beirut, 1983, p. 84.

32. Nagel, *Rechtleitung und Kalifat*, p. 320.

33. Cf. W. Montgomery Watt, *The Formative Period of Islamic Thought*, Edinburgh,

1973, pp. 245–46; R. Frank, "The Divine Attributes according to . . . Abu l-Hudhayl al-Allaf," in *Le Muséon*, LXXXII (1982), pp. 451–506, esp. pp. 459ff.

34. Nagel, *Problem der Orthodoxie im frühen Islam*, p. 34; regarding additional theories on the term's origin, see van Ess, *Theologie und Gesellschaft*, vol. 2, pp. 336ff.

35. It is utterly impossible to describe exhaustively the many ramifications of the Mu'tazila, which had numerous local schools. Here is only room for its main lines of argument. For further reading, I refer to the works of Josef van Ess, "Lecture à rebours de l'histoire du Mutalizisme," in *Revue des Etudes Islamiques*, XLVI (1978), pp. 163–240, and XLVII (1979), pp. 19–69; *Theologie und Gesellschaft im 2. und 3. Jahrhundert Hidschra*, vol. 2, pp. 310ff.

36. W. Montgomery Watt, *The Formative Period of Islamic Thought*, p. 195.

37. Watt, ibid.

38. Al-Ashari, *Maqalat al-islamiyin*, ed. H. Ritter, Instanbul, 1929–30, pp. 166ff.

39. Joseph Schacht, *Der Islam mit Ausschluß des Qo'rans*, pp. 54–55.

40. See above, p. 85.

41. Josef van Ess, "Dirar ibn 'Amr and the Jahmiyya," in *Der Islam*, XLIII (1967), pp. 247–48.

42. At-Tabari, *Annales*, series 3, pp. 1113–14, 1118–19.

43. This, incidentally, explains Yahya ibn al-Hysayn's predestinarian interpretation of al-Hasan ibn Muhammad's treatise that was mentioned above; cf. pp. 86f.

44. A. J. Wensinck, *The Muslim Creed*, Cambridge, 1932, pp. 102ff.

45. Al-Ashari, *Maqalat*, p. 132.

46. R. Frank, *Neoplatonism*, pp. 405–06.

47. See above, pp. 32, 47, 53f.

48. Nagel, *Rechtleitung und Kalifat*, pp. 98–100, 321–23, and 354.

49. See above, p. 108.

50. Van Ess, *Dirar ibn 'Amr*, pp. 270–71.

51. See above; cf. R. Frank, *Divine Attributes*, pp. 467–68. (See above, n. 33.)

52. Watt, *Formative Period*, pp. 233ff.

53. See above, p. 40.

54. On the denial of the concept of a soul, see J. R. T. M. Peters, *God's Created Speech*, Leiden, 1976, pp. 165–66.

55. The entire human being could be considered "matter" containing certain accidentals such as the faculty to act (Hans Daiber, *Das theologisch-philosophische System des Mu'ammar b. 'Abbad as-Sulami*, Beirut, 1975, p. 362; pp. 322–70 contain a graphic description of an example from Mu'tazilite physics and metaphysics).

56. Peters, *God's Created Speech*, p. 106, n. 3.

57. W. Montgomery Watt, *Islamic Philosophy and Theology*, Islamic Surveys 1, Edinburgh, 1979, p. 68.

58. Nagel, *Rechtleitung und Kalifat*, pp. 266ff.

59. Nagel, *Problem der Orthodoxie*, p. 42.

60. Examples in Josef van der Ess, "Das Kitab an-nakt des Nazzam," in *Abhandlungen der Göttinger Akademie der Wissenschaften*, Phil.-hist. Klasse, 3. Folge, no. 79, Göttingen, 1972.

61. Cf. on this issue Lecomte (tr.), *Le traité des divergences du hadith d'Ibn Qutayba (mort an 889)*, Damascus, 1962.

62. See above, p. 75.

63. Following Joseph Schacht, *Der Islam mit Ausschluß des Qo'rans*, p. 19; Arabic text

in Louis Pouzet, S.J., *Le commentaire des Arba'un al-Nawawiya*, Beirut, 1982, p. 38.

64. Muad ibn Jabal, Muhammad's representative in Hadramaut (J. Wellhausen, *Skizzen und Vorarbeiten*, Heft 6, Berlin, 1899, p. 30).

65. Following Schacht, *Der Islam . . .*, p. 22; Pouzet, *Le commentaire . . .*, pp. 47–48.

66. Nagel, *Rechtleitung und Kalifat*, pp. 447–49.

67. Nagel, *Staat und Glaubensgemeinschaft*, vol. 1, p. 314.

68. Ahmad ibn Muhammad al-Barqi, *Kitab al-mahasin*, ed. al-Husaini, vol. 1, Nedjef, 1964, pp. 285 and 423.

69. See above, pp. 77f.

70. Al-Barqi, *Kitab al-mahasin*, vol. 1, pp. 222–23.

Chapter V (pp. 125–170)

1. Nagel, *Rechtleitung und Kalifat*, p. 465.

2. Rainer Glagow, *Das Kalifat des al-Mu'tadid billah (892–902)*, Bonn, 1968, pp. 156ff.

3. Miskawayh, *Tajarib al-umam*, ed. Amedroz, vol. 2, Cairo, 1914–15, p. 73.

4. Heinz Halm, *Das Reich des Mahdi: Der Aufstieg der Fatimiden*, Munich, 1991, pp. 361ff.

5. Tilman Nagel, *Die Festung des Glaubens*, Munich, 1988, p. 73.

6. Tilman Nagel, "Über die Ursprünge der Religionspolitik der ersten seldschukischen Sultane," in *Zeitschrift der ersten morgenländischen Gesellschaft*, Supplement 2, Wiesbaden, 1974, pp. 241ff.

7. Shahfur Tahir al-Isfara'ini, *At-Tabsir fi d'din*, ed. al-Kautari, Cairo, 1955, pp. 108ff.

8. See above, p. 68.

9. Arabic: *niyya*. In Islamic ritual law acts have religious merit only after the *niyya* has been formulated; the worship of God, to which human beings are obligated, must not be performed thoughtlessly.

10. See above, p. 119.

11. Nagel, *Rechtleitung und Kalifat*, pp. 329–32.

12. See above, p. 81.

13. A. J. Wensinck, *The Muslim Creed*, Cambridge, 1932, p. 103 (article 1: No one's belief may be questioned on account of sin); ibid., p. 125 (article 2: contains the phrasing criticized by Sufyan ibn 'Uyayna).

14. Al-Humaydi, *Musnad*, Appendix, pp. 546ff.

15. "Sorcerer," or "magician" (Arabic: *majus*) refers to the Zoroastrians, who believed a good and an evil principle were at work in the world; in the *hadith*, the Qadarites are denounced as "sorcerers of this (Islamic) community," because they believed in a second independent actor—man—besides God.

16. Ibn abi Ya'la, *Tabaqat a-hanabila*, ed. Muhammad Hamid al-Fiqi, vol. 1, Cairo, 1952, pp. 25–26.

17. Ibid., p. 31.

18. See above, pp. 112f..

19. Ibn abi Ya'la, *Tabaqat . . .*, vol. 1, p. 29.

20. Ibid., p. 31.

21. Ibid., p. 36.

22. Ibn Khuzayma, *Kitab at-tauhid wa-ithbat sifat ar-Rabb*, ed. M. Kh. Harras, Beirut, 1983, pp. 10–11 and 22–23. Cf. Joseph Schacht, *Der Islam mit Ausschluß des Quo'rans*, pp. 41–42. Al-Baihaqi's (d. 1066) *Kitab al-asma was-sifat* (Beirut, Dar al-kutub al-ilmiya, c. 1985), presents an additional impressive example of the way Sunni theology was practiced in Nishapur. Al-Baihaqi, however, focuses his arguments even more on the *hadith* than Ibn Khuzayma.

23. See above, p. 119.

24. Ibn abi Ya'la, *Tabaqat . . .*, vol. 1, p. 29.

25. Johann Fück, "Spuren des Zindiqtums in der islamischen Tradition," in *Festschrift Paul Kahle*, Leiden, 1935, pp. 97–98.

26. Cf. G. Lecomte, *Le traité des divergences* (seech. 4, n. 61), nos. 15, 229, and 295.

27. Ibn Qutayba, *Al-Ikhtilaf fi l-lafz*, ed. Al-Kathauri, Cairo, 1349 h.

28. See above, pp. 128f. Nagel, *Rechtleitung und Kalifat*, pp. 331–32. Cf., however, below, n. 107. In chapter 3 of my book, *Medinensische Einschübe in mekkanischen Suren*, I explain Muhammad's teachings about the relation between the essence of the revelation and the "Book."

29. See above, p. 121.

30. See above, p. 66.

31. Tilman Nagel, *Die Festung des Glaubens*, pp. 200ff.

32. Abu 'Abd ar-Rahman as-Sulami, *Tabaqat as-sufiya*, ed. Shurayba, 2nd ed., Cairo, 1969, p. 33.

33. Ibid., p. 285.

34. Ibid, p. 282.

35. Ibid., p. 247; incidentally, as-Sulami introduced almost all Sufis he discussed as knowledgeable in the *hadith*.

36. Josef van Ess, *Die Gedankenwelt des Harit al-Muhasibi*, Bonn, 1961, pp. 3 and 5.

37. Ibid., pp. 186–87.

38. Ibid., pp. 113–14.

39. Zabihollah Safa, ed., *Ganjine-yi sukhan*, vol. 1, Tehran, 1969, p. 195.

40. Cf. on this subject Ulrich Rudolph, *Al-Maturidi und die sunnitische Theologie in Samarkand*, part 1.

41. Ibid., chapter "Theologische Gegner."

42. Al-Maturidi, *Kitab at-Tauhid*, ed. Kholeif, Beirut, 1970, p. 56.

43. Ibid., p. 57.

44. Ibid., pp. 4–6.

45. Ibid., p. 48. As this indicates, Murjiite thought continued to thrive in the east of the Islamic empire (cf. above, pp. 57ff.

46. Ibid., pp. 120 and 169.

47. Ibid., p. 114; cf. ibid., pp. 124 and 164–69.

48. Ibid., p. 164.

49. For examples of this, see Hans Leisegang, *Die Gnosis*, 5th ed., Stuttgart, 1985.

50. Al-Maturidi, *At-Taurid*, pp. 18ff. and 28.

51. Ibid., p. 29; cf. also p. 129.

52. Ulrich Rudolph, *Al-Maturidi . . .*, ch. 2, 2.2.1.

53. Al-Maturidi, *At-Tauhid*, pp. 82ff. Ultimately al-Maturidi argues from the Jahmite view of God's unlimitable omnipresence, to which Abu Hanifa had subscribed as well (cf. above, pp. 102f.

54. Ibid., p. 85.

55. See above, p. 117.
56. Al-Maturidi, *Al-Tauhid*, pp. 86–89.
57. Ibid., pp. 141–42; cf. p. 157.
58. Ulrich Rudolph, *Al-Maturidi* . . ., ch. 3B, 1.2.1.
59. Al-Maturidi, *At-Tauhid*, pp. 215–16.
60. See above, pp. 59f.
61. See above, pp. 141f.
62. Al-Maturidi, *At-Tauhid*, p. 237.
63. Ibid., 227–30.
64. Nagel, *Die Festung des Glaubens*, p. 108ff.
65. See above, pp. 138f.
66. Taj ad-Din as-Subki, *Tabaqat ash-shafiʻyya*, ed. at-Tanahi and al-Hilw, vol. 3, Cairo, 1964ff., pp. 347ff.
67. Henri Laoust, ed., *La profession de foi d'Ibn Batta*, Damascus, 1958, Arabic text, pp. 54–55.
68. Al-Ashʻari, *Al-Ibana ʻan usul ad-diyana*, ed. Fauqiya Husayn Mahmud, Cairo, 1977, pp. 241ff.
69. See above, pp. 130f.
70. Al-Ashʻari, *Risalat istihsan al-haud fi ʻilm al-kalam*, edition Haydarabad, 1344 h.
71. On this, see Daniel Gimaret, *Les noms divins en Islam*, Paris, 1988.
72. Fakhr ad-Din ar-Razi, *Muhassil afkar al-mutaqaddimin wal-muta'akhkhirin*, ed. Cairo, 1323 h, p. 55; R. Frank, "Abu Hashim's Theory of 'States,'" in *Actas do VI congresso de estudos árabes e islâmicos* (Coimbra and Lisbon, 1968), Leiden, 1971, pp. 85–100.
73. Al-Ashʻari, *Al-Ibana*, pp. 120–21.
74. Ibn Furak, *Mujarrad maqalat al-Ashʻari*, ed. Daniel Gimaret, Beirut, 1987, p. 44.
75. Ibid., pp. 49–50.
76. Cf. Geo Widengren, *Mani und der Manichäismus*, Stuttgart, 1961, pp. 50–51.
77. Ibn Furak, *Mujarrad* . . . , p. 57.
78. Ibid., pp. 57ff.
79. Nagel, *Die Festung des Glaubens*, p. 241.
80. Ibn Furak, *Mujarrad* . . . , pp. 80–81.
81. Ibid., pp. 289–90.
82. Ibid., p. 76.
83. Ibid., p. 83.
84. See above, p. 113.
85. Ibn Furak, *Mujarrad* . . . , pp. 93–94.
86. Ibid., p 84.
87. Ibn Khaldun, *Al-Muqaddimah*, tr. Franz Rosenthal, vol. 3, New York, 1958, p. 154.
88. Richard Frank, "The *kalam*, an Art of Contradiction-Making or Theological Science?" in *Journal of the American Oriental Society* 88, p. 309.
89. Ulrich Rudolph, *Al-Maturidi* . . . , ch. 3A1.
90. Ulrich Rudolph, "Christliche Bibelexegese und muʻtazilitische Theologie," lecture delivered at the congress of the Union Européenne d'Arabisants et Islamisants, Salamanca, 1992.
91. Ulrich Rudolph, *Al-Maturidi und die sunnitische Theologie in Samarkand*, ch. 3A1.
92. Nagel, *Die Festung des Glaubens*, p. 159.
93. See below, pp. 194ff.

94. Ibn al-Baqillani, *Kitab at-tamhid*, ed. MacCarthy, Beirut, 1957, pp. 15–16, par. 30.
95. Ibid., p. 6, par. 5.
96. See above, p. 116.
97. See above, pp.151ff.
98. On this, see Fray Luciano Rubio's monography *El "occasionalismo" de los teologos especulativos islamicos*, Madrid, 1987.
99. Ibn al-Baqillani, *Kitab at-tamhid*, pp. 191ff., pars. 325–29.
100. Al-Baihaqi (d. 1066) ventured to do this for a part of it—"names and qualities of God"—but in this area Koran and *hadith* contain a great many, and significant, statements (al-Baihaqi, *Kitab al-asma' was-sifat*, Beirut, n.d., cf. above, n. 22).
101. Al-Juwayni, *Kitab al-burhan fi usul al-fiqh*, ed. ad-Dib, Cairo, 1400 h, pp. 124ff., pars. 45ff.; Nagel, *Die Festung des Glaubens*, pp. 245ff.
102. Cf. al-Juwayni, *Ash-Shamil fi usul ad-din*, ed. an-Nashshar, Alexandria, 1969, pp. 18ff.
103. Nagel, *Die Festung des Glaubens*, pp. 141ff.
104. Ibid., pp. 142–43.
105. Ibid., pp. 240ff.
106. Ibid., pp. 263ff.
107. Josef van Ess, "Ibn Kullab und die Mihna," in *Oriens* XVIII (1965), pp. 92–142 (pp. 103–07).
108. Nagel, *Die Festung des Glaubens*, pp. 236ff.
109. Ibid., pp. 179ff.
110. Ibid., pp. 82ff. and 111ff.
111. On this, see Claude Gilliot's study *Exégèse, langue et théologie en islam*, Etudes musulmanes XXXII, Paris, 1990.
112. See above, pp. 30f.
113. Nagel, *Die Festung des Glaubens*, pp. 229ff.
114. See above, pp. 131f.
115. See above, pp. 148ff.; cf. Ibn Furak, *Mujarrad maqalat al-Ash'ari*, p. 302.
116. See above, p. 161.
117. Nagel, *Die Festung des Glaubens*, p. 147.
118. Az-Zajjaji, *Kitab al-idah*, ed. Mazin al-Mubarak, Cairo, 1959, p. 64.
119. Ibn al-Anbari, *Die grammatischen Streitfragen der Basrer und Kufer*, ed. Gotthold Weil, Leiden, 1913, p. 31.
120. Ibn Hazm, *Al-Ihkam fi usul al-ahkam*, ed. Ahmad Shakir, vol. 1, Cairo, n.d., pp. 30–31. Cf. Roger Arnaldez, *Grammaire et théologie chez Ibn Hazm de Cordoue*, Paris, 1956, and T. Nagel, "Bemerkungen zur Sprache im Lichte der islamischen Theologie," in *Die arabische Sprache in Forschung und Unterricht*.

Chapter VI (pp. 171–214)

1. See above, p. 90.
2. Ibn Khaldun, *The Muqaddimah*, tr. . . . Franz Rosenthal, vol. 3, New York, 1958, pp. 50–51.
3. Ibid., p. 144.
4. Ibid., pp. 52-53; Nagel, *Die Festung des Glaubens*, p. 148; cf. above, p. 169.

5. Von Campenhausen, *Griechische Kirchenväter*, Stuttgart, 1955, p. 17.
6. On the relationship between jurisprudence and theology, see Tilman Nagel, *Die Festung des Glaubens*, Munich, 1988, pp. 264ff.
7. Ibn Rushd, ed., *Fasl al-maqal*, 3rd ed., Nadir, Beirut, 1973, pp. 35–36.
8. Ibid., pp. 41–42.
9. Ibid., p. 43.
10. Ibid., pp. 45ff.
11. This complex issue is discussed in many of its aspects in the book by Tilman Nagel, *Die Festung des Glaubens*; cf. also Nagel, *Timur der Eroberer*, Munich, 1993, chapter "Kairo."
12. See above, pp. 128ff.
13. Nagel, *Die Festung des Glaubens*, p. 177.
14. On the assassins, see M. G. S. Hodgson, *The Order of the Assassins*, The Hague, 1955.
15. Nizam al-Mulk, *Siyasat-nama: Gedanken und Geschichten*, tr. Karl Emil Schabinger Freiherr von Schowingen, Munich and Freiburg, 1960, ch. 47.
16. Bayard Dodge (tr.), *The Fihrist of al-Nadim*, New York and London, 1970, p. 471.
17. Shahfur Tahir al-Isfara'ini, *At-Tabsir fi d-din*, ed. al-Kautari, Cairo, 1955, p. 126.
18. Al-Ghazali, *Fada'ih al-batiniyyah*, ed. Badavi, Kuwait, n.d. (after 1964), pp. 55ff.
19. Ibid., pp. 198–99.
20. See above, p. 80.
21. Fritz Meier, "Abu Sa'id-i bu l-Hayr: Wirklichkeit und Legende," in *Acta Iranica* XI (1976), p. 137.
22. Fritz Meier (ed. and commentary), *Die fawa'ih al-gamal . . . des Nagm ad-Din Kubra*, Akademie der Wissenschaften und Literatur (Mainz), Veröffentlichungen der orientalistischen Kommission 9, Wiesbaden, 1957, p. 86.
23. Nagel, *Timur der Eroberer*, pp. 70ff.
24. Ibid., p. 73.
25. Cf., e.g., the laudatory phrase of a scholar being knowledgeable "in the sciences of Greek and theology," Qashani, *Tarikh-i Uljaytu*, ed. Hambly, Tehran, 1348 h, pp. 101, 219, and 221.
26. Gotthelf Bergsträsser, *Hunayn b. Ishaq: Die syrischen und arabischen Galen-Übersetzungen*, Abhandlungen zur Kunde des Morgenlandes XVII/2, Leipzig, 1925.
27. W. Montgomery Watt, *Islamic Philosophy and Theology*, Edinburgh, 1962, p. 44.
28. On this, cf. Ulrich Rudolph, *Die Doxographie des Pseydo-Ammonios*, Abhandlungen zur Kunde des Morgenlandes IL/1, Wiesbaden, 1989.
29. Rudolph, *Doxographie . . .*, p. 210.
30. A short summary can be found in de Boer, *Geschichte der Philosophie im Islam*, Stuttgart, 1901, p. 95.
31. *Encyclopedia of Islam*, 2nd ed., see al-Kindi.
32. Jean Jolivet, *L'intellect selon Kindi*, Leiden, 1971, p. 91.
33. Ibid., p. 96.
34. Ibid., p. 95.
35. Nagel, *Die Festung des Glaubens*, p. 295.
36. De Boer, *Geschichte der Philosophie im Islam*, pp. 104–106.
37. Ibid., p. 106.
38. Ibid., pp. 106–10.
39. Cf. Friedrich Dieterici (tr.), *Der Musterstaat des al-Farabi*, Leiden. 1900. p. 93;

Richard Walzer, *Greek into Arabic*, Oxford, 1962, pp. 19–20.

40. Dieterici, *Der Musterstaat des al-Farabi*, pp. 5–9.

41. Susanne Diwald (tr.), *Arabische Philosophie und Wissenschaft in der Enzyklopädie Kitab Ihwan as-safa' (III): Die Lehre von Seele und Intellekt*, Wiesbaden, 1975; cf. in the context of this chapter the book's introduction.

42. Abu Haiyan at-Tauhidi, *Al-Imta' wal-mu'anasa*, ed. Ahmad Amin and Ahmad az-Zain, vol. 2, Beirut, n.d., p. 14.

43. *EI2*, see Abu Sulayman al-Mantiki.

44. See above, p. 178.

45. Abu Haiyan a-Tauhidi, *Al-Imta' wal-mu'anasa*, vol. 2, pp. 6–12.

46. Roger Arnaldez, *Grammaire et théologie chez Ibn Hazm de Cordoue*, Paris, 1956, pp. 46–47 and 62ff.; A. G. Cheine, *Ibn Hazm*, Chicago, 1982, pp. 56ff.; on Ibn Hazm's works on logic, see ibid., pp. 167ff. See above, pp. 169f.

47. W. Montgomery Watt, *Muslim Intellectual: A Study of al-Ghazali*, Edinburgh, 1963, pp. 65ff.

48. Nagel, *Die Festung des Glaubens*, p. 359. Cf. al-Ghazali, *Der Erretter aus dem Irrtum*, tr. from the Arabic by A. A. Elschazli, Hamburg, 1988, pp. 40ff. and 55ff.

49. Nagel, *Die Festung des Glaubens*, pp. 217, 226, and 240; cf. also ibid., pp. 154–55.

50. See above, p. 178f.

51. Al-Ghazali, *Iljam al-'amm 'an al-khaud fi 'ilm al kalam*, ed. M. M. al-Baghdadi, Beirut, 1985.

52. Cf. sura 16, verses 1–2.

53. J. M. S. Baljon, "The 'Amr of God' in the Koran," in *Acta Orientalia* XXIII (1958), pp. 7–18; see above.

54. Fahr ad-Din ar-Razi, *Mafatih al-jayb*, vol. 21, pp. 37–38.

55. Ibid., p. 40.

56. Cf. ibid., p. 46, ll. 7ff.

57. Ibid., p. 45.

58. Ibid., p. 45, l. 20.

59. Here the concept of "mutual hindrance," with which the Mutazilites and Asharites had attempted to prove God's oneness (Nagel, *Die Festung des Glaubens*, pp. 123ff.), is transferred to the human individual—this single example illustrates the monumental shift in perspective!

60. Fakhr ad-Din ar-Razi, *Mafatih al-jayb*, vol. 21, p. 50.

61. E.g., ibid., p. 43 above; placement of knowledge: al-Ghazali, *Tahafut al-falasifa*, ed. Dunya, Cairo, n.d., pp. 243ff.

62. Ernst Behler, *Die Ewigkeit der Welt*, Munich, 1965, p. 138.

63. Al-Ghazali, *Fada'ih al-batiniyyah*, p. 242.

64. Ibid., pp. 66–67 and 70.

65. Ibid., p. 68.

66. Ibn Sina, *Al-Isharat wat-tanbihat*, ed. Dunya, vol. 2, n.p., 1948, pp. 343ff.

67. Shlomo Pines, *Studies in Abu l-Barakat al-Baghdadi: Physics and Metaphysics*, Jerusalem and Leiden, 1979, pp. 188ff., 199ff., 223, 227, and 247.

68. Tilman Nagel, "Ibn al-Arabi und das Ascharitentum," in *Festschrift für Abdoljavad Falaturi*, Cologne and Vienna, 1991, pp. 207–45 (p. 229).

69. Ibid., pp. 230–31.

70. Ibid., pp. 235ff.

71. Tilman Nagel, *Timur der Eroberer*, Book 2 ("Chaos und Kosmos").
72. Fakhr ad-Din ar-Razi, *Mafatih al-ghaib*, vol. 3, p. 213.
73. See below, "Islamic Orthodoxy."
74. On him, cf. Gimaret and Monnot (tr.), *Shahrastani: Livre des religions et sectes*, vol. 1, Unesco, 1986, pp. 52ff.
75. Ash-Sharastani, *Nihayat al-iqdam*, ed. Guilleaume, reprint, n.p., n.d., p. 89.
76. See above, pp. 195ff.
77. Nagel, *Die Festung des Glaubens*, p. 148.
78. Ibid., pp. 241ff.
79. Fakhr ad-Din ar-Razi, *Muhassil afkar al-mutaqaddimin . . .*, p. 29.
80. According to Avicenna, every thing is perceived as "either existing in (the form of) essences or as imagined in the mind" (A.-M. Goichon, *Lexique de la langue philosophique d'Ibn Sina*, Paris, 1938, p. 133; additional examples of Avicenna's use of *dhihn* can be found there).
81. Fakhr ad-Din ar-Razi, *Al-Mabahith al-mashriqiyya*, vol. 1, ed. Tehran, 1966, pp. 41–42.
82. Fakhr ad-Din ar-Razi, *Muhassil al-afkar al-mutaqaddimin wal-muta'akhkhirin*, p. 45.
83. The following discussion is based on Richard Frank, *Creation and the Coranic System: Al-Ghazali and Avicenna*, Abhandlungen der Heidelberger Akademie der Wissenschaften, philosophisch-historische Klasse 1992/i, Heidelberg, 1992. A significant part of my 1993 book *Timur der Eroberer*, which was written independently of that work, rests on similar conclusions and insights.
84. Cf. above, p. 155; Nagel, *Festung des Glaubens*, pp. 142–47.
85. Frank, *Creation and the Coranic System*, p. 21.
86. Nagel, *Timur der Eroberer*, pp. 358ff.
87. Frank, *Creation and the Coranic System*, p. 21, n. 27.
88. As J. van Ess ("The Logical Structure of Islamic Theology," in G. E. V. Grunebaum [ed.], *Logic in Classical Islamic Culture*, First Giorgio Levi della Vida Biennial Conference, Wiesbaden, 1970, pp. 21–50) makes clear, the *kalam*, which centers around the creation as a system of signs, was bound to a logic that in many respects was reminiscent of Stoicism. Al-Ghazali, however, had practiced Aristotelian logic.
89. Cf. Nagel, "Theologie und Ideologie im modernen Islam," in *Der Islam*, vol. 3, *Die Religionen der Menschheit*, vol. 25/iii, Stuttgart, 1990, p. 5.
90. Frank, *Creation and the Coranic System*, p.43.
91. Ibid., pp. 65–68.
92. Ibid., p. 82.
93. Fakhr ad-Din ar-Razi, *Kitab an-nafs war-ruh wa-sharh quwa-huma*, ed. al-Masumi, Istanbul, 1968.
94. Ala ad-Din at-Tusi, *Tahafut al-falasifa*, ed. R. Saada, 3rd ed., Beirut, p. 387.

Chapter VII (pp. 215–234)

1. Hans Leisegang, *Die Gnosis*, Stuttgart, 1985, p. 20.
2. Hans Jonas, *Gnosis und spätantiker Geist*, new ed., Göttingen, 1988, p. 98.
3. Ibid., pp. 157 and 162.

4. Cf. Helmer Ringgren, *Studies in Arabian Fatalism*, Uppsala and Wiesbaden, 1955.

5. Jonas, *Gnosis und spätantiker Geist*, p. 145.

6. See above, pp. 4f.

7. Kurt Rudolph, *Die Gnosis: Wesen und Geschichte einer spätantiken Religion*, Leipzig, 1977, pp. 70–71.

8. Arabic: *min tahti-ha* (sura 2, verse 22, and *passim*). Following the translation by Paret, the meaning is "in the lowlands," but Paret adds that this frequently recurring *topos* is unclear.

9. Cf. Mark Lidzbarski (tr.): *Ginza: Der Schatz oder Das große Buch der Mandäer*, Göttingen and Leipzig, 1925, pp. 292, 479, 510, 527, and *passim*.

10. Kurt Rudolph, *Die Gnosis*, p. 76.

11. Tilman Nagel, "Der Koran als Zeugnis einer Zeitenwende," in *Zeitschrift für Missionswissenschaft und Religionswissenschaft* LXVII (1983), pp. 97–109.

12. Abu l-Hasan al-Amiri, *Kitab al-i'lam bi-manaqib al-islam*, ed. Ghorab, Cairo, 1967, pp. 163ff.

13. See above, p. 97f.

14. See above, ch. 5, n. 15.

15. See below, pp. 269f.

16. Carsten Colpe, "Der Manichäismus in der arabischen Überlieferung," Dissertation, University of Göttingen, 1954. p. 184.

17. Ibid., pp. 187–88.

18. *EI2*, see Abu 'Isa al-Warrak.

19. Colpe, "Der Manichäismus in der arabischen Überlieferung," pp. 63–64.

20. On an-Nazzam, see above, pp. 107–108 and 114.

21. Al-Khayat, *Kitab al-intisar*, ed. S. Nyberg, Cairo, 1925, pp. 30–31.

22. On the decline of Manichaeism in the Islamic world, cf. Bayard Dodge (ed.), *The Fihrist of al-Madim*, New York and London, 1970, p. 802. The Zoroastrians emigrated from Iran to India in large numbers as early as the eighth century.

23. On this, see the following chapter.

24. Unfortunately, the term "Gnosis" is often used quite unspecifically in reference to certain forms of the late Middle Ages' theology of the "oneness of being."

25. The tenth century, a period of Byzantium's great expansion of power, witnessed Johannes Tzimiskes's advance to the vicinity of Jerusalem in 975 (Georg Ostrogorski, *Geschichte des byzantinischen Staates*, 3rd ed., Munich, 1963, pp. 236–49; *Nikephoros Phokas und Johannes Tzimiskes: Die Zeit von 959–76 in der Darstellung des Leon Diakonos*, tr. Franz Loretto, Byzantinische Geschichtsschreiber X, Graz, 1961).

26. Susanne Diewald (tr.), *Arabische Philosophie und Wissenschaft in der Enzyklopädie Ihwan as-sarfa' (III): Die Lehre von Seele und Intellekt*, Wiesbaden, 1975, pp. 142–43.

27. Ibid., pp. 314–15.

28. Ibid., pp. 330–31.

29. William E. Gohlman (tr.), *The Life of Ibn Sina*, Albany, 1974, pp. 18–20.

30. On account of Avicenna's statement that he did not let the Isma'ilites visiting his parents' home impress him, Dimitri Gutas (*Avicenna and the Aristotelian Tradition*, Leiden, 1988, pp. 192–93) seems to rule out the influence of Ismailite thought on Avicenna. Yet is it permissible to dismiss this difficult issue without any reference to the content of Avicenna's writings?

31. Diwald, *Arabische Philosophie und Wissenschaft*, pp. 9–14.
32. Heinz Halm, *Die islamische Gnosis*, Zurich and Munich, 1982, pp. 72–73; incidentally, it is worth mentioning that Islam's Gnostic movements partly knew the concept of the transmigration of souls (on this, see Rainer Freitag, *Seelenwanderung in der islamischen Häresie*, Islamkundliche Untersuchungen 10, Berlin, 1985).
33. Heinz Halm, *Kosmologie und Heilslehre der frühen Isma'iliya: Eine Studie zur Islamischen Gnosis*, Abhandlungen zur Kunde des Morgenlandes XLIV/1, pp. 20–21.
34. Ibid., pp. 29–30.
35. Ibid., pp. 110–11; cf. Geo Widengren, *Mani und der Manichäismus*, p. 59.
36. Nagel, *Staat und Glaubensgemeinschaft*, vol. 1, pp. 247ff.
37. A detailed study on the life of a Fatimid agent, which however mentions the religio-political content of these ideas only marginally, is the book by Verena Klemm: *Die Mission des fatimidischen Agenten al-Mu'ayyad fi d-Din in Siraz*, Europäische Hochschulschriften, series XXVII, no. 24, Frankfurt/Main, 1989.
38. Bernard Lewis, *The Assassins: A Radical Sect in Islam*, London, 1967.
39. Ignaz Goldziher, *Die Streitschrift des Gazali gegen die Batinijja Sekte*, Leiden, 1916, pp. 52–60.
40. Ibid., p. 47.
41. Heinz Halm, *Die Schia*, Darmstadt, 1988, pp. 172–73.
42. On the milieu in which Druzedom developed, see Josef van Ess, *Chiliastische Erwartungen und die Versuchung der Göttlichkeit*, Abhandlungen der Heidelberger Akademie der Wissenschaften, philosophisch-historische Klasse, 1977, Abhandlung 2. A basic text on the history of the Druzes is the book by Werner Schmucker: *Krise und Erneuerung im libanesischen Drusentum*, Bonner Orientalistische Studien 27/iii, Bonn, 1979.
43. Halm, *Die Schia*, pp. 234ff.
44. Even the early Shia contained the idea that Ali was the gate to knowledge that guaranteed the good next world and was even the gate to the next world itself (Nagel, *Rechtleitung und Kalifat*, p. 185). Saiyid Ali Muhammad (1821–1850) from Shiras, the precursor of the founder of Baha'ism, also called himself a "gate" (*bab*) (*EI2*, see Bab).
45. Rudolph Strothmann, *Gnosis-Texte der Ismailiten*, Göttingen, 1943, pp. 20–21 and 43.
46. Heinz Halm, *Die Schia*, pp. 118–19.

Chapter VIII (pp. 235–252)

1. See above, p. 56
2. Tilman Nagel, *Die Festung des Glaubens*, pp. 48ff.
3. See above, pp. 75ff.
4. Tilman Nagel, "Das Problem der Orthodoxie im frühen Islam," in *Studien zum Minderheitenproblem im Islam*, Bonner Orientalistische Studien 27, Bonn, 1973, pp. 37ff.
5. See above, p. 128, the earlier example of al-Humaydi.
6. On *bid'a*, see above, p. 67.

7. See above, p. 207.

8. Ibn abi Ya'la, *Tabaqat al-hanabila*, ed. al-Faqi, vol. 1, Cairo, 1952, pp. 342–45.

9. Henri Laoust, *La profession de foi d'Ibn Batta*, Damascus, 1958, p. xxx.

10. In the tenth century general consensus had been established on what Islam was (cf. on this issue the book by Claude Gilliot in the recommendations for further reading in chapter five).

11. Nagel, *Die Festung des Glaubens*, p. 347.

12. Ibn abi Ya'la, *Tabaqat al-hanabila*, ed. al-Faqi, vol. 2, pp. 19 and 22; on 9 Du l-Hijja the pilgrims to Mecca remain near 'Arafa; see below, p. 238.

13. See above, p. 44.

14. Laoust, *La profession . . .*, pp. lxxxff.

15. Nagel, *Staat und Glaubensgemeinschaft*, vol. 1, pp. 331ff.

16. On this, see above, pp. 99f., a detailed analysis and description of al-Ma'mun's endeavors within the context of his time is in Nagel, *Rechtleitung und Kalifat*, pp. 400ff.

17. Nagel, *Die Festung des Glaubens*, pp. 21ff.

18. Ibid., pp. 56ff.

19. On Abu Isma'il `Abdallah al-Harawi, cf. Ignaz Goldziher, "Zur Geschichte der hanbalitischen Bewegungen," in *Gesammelte Schriften*, vol. 5, Hildesheim, 1970, pp. 135–62, esp. pp. 144ff.

20. Nagel, *Die Festung des Glaubens*, pp. 168ff. and 307ff.

21. Goldziher, "Zur Geschichte der hanbalitischen Bewegungen," pp. 158-59.

22. Henri Laoust (tr.), *Le traité de droit public d'Ibn Taimija*, Beirut, 1948.

23. Cf. the treatises in Ibn Taimiyya, *Magmu'at ar-rasa'il wal-masa'il*, vol. 1, ed. Beirut, 1983.

24. Nagel, *Staat und Glaubensgemeinschaft*, vol. 1, pp. 112ff.

25. Carl Brockelmann, *Geschichte der arabischen Literatur*, G I, pp. 262 and 442; S I, p. 792; S II, p. 280; cf. Ibn Abidin, "Ijabat al-gauth bi-bayan hal an-nuqaba' . . . ," in Ibn 'Abidin, *Majmu'at rasa'il Ibn 'Abidin*, reprint, vol. 2, n.p., n.d., pp. 264–81.

26. See above; Ibn 'Abidin, "Sall al-husam al-hindi . . . ," in *Majmu'at rasa'il Ibn 'Abidin*, vol. 2, pp. 284–315.

27. Nagel, *Timur der Eroberer*, pp. 303ff.

28. See above, p. 212f.

29. Oskar Rescher (tr.), *es-Saqa'iq an-No'manijje von Tasköprüzade*, translated from the Arabic with addenda and notes, Constantinople and Stuttgart, 1927–34, pp. 191–94. Cf. also the study by Hedda Reindl, *Männer um Bayezid*, Islamkundliche Untersuchungen 75, Berlin, 1983, where the aspects relating to the history of the mind, however, are mentioned only in passing.

30. Gibb and Bowen, *Islamic Society and the West*, vol. 1/ii, Oxford University Press, 1957, pp. 121ff.

31. Ibid., pp. 76 and 198; on the history of the order of Naqshbandiyya—although with an emphasis on Central Asia—cf. Jürgen Paul, *Die politische und soziale Bedeutung der Naqshbandiyya in Mittelasien im 15. Jahrhundert*, Berlin and New York, 1991.

32. Heinz Halm, *Die Schia*, pp. 205ff.

33. Nagel, *Staat und Glaubensgemeinschaft*, vol. 1, pp. 218–19.

34. Ibid., pp. 267-72.

35. Heinz Halm, *Die Schia*, pp. 124ff.

Chapter IX (pp. 253–276)

1. On France's attack on Egypt and Muhammad 'Ali's rise, cf. Arnold Hottinger's German translation of a contemporary chronicle by al-Jabarti, *Bonaparte in Ägypten*, Bibliothek des Morgenlandes im Artemis Verlag, Zurich and Munich, 1983.
2. Ulrich Haarmann (ed.), *Geschichte der arabischen Welt*, Munich, 1987, p. 388.
3. Muhammad 'Abduh, *Mudhakkirat al-imam Muhammad 'Abduh*, ed. at-Tanahi, Cairo, n.d., pp. 39ff.
4. Alexander Schölch, *Ägypten den Ägyptern! Die politische und gesellschaftliche Krise der Jahre 1878–82 in Ägypten*, Zurich and Freiburg, n.d.
5. Cf. Ibn 'Abidin, *Majmu'at ar-rasa'il*, vol. 1, reprint, n.p., n.d., pp. 2–8.
6. Albert Hourani, "Shaikh Khalid and the Naqshbandi Order," in *Islamic Philosophy and the Classical Tradition: Festschrift Richard Walzer*, University of South Carolina Press, 1972 (pp. 89–103), p. 96.
7. Al-Baytar, *Hilyat al-bashar*, ed. Damascus, 1961–63, p. 1239.
8. Cf. Carl Brockelmann, *Geschichte der arabischen Literatur*, supplement vol. 2, p. 643; Ibn 'Abidin's excerpt "Al-'Uqud ad-Durriyya" was reprinted many times (Brockelmann, ibid.).
9. Ibn Abidin, *Majmu'at ar-rasa'il*, vol. 1, p. 325, l. 7.
10. Ibid., pp. 338–39.
11. Brockelmann, *Geschichte der arabischen Literatur*, supplement vol. 2, p. 225.
12. Ibn 'Abidin, *Majmu'at ar-rasa'il*, vol. 1, p. 328.
13. Ibid., p. 329.
14. Ibid., p. 335.
15. Ibid., p. 336.
16. Ibid., p. 348.
17. Ibid., p. 338. According to Ibn 'Abidin, Hanafite law contains no basis for executing the man who had insulted the Prophet; therefore Ibn 'Abidin recommended to the judges of that school that they leave the verdict in cases of such offenses up to the Qadis of other schools so that the verdict could always be reached that in his opinion would be most useful to the Muslims (ibid., p. 351). On this issue, of which the Western world has become aware through the Rushdie case, cf. T. Nagel, "Die Tabuisierung der Person des Propheten Muhammad," in *Festschrift Kurt Rudolph*, 1994.
18. On al-Ghazali's view of the position of mathematics within the sciences, cf. al-Ghazali, *Tahafut al-falasifa*, ed. S. Dunja, Cairo, n.d., pp. 70–71; cf. also above, p. 201.
19. This is the argument of, e.g., Khair ad-Din at-Tunisi (1823–90); cf. Nagel, "Theologie und Ideologie im modernen Islam," in *Der Islam III*, Religionen der Menschheit 25/iii, Stuttgart, 1990, p. 14.
20. Jürgen Paul, *Die politische und soziale Bedeutung der Naqsbandiya in Mittelasien*, pp. 26-38; on the expansion of this order in the Ottoman Empire, see Gibb and Bowen, *Islamic Society and the West*, vol. 1/ii, pp. 196-97.
21. Brockelmann, *Geschichte der arabischen Literatur*, vol. 2, pp. 264ff.; cf. above, p. 234.
22. Ibn 'Abidin, *Majmu'at ar-rasa'il*, vol. 2, pp. 284ff.
23. Albert Hourani, "Shaikh Khalid . . . ," (see n. 6).
24. B. G. Martin, *Muslim Brotherhoods in Nineteenth Century North Africa*, Cambridge

University Press, 1976, pp. 99ff.; R. S. O'Fahey, *The Enigmatic Saint*, London, 1990, pp. 58 and 130ff.

25. Nicola Ziadeh, *Sanusiyah: A Study of the Revivalist Movement in Islam*, Leiden, 1958, pp. 41–44.

26. Cf. ibid., pp. 81ff.

27. See above, p. 245.

28. As-Sanusi, *Iqaz al-wasanan*, ed. of the Libyan Ministry of Information and Culture, 1968, p. 129.

29. Johann Ludwig Burckhardt, *Reisen in Arabien*, Weimar, 1830, pp. 265ff.; C. Snouck Hurgronje, *Mecca in the Latter Part of the Nineteenth Century*, Leiden, 1931.

30. Gerd Rüdiger Puin, "Aspekte der wahhabitischen Reform," in *Studien zum Minderheitenproblem im Islam*, Bonner Orientalistische Studien 27, Bonn, 1973, pp. 45–99.

31. See above, p. 24.

32. Richard Hartmann, "Die Wahhabiten," in *ZDMG* LXXVIII (1924), pp. 179-84; since the waning tenth century the difference of opinion among scholars was considered an expression of grace (Nagel, *Die Festung des Glaubens*, p. 319).

33. Hartmann, "Die Wahhabiten"; on the Wahhabites' teachings see also Henri Laoust, *Les schismes dans l'islam*, Paris, 1965, pp. 321-32.

34. Nagel, *Festung des Glaubens*, pp. 365-66.

35. Ibn Taymiyya, *Muwafaqat sahih al-manqul li-sarih al-ma'qul*, 2 vols., ed., Beirut, 1985.

36. On him, see Brockelmann, *Geschichte der arabischen Literatur*, supplement vol. 3, pp. 315ff.; Malcolm H. Kerr, *Islamic Reform*, Los Angeles and Cambridge, 1966, pp. 103ff.

37. Muhammad 'Abduh, *Al-A'mal al-kamila*, vol. 3, ed. 'Ammara, Cairo, pp. 262 and 282–83. Averroes had also demanded that the revelation be interpreted until its content coincided with that of reason; but the fundamental difference to 'Abduh was that he was not familiar with the special ontological category of the "world as a whole" and therefore, following the Ash'arist doctrine, allowed that everything that was not God was directly determined by Him (cf. above, p. 176). In contrast, in 'Abduh's work al-Ashari's legitimization of rationalism within Sunnism has turned into a legitimization of rationalism within a framework of "names" that God taught (sura 2, verse 29) and that could no longer be determined, which opens the door wide to intellectual dishonesty.

38. See above, p. 89.

39. Arabic: *fard al-kifaya*, a duty imposed on the community of Muslims by God, which, however, need not be carried out by all but only a sufficient number of believers.

40. Muhammad 'Abduh, *Al-A'mal al-kamila*, vol. 3, pp. 15-22; Nagel, "Theologie und Ideologie im modernen Islam," p. 17.

41. Muhammad 'Abduh, *Al-A'mal al-kamila*, vol. 4, pp. 138–40.

42. Ibid., vol. 5, pp. 21–22.

43. Cf. above, p. 170.

44. Cf. above, pp. 154-62.

45. Cf. above, pp. 210f.

46. Walther Braune, *Der islamische Orient zwischen Vergangenheit und Zukunft*, Berne and Munich, 1960, pp. 129–30; Nagel, "Theologie und Ideologie im modernen Islam," pp. 29–31.

47. Tilman Nagel, "Zum Menschenbild im modernen Islam," in *ZDMG*, suppl. vol. III/1, XIXth Deutscher Orientalistentag, lectures, pp. 559–65.
48. Nagel, *Der Koran*, pp. 130ff.
49. Cf. Franz Rosenthal, *Knowledge Triumphant*, Leiden, 1970, p. 245.
50. This is also true of the Shiite version of fundamentalism, cf. Nagel, *Staat und Glaubensgemeinschaft*, vol. 2, pp. 315–16.
51. Cf. the manuscript Ahlwardt no. 3637.
52. Nagel, "Theologie und Ideologie im modernen Islam," pp. 37ff.; Nagel, "Abkehr von Europa: Der ägyptische Literat Taha Husain und die Umformung des Islams in eine Ideologie," in *ZDMG* CXLIII (1993), pp. 383–98.
53. See above, p. 67.

Epilogue (pp. 277–284)

1. Bo Holmberg, *A Treatise on the Unity and Trinity of God by Israel of Kashkar (d. 872)*, Lund, 1989, as well as the literature referenced there; a pioneering work in the area of comparative theology is Seppo Rissanen, *Theological Encounter of Oriental Christians with Islam during Early Abbasid Rule*, Abo Akademis Förlag, 1993.
2. Khalil Samir S.J. (ed.), *Traité de Paul de Bus sur l'unité et la trinité, l'incarnation et la vérité du christianisme*, Patrimoine arabe chrétien 4, Couvent St. Michel, Lebanon, 1983.
3. We have learned tremendously in this area from Georges Vajda (1908–81); his most important essays are now easily accessible in G. E. Weil (ed.), *Mélanges Georges Vajda*, Hildesheim, 1982, and David R. Blumenthal (ed.), *Al-Kitab al-muhtawi de Yusuf al-Basir . . . par Georges Bajda*, Leiden, 1985. A short summary of these issues is in S. Simon and M. Simon, *Geschichte der jüdischen Philosophie*, Munich, 1984, pp. 37–59.
4. Al-Juwayni, *Ash-Shamil fi usul ad-din*, ed. An-Nashshar, Alexandria, 1969, pp. 252ff., esp. pp. 258–59; Harry A. Wolfson, *The Philosophy of the kalam*, Harvard University Press, 1976, pp. 48ff.
5. One example is the book by Wolfson referenced in the previous endnote; in addition, a book by Gardet and Anawati deserves mention: *Introduction à la théologie musulmane: Essai de théologie comparée*, Paris, 1948. The authors draw numerous parallels between medieval Christian and Islamic theology; however, the book is more systemically oriented, and consequently, the historical development of both fields and areas where they might overlap or deviate from one another are not examined sufficiently.
6. Tilman Nagel, *Timur der Eroberer*, Munich, 1993, pp. 233 and 263ff.

Recommendations for Further Reading

Chapter I

Various English translations of the Koran are available. All quotes in this book are taken from A. J. Arberry's translation (see note to Preface). The following should also be mentioned: *The Koran: Text, Translation and Commentary* by A. Yusuf Ali (Washington, D.C.: American International Printing Company, 1946); *The Quran, Translated with a Critical Rearrangement of the Surahs* by Richard Bell, 2 vols. (Edinburgh: T. T. Clark, 1937–39); *The Koran* by N. J. Dalwood (Baltimore: Penguin, 1961); *The Quran*, by T. B. Irving (Brattleboro, Vermont: Amana Books, 1985); and *The Meaning of the Glorious Koran*, by Mohammed Marmaduke Pickthall (New York: New American Library and Mentor Boks, n.d.).

The highly detailed article, "al-Kur'an," in the *Encyclopedia of Islam*, vol. 5, pp. 400–32, offers an overview of the state of Koran research. The general (German-speaking) reader will find an explanation of the Koran's main themes in T. Nagel, *Der Koran: Einführung, Texte, Erläuterungen*, 2nd ed., Munich, 1991.

On Muhammad's life, I recommend: Rudi Paret, *Mohammed und der Koran*, Stuttgart, 1957 (numerous subsequent editions), as well as the far more extensive works by W. Montgomery Watt: *Muhammad at Mecca*, Oxford, 1953; *Muhammad at Medina*, Oxford, 1956; and *Muhammad, Prophet and Statesman*, Oxford, 1961.

In his book *The Event of the Qur'an* (London, 1971), Kenneth Cragg examines the Koran as a living document of a religious experience. The same author deals with the issue of how the Muslims convey that specific experience in *The Mind of the Qur'an: Chapters in Reflection*, London, 1973.

Helmut Gätje offers a look at Muslim Koran exegesis in his book *Koran und Koranexegese* (Zurich and Stuttgart, 1971), which contains a wealth of sources and focuses on the core topics of Islamic faith.

Chapter II

The following works provide the clearest information on the historical background: Julius Wellhausen, *Das Arabische Reich und sein Sturz*, 2nd ed., Berlin, 1960, and Wellhausen, "Die religiös-politischen Oppositionsparteien im alten Islam," in *Abhandlungen der geisteswissenschaftlichen Klasse der Göttinger Akademie der Wissenschaften*, Neue Folge 5; and Albrecht Noth, "Früher Islam," in U. Haarmann, ed., *Geschichte der arabischen Welt*, 2nd ed., Munich, 1991. W. Montgomery Watt and Michael Marmura, *Der Islam II*, Stuttgart, 1985 stresses the theological and religiopolitical aspects; the passages about early Islam were taken from Watt's book *The Formative Period of Islamic Thought*, Edinburgh, 1973.

A brief description of Shiite Islam considering the latest research is offered by Heinz Halm, *Shia Islam: From Religion to Revolution*, tr. Allison Brown, Princeton Series on the Middle East, Markus Wiener Publishers, Princeton, 1997. We are lacking a similar study both on the Kharijites—I would like to refer to Karl-Heinz Pampus, *Über die Rolle der Harigiya im frühen Islam*, Bonn, 1980, and Werner Schwartz, *Die Anfänge der Ibaditen in Nordafrika*, Bonn, 1983—and Sunnism (see, however, the following chapter!).

Tilman Nagel, *Rechtleitung und Kalifat: Versuch über eine Grundfrage der islamischen Geschichte*, Bonn, 1975, presents and interprets the history of early Islam until the turn of the ninth century by looking at the entanglement of political power and theology.

Chapter III

The entries *hadith* and *'Ilm al-kalam* in *Encyclopedia of Islam* briefly summarize the most important issues.

Translated samples of *hadiths* and texts from the *kalam* can be found in the following works: Joseph Schacht, *Der Islam mit Ausschluß des Qor'ans*, Tübingen, 1931 (*Religionsgeschichtliches Lesebuch*, ed. Alfred Bertholet, 2nd, expanded edition, no. 16); Arthur Jeffrey, *A Reader on Islam*, 's-Gravenhage, 1962.

Chapter IV

For German translations of sources on the topic of this chapter see, apart from the references in chapter 3: Joseph Hell (tr.), *Die Religion des Islam I: Von Mohammed bis Ghazali*, Religiöse Stimmen der Völker, ed. Walter Otto, Jena, 1915; and those volumes that have so far been published of Josef van Ess, *Theologie und Gesellschaft im 2. und 3. Jahrhundert Hidschra*, Berlin, 1991ff.

A translation of 'Abd al-Qahir al-Baghdadi's (d. 1037) treatise on the religious movements in Islam illustrates the way a medieval Sunnite scholar sees the history of early Islamic theology: Kate Chambers Seelye (tr.), *Moslem Schisms and Sects*, Columbia University Oriental Studies XV, 2nd ed., New York, 1966.

We are still lacking comprehensive studies of early Islamic rationalism. A brief outline is in W. Montgomery Watt, *Islamic Philosophy and Theology*, Islamic Surveys 1, paperback edition, Edinburgh, 1979; I also want once again to refer to the works listed in chapter 2 (Watt, *The Formative Period of Islamic Thought*; Nagel, *Rechtleitung und Kalifat*). An inventory of the Mu'tazila's early history can be found in Josef van Ess, "Une lecture à rebours de l'historie du Mu'tazilisme," in *Revue des Etudes Islamiques* XLVI (1978), pp. 163–240 and XLVII (1979), pp. 19–69. Hans Daiber has written a very extensive monograph on a representative of early rationalism, which sometimes lacks a certain clarity owing to its great emphasis on details: *Das theologisch-philosophische System des Mu'ammar ibn 'Abbad as-Sulami (gest. 830 n. Chr.)*, Beiruter Texte und Studien 19, Beirut, 1975.

Chapter V

Daniel Gimaret wrote monographs on the core topics of Ash'arite theology with an emphasis on the history of its dogmas: *Théories de l'acte humain en théologie musulmane*, Paris, 1980, and *La doctrine d'al-Ash'ari*, Paris, 1990. A study of the development of an interpretation of the Koran that was prerequisite for an understanding of the history of dogmas proper, which thus also established an agreement on what is Islam and an Islamic way of life, was accomplished by Claude Gilliot in *Exégèse, langue et théologie en islam: L'exégèse coranique de Tabari*, Etudes musulmanes XXXII, Paris, 1990. In this context early Islamic Sufism is particularly significant; basic information on Sufism is provided in Annemarie Schimmel, "Sufismus und Volksfrömmigkeit," in *Der Islam III*, Stuttgart, 1990 (Die Religionen der Menschheit 25/iii), pp. 157–242. As an introduction to Sufi thought I recommend Richard Gramlich (tr.), *Schlaglichter über das Sufitum: Abu Nasr as-Sarrags Kitab al-luma'*, introduced, translated, and with a commentary, Freiburger Islamstudien XIII, Stuttgart, 1990, and Richard Hartmann, *Al-Kuschairis Darstellung des Sufitums*, Berlin, 1914. The book by Tilman Nagel, *Die Festung des Glaubens: Triumph und Scheitern des islamischen Rationalismus im 11. Jahrhundert*, Munich, 1988, contains an analysis of the thought of the Ash'arite al-Juwayni against the backdrop of the turbulent political history of the eleventh century, and traces interconnections between mature Ash'arite theology and metaphysics and contemporary Islamic jurisprudence and political science.

Chapter VI

Several histories of philosophy of Islam are available. The short book in German by T. J. de Boer, *Geschichte der Philosophie im Islam*, Stuttgart, 1901, can still serve as the first introduction to the subject, even though it is obsolete in many details. The two-volume collection by M. M. Sharif (ed.), *A History of Muslim Philosophy*, Wiesbaden, 1963–1966, was penned by a number of mostly Muslim authors. Very useful, as it focuses on the most significant controversies, is Oliver Leaman's study *An Introduction to Medieval Islamic Philosophy*, Cambridge University Press, 1985.

There is still an insufficient number of works on individual philosophers or their works. The following should be mentioned: Jean Jolivet, *L'intellect selon al-Kindi*, Leiden, 1971; Dimitri Gutas, *Avicenna and the Aristotelian Tradition*, Leiden, 1988; Miguel Cruz Hernandez, *Abu Walid Ibn Dushd (Averroes): Vida, obra, pensamiento, influencia*, Cordoba, 1986; Oliver Leaman, *Averroes and His Philosophy*, Oxford, 1988.

We are still lacking a history of the debate between Muslim philosophy and Islamic theology. Aside from the two books by W. Montgomery Watt, *Islamic Philosophy and Theology*, Edinburgh, 1962 (and later), and *Muslim Intellectual: A Study of al-Ghazali*, Edinburgh, 1963, I recommend the already mentioned book by Oliver Leaman, *An Introduction . . .*, as well as this very detailed study on the theodicy: Eric L. Ormsby, *Theodicy in Islamic Thought: The Dispute over al-Ghazali's "Best of All Possible Worlds,"* Princeton University Press, 1984.

Chapter VII

An excellent introduction to this topic is the collection of translated sources with commentaries by Heinz Halm: *Die islamische Gnosis: Die extreme Schia und die Alawiten*, Die Bibliothek des Morgenlandes im Artemis Verlag, Zurich and Munich, 1982.

Chapter IX

There is no comprehensive analysis of the development of the theology of modern Islam. The historical background where such a study would have to begin, on the other hand, has been examined from various angles. The following books can be recommended: Bassam Tibi, *Die Krise des modernen Islams: Eine vorindustrielle Kultur im wissenschaftlich-technischen Zeitalter*, Munich, 1982; Wilfred Cantwell Smith, *Islam in Modern History*, Princeton: Princeton University Press, 1957.

The following works strongly emphasize the history of ideas: Albert Hourani, *Arabic Thought in the Liberal Age*, revised ed., New York: Oxford University Press, 1967; Malcolm H. Kerr, *Islamic Reform: The Political and Legal Theories of Muhammad 'Abduh and Rashid Rida*, Los Angeles and Cambridge, 1966; Walther Braune, *Der islamische Orient zwischen Vergangenheit und Zukunft*, Berne and Munich, 1960; and Keneth Cragg, *Counsels in Contemporary Islam*, Islamic Surveys 3, Edinburgh, 1965.

A French translation of the *Risalat at-Tauhid*, Muhammad 'Abduh's most important theological work, was published by B. Michel and Moustapha Abdel Raziq in Paris in 1925. The following shorter works are devoted more specifically to theological issues: Henri Laoust, *Les schismes dans l'islam: Introduction à une étude de la religion musulmane*, Paris, 1965, ch. 11; Laoust, "Le réformisme Orthodoxe des 'Salafiya' et les charactères généraux de son orientation actuelle," in *Revue des études islamiques* 1932, pp. 175–224; Tilman Nagel, "Theologie und Ideologie im modernen Islam," in *Der Islam III, Die Religionen der Menschheit* 25/iii, Stuttgart, 1990.

Glossary of Arabic Terms

1. Arabic Terms

al-ʿadl—justice (i.e., of God); one of the basic principles of Muʿtazilite theology

al-afʿāl (sg. *al-fiʿl*)—actions as the real or metaphorical results of an actors' deeds; also loss of (the creature's) power, freedom to act, predestination, righteousness of one's deeds

al-ahwaʾ (sg. *al-hawā*)—one's own views (not founded on the revelation or on reason); emotions (not restrained by the revealed law); also reason

Allāh—the (one) God; usually rendered as "God" in this book; the Arabic term for God is used to refer to (a) the superior god worshiped at the Kaaba, and (b) the specifically Islamic nouminous fullness of being of the one God

amīr al-muʾminīn—commander of the believers; ruler's title established by Umar; cf. also *haīfat Allāh; halīfat rasūl Allāh*

al-amr—providence emitted by God, penetrating and ruling His continuous work of creation; also providence

al-annīyya—God's (pure) existence (without attached attributes); also *al-māhīya*

al-ʿaql— reason

al-ʿaql—intellect (in Islamic Neoplatonism)

al-aʿrāḍ (sg. *alʿaraḍ*)— *accidentes*

al-aṣlaḥ—the best, most useful things for human beings or creation in general; in the Muʿtazilite view, yardstick for God's actions

aslama— *al-islām*

al-badāʾ—God's opportunity to revise His statements (Shiite)

al-bāṭin—the esoteric meaning of the revelation or God's law, respectively (Shiite); *aẓ-ẓāhir*

al-bāṭin—the deeper, real meaning of God's word, which according to

317

Averroes must be detected by human reason

al-bāṭinīyya—movement of the intrinsic meaning; within Sunnism, common term for the Sevener Shia

al-bidʿa (pl. *al-bidaʿ*)— innovation not backed by the tradition on the Prophet and therefore problematical; opposite: *as-sunna*

ad-dajjal—the great seducer, a sort of Antichrist of Islamic millenarianism

aḏh-ḏhihn—the human intellect as the domain of merely imagined or conceivable being; also *al-hārij*

ad-dīn—the totality of the rules of how to live and of conduct given and intended by God

al-fāʿil—the actor; cf. *al-afʿāl*

al-fitna—politically: discord of the community of believers (*al-jamāʿa*); religiously: enticement to abandon a life following *ad-dīn*

al-fiṭra—the human destination toward God, the creator, which is destructible

al-ġayb—the domain of the unseen, in contrast to the ontological domain of the *aš-šhāhid*

al-ġulūw—exaggeration, leaving the [idealized] middle course in matters of faith

al-jabbar—the tyrant who does not feel bound by God's law

al-ḥadīth—the tale, i.e., the body of traditions, of Muhammad's standard-setting speeches and actions; also used as term for the individual standard

al-ḥanīf—God-seeker

al-ḥaqq—truth, true being (term for God); also *al-wāḥid al-ḥaqq*

al-haya'—bashfulness (cf. *al-ahwa'*, *ad-dīn*)

al-hijā'—invective, invective poem

al-ḥujja—argument (i.e., of God directed against the unbelievers who excuse their wrongful doings by pleading ignorance); the Shia's redeemer imam, also imamate

al-ijtihād—independent (to a certain degree even independent of the revelation) search for legal (*ash-shariʿa*, *at-taqlīd*) decisions

al-ikhtiyyār—the acting human being's freedom to choose

iktasaba— *al-iktisab*

al-iktisāb—a human being's acquisition of an act originated by God *al-ilāhīyya*—divinity, fifth state of divine being

al-ʿilla—cause; also causality, innerworldly

al-ʿilm— knowledge; knowledge going back to God, which cannot be expanded by human beings

al-ʿilm as-sābiq—divine prescience

al-imām—leader (imamate) of a religiously based community; also *al-umma*

imāmat al-mafḍūl— imamate of someone who is not the most virtuous of the community (Zaydi Shia)

al-īmām— faith; opposite: *al-islām*; also Islam (piousness of rites)

al-irāda— will

al-irjāʾ—postponement; also Murjiites

al-islām—turning one face toward the (one) God; also Islam (piousness of rites); opposite: *al-īmān*

al-isnād—the chain of men who passed on traditions, *al-ḥadīth*

al-istiṭāʿa— ability to perform an action

al-iʿtizāl—withdrawal from the partisan conflict concerning the civil war. also Mutazila, *al-liʿan*

al-jabriyya—belief in the divine predetination of human actions; those profess this belief

al-jabrut—tyranny; cf. *al-jabbar*

al-jahiliyya—the period of ignorance of the divine law; Arab antiquity before Muhammad's appointment

al-jamaʿa—the community of believers, united (by *islam*)

al-jauhar—the substance to which *accidentes* (*al-aʿrad*) must be attached

al-jihad—the holy war; in a figurative sense: the battle against the emotions (al-ahwa') for the realization of the order God has intended (*ad-din*)

al-kalām—Islamic theology using rational arguments

al-khabar—term for the individual news on the Prophet passed on in the *hadith*

al-khalifa—God's deputy (in creation), i.e., man

khalifat Allah—God's deputy; also caliphate

khalifat rasul Allah— deputy of God's messenger; also caliphate

khaliq—creating; attribute of God, contrasting Him ontologically to creation (*makhluq*)

al-kharij—the world of things as opposed to the mental world (*adh-dhin*)

laṭīf—kind, merciful (God); cf. *al-aṣlaḥ*

al-liʿān—the husband's malediction of his wife, uttered without proof of the wife's offense; in the Mutazila, figure of thought used to justify neutrality in the partisan conflict in early Islam; also *al-iʿtizāl*

al-maʿād—return (of the bodies and souls, respectively, into existence) on the Last Day

al-madīḥ—praise, panegyric, eulogy

al-mahdī—rightly guided person; Islamic ruler at the end of time (cf. *ad-dajjāl* and rightly guided caliphs)

al-māhīyya—God's essence, the not concretely definable nature or essence of God; cf. *al-anniyya*

al-māhīyya—quiddity

makhluq—created; the creature's ontological status as opposed to God's (*khāliq*)

al-maʿrifa—intuitive knowledge that cannot be gained by way of discourse

al-maʿrifa—Gnosis, Gnosticism

al-muʿaṭṭila— *at-taʿṭīl*

al-mujassima— *at-tajsim*

al-mujtahid—person capable of *al-ijtihād*

muḥdath—created in time, bound to time, contingent

al-muʾminūn—the believers, also *al-īmān*

al-murjiʾa— *al-irjāʾ*

al-musauwir—the shaper, one of the names of God

al-muslim—person performing *al-islām*

al-mutakallim (pl. *al-mutakallimūn*)—person engaged in *al-kalām*; in the high and late Middle Ages often proponent of a materialistic view of the world

an-nuṭaqāʾ (sg. *an-nāṭiq*)—speaker-prophets of the Sevener Shia

al-qadar—determining force; the power to lead actions to their intended goal; also freedom of action, Qadariyya

al-qibla—direction of prayer

al-qudra—force or power to perform an action; *al-qadar*

ar-rafḍ—rejection of the caliphates of Abu Bakr, Umar, and Uthman; the Sunnites' invective for the Shiites originates from this term: *ar-rāfia ar-rūḥ*—the spirit, a medium originating in God, conveyor of the revelation, typically personified as an angel; also *al-amr*

aṣ-ṣabr—the virtue of waiting patiently

ash-shahāda—the ontological realm that is accessible to the senses; opposite: *al-ġaib*

ash-shāhid—the visible; cf. *ash-shahada*

ash-shai²—the thing

as-sharī'a—the law God imposed on human beings, given them in the Koran and the standard-setting example of Muhammad (law, Koran, *as-sunna, ad-dīn*)

shī'a(t 'Alī)—'Ali's followers, Shiites

as-sunna—the ancestors' path; the original community's custom; Muhammad's norm-setting speeches, actions, and tacit approval; also *al-ḥadīth*, Sunnites

at-tajsīm—concept of God as a corporeal being; also anthropomorphism

at-taklif—the burdening of human beings with the law

at-tanzīl—the sending down of the revelation

at-taqlīd—the adoption of legal decisions waiving *al-ijtihad*

at-ta'ṭīl—deflating the concept of God of any content that could be described in human terms; also *Jahmiyya*

at-tauḥīd—God's oneness, one of the basic principles of Mu'tazilite theology; in a general sense, the most important statement of Islamic theology

tawallā—to show unconditional loyalty to a religiopolitical leader, declare one's unreserved loyalty to that person; also Kharijites

at-tawallud—things and events evolving from analyzable facts; also causality, innerworldly

at-ta²wīl—the interpretation of the revelation or the law that is independent of the tradition

at-ta²wīl—the authoritative interpretation of the revealed law by the imam; also Shia

ath-thubūt—the affirmability of a fact, whether in the world of things (*al khārij*) or in the imagination (*adh-dhin*)

al-'ulama² (sg. *al-'ālim*)—the scholars; cf. *al-'ilm*

ūlū l-'azm—the resolute ones (among Muhammad's predecessors); in the Sevener Shia, epithet for the *an nuṭaqā² al-umma*—community of believers gathered around a prophet or imam, particularly the Islamic community around Muhammad

al-ʿumra—the "lesser" pilgrimage to Mecca, which can be made independent of the calendar of holy days

waḥdat al-wujūd—the oneness (and divinity) of all being

al-wāḥid al-ḥaqq—the one true one, in Islamic philosophy paraphrase for the supreme, the divine being; also *al-ḥaqq*; cf., in contrast, personal God in the Koran and the *kalām*

al-waṣī—someone entitled to inherit from a prophet or imam, owing to an explicit testament; Shia, view of history

al-waṣīyya—a prophet's or imam's declaration of intent determining a *wasi*

al-wujūd—being, existing; existence

aẓ-ẓāhir—exoteric meaning; opposite: *al-bāṭin*

aẓ-ẓulm—injustice; action of the powerful not protected by the *ash-sharīʿa*

Index

1. Persons

Aaron 53
'Abbas 35, 50, 98, 120, 287
'Abdallah ibn 'Amr ibn al-'As 79
'Abdallah al-Harawi 242, 309
'Abdallah ibn Harb 229-230
'Abdallah ibn Ibad 45-47, 67, 74, 293
'Abdallah ibn Mubarak 121, 136
'Abdallah ibn al-Muqaffa' 90, 298
'Abdallah ibn Saba' 50, 52, 54
'Abdallah ibn 'Umar ibn al-Khattab 64
'Abd al-Malik ibn Marwan 37, 40, 44, 49, 60, 64, 67, 85
'Abd al-Qahir al-Baghdadi 240, 314
'Abd ar-Rahman ibn 'Auf 237
Abel 53
Abraham 5-7, 10, 16-17, 20-21, 101, 230
Abu 'Ali al-Jubba'i 148-150, 153, 155
Abu Bakr 28, 30-32, 45, 47-48, 53, 55-56, 61-62, 67, 119, 133, 180, 237, 296, 320
Abu l-Barakat al-Baghdadi 203, 305
Abu Hanifa 104, 110, 129, 141, 146, 257-258, 301
Abu Hashim al-Jubba'i 149
Abu l-Hudhayl al-'Allaf 104, 106, 111, 113, 130
Abu l-Husain al-Basri 153
Abu 'Isa al-Warraq 223
Abu Jandal 74, 77
Abu Lahab 112
Abu Sa'id ibn abi l-Khair 182
Abu Sa'id al-Khudari 80
Abu Sulaiman al-Mantiqi 192
Abu Talib 9
Abu 'Ubaida 237
Abu Yusuf 257
Adam 19-20, 53, 59, 67, 73, 75-76, 135, 170, 188, 193, 204, 229-230, 239, 258-259, 269-270, 272-273, 280, 288
Ahmad ibn Hanbal 76, 119, 125, 129-131, 133-134, 136, 138, 148, 151-152, 178, 236-238, 240, 242, 244, 295-296
Ahmad ibn Idris al-Fasi 262, 280
'A'isha 31-32
Aiyyub as-Sakhtiyyani 78
'Ala' ad-Din at-Tusi 213, 247, 259, 306
Alexander 293, 296, 310
'Ali ibn abi Talib 28, 31, 36, 42, 64, 237, 240, 250, 255, 286
Alp Arslan 243
al-A'mash 80
al-Amin 93, 99, 138
Ammonios Hermeneiou 185
'Amr ibn 'Ubaid 112-113
Aristotle 175, 177, 184, 189, 210, 222
al-Ash'ari 112, 148-160, 163, 165, 169, 171-173, 179, 187-188, 192, 235, 243, 302-303, 315
'Ata' ibn abi Rabah 81
'Ata' ibn as-Sa'ib 79-80
Averroes (Ibn Rushd) 175-177, 184, 192, 196, 201, 226, 304, 311, 315, 317
Avicenna (Ibn Sina) 202-204, 208, 210-212, 227-228, 288, 306-307, 315

Bayazid II 248
al-Bazzazi 256-258

Cain 53
Christ, see Jesus
Cusa, Nicholas of 282

ad-Darimi 102-103, 298
Da'ud ibn Marwan al-Muqammis 282
Dirar ibn 'Amr 106-108, 111-114, 140, 299
Dhu Nuwas 3

Eve 19, 59
Ezra 20

Fakhr ad-Din ar-Razi 195, 206-207, 211-212, 226, 269, 271, 302, 305-306

al-Farabi 188-191, 193, 203, 207, 304-305
al-Fath ibn Khaqan 93-95
Fatima 28, 49

Gabriel 15, 230
Ghailan 40
Galen 184
al-Ghazali 180-181, 183, 193, 195, 200-203, 210-212, 232, 246, 259, 264, 269, 272, 280, 304-306, 310, 315

al-Hajjaj ibn Yusuf 38
al-Hakim an-Naisaburi 76
Hamid ibn Muhammad al-Qastamuni 256
al-Harith al-Muhasibi 138
Harun ar-Rashid 99, 106
al-Hasan ibn 'Ali 49, 55, 235, 255
al-Hasan al-Basri 38, 40-41, 45, 55, 60, 66, 74, 111, 113, 135, 294
al-Haskafi 256
al-Humaydi 78-79, 81, 128-130, 152, 290, 296, 300, 308
Hunain ibn Ishaq 184

Ibn (al-)'Arabi 261
Ibn al-Baqillani 88-90, 160-166, 172-174, 297, 303
Ibn Batta 240, 302, 309
Ibn al-Farid 246, 266
Ibn Furak 157, 302-303
Ibn Hazm 170, 192-193, 290, 303, 305
Ibn Khaldun 158, 171-173, 175, 302-303
Ibn Khuzayma 131-132, 134, 169, 301
Ibn al-Muqaffa' 90, 98, 220-222, 298
Ibn Nujaym 273
Ibn Qutayba 132-135, 138-140, 149, 196, 299, 301
Ibn Taymiyya 104, 243-247, 264-265, 267, 272, 280, 298, 311
Ibn Tufayl 201
Ibn Tumart 245
Ibrahim an-Nazzam, see an-Nazzam
Ibrahim ibn 'Uyayna 128
Ismael 94
Isma'il (Safavid) 94, 251, 309

Jabir ibn Zaid al-Azdi 45
Ja'd ibn Dirham 101

Ja'far as-Sadiq 52-53, 122, 240
al-Jahiz 83, 89, 93-97, 278, 298
Jahm ibn Safwan 101-102, 110-111, 114, 298
Jesus 1, 20, 52, 100, 174, 230, 233
John Philoponus 282
Joshua 53
Justinus Martyr 174, 188
al-Juwayni 164-169, 172-174, 179, 193, 195, 207, 235-236, 282, 303, 312, 315

al-Ka'bi 144
al-Khayyat 223-224
al-Kindi 185-188, 304, 315

Mahmud of Ghaznah 127
Maimonides 282
al-Malik al-Mansur Lajin 244
Malikshah 179, 243
al-Ma'mun 93, 99-100, 106, 109, 125, 127, 133, 138, 185, 187, 235, 241, 309
al-Mansur 98, 244
Mansur ibn Nuh 141
Marwan II 101
al-Maturidi 140-150, 155, 157-159, 188, 196, 297, 301-302
Mehmed II 213
Moses 1, 10, 12, 39, 46, 53, 101, 130, 159, 206, 230
Moses bar Kepha 159
Mu'adh ibn Jabal 120
Mu'ayyad-zade 248
Mu'awiya (ibn abi Sufyan) 28-29, 32-34, 36, 42-43, 46-47, 49, 51, 54-55, 64, 89, 118-119, 133
Muhammad x-xi, 4, 6-16, 18, 21-25, 27-37, 42, 44-63, 65-70, 74-76, 78-82, 84-88, 90, 96-99, 105, 118-120, 122-123, 126, 128, 130, 133, 135, 137, 145, 149-152, 159, 170, 174, 177, 183, 188, 191-192, 196, 204, 212, 215, 218, 230, 235-236, 241, 247, 251, 261, 271, 277, 285-286, 288-293, 295, 299-301, 313, 318-319, 321
Muhammad ibn 'Abd al-Wahhab 264-266, 268
Muhammad 'Abduh 254-255, 268, 274,

310-311, 316
Muhammad 'Ali 49-50, 52, 54-55, 253-255, 262, 264, 266, 274, 280, 308, 310
Muhammad ibn 'Ali as-Sanusi 262, 266, 274, 280
Muhammad ibn al-Hanafiyya 49, 58, 297
Muhammad al-Muntazar 249
al-Mukhtar ibn abi 'Ubayd 49
Musaylima 50
al-Mu'tadid 125, 300
al-Mu'tasim 93-95, 185, 187
al-Mu'tawakkil 73, 99, 125, 237

an-Najashi ibn al-Harith ibn Ka'b 54
Najm ad-Din Kubra 182
Napoleon 253
an-Nazzam 107, 115, 128, 224, 307
Nizam al-Mulk 127, 173, 178-179, 181, 193, 207, 243, 304
Noah 10, 53, 180, 230

Plato 174, 177
Potiphar 217

al-Qadir 241-242
al-Qa'im 241
al-Qashani 246, 261-262, 280
Qusayy 3-4, 6, 11, 34

Saadya 282
Sa'd ibn abi Waqqas 237
as-Saffah 50, 298
Sahl ibn Hunayf 73-74, 77, 82
Sa'id ibn Zayd 237
Salim ibn 'Abdallah ibn 'Umar 74
Sayf ad-Daula 188

ash-Shafi'i 82
Shahfur Tahir al-Isfara'ini 128, 159, 300, 304
ash-Shahrastani 206
ash-Shaybani 257
Shaykh Khalid 256, 261
Seljuq 179
Sirma ibn Malik 9
Sufyan ibn 'Uyayna 78-81, 128-129, 135-136, 196, 300
Süleyman II 256

at-Tabari 140, 293-294, 298-299
at-Tahtawi 254
Talha 31, 50, 237
at-Tirmidhi 120
Togrilbeg 127

'Ubaydallah al-Mahdi 231
'Ukasha ibn Muhsin 94
Umayya ibn abi s-Salt 196
'Umar ibn al-Khattab 30, 36, 64, 73-75, 77, 82, 286
'Uthman ibn 'Affan 286

al-Walid 40, 240, 293

Yahya ibn al-Husayn 84-85, 87, 297
Ya'la ibn Umayya 81-82
Yazid ibn Mu'awiya 50, 64
Yusuf al-Basir 282, 312

Zayd ibn 'Ali 55
az-Zajjaji 169, 303
Ziyad ibn abi Sufyan 43
az-Zubayr 31, 50, 237, 292
az-Zuhri 80

2. Concepts and Goups

Abbasids 35, 50, 81, 93, 99, 112, 125-127, 249

accidentes (al-a'rad) 86, 116-117, 145-146, 161-162, 172, 199, 202, 211-212, 317, 319

acquisition (of actions) (al-iktisab) 108-109, 130, 141, 147, 157, 184, 261, 269, 273, 318

actions, human 13-16, 21-23, 35, 37-40, 47, 58-62, 70, 73-75, 86-90, 109-117, 122-123, 129-138, 146-147, 149-150, 192-200, 202-207, 210-213, 219-222, 224-226, 260

actor (al-fa'il) 88, 104, 107, 110, 113-114, 142, 163, 186, 221, 224, 300, 318

Aghlabids 125

Alamut 179, 232

Alawis 232

Almohads 245

alms tax 65

Amasya 248

analogies 103, 117, 131, 152, 165, 175, 189, 238, 282

anarchy 43

angels 15, 66, 103, 134, 180, 189, 196, 211, 223, 229, 269-270

anthropomorphism 133, 244, 321

apologia 158-172

apostate (or renegade) 46, 169, 257

argument of God al-hujja 318

arbitrary will, God's 157, 185, 196, 210-213

Ash'arites 163, 167, 171-172, 175-177, 179, 194, 197, 201, 207, 211-212, 225, 240, 242-245, 278-279

atomism 158, 287

auditores and electi 220, 226

Aws 4, 9-10, 50, 291

Banu 'Abd al-Muttalib 94

Banu 'Abd Qays 65

Banu 'Abd Shams 49, 63, 286

Banu 'Adi ibn an-Najjar 9, 285

Banu Hanifa 49-50

Banu Hashim 9, 32, 63, 285

Banu Kinda 4

Banu n-Nadir 3

Banu Qurayza 3

Banu Tamim 3-4, 6

Banu Tayy 94

Banu Thaqif 49

Barmakids 99, 106

Battle of the Camel 32

being of God 146

body and soul, issue of 199, 202

Buddhism 102

Bukhara 125

Buyids 126-127, 243

caliph, caliphate x, 28-29, 31, 33-36, 38, 40-41, 43-50, 52, 55-56, 58, 60, 64, 66-68, 93-100, 106, 109, 119, 125-127, 179, 220, 232-3, 235, 237, 243, 249, 286-287, 292, 298

causality, innerworldly 91, 114, 116, 142, 157-158, 185, 188, 318, 321

charismatic rule 50

choice, freedom to choose 41, 67, 87, 111, 135, 157, 185, 188, 224-225, 318

Christians 2, 20, 27, 90, 174, 272, 282, 294, 312

community of blood 2, 94

community, Islamic 43, 45, 69, 90, 118, 164, 268, 300, 321

community, Medinese (original community) 29-30, 50, 61, 279, 286

complementarity of God and the world 206-210

conveyor of salvation, see redeemer

cosmos 160, 179, 187-191, 196, 210, 216-220, 225, 259

created makhluq 16, 320

createdness of the Koran 100, 103, 107-109, 111, 118, 122, 128, 157, 291

Day of Judgment (also Last Day) 2, 7-8, 15, 51-52, 58-59, 69, 87, 122, 215, 237, 258, 287

demiurge 100, 215

destination for salvation (al-fitra) 318

direction of prayer 7, 74, 277, 295, 320

domain of the intellect (adh-dhihn) 318

dualism 45, 146, 222

ego consciousness 198-199, 203-204, 206
epistemology 160, 173
eternity of the world 222, 282
evil 17, 21, 27, 38-40, 49, 55, 67-68, 100,
    110, 120, 128-129, 135, 143, 146-
    147, 180, 215-217, 219, 221-222,
    224-225, 228, 238, 242, 250, 300

family of the Prophet (also kinship with
    the Prophet) 236
fasting 120, 180
Fatimids 126-128, 231, 241, 249
final act 76
forgiveness, God's 23, 70
freedom to act, power to act 88-89, 105,
    109, 117, 142, 146, 196, 317

genealogy 94
Ghassanids 4
Ghaznawids 127
Gnosticism 215-223, 225-226, 228, 231,
    233, 320
God-seeker (al-hanif) 16, 318

Hanbalites 176, 243, 267
Harran 185
Hashimiyya movement 50, 97-99, 178
Hawazin Khazraj 11
hell 8, 17, 21, 23, 39-40, 56, 58-60, 67,
    69, 73-76, 113, 115, 118, 120, 130,
    150, 152, 177, 180, 219, 239, 266,
    314
herd (subjects) 36-38, 71
hijra 9, 31, 174, 285-286, 291
hijra calendar 31, 286
Himyarites 5
Hira 3
Hirmi 4
holy war 46, 244, 296, 319
Hudaybiyya 63, 74
Hums, association of 4-6, 9
Hunayn 81, 304

imam, imamate (al-imam) 33, 45, 47, 51-
    53, 56, 58, 61, 67, 84, 100, 106, 118-
    119, 121-123, 125-126, 133, 180,
    191, 232, 235, 240, 245, 249-251,
    263, 279, 294, 297, 310, 318-319,
    321-322
immanence 279
infidels, unbelievers 20, 33, 42, 47, 55-
    56, 64, 68, 130, 180, 228, 266, 290,
    293, 318
inquisition 99, 125, 128, 131, 135, 138,
    168, 179, 241, 287
intellect (al'aql) 317
intercession 130, 149-152
Islam (connectedness of creature with the
    creator) (al-islam) 2, 206
Islam (piousness of rites) 58, 60, 80, 97,
Islamization (of society) 82-83, 95, 98,
    265, 296
Isma'iliyya, Sevener Shia 179-181, 183-
    184, 228, 231-232, 249, 317, 320-
    321

Jahmiyya 102-104, 106, 108, 111-113,
    116, 128, 299, 321
Jerusalem 7, 290, 292, 305, 307
Jews 2, 20, 27, 90, 272, 281-282, 294
al-Ji'rana 81-82
judgment, Day of Judgment 2, 7-8, 15,
    51-52, 58-59, 69, 87, 122, 215, 237,
    258, 287
judgment, God's (of human beings) 58,
    62, 111, 150

Kaaba 4-8, 34, 104, 120, 285, 289-291,
    317
Karbala 49
Kasrawan 244
Kharijites 33, 41-49, 51-52, 54, 56-58,
    61, 63, 66, 68, 77, 82, 109, 129, 240,
    266, 286, 314, 321
Khurasan 93
Kufa 33, 42, 50, 56, 79-80, 101

Lakhmids 3
Last Day (Day of Judgment) 2, 7-8, 15,
    20, 51-52, 58-59, 69, 87, 118, 120-
    122, 130, 149-150, 201, 209, 215,
    237, 258, 287
al-Lat 5
Libya 48, 263
logos xi, 174

Ma'dd 3
Mamluks 253, 288

...

Manat 5
Manichaeism 100, 215, 220, 223-224,
    231, 307
martyr's death 49
matter ix, 8, 23, 33, 70, 74, 76, 79, 86,
    88, 100, 116-117, 120, 142, 146-148,
    156, 161-162, 169, 172, 176, 187-
    190, 193, 198, 200-201, 205, 211,
    223, 231, 237, 244, 270, 299
Mecca 3-4, 6-7, 9-13, 17, 22, 29-31, 37,
    44, 60, 63, 79, 81, 104, 193, 204,
    262, 264, 277, 285-286, 289-291,
    309, 311, 313
Medina 3, 7, 9-13, 15, 17, 20, 22-23, 30,
    32-33, 35, 37, 44, 50, 52, 54, 56, 64-
    65, 75, 97, 133, 174, 277, 285-286,
    291, 294-297, 313
metaphysics ix, 83, 97, 115, 117, 157,
    163-164, 167, 173, 189, 194, 198-
    201, 211-212, 222, 238, 248, 281,
    299, 305, 315
millenarianism 52, 122, 237, 245, 250-
    251, 318
miracle 1
Mongols 127, 244
monotheism, affective 5-6, 8-9, 19-20,
    100, 272, 285, 292
morality 8
Mu'tazilites 105, 107, 109, 111, 114,
    117-119, 122, 125, 128, 130, 132,
    140-142, 144-147, 149-153, 157-158,
    160-161, 163, 165, 167, 169, 171-
    172, 178-179, 187, 189, 192, 194,
    209, 212, 221, 223, 237, 240, 266
Mufti 248, 256
Murjiites, see al-irja' 62, 77, 89, 109,
    129-131, 147, 266, 286, 319
Mustaganim 262
mystical union unio mystica 192-193,
    263

Nahrawan 77
Najran 3
names of God (also attributes, attributes of
    works) 311, 320
Nashbandiyya order 280
natural philosophy 90, 158, 184
nature of God being of God 18
Nedjd 264
Neoplatonism 187, 231, 299, 317

Northern Africa 43, 47, 125, 235, 263

obedience 23, 35-38, 40, 62, 68, 94, 150,
    224, 229, 250
obedience (toward God, toward the
    caliphs)
Oman 47
omnipotence of God 60, 90, 101, 116,
    150-155
oneness of God (at-tauhid) 118, 281,
    301-302, 316, 321
ontology, being 16, 117, 136, 159-160,
    164, 194, 208-209
original sin (al-fitra) 20, 229, 318
Ottoman Empire 247-248, 255-256, 261,
    264, 288, 310

pantheism 109
paradise 8, 17, 19-21, 40, 42-43, 48, 53,
    59-60, 65, 67, 69, 73-75, 78, 94, 99,
    106, 113, 115, 118, 120-121, 130,
    134, 144, 149-151, 159, 168, 177,
    180, 183, 194, 217-219, 237, 250
particle (of matter) 117, 161-162, 169,
    172, 199-200
philology, Arabic 168-170
pilgrim, pilgrimage 4-5, 9, 22, 81-82,
    120, 193, 262, 264, 266, 285
polytheism 7, 20, 59, 68, 129, 277
postponement (al-irja') 61-62, 66, 110,
    319-320
prayer, ritual 4, 6-8, 16-17, 24-25, 29-30,
    34, 55, 61, 63, 65, 74, 78, 81, 95,
    104, 120, 129, 137, 180, 242, 274,
    277, 290, 292, 295, 300, 320
predestination 39, 61, 69-70, 75, 82, 85-
    86, 119, 129-130, 317
Prophet (Muhammad) xi, 2, 4, 7-14, 18,
    20-25, 27-38, 41-42, 44-57, 60-66,
    70, 73-83, 85, 87, 90, 94-99, 104,
    108, 110-111, 118-120, 123, 128-
    129, 131-133, 135-140, 147-149,
    151-152, 171, 178, 180-181, 187,
    190, 195-196, 206, 215, 217-218,
    230, 235-241, 243-245, 256, 258,
    262-267, 269-270, 272, 274, 277-
    280, 285-287, 290-291, 295-296,
    310, 313, 318-319, 321-322
prophets (before Muhammad) 11, 20, 53,
    59, 110-118, 188, 192, 204, 226-228,

288
providence, divine 135-136, 196-199,
    203-205, 232, 286-288, 299, 317-319
Pure Brothers 191, 226-228, 231-232

Qadarites 38, 40-41, 43-44, 46, 48, 58-
    62, 67-68, 73-74, 77, 79, 82, 84-85,
    109, 112-113, 131, 140, 142, 221,
    286, 297, 300
Qadi 181, 244, 248
Quraysh 3-4, 6-11, 28-34, 36, 40-42, 44,
    50-51, 54, 57, 64, 94, 215, 285-286,
    289-290, 293-294

rationalism (in theology) 93, 95, 97, 99,
    101, 103, 105, 107-109, 111, 113,
    115, 117, 119, 121, 123, 125, 127,
    129-133, 135-137, 139-141, 143,
    145, 147-149, 151-153, 155, 157,
    159, 161, 163, 165, 167-169, 171,
    174, 177-178, 188, 195, 221, 238,
    240, 287, 311, 314
rationality, utilitarian 89, 104, 146-147,
    255, 297
redeemer, redemption 53, 226, 229, 318
reform of Islam 242-248
resurrection 20-21, 53, 66, 69, 75, 87,
    161, 200, 213, 223, 228, 232, 239
Rumelia 248

Safavids 251
saints 54, 119, 246-247, 261, 267, 279,
    288
Saljuqs 128, 235, 243
Samanids 126, 140
Sasanids 41, 43, 50
Satan 18-19, 23, 42, 46, 65, 78, 154, 292
scrupulousness 143, 182
Sevener Shia 179-181, 183-184, 249,
    317, 320-321
Sharia (ash-shari'a) 175, 178, 180-184,
    191-192, 195, 201-202, 205-207,
    230, 237, 242, 245, 247, 251, 256,
    258, 273, 278-279, 318, 322
Shiites 28-29, 46, 48-52, 54-58, 61, 66,
    82, 99, 109, 118-119, 121-122, 126-
    128, 180-181, 191, 230, 232-233,
    235-236, 240-241, 244-245, 249-250,
    266, 286, 320-321
Shiras 248, 308

Siffin 33, 46, 54, 64, 66, 73-74, 77, 295
spatiality of God 162
spirit 15, 42, 63, 89, 185-187, 189-190,
    196-198, 213, 217, 247, 249-250,
    259, 261-262, 298, 320
ar-ruh 196, 320
state, Islamic 49, 127, 150, 241
substratum 88, 116, 157, 163, 166-167,
    207
Sufis, Sufism 60, 136-137, 141, 153, 168,
    181-183, 187, 195, 201, 225, 247,
    262, 264, 301, 315
Sunnites, Sunnism 28-29, 63, 67-68, 70,
    75-77, 89, 99, 118-119, 121, 123,
    128-130, 132-134, 121, 123, 125-
    126, 128-135, 137, 148-149, 151-
    152, 160, 164, 168, 172, 178-181,
    184, 188, 195, 232-233, 235-238,
    240-244, 246, 251, 261, 263, 278,
    287, 311, 314, 317, 320-321
syllogism 175

testamentary disposition 50
throne, God's 162, 230
Tirmidh 101-102
transcendence, God's 63, 110-111
Twelver Shia 250-251

Umayyads 28-29, 34, 36, 40, 43, 48-52,
    54, 57-59, 63-64, 98, 112, 125, 137,
    286, 298
uncreatedness (of God's speech, the
    Koran) 242
unimitability (of God's speech, the Koran)
    1-2
unio mystica, mystical union 183, 262
universal religions 90
al-'Uzza 5

visio beatifica 129, 150, 156, 181

Wahhabites 255, 264, 311
Wasit 101
will, human 1, 111, 266, 277

Zaydites 56, 121
Zoroastrianism 90